RIGHTSTA
MATHEMATICS

by Joan A. Cotter, Ph.D.
with Tracy Mittleider, MSEd

LEVEL C LESSONS

Second Edition

Activities for Learning, Inc.

A special thank you to Kathleen Cotter Lawler for all her work on the preparation of this manual.

Note: Rather than use the designations, Kindergarten, First Grade, ect., to indicate a grade, levels are used. Level A is kindergarten, Level B is first grade, and so forth.

Printed in the United States of America

www.RightStartMath.com

For more information: info@RightStartMath.com
Supplies may be ordered from: www.RightStartMath.com

Activities for Learning, Inc.
321 Hill Street
Hazelton, ND 58544-0468
United States of America
888-775-6284 or 701-782-2000
701-782-2007 fax

ISBN 978-1-931980-70-8
November 2020

RightStart™ Mathematics Objectives for Level C

Name ______________________________ Year __________

Numeration	Quarter 1	Quarter 2	Quarter 3	Quarter 4
Can skip count by 2s, by 5s, by 10s, and by 100s to 1000				
Can compare numbers up to 1000 using <, =, and >				
Can read and construct Roman numerals to 1000				
Understands place value and can write numbers to 9999 with numerals, words, and expanded form				
Addition				
Knows addition facts				
Can add 2-digit numbers mentally				
Can add 4-digit numbers				
Subtraction				
Understands subtraction	N/A			
Knows subtraction facts	N/A			
Can subtract 2-digit numbers mentally	N/A			
Can subtract 4-digit numbers	N/A			
Multiplication				
Understands multiplication as arrays	N/A			
Knows multiplication facts to 5 × 5	N/A	N/A		
Problem Solving				
Solves problems in more than one way				
Persists in solving problems				
Can solve addition and subtraction problems	N/A			
Can solve compare problems	N/A	N/A		
Time and Money				
Can tell time to the minute	N/A	N/A		
Can find the value of up to five coins and make change	N/A	N/A	N/A	
Measurement				
Can measure in inches, feet, centimeters, and meters	N/A	N/A	N/A	
Can find perimeter and area in customary and metric	N/A	N/A	N/A	
Can read a ruler to halves	N/A	N/A	N/A	
Geometry				
Can identify basic 2D and 3D shapes	N/A	N/A	N/A	
Can determine number of angles, sides, and faces in shapes	N/A	N/A		
Fractions				
Understands fractions as a type of division	N/A	N/A	N/A	
Knows unit fractions up to 1/10	N/A	N/A	N/A	
Data				
Gathers and shows data with line plots and intreprets results	N/A	N/A	N/A	
Calculator				
Can add, subtract, and multiply whole numbers	N/A	N/A	N/A	
Can solve two-step problems	N/A	N/A	N/A	

Materials needed but not included in the RS2 Math Set

Occasionally within the lessons materials list, you will see items in bold that are not included in the RS2 Math Set. Below is a list of the items that will be needed to teach those lessons.

Lesson 2 – Large calendar with 12 months
Lessons 4, 80 – Slips of paper
Lesson 61 – Mechanical pencils and erasers (this is the first drawing lesson, will be used again)
Lessons 67, 123, 125 – Scissors
Lessons 69, 73, 76, 125 – Colored pencils, crayons or markers
Lessons 70, 104, 106 – Extra paper, preferably 8.5 by 11
Lesson 78 – Thermometer
Lesson 82 – Digital clock
Lessons 96, 98 – Cash box (there are directions on how to make one if one is not available)
Lesson 107 – Measuring tape
Lesson 123 – Wide paper, preferably 36" by 36"
Lesson 125 – Tape

How This Program Was Developed

We have been hearing for years that Japanese students do better than U.S. students in math in Japan. The Asian students are ahead by the middle of first grade. And the gap widens every year thereafter.

Many explanations have been given, including less diversity and a longer school year. Japanese students attend school 240 days a year.

A third explanation given is that the Asian public values and supports education more than we do. A first grade teacher has the same status as a university professor. If a student falls behind, the family, not the school, helps the child or hires a tutor. Students often attend after-school classes.

A fourth explanation involves the philosophy of learning. Asians and Europeans believe anyone can learn mathematics or even play the violin. It is not a matter of talent, but of good teaching and hard work.

Although these explanations are valid, I decided to take a careful look at how mathematics is taught in Japanese first grades. Japan has a national curriculum, so there is little variation among teachers.

I found some important differences. One of these is the way the Asians name their numbers. In English we count ten, eleven, twelve, thirteen, and so on, which doesn't give the child a clue about tens and ones. But in Asian languages, one counts by saying ten-1, ten-2, ten-3 for the teens, and 2-ten 1, 2-ten 2, and 2-ten 3 for the twenties.

Still another difference is their criteria for manipulatives. Americans think the more the better. Asians prefer very few, but insist that they be imaginable, that is, visualizable. That is one reason they do not use colored rods. You can imagine the one and the three, but try imagining a brown eight–the quantity eight, not the color. It cannot be done without grouping.

Another important difference is the emphasis on non-counting strategies for computation. Japanese children are discouraged from counting; rather they are taught to see quantities in groups of fives and tens.

For example, when an American child wants to know 9 + 4, most likely the child will start with 9 and count up 4. In contrast, the Asian child will think that if he takes 1 from the 4 and puts it with the 9, then he will have 10 and 3, or 13. Unfortunately, very few American first-graders at the end of the year even know that 10 + 3 is 13.

I decided to conduct research using some of these ideas in two similar first grade classrooms. The control group studied math in the traditional workbook-based manner. The other class used the lesson plans I developed. The children used that special number naming for three months.

They also used a special abacus I designed, based on fives and tens. I asked 5-year-old Stan how much is 11 + 6. Then I asked him how he knew. He replied, "I have the abacus in my mind."

The children were working with thousands by the sixth week. They figured out how to add 4-digit numbers on paper after learning how on the abacus.

Every child in the experimental class, including those enrolled in special education classes, could add numbers like 9 + 4, by changing it to 10 + 3.

I asked the children to explain what the 6 and 2 mean in the number 26. Ninety-three percent of the children in the experimental group explained it correctly while only 50% of third graders did so in another study.

I gave the children some base ten rods (none of them had seen them before) that looked like ones and tens and asked them to make 48. Then I asked them to subtract 14. The children in the control group counted 14 ones, while the experimental class removed 1 ten and 4 ones. This indicated that they saw 14 as 1 ten and 4 ones and not as 14 ones. This view of numbers is vital to understanding algorithms, or procedures, for doing arithmetic.

I asked the experimental class to mentally add 64 + 20, which only 52% of nine-year-olds on the 1986 National test did correctly; 56% of those in the experimental class could do it.

Since children often confuse columns when taught traditionally, I wrote 2304 + 86 = horizontally and asked them to find the sum any way they liked. Fifty-six percent did so correctly, including one child who did it in his head.

The following year I revised the lesson plans and both first grade classes used these methods. I am delighted to report that on a national standardized test, both classes scored at the 98th percentile.

Joan A. Cotter, Ph.D.

Some General Thoughts on Teaching Mathematics

1. Only five percent of mathematics should be learned by rote; 95 percent should be understood.
2. Real learning builds on what the child already knows. Rote teaching ignores it.
3. Contrary to the common myth, "young children can think both concretely and abstractly. Development is not a kind of inevitable unfolding in which one simply waits until a child is cognitively 'ready.'" —*Foundations for Success* NMAP
4. What is developmentally appropriate is not a simple function of age or grade, but rather is largely contingent on prior opportunities to learn." —Duschl & others
5. Understanding a new model is easier if you have made one yourself. So, a child needs to construct a graph before attempting to read a ready-made graph.
6. Good manipulatives cause confusion at first. If a new manipulative makes perfect sense at first sight, it is not needed. Trying to understand and relate it to previous knowledge is what leads to greater learning. —Richard Behr & others.
7. According to Arthur Baroody, "Teaching mathematics is essentially a process of translating mathematics into a form children can comprehend, providing experiences that enable children to discover relationships and construct meanings, and creating opportunities to develop and exercise mathematical reasoning."
8. Lauren Resnick says, "Good mathematics learners expect to be able to make sense out of rules they are taught, and they apply some energy and time to the task of making sense. By contrast, those less adept in mathematics try to memorize and apply the rules that are taught, but do not attempt to relate these rules to what they know about mathematics at a more intuitive level."
9. Mindy Holte puts learning the facts in proper perspective when she says, "In our concern about the memorization of math facts or solving problems, we must not forget that the root of mathematical study is the creation of mental pictures in the imagination and manipulating those images and relationships using the power of reason and logic." She also emphasizes the ability to imagine or visualize, an important skill in mathematics and other areas.
10. The only students who like flash cards are those who do not need them.
11. Mathematics is not a solitary pursuit. According to Richard Skemp, solitary math on paper is like reading music, rather than listening to it: "Mathematics, like music, needs to be expressed in physical actions and human interactions before its symbols can evoke the silent patterns of mathematical ideas (like musical notes), simultaneous relationships (like harmonies) and expositions or proofs (like melodies)."
12. "More than most other school subjects, mathematics offers special opportunities for children to learn the power of thought as distinct from the power of authority. This is a very important lesson to learn, an essential step in the emergence of independent thinking." —*Everybody Counts*

13. The role of the teacher is to encourage thinking by asking questions, not giving answers. Once you give an answer, thinking usually stops.
14. Putting thoughts into words helps the learning process.
15. Help the children realize that it is their responsibility to ask questions when they do not understand. Do not settle for "I don't get it."
16. The difference between a novice and an expert is that an expert catches errors much more quickly. A violinist adjusts pitch so quickly that the audience does not hear it.
17. Europeans and Asians believe learning occurs not because of ability, but primarily because of effort. In the ability model of learning, errors are a sign of failure. In the effort model, errors are natural. In Japanese classrooms, the teachers discuss errors with the whole class.
18. For teaching vocabulary, be sure either the word or the concept is known. For example, if a child is familiar with six-sided figures, we can give him the word, hexagon. Or, if he has heard the word, multiply, we can tell him what it means. It is difficult to learn a new concept and the term simultaneously.
19. Introduce new concepts globally before details. This lets the children know where they are headed.
20. Informal mathematics should precede paper and pencil work. Long before a child learns how to add fractions with unlike denominators, she should be able to add one half and one fourth mentally.
21. Some pairs of concepts are easier to remember if one of them is thought of as dominant. Then the non-dominant concept is simply the other one. For example, if even is dominant over odd, an odd number is one that is not even.
22. Worksheets should also make the child think. Therefore, they should not be a large collection of similar exercises, but should present a variety. In RightStart™ Mathematics, they are designed to be done independently.
23. Keep math time enjoyable. We store our emotional state along with what we have learned. A person who dislikes math will avoid it and a child under stress stops learning. If a lesson is too hard, stop and play a game. Try the lesson again later.
24. In Japan students spend more time on fewer problems. Teachers do not concern themselves with attention spans as is done in the U.S.
25. In Japan the goal of the math lesson is that the student has understood a concept, not necessarily has done something (a worksheet).
26. The calendar must show the entire month, so the children can plan ahead. The days passed can be crossed out or the current day circled.
27. A real mathematical problem is one in which the procedures to find the answer are not obvious. It is like a puzzle, needing trial and error. Emphasize the satisfaction of solving problems and like puzzles, of not giving away the solution to others.

RightStart™ Mathematics

Ten major characteristics make this research-based program effective:

1. Refers to quantities of up to 5 as a group; discourages counting individually. Uses fingers and tally sticks to show quantities up to 10; teaches quantities 6 to 10 as 5 plus a quantity, for example 6 = 5 + 1.
2. Avoids counting procedures for finding sums and differences. Teaches five- and ten-based strategies for the facts that are both visual and visualizable.
3. Employs games, not flash cards, for practice.
4. Once quantities 1 to 10 are known, proceeds to 10 as a unit. Temporarily uses the "math way" of naming numbers; for example, "1 ten-1" (or "ten-1") for eleven, "1-ten 2" for twelve, "2-ten" for twenty, and "2-ten 5" for twenty-five.
5. Uses expanded notation (overlapping) place-value cards for recording tens and ones; the ones card is placed on the zero of the tens card. Encourages a child to read numbers starting at the left and not backward by starting at the ones.
6. Proceeds rapidly to hundreds and thousands using manipulatives and place-value cards. Provides opportunities for trading between ones and tens, tens and hundreds, and hundreds and thousands with manipulatives.
7. Teaches mental computation. Investigates informal solutions, often through story problems, before learning procedures.
8. Teaches four-digit addition on the abacus, letting the child discover the paper and pencil algorithm.
9. Introduces fractions with a linear visual model, including all fractions from 1⁄2 to 1/10. "Pies" are not used initially because they cannot show fractions greater than 1. Later, the tenths will become the basis for decimals.
10. Teaches short division (where only the answer is written down) for single-digit divisors, before long division.

Second Edition

Many changes have occurred since the first RightStart™ lessons were begun in 1994. First, mathematics is used more widely in many fields, for example, architecture, science, technology, and medicine. Today, many careers require math beyond basic arithmetic. Second, research has given us new insights into how children learn mathematics. Third, kindergarten has become much more academic, and fourth, most children are tested to ensure their preparedness for the next step.

This second edition is updated to reflect new research and applications. Topics within each level are always taught with the most appropriate method using the best approach with the child and teacher in mind.

Daily Lessons

Objectives. The objectives outline the purpose and goal of the lesson. Some possibilities are to introduce, to build, to learn a term, to practice, or to review.

Materials. The Math Set of manipulatives includes the specially crafted items needed to teach RightStart™ Mathematics. Occasionally, common objects such as scissors will be needed. These items are indicated by boldface type.

Warm-up. The warm-up time is the time for quick review, memory work, and sometimes an introduction to the day's topics. The dry erase board makes an ideal slate for quick responses.

Activities. The Activities for Teaching section is the heart of the lesson; it starts on the left page and continues to the right page. These are the instructions for teaching the lesson. The expected answers from the child are given in square brackets.

Establish with the children some indication when you want a quick response and when you want a more thoughtful response. Research shows that the quiet time for thoughtful response should be about three seconds. Avoid talking during this quiet time; resist the temptation to rephrase the question. This quiet time gives the slower child time to think and the quicker child time to think more deeply.

Encourage the child to develop persistence and perseverance. Avoid giving hints or explanations too quickly. Children tend to stop thinking once they hear the answer.

Explanations. Special background notes for the teacher are given in Explanations.

Worksheets. The worksheets are designed to give the children a chance to think about and to practice the day's lesson. The children are to do them independently. Some lessons, especially in the early levels, have no worksheet.

Games. Games, not worksheets or flash cards, provide practice. The games, found in the *Math Card Games* book, can be played as many times as necessary until proficiency or memorization takes place. They are as important to learning math as books are to reading. The *Math Card Games* book also includes extra games for the child needing more help, and some more challenging games for the advanced child.

In conclusion. Each lesson ends with a short summary called, "In conclusion," where the child answers a few short questions based on the day's learning.

Number of lessons. Generally, each lesson is to be done in one day and each manual, in one school year. Complete each manual before going on to the next level.

Comments. We really want to hear how this program is working. Please let us know any improvements and suggestions that you may have.

Joan A. Cotter, Ph.D.
info@RightStartMath.com
www.RightStartMath.com

Level C: Table of Contents

Level C: Table of Contents

Level C: Table of Contents

Level C: Table of Contents

Review Lesson 1: Subitizing Quantities 1 to 7

OBJECTIVES:

1. To construct and subitize quantities 1 to 7 on fingers, with tally sticks, tiles, and on the AL Abacus

MATERIALS:

1. *Yellow is the Sun* book and music (Appendix p. 1, available via QR code, or online at RightStartMath.com)
2. Tally sticks
3. 1" × 1" colored tiles
4. AL Abacus

ACTIVITIES FOR TEACHING:

Warm-up. Teach the child the song "Yellow is the Sun." If available, read the book *Yellow is the Sun* to her. Ask the child to raise the corresponding fingers at the appropriate words. (See the right column.)

Identifying small quantities. Tell the child that a scientist, Dr. Karen Wynn, discovered that babies 5 months old could tell the difference between groups of one, two, and three objects. If the child is interested, tell her how Dr. Wynn did her research:

> Dr. Wynn found that babies will look at something new for a longer time than something they've seen before. She showed the baby one teddy bear. Then she covered the teddy bear with a screen that hid the bear.
>
> Next she showed the baby another teddy bear and put it behind the screen. When she removed the screen, the baby saw two teddy bears. The baby didn't look very long because the baby expected to see two teddy bears.
>
> Dr. Wynn did the experiment again, but this time she tricked the baby. Without the baby seeing, she put an extra teddy bear behind the screen. When the screen was removed, the baby saw three teddy bears. The baby looked much longer, trying to figure out where the extra bear came from.
>
> By timing how long the babies looked, Dr. Wynn learned that babies could tell the difference between one, two, or three teddy bears. Other researchers found some older babies could tell up to four teddy bears.

Showing quantities 1 to 5. Tell the child to show 2 with the fingers on her left hand. Repeat for 3, 4, 5, and 1. Explain: Naming quantities without counting is called *subitizing.* Repeat in random order. Also, raise various fingers on your hand using quantities from 1 to 5 and ask her to name the amount as a group.

Comparing 4 with 5. Show a group of 4 tally sticks and another group with 5. See top of the next page. Ask: Which group has a middle, 4 or 5? [5]

EXPLANATIONS:

These Review Lessons are designed for a child who have not previously used the RightStart™ approach.

The words for *Yellow is the Sun* are as follows:

Yellow is the Sun

Yellow is the sun.
This is only one. (Raise 1 finger on left hand.)

Why is the sky so blue?
Let me show you two. (Raise 2 fingers.)

Salty is the sea.
One more and it's three. (Raise 3 fingers.)

Hear the thunder roar.
Here's the mighty four. (Raise 4 fingers.)

Ducks will swim and dive.
My whole hand makes five. (Raise 5 fingers.)

Yellow is the sun.
Six is five and one. (5 on left hand; 1 on right.)

Why is the sky so blue?
Seven is five and two. (5 on left; 2 on right.)

Salty is the sea.
Eight is five and three. (5 on left; 3 on right.)

Hear the thunder roar.
Nine is five and four. (5 on left; 4 on right.)

Ducks will swim and dive.
Ten is five and five. (5 on left; 5 on right.)

The article by K. Wynn, "Addition and Subtraction by Human Infants" was published August 27, 1992 in Nature, Vol. 358, p. 749-750.

The child can use any fingers on her left hand to show the quantity.

Use your right hand when you are across from the child so she sees the quantity on her "left".

ACTIVITIES FOR TEACHING: | **EXPLANATIONS:**

4 has no middle.

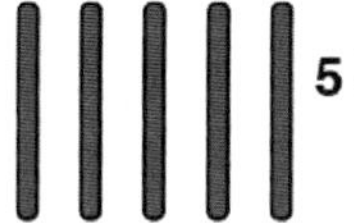

5 has a middle.

The quantities 6 and 7. Tell the child to show 6 with her fingers as shown below on the left. Then ask her to make 6 with tally sticks as shown below.

Be sure the child uses her left hand for five and her right hand for amounts over five.

Six.

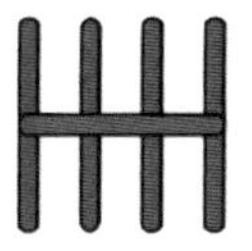

Six.

Repeat the above activities for 7.

Practice with her to construct quantities from 1–7 using the tally sticks. She needs only to change the quantity to reflect the new number, not start from scratch.

Quantities with tiles. Ask the child to take 10 tiles, 5 each of two different colors. Ask her to construct 6 like our hands, as shown below. Explain that in order to use our eyes instead of counting, we need to group in fives like our fingers. Repeat with 7.

Subitizing beyond five by grouping is called *conceptual subitizing.*

Six.

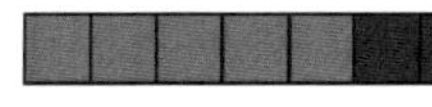

Seven.

Introducing the AL Abacus. Tell the child to place her abacus flat with the wires horizontal and the logo on the top right. Tell her to clear the abacus by lifting the left edge so the beads fall to the right side near the logo.

Ask her to enter 3 on the abacus by sliding 3 beads on the top wire to the left edge. Now ask her to clear the abacus and to enter 6. Repeat for 7. See the figures below.

The beads must be moved together as a unit, not one by one.

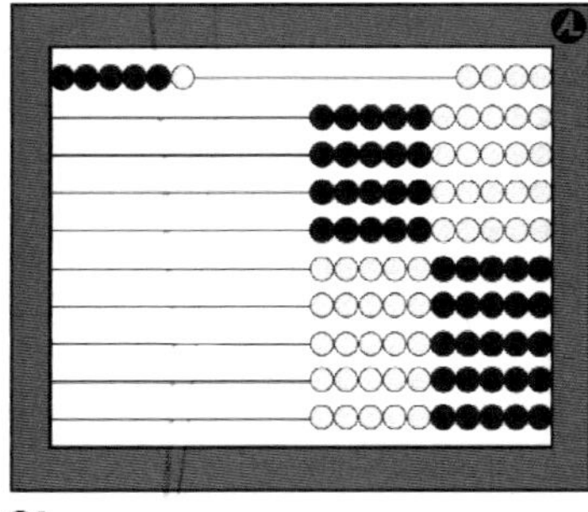

Six.

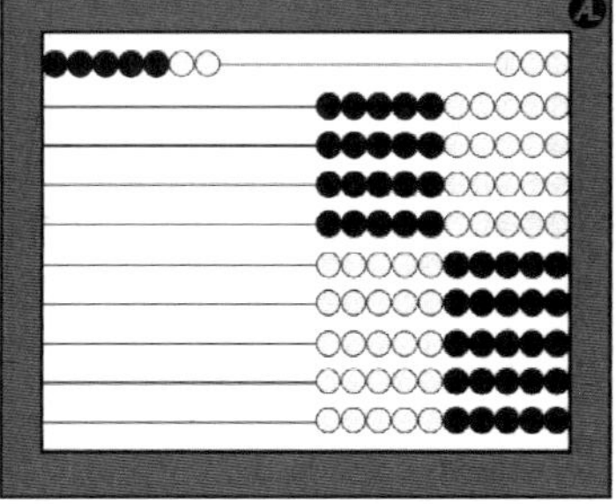

Seven.

Now ask her to enter numbers 1 to 7 in random order as quickly as she can, without clearing the previous number and before making the new number.

Not all children respond well to answering quickly. For some it creates stress which interferes with learning.

In conclusion. Ask: How is 7 made the same with fingers, tally sticks, tiles, and the abacus? [5 and 2] Do you need to count to see how much it is? [no]

Conclusions may be a summary of the day's lesson or an expansion of the lesson to challenge higher level thinking.

Review Lesson 2: Subitizing Quantities 8 to 10

OBJECTIVES:

1. To review the months
2. To subitize quantities 8–10 by grouping in 5s

MATERIALS:

1. Music for "Yellow is the Sun"
2. **Calendar with 12 months, one per page**
3. Tally sticks
4. Tiles
5. AL Abacus
6. *Math Card Games* book, A3*

ACTIVITIES FOR TEACHING:

Warm-up. Sing *Yellow is the Sun.* Tell the child to show the correct fingers at the appropriate words.

Say numbers 1 to 7 and ask the child to show the quantities with her fingers. Do the inverse: Show the child quantities 1 to 7 with your fingers and ask her to name them.

Teach the child the song, "The Months." Sing it to the tune of "Michael Finnegan." Turn to each month on the calendar as it is sung.

The Months

January, February, March, and April,
May, June, July, and August,
September, October, November, December.
These are the months of the year.

Quantities 8–10 with fingers. Demonstrate to the child how to show 8 with her fingers. See below. Then ask her to show 8 with her fingers, five with the left hand and 3 with the right hand. Repeat for 9 and 10.

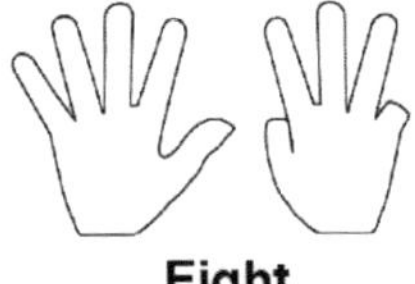

Eight.

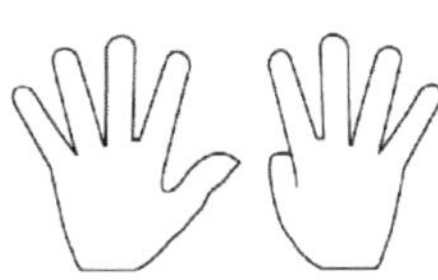

Nine.

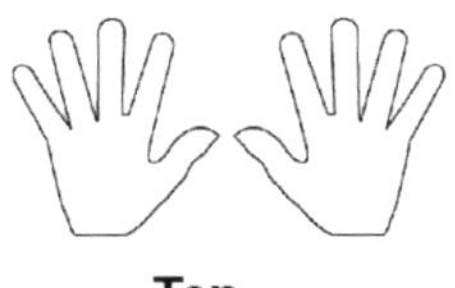

Ten.

Ask: What makes 10 a special number? [all the fingers, two groups of five]

Quantities 8–10 with tally sticks. Tell the child to construct 8 with tally sticks. Remind her to group 8 as a five and a three. See the left figure below. Then tell her to construct 9. Next tell her to construct 10. See the figures below.

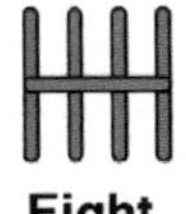 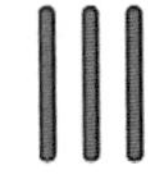

Eight.

Nine.

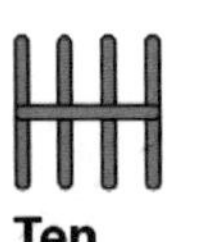 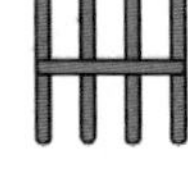

Ten.

EXPLANATIONS:

*The Fifth Edition of the *Math Card Games* book is needed for this manual.

The book is arranged in chapters as follows:

1. Number Sense (N)
2. Addition (A)
3. Clocks (C)
4. Multiplication (P)
5. Money (M)
6. Subtraction (S)
7. Division (D)
8. Fractions (F)

The games are numbered sequentially within each chapter. For example, A3 is the third game in the Addition chapter and N4 is the fourth game in the previous chapter, Number Sense.

Within each chapter the games get progressively harder.

Often, eight is the hardest quantity for a child to recognize.

ACTIVITIES FOR TEACHING:

Say random numbers 6–10 for her to make quantities with the tally sticks, concentrating especially on 8–10.

Quantities 8–10 with tiles. Tell the child to take 10 tiles, 5 each of 2 different colors. Ask her to construct 8, shown below. Also ask her to construct 9 and 10. Then give her random numbers to construct.

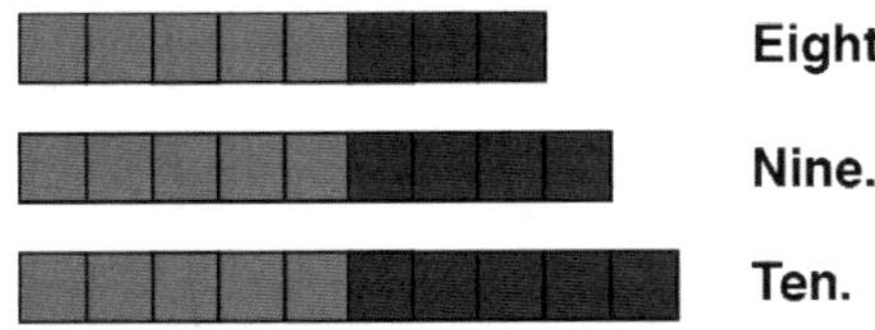

Eight.

Nine.

Ten.

Quantities 8–10 with the abacus. Ask the child to enter 8 on the abacus. See the left figures below. Repeat for 9 and 10.

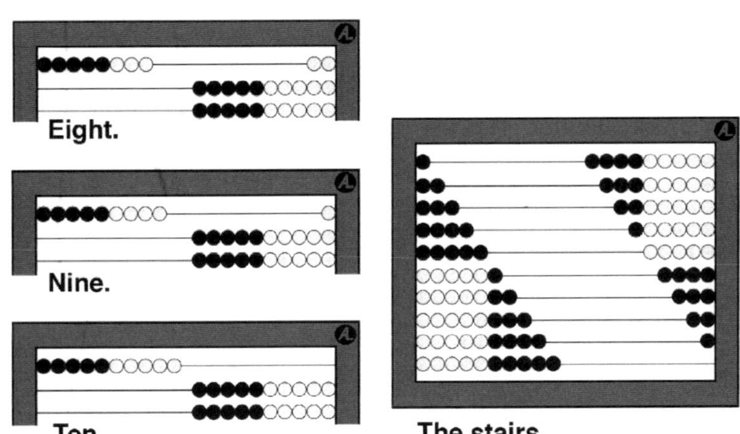

Eight.

Nine.

Ten.

The stairs.

The stairs. Ask the child to build the stairs by entering 1 on the first wire, 2 on the second wire, and so forth. See the right figure above. Ask her to read the quantities from top to bottom. [1, 2, 3, . . . , 10] Ask her to point to 8, to 10, to 6, to 9, and other quantities.

Tell her to find 5. Then ask her to find the other 5. [on the right side of the abacus] Ask: Can you find both 2s? Point to both. Repeat for other quantities at random.

Ask: When 8 is entered, how many beads are on the right side of the wire? [2] When 4 is entered, how many are on the right side? [6] Repeat for other quantities.

Go to the Dump game. Play Go to the Dump found in the *Math Card Games* book, A3. Use the abacus to find the matches.

In conclusion. Ask: What are the ways to make 10? [9 & 1, 8 & 2, 7 & 3, 6 & 4, 5 & 5, 4 & 6, 3 & 7, 2 & 8, 1 & 9, 0 & 10]

EXPLANATIONS:

It is critically important that the child enter these quantities without counting.

For a child having difficulty constructing the stairs, use the following method:

Tell her to enter 1 on the first wire.

Tell her to copy what is on the first wire and enter it on the next wire. [1] Then tell the child to add one more. [2]

For the next wire, copy what is above and add one more. [3]

Continue for remaining wires.

Review Lesson 3: Tens and Ones on the Abacus

OBJECTIVES:

1. To enter tens and ones on the abacus
2. To compose numbers 1 to 99 with place-value cards

MATERIALS:

1. AL Abacus
2. Place-value cards, 1 to 9 and 10 to 90
3. *Math Card Games* book, N43

ACTIVITIES FOR TEACHING:

Warm-up. Ask the child to name the ways to make 10. [9 & 1, 8 & 2, 7 & 3, 6 & 4, 5 & 5, 4 & 6, 3 & 7, 2 & 8, 1 & 9, 0 & 10]

Tens on the abacus. Tell the child to enter 10 on her abacus. Then tell her to enter another 10 on the second wire. Ask: How many beads are entered? [twenty] Say: If you lived in Asia, you would say 2-ten. So, for today we will use these names, and call it the "math way" of number naming.

Tell her to enter another 2-ten. Ask: How much do you have now? [4-ten] Tell her to enter another 2-ten. Ask: How much do you have now? [6-ten] How can you tell it is 6-ten without counting? Make sure she sees that the color changes after 5-ten. Repeat for 8-ten.

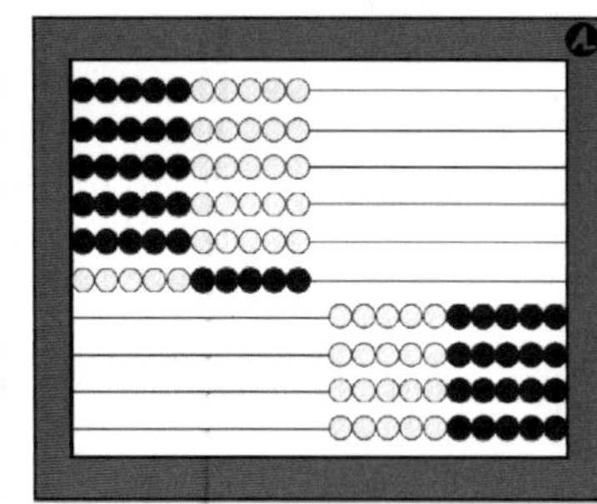

2-ten (twenty) entered.

6-ten (sixty) entered.

Practice the inverse. Enter various tens on the abacus and ask the child to name them. It is more difficult for a child to see the beads changing colors after 5-ten than changing colors after five in a row. Enter 7-ten and ask: How much it is? [7-ten]

Place-value cards. With 2-ten entered, show the child the place value card "20" and tell her this is how we record, or write, 2-ten; point to the "2" while saying "two" and to the "0" while saying "ten." See the figure on the right.

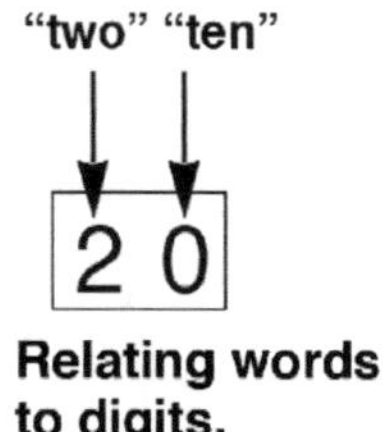

Relating words to digits.

EXPLANATIONS:

The first half of these RightStart™ Mathematics lessons refers to the child as a female and the second half refers to the child as a male.

The math way of number naming was used in RightStart™ Mathematics Level A and Level B.

ACTIVITIES FOR TEACHING:

Combining tens and ones. Ask the child: Can you enter 3-ten and 6? If necessary, tell her that the 6 is entered on the wire immediately below the last ten. See the left figure below.

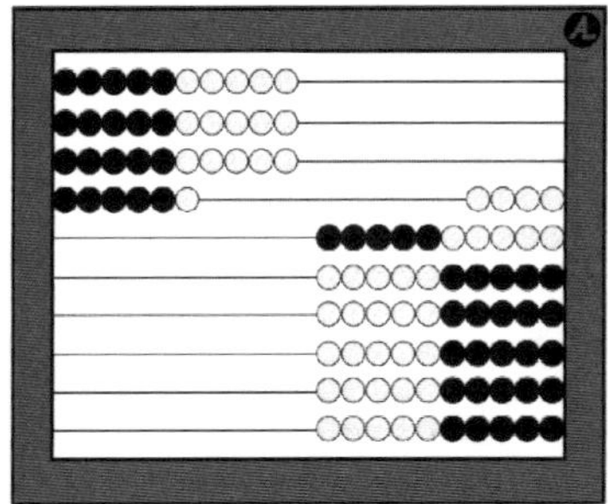

3-ten 6 (thirty-six) entered.

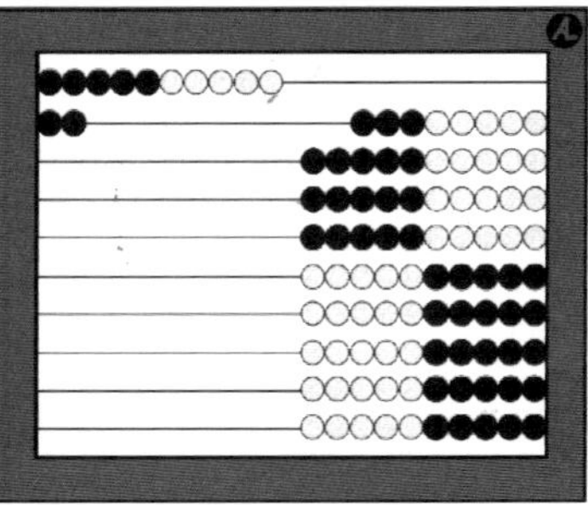

1-ten 2 (twelve) entered.

Ask the child to enter 1-ten 2. See the right figure above. Repeat for 6-ten 1 and 4-ten 8.

Naming quantities. Enter various quantities on the abacus for the child to name: 2-ten 7, 7-ten 2, 1-ten 1, and so forth.

Place-value cards with tens and ones. Explain that we will use the place-value cards to compose numbers. Enter 3-ten 6 on the abacus and find the place-value cards for 3-ten and 6. Then ask the child to watch. Take the cards and stack the 6 on top of the 3-ten as shown. See the figure below. Ask her to read it. [3-ten 6]

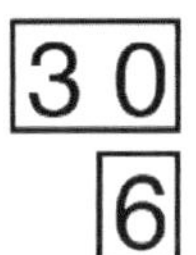

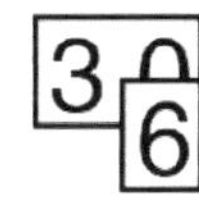

Stacking the cards to compose 3-ten 6.

Ask her to enter 1-ten 4 on her abacus and to compose the number with place-value cards. Repeat for other numbers, such as 6-ten 9, 3-ten 7, 2-ten 5, and more as needed.

Can You Find game. Play the Can You Find game Levels 1–3 found in the *Math Card Games* book, N43. Use both the math way and the regular names when asking for quantities.

Play the game again, but this time enter the quantities on the abacus for the child to read and find the corresponding cards.

In conclusion. Ask: What is the math way name for thirteen? [1-ten 3] For nineteen? [1-ten 9] What is the regular name for 1-ten 5? [fifteen] For 5-ten 1? [fifty-one]

EXPLANATIONS:

Thinking of numbers in columns hampers a full understanding of place value. That model requires first looking at the ones and then proceeding to the left, that is, reading numbers backward.

asked for break. didn't feel like game.

8·10·2021

Review Lesson 4: Hundreds on the Abacus

OBJECTIVES:

1. To enter hundreds on the AL Abacus
2. To compose 3-digit numbers with place-value cards

MATERIALS:

1. AL Abacus
2. Place-value cards
3. Abacus Tiles
4. *Math Card Games* book, N43

ACTIVITIES FOR TEACHING:

Warm-up. Ask the child to enter quantities on the abacus, such as 8-ten, seven, and thirteen. Make various numbers with place-value cards and ask her to enter the quantities on the abacus.

Ones. Enter 3 on the abacus and ask: How much is it? [3] With a smile, ask: Three what—is it 3-ten? [no] Tell the child that instead of calling it "just 3," we call it "3 ones." Ask: Why do you think it is called ones? [because we are thinking about ones, not tens]

Tens. Tell the child to enter 10 on her abacus. See the left figure below. Ask: How many ones is it? [10] How many tens? [1]

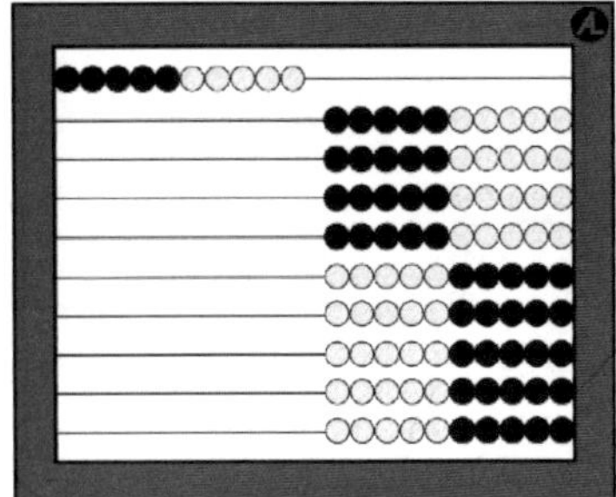

Ten.

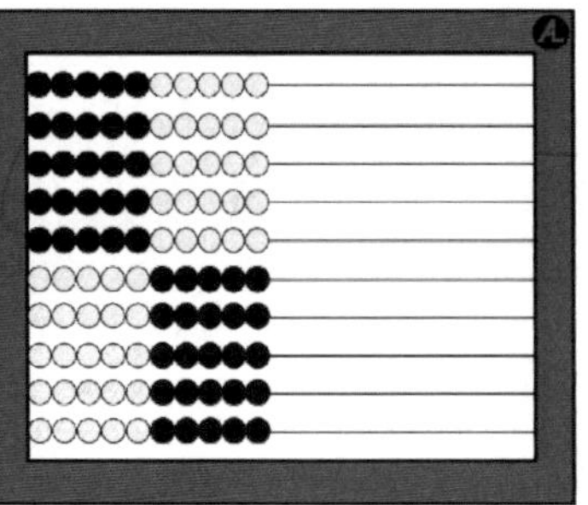

Hundred.

Hundreds. Tell the child to enter 10 tens on her abacus. See the right figure above. Remind her it has another name, *one hundred*. How many tens are in 1 hundred? [ten] How many ones are in one hundred? [100]

More hundreds. Ask: How could you show 2 hundred? [2 abacuses] Tell the child we will use two abacus tiles, which are pictures of 100 on the abacus. See the left figure below. Ask her to make 4 hundred. [4 abacus tiles]

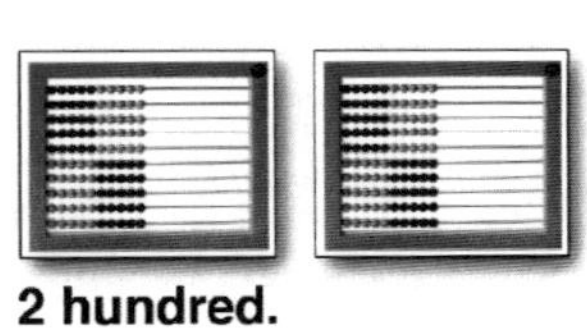

2 hundred.

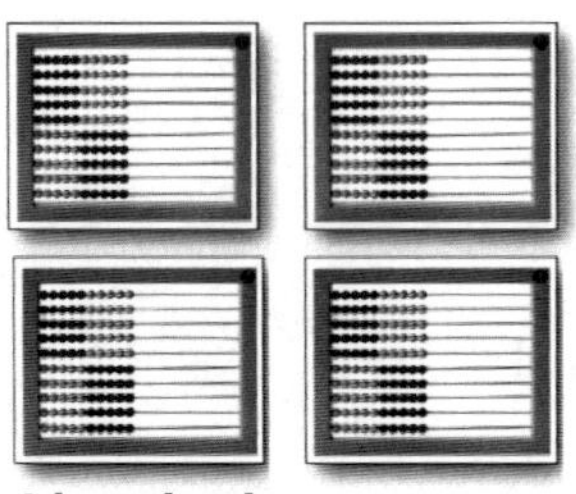

4 hundred.

EXPLANATIONS:

>did 9-tens starting at bottom ob abacus

>lots of Number blocks songs-GREAT!

It is important that the child identify a "ten" by noting that a digit follows it. This allows her to read numbers from left to right, the normal order. Later it will help her see 120 as 12 tens.

ACTIVITIES FOR TEACHING: | **EXPLANATIONS:**

Ask: Can you make 7 hundred? How could a person tell it was 7 hundred without counting them? [They could group five and two together.] See below on the left. Continue with 8 hundred and 10 hundred.

Recording hundreds. Show two abacus tiles and ask: How much is this? [2 hundred] Write 200 and say: This is how we write 200. Point to the 2 while saying two; point to the first 0 while saying "hun"; and point to the second 0 while saying "dred." See the figure on the right. Tell her this number has 3 digits: 2, 0, and 0.

2 0 0
two hun-dred

Ask the child to enter 48 on the abacus and set it next to seven abacus tiles. See the figure below. Ask: How many beads are shown? [748] Tell the child to find the place-value cards for the quantity. Ask: How many digits are in 748? [3] See below. Demonstrate how to stack the cards.

The seventh abacus tile can be on either the left or right side.

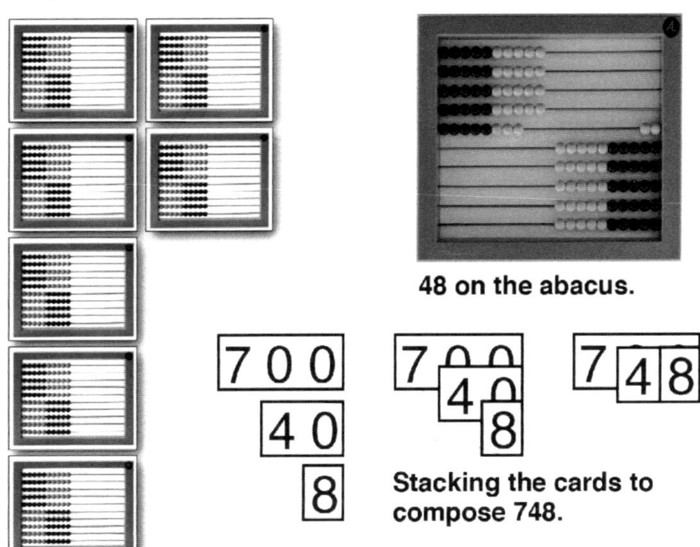

48 on the abacus.

Stacking the cards to compose 748.

700 with abacus tiles.

Can You Find game. Play the Can You Find game in the *Math Card Games* book, N43, but include the place-value cards for the hundreds, as well as the tens and ones.

Below are suggested numbers to say. With these numbers, all the cards will be picked up at the end of the game.

1. Can you find 400?
2. Can you find 43?
3. Can you find 104?
4. Can you find 57?
5. Can you find 629?
6. Can you find 760?
7. Can you find 215?
8. Can you find 998?
9. Can you find 371?
10. Can you find 502?
11. Can you find 86?
12. Can you find 830?

In conclusion. Ask: How many digits do you need after the 4 to write 400? [2] How many digits do you need after the 4 to write 40? [1] How many digits do you need after the 4 to write 4? [0]

Review Lesson 5: The Math Balance

OBJECTIVES:

1. To introduce the math balance
2. To review facts totaling 11

MATERIALS:

1. Math balance* and weights
2. Dry erase board
3. *Math Card Games* book, A24
4. AL Abacus

ACTIVITIES FOR TEACHING:

Warm-up. Sing "The Months" from a previous lesson.

Sing or recite "Yellow is the Sun."

Ask: How many digits do you need after the 6 to write 600? [2] How many digits do you need after the 6 to write 60? [1] How many digits do you need after the 6 to write 6? [0]

Math balance. Present the math balance shown below to the child. Give her two weights and ask her to make it balance. Avoid giving hints.

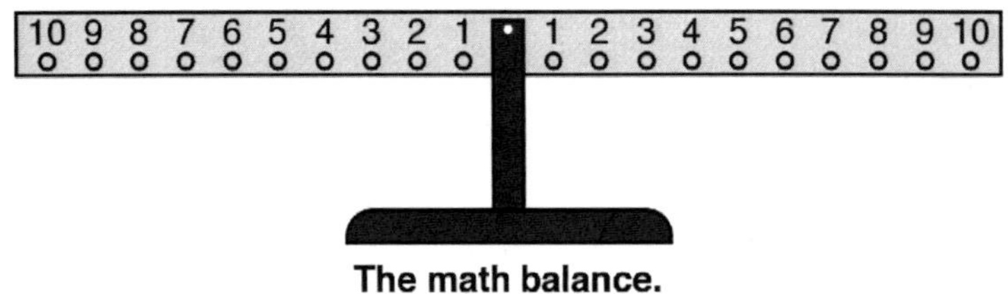

The math balance.

Remove the two weights and give them back to the child. Ask her to find another way to make it balance. Repeat.

Write:

10 = 10

Explain this is how we write the equation.

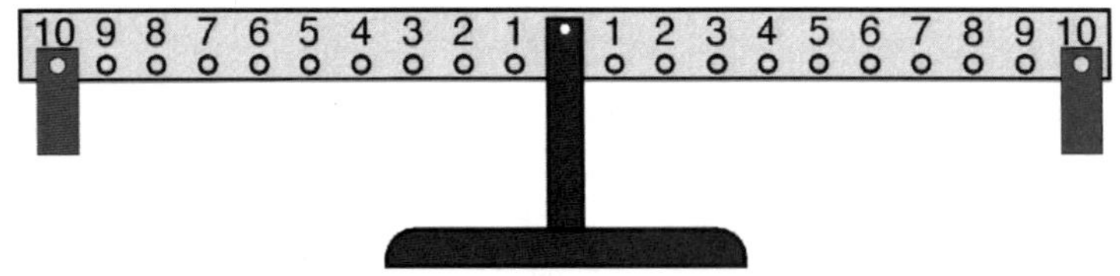

Balanced with two weights.

Next give the child three weights and ask her to make it balance. One possibility is shown on the next page. Ask: Why does it balance? [because the sides equal the same amount]

EXPLANATIONS:

*After the math balance is assembled, check to be sure it is level. If necessary, adjust it by moving the little white weights under the yellow beam.

All the weights are the same; ignore the numbers embossed on them.

For a person's first attempt, children usually choose the 10s, while adults usually choose a low number.

A person can make this discovery only once; so do not let anyone spoil it.

The white peg in the center is not a solution.

ACTIVITIES FOR TEACHING:

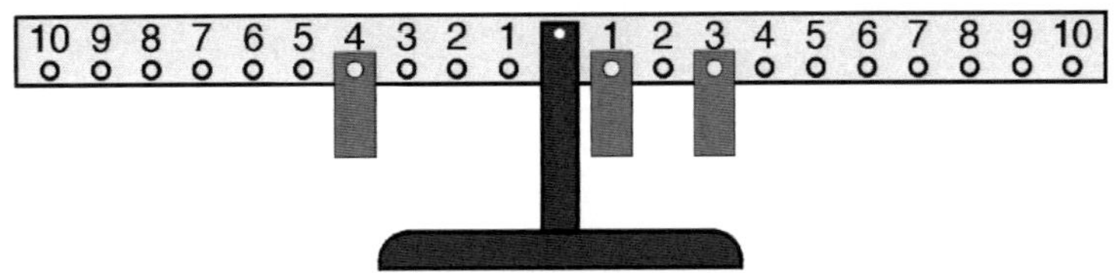

Balancing with three weights; 4 is 1 + 3.

Write:

$$4 = 1 + \_\_\_$$

Ask the child to complete the equation. [3]

Ways to make 10. Place a weight on the left 10. Give the child two weights and ask her to make it balance. See the figure below for one solution.

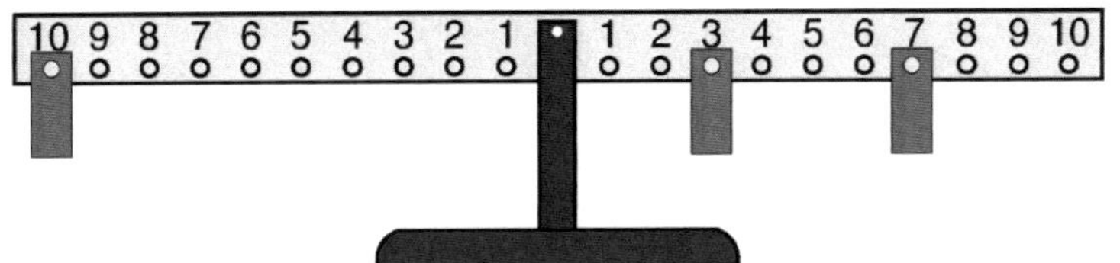

One way to make 10; 10 = 3 + 7.

Ask the child to write the equation on the dry erase board. [10 = 3 + 7]

Ask her to find a different solution to make it balance with 10. [10 = 1 + 9, 10 = 2 + 8, 10 = 4 + 6, 10 = 5 + 5] Tell the child to write it down on the dry erase board. Continue until all five ways are found and recorded.

Ways to make 11. Go back to 10 on the left and 3 and 7 on the right as shown above. Ask the child to move the weight from the 3-peg to the 4-peg. Then give her another weight and tell her to make it balance. See below. Ask the child for the equation [11 = 4 + 7] and then ask her to write it on the dry erase board.

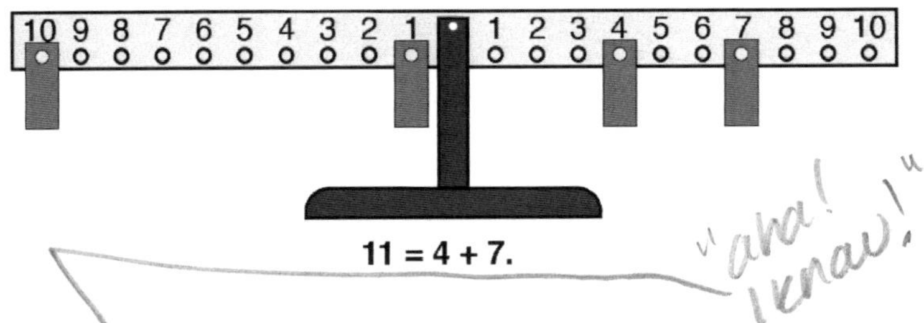

11 = 4 + 7.

Ask the child to find and write the other ways to equal eleven. [11 = 5 + 6, 11 = 3 + 8, 11 = 2 + 9, and 11 = 1 + 10]

Go to the Dump with Elevens. Play Go to the Dump with Elevens, found in *Math Card Games* book, A24. Encourage the child to use the abacus as needed.

In conclusion. Ask: What does an equal sign mean in an equation? [It shows balancing.]

EXPLANATIONS:

Flash cards are not a good way to drill the number facts. The only people who like flash cards are those who do not need them. Many adults today, because they could not respond fast enough to flash cards or time tests, became convinced as child that they have no math "ability." These people often develop math anxiety.

Flash cards are abstract; they require associating a symbol with two other symbols. On the other hand, a child familiar with the abacus thinks about the concrete beads when asked for a fact.

Another problem with flash cards is the false impression they give that mathematics is a subject that doesn't require thinking, or that it is just a tidy collection of "facts" that everyone must memorize.

The theory behind flash cards, going back to 1910, is based on the erroneous concept that a person learns these facts by associating a third symbol with two symbols. For example, if you see 8 and 7, you think 15. Brain research now tells us our brains do not work well that way. Rather, it is more natural to use a strategy. In this case they might take 2 from the 7, combine it with the 8 and change it into 10 and 5, or 15.

Also, even if the child did memorize 8, 7, 15, a few years later, the unfortunate child is expected to memorize 8, 7, 56. Many children find this very difficult.

Facts practice should always provide a strategy for the learner to figure out a forgotten answer. The AL Abacus provides a good way through visual representation, based on 5s and 10s.

Another reason to provide the abacus is to discourage counting. Counting is slow, unreliable, and habit forming. Those adding by counting dots on numerals are still counting dots decades later, although now it might be in their heads.

A 5-year-old was asked how much is 11 and 6. After he said 17 without counting, he was asked how he knew. He replied with a grin, "I have the abacus in my mind."

wednesday 8·18·2021

REVIEW LESSON 6: PART-WHOLE CIRCLE SETS

OBJECTIVES:

1. To identify the whole and its parts
2. To solve problems using part-whole circle sets

MATERIALS:

1. AL Abacus
2. Place-value cards
3. Worksheet 1, Part-Whole Circle Sets

ACTIVITIES FOR TEACHING:

Warm-up. Ask the child to enter quantities on the abacus, such as 8-ten, seven, and thirteen. Make various numbers with place-value cards and ask her to enter the quantities on the abacus.

Ask: How many digits do you need after the 7 to write 700? [2] How many digits do you need after the 7 to write 70? [1] How many digits do you need after the 7 to write 7? [0]

Part-whole circle sets. Draw a part-whole circle set as shown on the right. Explain that the larger circle is the whole and the smaller circles are the parts.

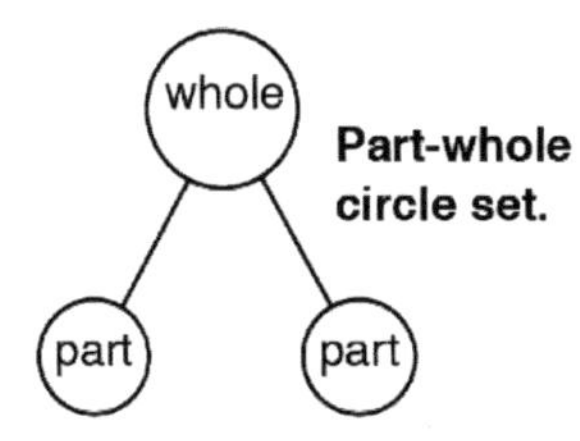

Part-whole circle set.

Write 10 in the whole-circle and 3 in the left part-circle. Ask: What is the other part? [7] Have the child write the answer. See the figures below.

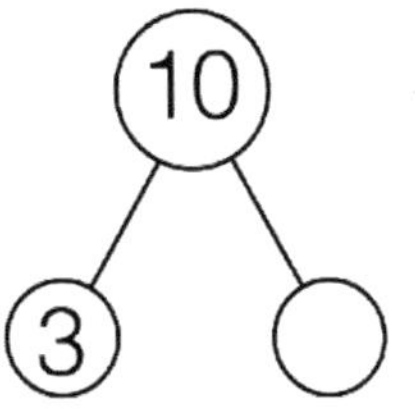

10 is a whole and 3 is a part.

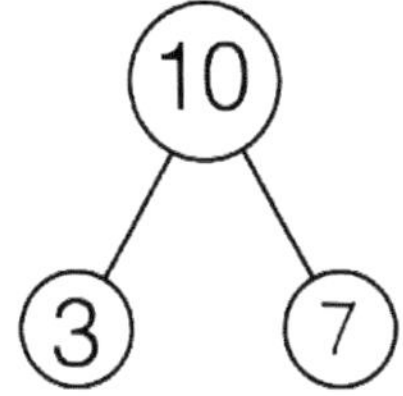

7 is the other part.

Ask her to say the equation. [3 + 7 = 10]

In the part-whole circle set, change the 10 to 11 and erase the 3. See the figures below. Ask: What is the missing part? [4] What is the equation? [11 = 4 + 7 or 4 + 7 = 11]

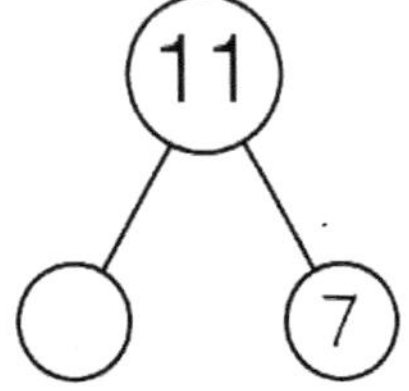

Find the other part.

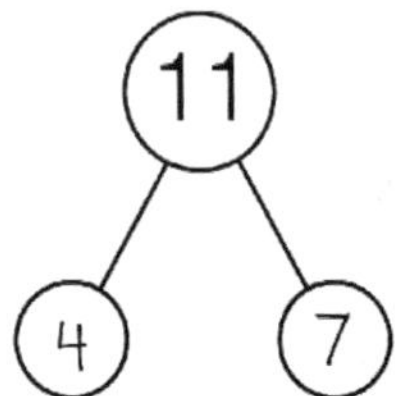

4 is the other part.

EXPLANATIONS:

Part-whole circle sets are a visual tool that help the child understand relationships. Research shows children using them do better when solving story problems.

ACTIVITIES FOR TEACHING:

Problem 1. Give the worksheet to the child and tell her to read the first problem.

> Eleven cherries were on the plate. Matthew ate some of them. Then there were eight cherries. How many cherries did Matthew eat? [3]

Tell the child to read the problem again. Then ask: Is the 11 a part or a whole? [whole] Tell her to write it in the whole-circle. See the left figure below.

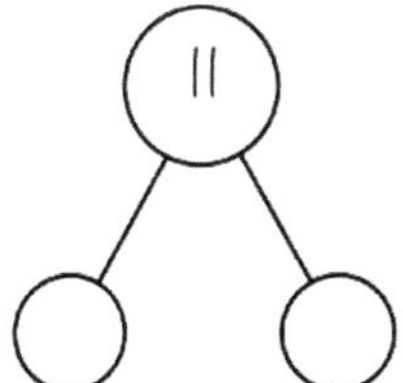

11 is the whole.

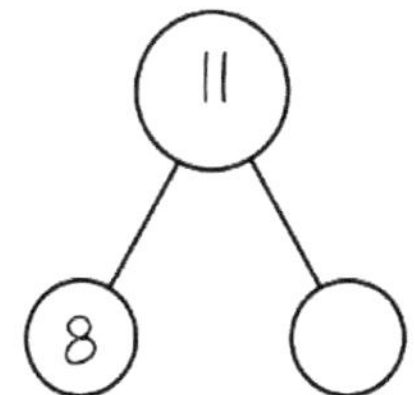

8 is a part.

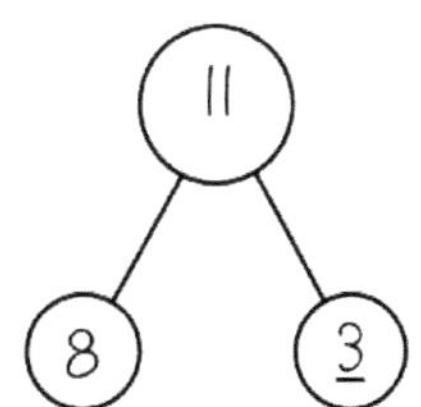

3 is the other part.

Ask: Is 8 a part or a whole? [part] Tell her to write it in a part-circle. See the middle figure above. Tell her to find the other part and write the equation, underlining the answer. Ask: Does your answer make sense? [yes]

Problem 2. Tell the child to read the second problem:

> Four crows were sitting on the grass. More crows flew there. Then there were ten crows. How many crows flew over to the first four? [6]

Ask: Is 4 a part or a whole? [part] Is 10 a part or a whole? [whole] Tell her to write the numbers in the appropriate circles and find the missing part. [6] See solution below.

Problem 3. Tell the child to read the third problem:

> Elizabeth had ten goldfish. For her seventh birthday, she received eight goldfish. How many goldfish does she have now? [18]

Tell the child to solve. Ask: Does her seventh birthday have anything to do with the goldfish? [no]

Problems 4 and 5. Tell the child to complete the worksheet. Answers are shown below.

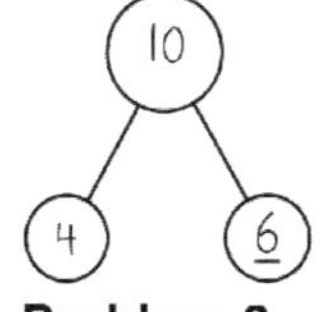

Problem 2.

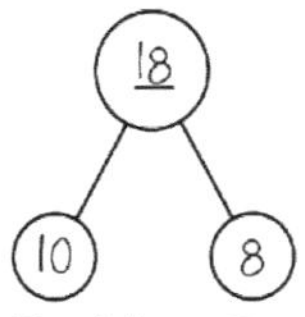

Problem 3.

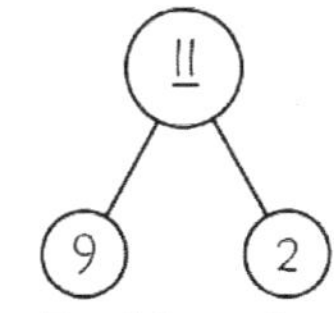

Problem 4.

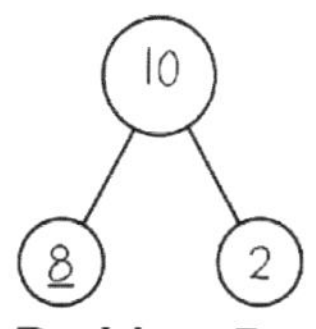

Problem 5.

In conclusion. Ask: What do the parts in a part-whole circle set add up to? [the whole]

EXPLANATIONS:

The 8 can be written in either the left or right part-circle.

> 2 #'s add up to the whole
* kind of caught up on #2 & #5 with wording "over" "fewer" we wanted to subtract.

Lesson 7: Ones Strategy on the Addition Table

OBJECTIVES:

1. To introduce the basic Venn diagram
2. To review the addition strategy of a Number Plus One and One Plus a Number
3. To learn about tables through constructing the addition table

MATERIALS:

1. Math journal, found in the back of the child's worksheets
2. Worksheet 2, Addition Tables
3. *Math Card Games* book, N35

ACTIVITIES FOR TEACHING:

Warm-up. Ask: What is 3 + 7? [10] What is 3 + 8? [11] Six and what makes 10? [4] Eight plus what equals 11? [3] Two plus what equals 11? [9]

Venn diagram. Draw a Venn diagram, consisting of a rectangle and two nonoverlapping circles, as shown below. In one circle write the phrase, "Girl Friends;" in the other circle write, "Boy Friends." Ask the child to write the names of friends in the correct circle. Those not fitting in either category, for example, pets, have their names inside the rectangle but outside the circles. See the figures below.

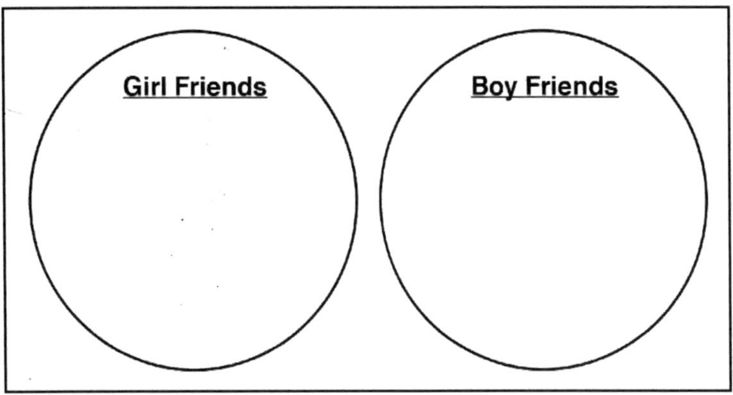

A basic Venn diagram.

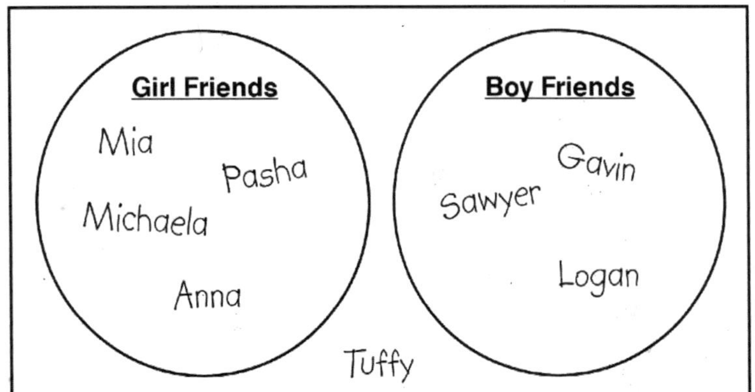

A Venn diagram with entries.

EXPLANATIONS:

The first half of these RightStart™ Mathematics lessons refers to the child as a female and the second half refers to the child as a male.

Venn diagrams are a way of representing relationships visually. They help sort and organize information with all subjects.

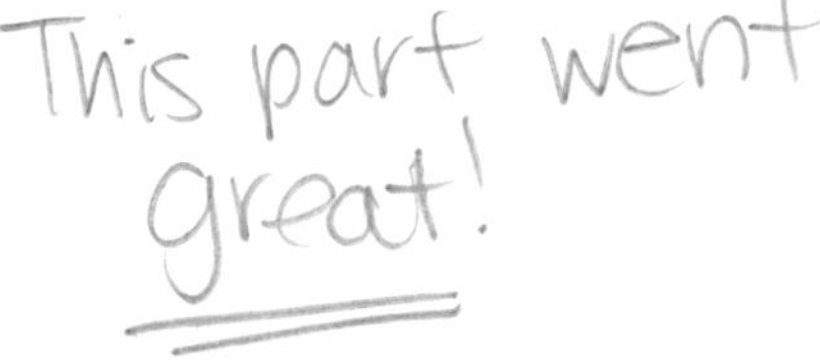

ACTIVITIES FOR TEACHING:

A Number Plus One. Ask the child to think of equations that starts with a number between 1 and 9 and adds 1. [1 + 1 = 2, 2 + 1 = 3, . . . , 9 + 1 = 10] Tell her to write all nine equations in her math journal. Ask: What is your strategy; how did you find the sums? [next number]

Worksheet 2. Give the child the worksheet. Explain: These are addition tables that will show the addition facts. Each table shows one type of strategy. A strategy is a way to remember some facts. Today you will work with the first table, Ones and Twos Strategies.

Demonstrate as follows: Let's write 3 + 1 = 4. Go across the top until you come to 3. Then go down in that column to the 1 on the side. That is the square where you write 4. See the figures below.

+	1	2	3	4	5	6	7	8	9
1									
2									
3									
4									
5									
6									
7									
8									
9									

+	1	2	3	4	5	6	7	8	9
1			4						
2									
3									
4									
5									
6									
7									
8									
9									

To write 3 + 1 = 4: Start at 3 and go down to 1. Write 4.

Ask the child to record the other facts she wrote in her math journal on her addition table. The table with these facts is shown below in the left figure.

+	1	2	3	4	5	6	7	8	9
1	2	3	4	5	6	7	8	9	10
2									
3									
4									
5									
6									
7									
8									
9									

Sums with a number + 1.

+	1	2	3	4	5	6	7	8	9
1	2	3	4	5	6	7	8	9	10
2	**3**								
3	**4**								
4	**5**								
5	**6**								
6	**7**								
7	**8**								
8	**9**								
9	**10**								

Sums with 1 + a number.

Next tell the child to write nine equations starting with 1 + a number. [1 + 1 = 2, 1 + 2 = 3, 1 + 3 = 4, . . . , 1 + 9 = 10] Ask her to record them on her addition table. See right figure above. Tell the child the other addition tables will be used during the next few days.

Slower Speed game. Play the Slower Speed game, found in the *Math Card Games* book, N35.

In conclusion. Ask: What is 49 plus 1? [50] What is 13 plus 1? [14] What is 1 plus 15? [16] What is 1 plus 79? [80]

EXPLANATIONS:

You might want the child to date her work in her math journal.

New entries to the table are shown in boldface.

Remind the child in some way that it is her responsibility to ask questions if she does not understand.

Conclusions may be a summary of the day's lesson or an expansion of the lesson to challenge higher level thinking.

Lesson 8: Twos Strategy on the Addition Table

OBJECTIVES:

1. To introduce an overlapping Venn diagram
2. To review the addition strategy of a Number Plus Two and Two Plus a Number

MATERIALS:

1. Music for "Thirty Days Has September" (Appendix p. 2, available via QR code, or online at RightStartMath.com)
2. AL Abacus
3. Math journal
4. Worksheet 2, Addition Tables
5. *Math Card Games* book, N37

ACTIVITIES FOR TEACHING:

Warm-up. Draw the Venn diagram with overlapping ellipses as shown below. Let the child read the statements and write names in the correct places. Friends who have both a brother and sister need to have their names written in the overlapping portion of the circles. Those with neither have their names outside the ellipses.

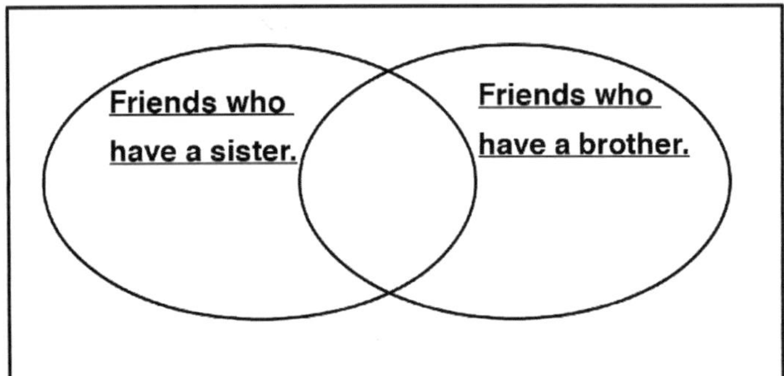

A Venn diagram with overlapping ellipses.

Ask: What is 39 plus 1? [40] What is 12 plus 1? [13] What is 1 plus 25? [26] What is 1 plus 69? [70] What is 1 plus 20? [21]

Ask the child to say the months in order. Sing or say "Thirty Days Has September."

Even Numbers Plus Two. Ask the child the enter twos on her abacus while naming the numbers. Stop at 20. [2, 4, . . . , 20] See the figure on the right. Ask the following: What is 2 + 2, [4] 4 + 2, [6] 6 + 2, [8] and 8 + 2? [10] What pattern do you hear? [next even number] Tell her to write these equations in her math journal.

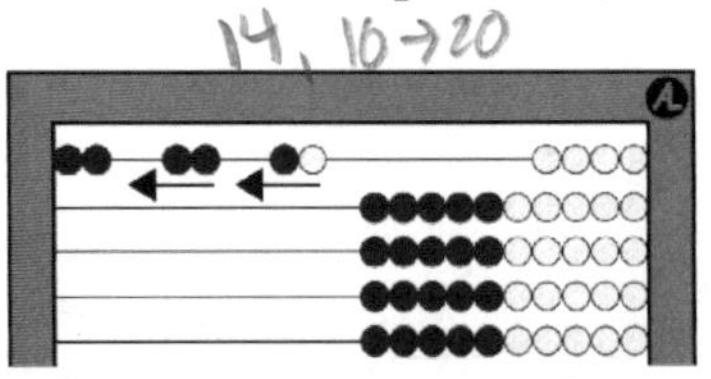

Adding 2s to even numbers.

Worksheet 2. Give the worksheet to the child and tell her to write these sums in her addition table, using the first table, Ones and Twos Strategies. See the left figure on the next page.

EXPLANATIONS:

QR code for "Thirty Days Has September."

A teacher's job in the past was to help the student get the right answer in the shortest amount of time. Today it is more important to know how a child arrives at the answer. The child should not attempt to memorize the number facts without efficient strategies.

ACTIVITIES FOR TEACHING:

+	1	2	3	4	5	6	7	8	9
1	2	3	4	5	6	7	8	9	10
2	3	**4**		**6**		**8**		**10**	
3	4								
4	5								
5	6								
6	7								
7	8								
8	9								
9	10								

Even number + 2.

+	1	2	3	4	5	6	7	8	9
1	2	3	4	5	6	7	8	9	10
2	3	4		6		8		10	
3	4								
4	5	**6**							
5	6								
6	7	**8**							
7	8								
8	9	**10**							
9	10								

2 + an even number.

EXPLANATIONS:

New entries to the table are shown in boldface.

Two Plus an Even Number. Ask: What is 2 + 2? [4] What is 2 + 4? [6] What is 2 + 6? [8] What is 2 + 8? [10] Ask: If you didn't know 2 + 6, how could you figure it out? [same strategy as 6 + 2] Ask her to write the 2 plus and even equations in her math journal and write the sums on her addition table. See the right figure above.

Odd Numbers Plus Two. Tell the child to enter 1 on her abacus and then enter 2s while naming the quantities. Stop at 11. [1, 3, . . . , 11] See the figure.

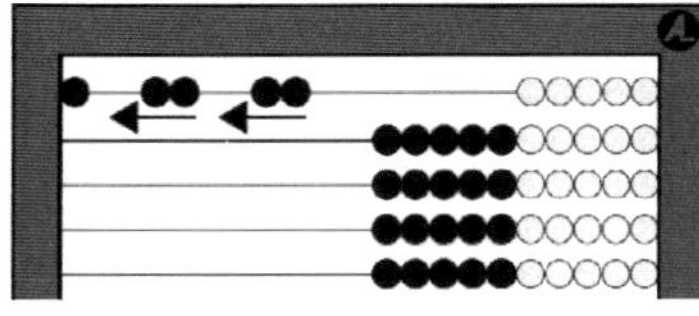

Adding 2s to odd numbers.

Ask: What is 1 + 2, [3] 3 + 2, [5] 5 + 2, [7] and 7 + 2? [9] What strategy do you hear? [next odd number] Tell her to write these equations in her math journal and to write them on her addition table. See the left figure below.

+	1	2	3	4	5	6	7	8	9
1	2	3	4	5	6	7	8	9	10
2	3	4	**5**	6	**7**	8	**9**	10	**11**
3	4								
4	5	6							
5	6								
6	7	8							
7	8								
8	9	10							
9	10								

Odd number + 2.

+	1	2	3	4	5	6	7	8	9
1	2	3	4	5	6	7	8	9	10
2	3	4	5	6	7	8	9	10	11
3	4	**5**							
4	5	6							
5	6	**7**							
6	7	8							
7	8	**9**							
8	9	10							
9	10	**11**							

2 + an odd number.

Next tell the child to write the five equations starting with 2 + an odd number. [2 + 1 = 3, 2 + 3 = 5, 2 + 5 = 7, 2 + 7 = 9, 2 + 9 = 11] Tell her to enter them on her addition table. See right figure above.

Slower Speed with Evens and Odds game. Play the Slower Speed with Evens and Odds game found in the *Math Card Games* book, N37.

In conclusion. Ask: What is 12 plus 2? [14] What is 18 plus 2? [20] What is 2 plus 13? [15] What is 2 plus 19? [21] What is 2 plus 29? [31] What is 2 plus 98? [100]

9.7.2021

Lesson 9: Tens and Near Tens on the Addition Table

OBJECTIVES:

1. To review the Tens Strategy
2. To review Near Tens Strategies

MATERIALS:

1. Math balance
2. Math journal
3. Worksheet 2, Addition Tables
4. *Math Card Games* book, A34
5. AL Abacus

ACTIVITIES FOR TEACHING:

Warm-up. Ask the child to say the months in order. Tell her to sing or say "Thirty Days has September."

Ask: What is 14 plus 2? [16] What is 8 plus 2? [10] What is 2 plus 15? [17] What is 2 plus 19? [21] What is 2 plus 29? [31] What is 2 plus 98? [100]

Tens Strategy on the math balance. Tell the child to put a weight on the left 10 and to use two weights to find all the ways to make it balance. See below for one solution.

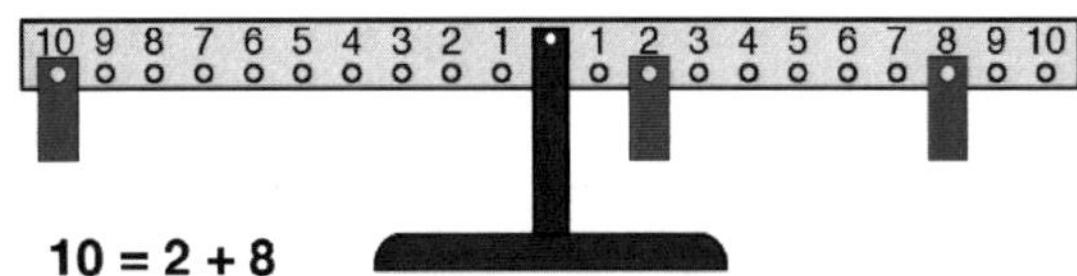

Ask the child to write the equations in her math journal as shown below on the left.

10	=	1	+	9
10	=	2	+	8
10	=	3	+	7
10	=	4	+	6
10	=	5	+	5
10	=	6	+	4
10	=	7	+	3
10	=	8	+	2
10	=	9	+	1

The tens equations.

+	1	2	3	4	5	6	7	8	9
1									10
2								10	
3							10		
4						10			
5					10				
6				10					
7			10						
8		10							
9	10								

The tens facts.

Worksheet 2. Give the child the worksheet and tell her to write the 10s facts on the second addition table, Tens and Near Tens Strategies. See the right figure above. Ask: What pattern do you see? [a diagonal]

Near Tens Strategy; elevens. Using the math balance, tell the child to balance 10 with 2 and 8 as shown on above. Say: Put another weight on the left side so it equals 11. Where could you move the weight on 8 to make it balance? [move it to 9] Tell her to try it. See figure on the next page.

EXPLANATIONS:

→ write these lyrics out.

→ thought it through and got them right.

looks like stairs.

Awesome! Got it!

ACTIVITIES FOR TEACHING:

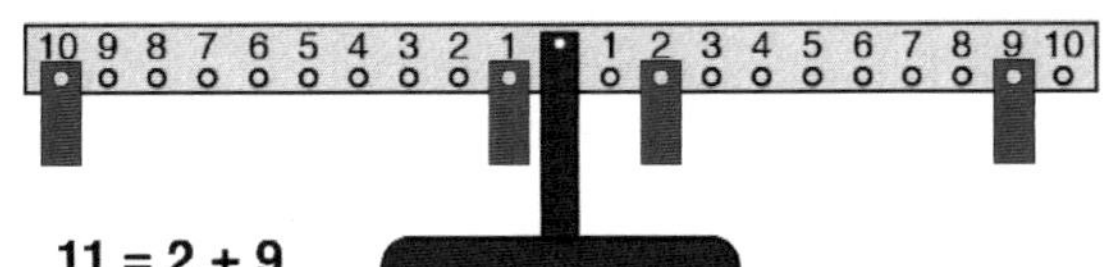

Tell her to put the weight back on 8. Ask: Where could you move the weight from 2 to make it balance? [move it to 3] Tell her to write the eight sums that equal 11 in her journal and in the second addition table. See below.

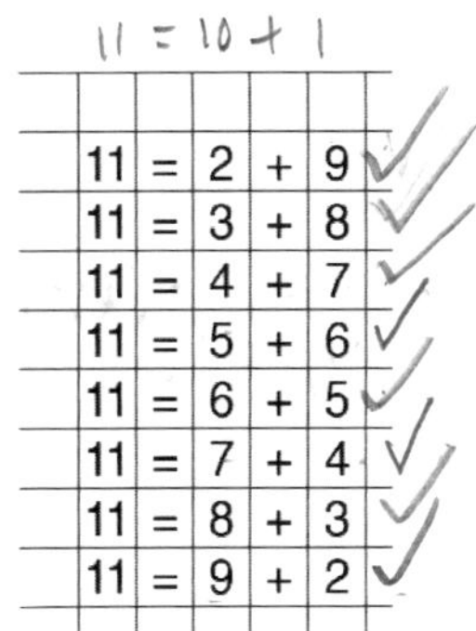

11	=	2	+	9
11	=	3	+	8
11	=	4	+	7
11	=	5	+	6
11	=	6	+	5
11	=	7	+	4
11	=	8	+	3
11	=	9	+	2

The 11s equations.

+	1	2	3	4	5	6	7	8	9
1									10
2								10	**11**
3							10	**11**	
4						10	**11**		
5					10	**11**			
6				10	**11**				
7			10	**11**					
8		10	**11**						
9	10	**11**							

The eleven facts.

Near Tens Strategy; nines. Using the math balance, tell the child to balance 10 with 2 and 8. Say: Now move the 10 weight to the 9. Ask: What do you need to do to make it balance? [Either move the 2-weight to 1 or the 8-weight to 7.] Tell her to find the eight 9s facts and to write them in her math journal and in the second addition table. See below.

Say: Use the addition table to find 8 + 1, [9] 8 + 2, [10] and 8 + 3. [11] Repeat for 5 + 4, [9] 5 + 5, [10] and 5 + 6. [11]

9	=	1	+	8
9	=	2	+	7
9	=	3	+	6
9	=	4	+	5
9	=	5	+	4
9	=	6	+	3
9	=	7	+	2
9	=	8	+	1

The 9s equations.

+	1	2	3	4	5	6	7	8	9
1								**9**	10
2							**9**	10	11
3						**9**	10	11	
4					**9**	10	11		
5				**9**	10	11			
6			**9**	10	11				
7		**9**	10	11					
8	**9**	10	11						
9	10	11							

The nine facts.

Go to the Dump with Nines. Play Go to the Dump with Nines, found in the *Math Card Games* book, A34. Encourage her to use the abacus as needed.

In conclusion. What do you need with 7 to make 10? [3] With 7 to make 11? [4] With 7 to make 9? [2] What do you need with 6 to make 11? [5] With 6 to make 9? [3]

EXPLANATIONS:

Lesson 10: Two-Fives Strategy on the Addition Table

OBJECTIVES:

1. To review the term *strategy*
2. To review the Two-Fives Strategy

MATERIALS:

1. AL Abacus
2. Math journal
3. Worksheet 2, Addition Tables
4. *Math Card Games* book, A44, Var. 2 using cards with numbers 5–9

ACTIVITIES FOR TEACHING:

Warm-up. Ask: What do you need with 6 to make 10? [4] With 6 to make 11? [5] With 6 to make 9? [3] What do you need with 5 to make 11? [6] With 5 to make 9? [4]

Ask the child to say the even numbers to 20 and the odd numbers to 19. Then ask her to say the even numbers backward from 10 and the odd numbers backward from 9. Use an abacus if necessary.

Ask the child to count by 10s to 200 [10, 20, 30, . . . , 200] and by 5s to 100. [5, 10, 15, . . . , 100]

Play the Comes Before game; ask the child what even number comes before the number you say: 6, [4] 10, [8] 8, [6] 2, [0] and 4. [2] Then ask the child what odd number comes before the number you say: 7, [5] 9, [7] 11, [9] 5, [3] and 3. [1]

Reviewing strategies. Ask: How many *strategies* can you think of? [adding 1, adding 2, making 10, making 11, and making 9]

The Two-Fives Strategy. Tell her that there is a strategy for adding two numbers when both numbers are between 5 and 9. Enter two 7s on the top two wires of the abacus as shown below on the left.

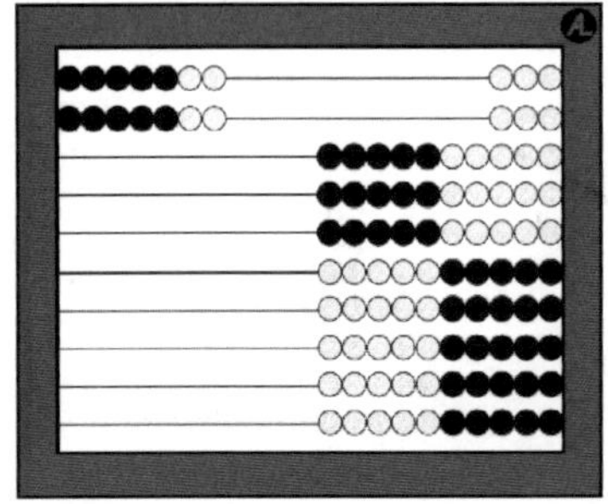

7 + 7 = ___.

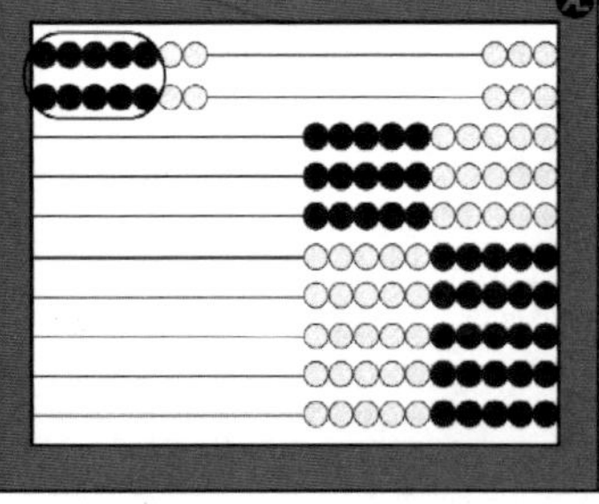

7 + 7 = 10 + 4 = 14.

Ask: Can see the 10? [the two groups of five beads] See the right figure above. Ask: How much is left over? [two 2s, or 4] How much is 7 + 7? [14]

EXPLANATIONS:

Children like names for concepts; hence, use term *strategy.*

Redo: call for help on 9.15.2021

ACTIVITIES FOR TEACHING:

Tell the child to use the Two-Fives Strategies to find 9 + 6. See the figures below. Ask the child to explain how she knows the sum. [Two-fives make 10 and the left overs equal 5, giving a sum of 15.]

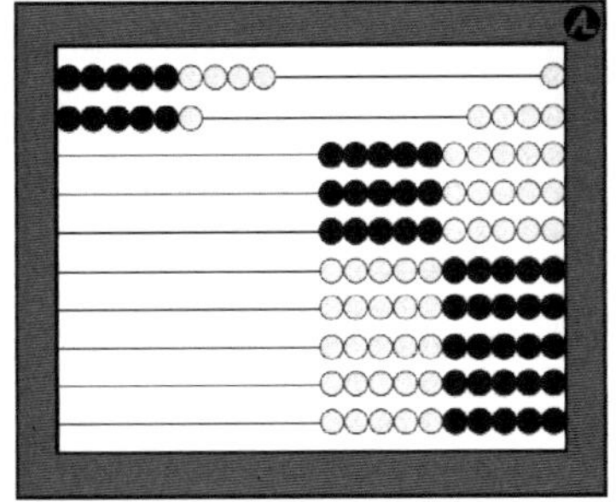

9 + 6 = ___.

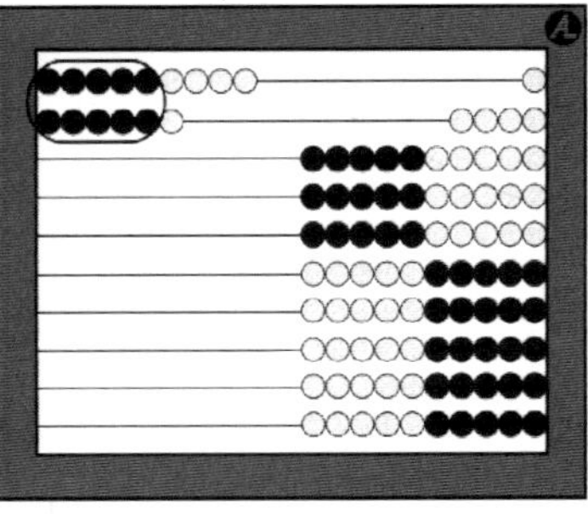

9 + 6 = 10 + 5 = 15 .

Reciting the Two-Fives Strategies. Tell the child to find the following by using her abacus: What is 5 + 5? [10] What is 5 + 6? [11] What is 5 + 7? [12] What is 5 + 8? [13] What is 5 + 9? [14] Continue with the 6s, but ask her to say the equations with you. [6 + 5 = 11, 6 + 6 = 12, . . . , 6 + 9 = 15] Repeat for the 7s, 8s, and 9s.

Writing the equations (optional). Tell the child to write the equations in her math journal. See below.

Worksheet 2. Give the child the worksheet and tell her to write the facts for using the Two-Fives Strategies on the third addition table, Two-Fives Strategy. See the figures below.

5	5	+	5	=	10
	5	+	6	=	11
	5	+	7	=	12
	5	+	8	=	13
	5	+	9	=	14
6	6	+	5	=	11
	6	+	6	=	12
	6	+	7	=	13
	6	+	8	=	14
	6	+	9	=	15
7	7	+	5	=	12
	7	+	6	=	13
	7	+	7	=	14
	7	+	8	=	15
	7	+	9	=	16
8	8	+	5	=	13
	8	+	6	=	14
	8	+	7	=	15
	8	+	8	=	16
	8	+	9	=	17
9	9	+	5	=	14
	9	+	6	=	15
	9	+	7	=	16
	9	+	8	=	17
	9	+	9	=	18

The Two-Fives facts written in the math journal.

+	1	2	3	4	5	6	7	8	9
1									
2									
3									
4									
5					10	11	12	13	14
6					11	12	13	14	15
7					12	13	14	15	16
8					13	14	15	16	17
9					14	15	16	17	18

The Two-Fives facts.

Addition War game. Play Addition War found in the *Math Card Games* book, A44, Var. 2. Use cards with 5–9.

In conclusion. Ask: What is 7 + 8? [15] What is 8 + 6? [14] What is 9 + 5? [14] What is 8 + 9? [17]

EXPLANATIONS:

said Abacus not really helpful.

Writing the equations is optional; it may be too much writing for some children.

→ look @ shape

→ play game. fun need to add more #'s

Lesson 11: Doubles Strategies on the Addition Table

OBJECTIVES:

1. To review the Doubles Strategy
2. To review the Near Doubles Strategy

MATERIALS:

1. AL Abacus
2. Math journal
3. Worksheet 2, Addition Tables
4. *Math Card Games* book, A17 (optional) and A19

ACTIVITIES FOR TEACHING:

Warm-up. Ask the child: What is 7 + 9? [16] What is 9 + 6? [15] What is 9 + 5? [14] What is 8 + 9? [17]

Ask: What do you need with 4 to make 10? [6] With 4 to make 11? [7] With 4 to make 9? [5] What do you need with 7 to make 11? [4] With 5 to make 9? [4]

Ask the child to say the even numbers to 30 [2, 4, 6, . . . , 30] and the odd numbers to 29. [1, 3, 5, . . . , 29] Use the abacus if necessary.

Ask the child to count by 10s to 200 [10, 20, 30, . . . , 200] and by 5s to 100. [5, 10, 15, . . . , 100]

Play the Comes Before game; ask the child what even number comes before the number you say: 6, [4] 10, [8] 8, [6] 2, [0] and 4. [2] Then ask the child what odd number comes before the number you say: 3, [1] 11, [9] 13, [11] 7, [5] and 9. [7]

Doubles Strategy. Ask the child: What could we call a strategy with facts like 2 + 2, 3 + 3, and 6 + 6? [Doubles Strategy] Tell her to enter the doubles on her abacus in order and to recite the sums. [1 + 1 = 2, 2 + 2 = 4, 3 + 3 = 6, . . . , 9 + 9 = 18] See figures below.

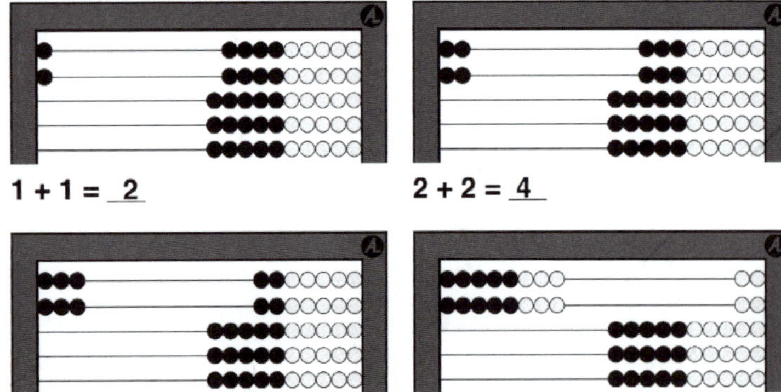

1 + 1 = 2 2 + 2 = 4

3 + 3 = 6 8 + 8 = 16

Tell the child to write the equations in her math journal. See the left figure on the next page.

EXPLANATIONS:

It is commonly thought that children learn the doubles easier than other facts. Research shows they are not easier to learn; the reason children seem to know them better is that teachers and parents drill them more often.

ACTIVITIES FOR TEACHING:

EXPLANATIONS:

Worksheet 2. Give the child the worksheet. Tell her to write the facts using the Doubles Strategies on the fourth addition table, Doubles and Near Doubles. See the right figure below. Ask: What patterns do you see? [diagonal and even numbers]

→like stairs.

1	+	1	=	2
2	+	2	=	4
3	+	3	=	6
4	+	4	=	8
5	+	5	=	10
6	+	6	=	12
7	+	7	=	14
8	+	8	=	16
9	+	9	=	18

The doubles facts.

+	1	2	3	4	5	6	7	8	9
1	2								
2		4							
3			6						
4				8					
5					10				
6						12			
7							14		
8								16	
9									18

The doubles facts.

Doubles Solitaire game (optional). Play Doubles Solitaire, found in the *Math Card Games* book, A17.

A child needing more practice with doubles needs to play this game.

STOP.

9.22.2021

Near Doubles Strategy. Tell her to make the stairs on the abacus. See the figure on the right. Ask: What near double do you see on the top two wires? [1 + 2] What near double do you see on the second and third wires? [2 + 3] Tell her to touch and say all the near doubles and their sums. [1 + 2 = 3, 2 + 3 = 5, . . . , 8 + 9 = 17]

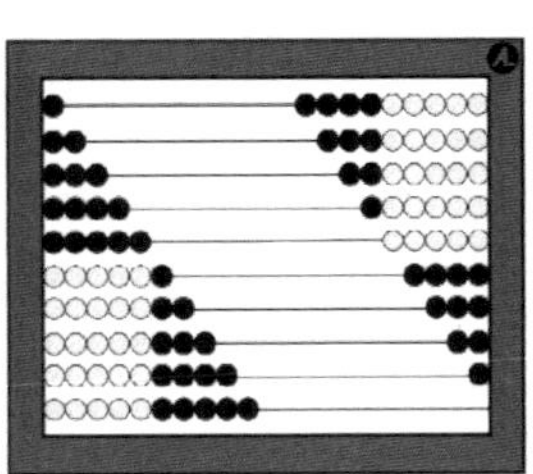

Near doubles facts.

→He wants to say "LOOK A like" Doubles.

Tell the child to write the equations in her math journal. See left figure below.

1	+	2	=	3
2	+	3	=	5
3	+	4	=	7
4	+	5	=	9
5	+	6	=	11
6	+	7	=	13
7	+	8	=	15
8	+	9	=	17

The near doubles facts.

+	1	2	3	4	5	6	7	8	9
1	2	3							
2	3	4	5						
3		5	6	7					
4			7	8	9				
5				9	10	11			
6					11	12	13		
7						13	14	15	
8							15	16	17
9								17	18

The near doubles facts.

Worksheet 2. Tell her to write the facts for the near doubles on the same addition table. See the figure above. Ask: What patterns do you see? [diagonal, odd numbers]

→odd numbers in a step shape.

Near Doubles Solitaire game. Play Near Doubles Solitaire found in the *Math Card Games* book, A19. Two can play, where they try to "beat the cards."

In conclusion. Ask: What is 7 + 7? [14] What is 7 + 8? [15] What is 6 + 6? [12] What is 6 + 7? [13]

–Master of the abacus! ♡

9.27.2021

Lesson 12: Making Ten Strategy on the Addition Table

OBJECTIVES:

1. To review adding 8 and 9 through Making Ten Strategy

MATERIALS:

1. AL Abacus
2. Math journal
3. Worksheet 2, Addition Tables
4. *Math Card Games* book, A55

ACTIVITIES FOR TEACHING:

Warm-up. Ask: What is 4 + 4? [8] What is 4 + 5? [9] What is 8 + 8? [16] What is 8 + 7? [15]

Ask: What is 7 + 9? [16] What is 9 + 6? [15] What is 9 + 5? [14] What is 8 + 9? [17]

Ask: What do you need with 7 to make 10? [3] With 7 to make 11? [4] With 7 to make 14? [7] What do you need with 7 to make 15? [8]

Ask the child to say the even numbers to 40 [2, 4, 6, . . . , 40] and the odd numbers to 19. [1, 3, 5, . . . , 19] 15

Ask: What is 4 + 4? [8] What is 4 + 5? [9] What is 8 + 8? [16] What is 8 + 7? [15]

EXPLANATIONS:

Still counting. used abacus

*do math drills - may help.

→ sang CC 2's song. 32 slave but did but did amazing.

mental math skills.

Adding 9 with the Making Ten Strategy. Tell the child to add 9 + 4 by entering 9 on the first wire and 4 on the second wire as shown below. Listen to her suggestions on how to solve the equation and then expand on the Take and Give Strategy by taking 1 from the 4 and giving it to the 9 to make 10 and 3. [13]

Sometimes the Making Ten Strategy is called Adding Nines and Eights Strategy.

Trading is best done using both hands simultaneously. One hand removes the bead(s) from the second wire while the other hand adds the same number of bead(s) to the first wire.

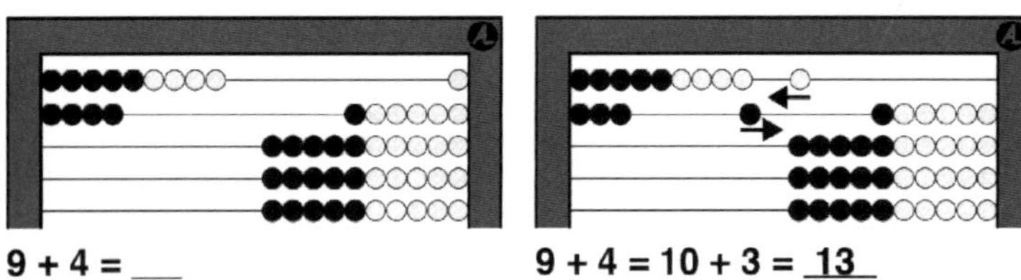

Next ask her to repeat for 9 plus 6. [15]

Now enter 9 and 3 on the abacus; ask the child to look at the abacus and move the beads in her head. [12] Continue with 9 + 9, [18] and other 9 facts. Also ask for 4 + 9, [13] 7 + 9, [16] and so forth.

Moving beads mentally is a step to help the child in developing a mental abacus.

STOP - too frustrated.

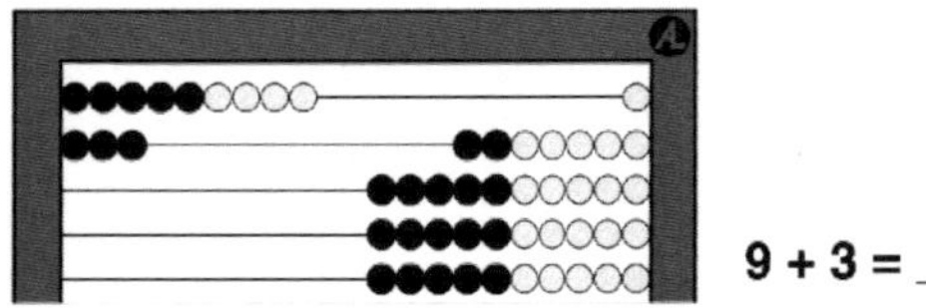

9 + 3 = ___

Tell the child to write the equations for 9 plus a number in her math journal. See the left figure on the next page.

ACTIVITIES FOR TEACHING:

EXPLANATIONS:

Worksheet 2. Distribute the worksheet and tell the child to write the facts for adding 9s by using the Making Ten Strategy. Use the fifth addition table, Making Ten Strategy. See the right figure below. Ask: What patterns do you see? [consecutive numbers in a row and a column]

9	+	1	=	10
9	+	2	=	11
9	+	3	=	12
9	+	4	=	13
9	+	5	=	14
9	+	6	=	15
9	+	7	=	16
9	+	8	=	17
9	+	9	=	18

The 9s facts.

+	1	2	3	4	5	6	7	8	9
1									10
2									11
3									12
4									13
5									14
6									15
7									16
8									17
9	10	11	12	13	14	15	16	17	18

The 9s facts.

Adding 8. Tell the child to enter 8 on the top wire and 3 on the next wire. Ask: How could you use the Making Ten Strategy to find the sum? [Take 2 from the 3 and give it to the 8.] Tell her to try it mentally and then do it on the abacus with her hands. Repeat for 8 plus 7.

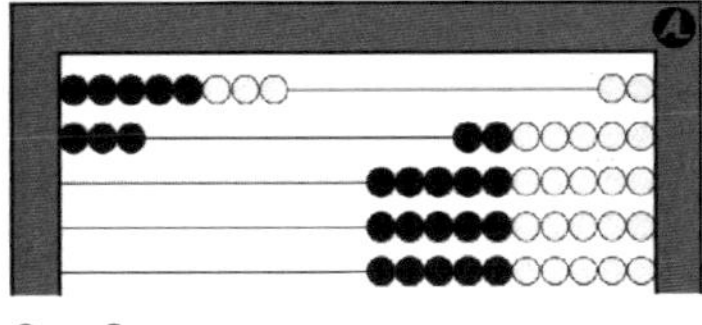

8 + 3 = ___

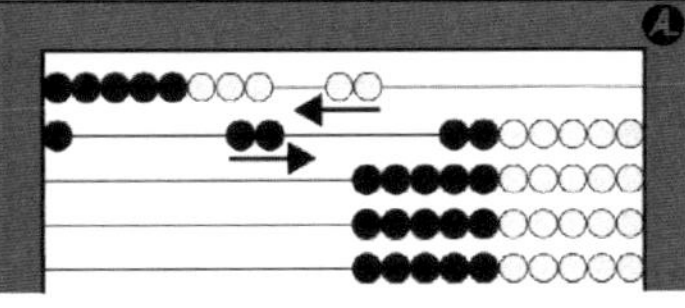

8 + 3 = 10 + 1 = 11

Tell the child to write the equations for 8 plus a number in her math journal.

Worksheet 2. Tell her to write the facts for the 8 plus a number on the same addition table. See figure below.

8	+	1	=	9
8	+	2	=	10
8	+	3	=	11
8	+	4	=	12
8	+	5	=	13
8	+	6	=	14
8	+	7	=	15
8	+	8	=	16
8	+	9	=	17

The 8s facts.

+	1	2	3	4	5	6	7	8	9
1								9	10
2								10	11
3								11	12
4								12	13
5								13	14
6								14	15
7								15	16
8	9	10	11	12	13	14	15	16	17
9	10	11	12	13	14	15	16	17	18

The 8s facts.

On the Number game. Play the On the Number game in the *Math Card Games* book, A55. Use 18 for the target.

In conclusion. Ask: What is 9 + 7? [16] What is 7 + 8? [15] What is 9 + 6? [15] What is 6 + 8? [14]

Lesson 13: The Completed Addition Table

OBJECTIVES:

1. To construct the complete addition table

MATERIALS:

1. Basic card decks
2. Worksheet 2, Addition Tables
3. *Math Card Games* book, A44

ACTIVITIES FOR TEACHING:

Warm-up. Ask: What is 3 + 3? [6] What is 3 + 4? [7] What is 6 + 6? [12] What is 6 + 7? [13]

Ask: What is 9 + 6? [15] What is 6 + 8? [14] What is 9 + 5? [14] What is 5 + 8? [13]

Draw a Venn diagram with overlapping ellipses as shown below. Be sure the overlapping area is large enough to accommodate almost two thirds of the facts.

Tell the child to read the statements and write two facts in each area without the sums. Facts using neither strategy need to be written outside the ellipses.

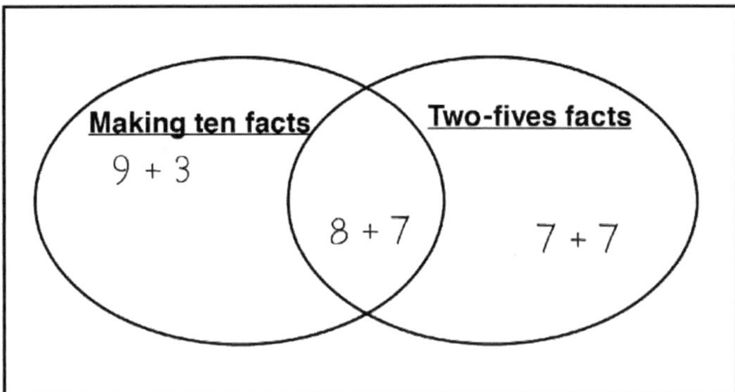

A Venn diagram with overlapping ellipses.

Play the Comes Before game; ask the child what even number comes before the number you say: 8, [6] 12, [10] 4, [2] 2, [0] and 10. [8] Then ask the child what odd number comes before the number you say: 5, [3] 11, [9] 13, [11] 9, [7] and 7. [5]

Finding Tens and Near Tens game. This simple game for two players provides practice in identifying the tens and near tens sums. Use six of each basic number card from 1–9.

Start by laying out face up a 3 × 3 array of cards as shown on the next page. The goal is to collect pairs that make 9, 10, or 11. The two cards must be in the same row or same column.

EXPLANATIONS:

It is interesting to note that slightly over 50 percent of the facts are included in these two strategies.

These cards can be used for the Addition War game to be played later.

ACTIVITIES FOR TEACHING:

EXPLANATIONS:

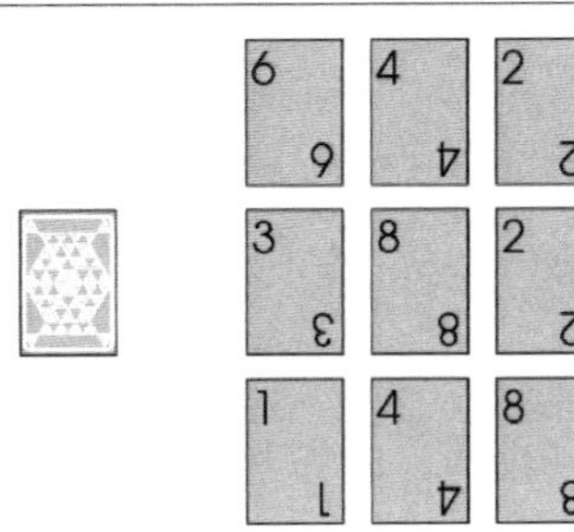

An array.

In the array above, the player could collect 6 and 3 in the first column. However, it would be better to take 6 and 4 from the first row and 3 and 8 from the second row. The player can also collect a 2 and 8 in the third column or 1 and 8 from the last row.

The player fills in the blank spaces before the second player takes a turn. If no one can play, replace the middle column. The winner is the player collecting the most cards. Be sure all players have the same number of turns by the end of the game.

Worksheet 2. Give the child the worksheet and tell her to write the sums for the last addition table as she plays the Addition War game. See below.

Addition War game. Play the Addition War game found in the *Math Card Games* book, A44. Each time the players pick up their two cards, they enter the sum in their addition tables, unless it is already entered. For example, if a player's cards are 4 and 8, they write 12 in the rectangle for 4 + 8 and in the rectangle for 8 + 4. The first player to complete their addition table is the winner.

+	1	2	3	4	5	6	7	8	9
1	2	3	4	5	6	7	8	9	10
2	3	4	5	6	7	8	9	10	11
3	4	5	6	7	8	9	10	11	12
4	5	6	7	8	9	10	11	12	13
5	6	7	8	9	10	11	12	13	14
6	7	8	9	10	11	12	13	14	15
7	8	9	10	11	12	13	14	15	16
8	9	10	11	12	13	14	15	16	17
9	10	11	12	13	14	15	16	17	18

Completed addition table.

In conclusion. Ask: What does the addition table show? [all the addition facts up to 9 + 9]

Lesson 14: Evens and Odds

OBJECTIVES:

1. To recognize even and odd numbers
2. To discover the even and odd rules for adding

MATERIALS:

1. Tiles
2. Worksheet 2, Addition Tables
3. Math journal

ACTIVITIES FOR TEACHING:

Warm-up. Draw the Venn diagram with overlapping ellipses and write "Write a number < 30" sentence at the top as shown below. Have the child write the numbers.

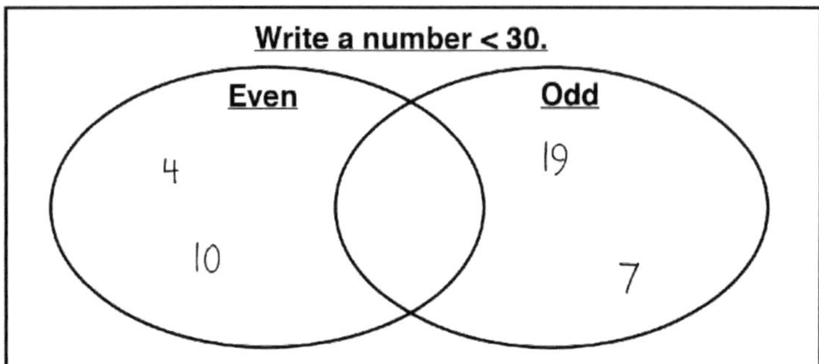

A Venn diagram for writing even and odd numbers.

Point to the "<" and ask: What does the this symbol mean? [less than] Why are there not any numbers written in the area where the circles overlap? [No number can be both even and odd.]

Ask the child to count by 10s to 200 [10, 20, 30, . . . , 200] and by 5s to 100. [5, 10, 15, . . . , 100]

Ask the child to say the even numbers to 20 [2, 4, 6, . . . , 20] and the odd numbers to 39. [1, 3, 5, . . . , 39]

Play the Comes Before game and ask the child: What even number comes before 10? [8] Before 6? [4] Before 8? [6] Before 2? [0] Before 4? [2] Then ask: What odd number comes before 11? [9] Before 7? [5] Before 3? [1] Before 9? [7] Before 5? [3]

Reviewing even or odd. Give the child Worksheet 2, from a previous lesson, and between 5 to 10 tiles in two colors. Tell her to arrange her tiles so someone could tell if they were even or odd without counting. See figures below. Ask: Do you have an even or odd amount? How do you know?

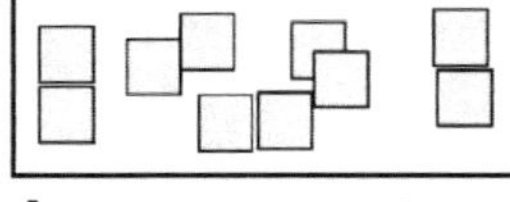

An even amount.

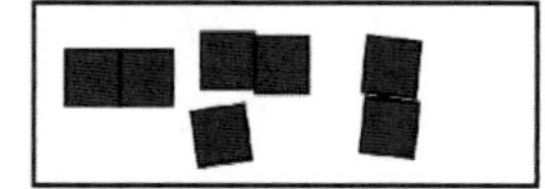

An odd amount.

EXPLANATIONS:

Many children see evenness as having a partner. Therefore, an odd number means one object stands alone.

ACTIVITIES FOR TEACHING:

Adding two even numbers. Now ask the child to make two even numbers less than 10 with tiles. Then ask her to add her two numbers together to see if it is even or odd. See the figure below. Ask the child: Is your sum even or odd? [even] Ask her to explain why. [All the groups of two tiles stay together.]

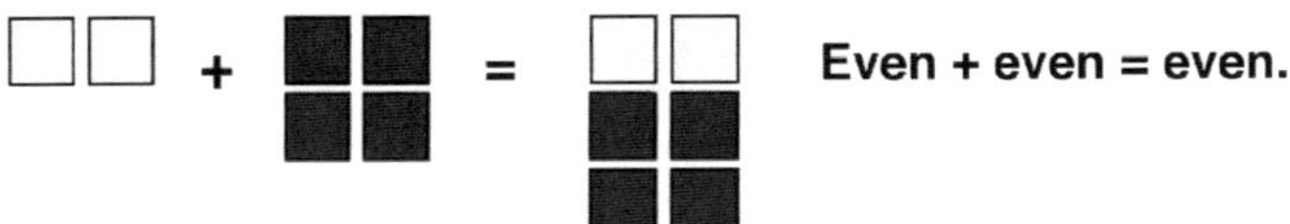

Ask her to find examples of adding two even numbers on the addition table from Worksheet 2. [for example 2 + 2 = 4]

Adding two odd numbers. Ask the child to make two odd numbers less than 10. Then ask her to add her tiles together. See the figure below. Ask the child: Is your sum even or odd? [even] Ask her to explain why. [The extra ones formed a pair.]

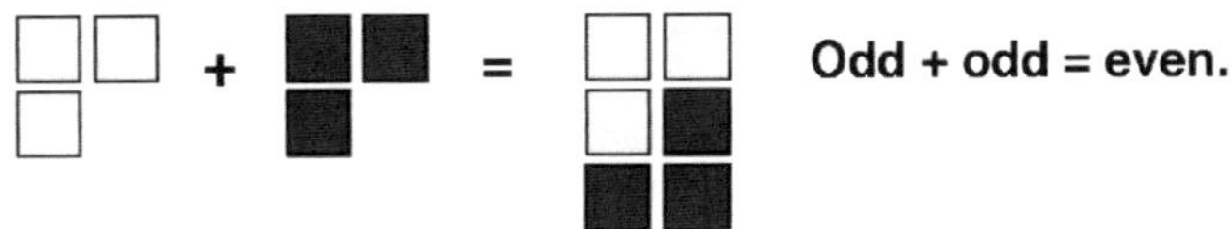

Now ask her to find examples of adding two odd numbers on the addition table. [for example 1 + 3 = 4]

Adding an even and an odd number. Ask: What happens if we add an even number and an odd number? Then tell her to try it by making an even number and an odd number and adding them together. See the figure below. Ask: What happens when you combined them? [odd] Ask her to explain. [The extra 1 from the odd number could not find a partner.]

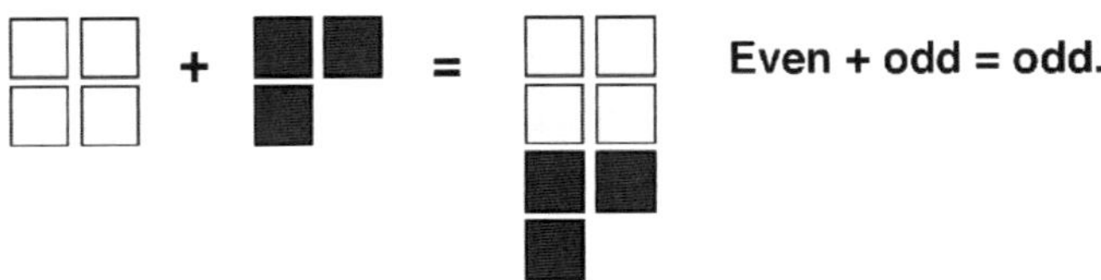

Ask her to find examples of adding one even number and one odd number on the addition table. [for example 2 + 3 = 5]

Writing about evens and odds. Ask her to write the results she found in her math journal and to explain with pictures and words why they work.

In conclusion. Ask the following:

What is even + even = ______ [even]
What is odd + odd = ______ [even]
What is even + odd = ______ [odd]

EXPLANATIONS:

Do not teach this as a rule. The child must truly understand it.

Lesson 15: Early Roman Numerals from 1 to 49

OBJECTIVES:

1. To review the number system through early Roman numerals
2. To use inductive reasoning when writing Roman numerals

MATERIALS:

1. Dry erase board
2. AL Abacus
3. Math journal

ACTIVITIES FOR TEACHING:

Warm-up. Ask the following:

What is even + even = ______ [even]
What is odd + odd = ______ [even]
What is even + odd = ______ [odd]

Ask the child to write her answers to the following questions on the dry erase board: What is 12 + 2, [14] 14 + 2, [16] 16 + 2, [18] 18 + 2, [20] 20 + 2, [22] 22 + 2, [24] 24 + 2, [26] and 26 + 2? [28]

Ask: How many ones are in a ten? [10] How many tens are in a hundred? [10] How many ones are in a hundred? [100] How many ones are in a thousand? [1000]

Roman numeral history. Tell the child that many years ago, the Romans did not have numbers like ours. Instead they used seven letters: I, V, X, L, C, D, and M. The people also used a different kind of abacus to do their number work. Sometimes people still use these Roman numbers, called *Roman numerals*, on clocks, on pages of books, for the date in years, and with the Olympic games.

Roman numerals 1 to 9. Tell the child that today she will learn how to write the Roman numerals to 49. Ask her to enter 1 on her abacus. Write the I and say: We write 1 with the letter I. Tell her to write it on her dry erase board.

Ask her to enter 2 on her abacus. Write II and say: We write 2 with two II's. Ask her to write it. Continue to 4. See the figures below.

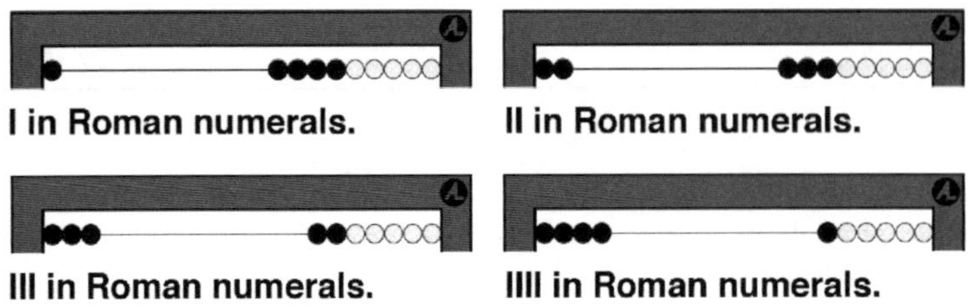

I in Roman numerals. **II in Roman numerals.**

III in Roman numerals. **IIII in Roman numerals.**

EXPLANATIONS:

Learning Roman numerals has several benefits. In addition to their occasional use in daily life, they give the child a look at another system of grouping numbers based on fives and tens.

Roman numerals can be written in either capital or lower case letters.

The child will first learn the early Roman numerals where 4 is written as IIII, not IV.

ACTIVITIES FOR TEACHING:

Ask the child to enter 5. Tell her 5 looks special and the Romans thought so too, so they used a different letter. Write a V and say: We write five with a V. You might say that some people remember the V by making a V with their four fingers and thumb as shown on the right. They might also think that the word five has a V in it. See the figures below.

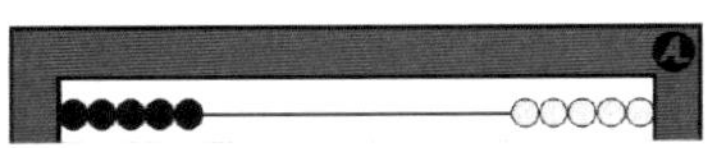

V in Roman numerals.

A way to remember Roman numeral V.

Ask the child to enter 6 and ask her to guess how to write 6. [VI] Emphasize that 6 is 5 and 1, so that is the way the Romans wrote it. Continue to 9. [VII, VIII, VIIII] See the figures below.

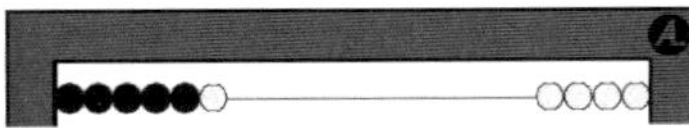

VI in Roman numerals.

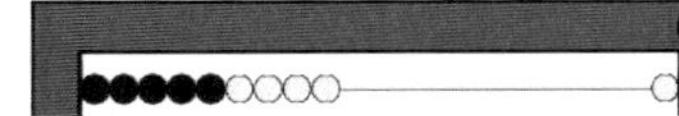

VIIII in Roman numerals.

Roman numerals 10 to 49. Tell her to enter 10 on her abacus. Ask: Do you think we could write ten as VIIIII? [no] Why not? [too hard to read, 10 is special] Tell her that the Romans used an X. Ask her to think of a way to remember that X means ten. One way is to think of the X as 2 V's, meaning two 5s.

Tell her to enter 2 tens. Ask: If 10 is X, how do you think the Romans wrote 20? [XX] Tell her to write it. Give her two more examples.

Ask her to enter 33 and write XXXIII. See below. Repeat for 48 as XXXXVIII.

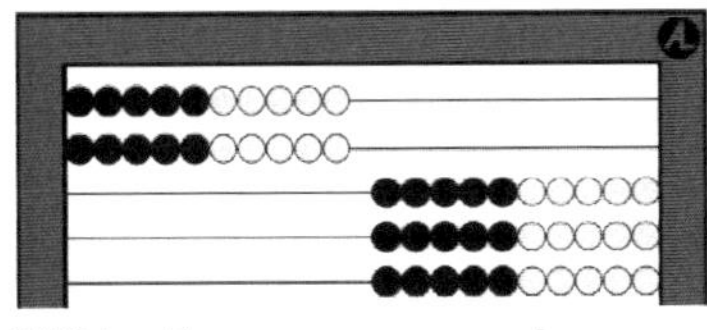

XX in Roman numerals.

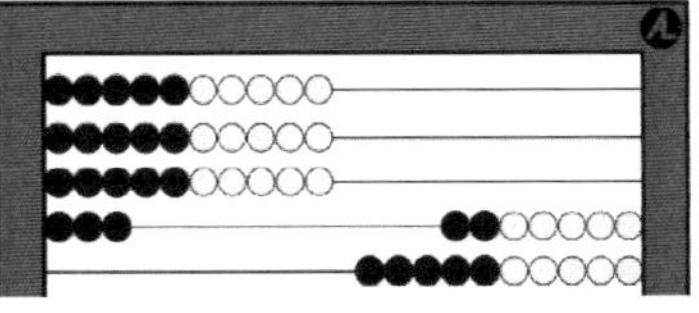

XXXIII in Roman numerals.

Writing the Roman numerals. Ask the child to write the Roman numerals to 49 in her math journal. See the figure at the right.

In conclusion. Ask: Do you think the Roman numerals are easier or harder to learn? Are they easier or harder to write?

EXPLANATIONS:

The child is learning the early Roman numerals where 9 is written as VIIII, not IX.

I	XI	XXI	XXXI	XXXXI
II	XII	XXII	XXXII	XXXXII
III	XIII	XXIII	XXXIII	XXXXIII
IIII	XIIII	XXIIII	XXXIIII	XXXXIIII
V	XV	XXV	XXXV	XXXXV
VI	XVI	XXVI	XXXVI	XXXXVI
VII	XVII	XXVII	XXXVII	XXXXVII
VIII	XVIII	XXVIII	XXXVIII	XXXXVIII
VIIII	XVIIII	XXVIIII	XXXVIIII	XXXXVIIII
X	XX	XXX	XXXX	

1 to 49 in Roman numerals.

Lesson 16: Early Roman Numerals from 1 to 499

OBJECTIVES:

1. To learn the Roman numeral for 50, L, and for 100, C
2. To practice writing and reading the early Roman numerals

MATERIALS:

1. AL Abacus
2. Dry erase board
3. Worksheet 3: Early Roman Numerals from 1 to 499
4. Abacus Tiles

ACTIVITIES FOR TEACHING:

EXPLANATIONS:

Warm-up. Tell the child to say the multiples of 2, that is, to count by 2s to 30. [2, 4, 6, . . . , 30]

Tell her to say the multiples of 5, that is, to count by 5s to 30. [5, 10, 15, . . . , 30]

Ask: Is 6 a multiple of 2? [yes] Is 10 a multiple of 2? [yes] Is 10 a multiple of 5? [yes] Is 13 a multiple of 2? [no] Is 13 a multiple of 5? [no]

Ask: How many ones are in a ten? [10] How many tens are in a hundred? [10] How many ones are in a hundred? [100] How many ones are in a thousand? [1000]

Reviewing Roman numerals. Write XX and ask the child to enter it on her abacus. [20] Repeat for VII, [7] XIII, [13] XXXXV, [45] and XXXVIIII. [39]

Remember, we are working with early Roman numerals.

Worksheet 3. Distribute the worksheet and tell the child to look at the chart at the top of page. Ask: What is the Roman numeral for 50? [L] Tell the child to enter that amount on her abacus without counting.

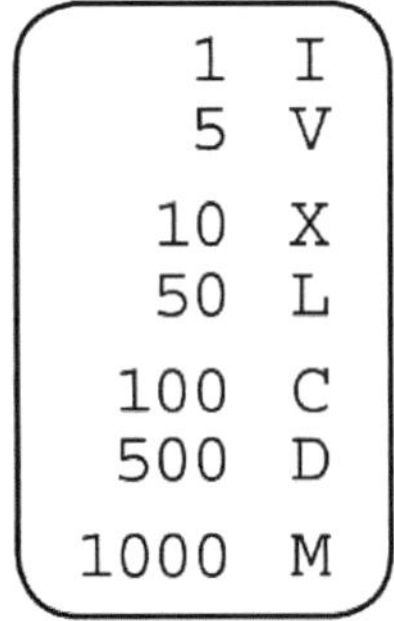

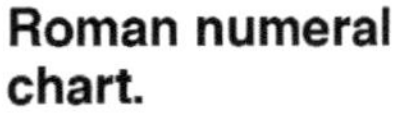
Roman numeral chart.

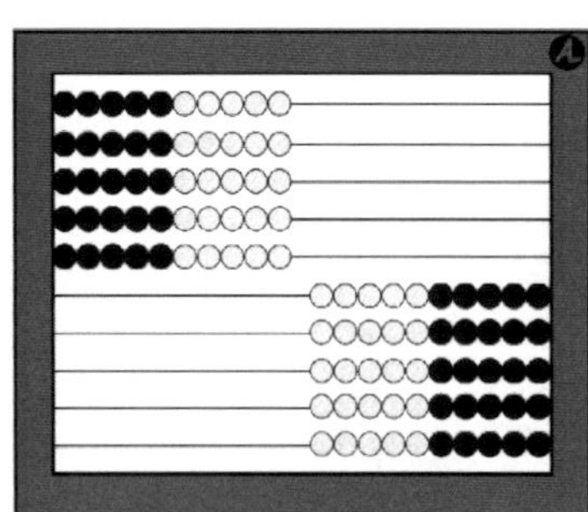

L in Roman numerals.

Roman numerals 50 to 99. Tell the child you want to write 68 in Roman numerals. Write:

LVIII

Ask: Is this correct? [no, it says 58] Write an X in front.

XLVIII

Ask: Is this correct? [no, wrong order] Let the child make the correction. [LXVIII] Again ask: Is this correct?

ACTIVITIES FOR TEACHING:	EXPLANATIONS:

Ask: How do you write 99? [LXXXXVIIII] Ask the child to write it. Repeat for 71 [LXXI] and 80. [LXXX]

Roman numerals 100 to 499. Enter 100 on the abacus and tell the child the Roman numeral for 100 is C. Tell her the Romans used C because it reminded them of 100. They had the word *century,* which starts with a C and means 100 years. They also had a word similar to *cent*; 100 cents makes a dollar. See the figure on the right.

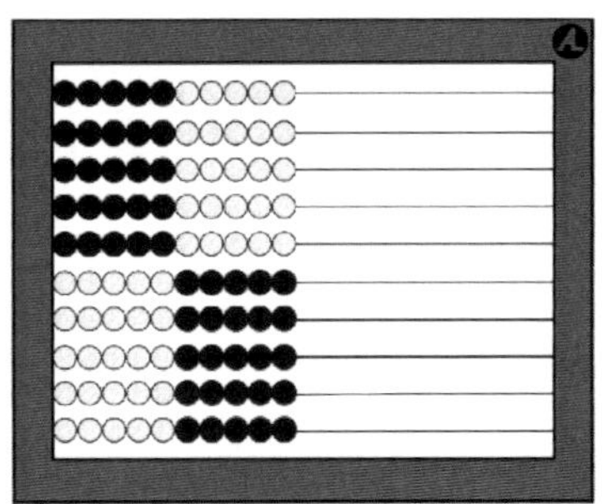

C in Roman numerals.

Show 132 using an abacus tile for 100 and using the abacus for 32. Ask the child to write the Roman numerals for this number on the dry erase board. [CXXXII] See below.

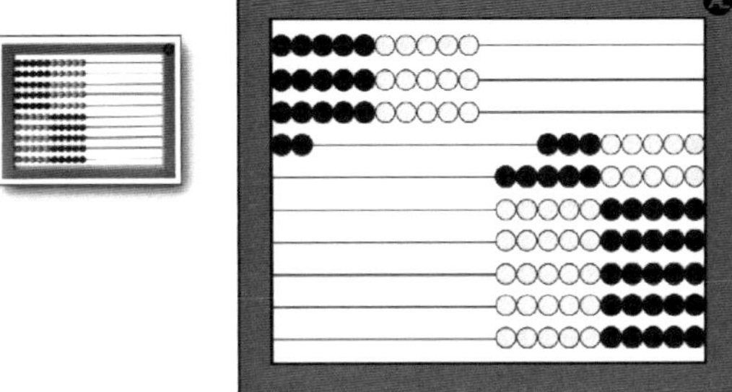

Write CCCLXXIII [373] and ask the child to show the amount with abacus tiles and the abacus. [It takes three abacus tiles to show the 300 and the abacus with 73 entered.]

Roman to Hindu-Arabic numerals. Write:

CCLXXXV

Ask the child to write the number using the regular numbers. [285] Explain that these are called *Hindu-Arabic* numerals and that most of the world uses them.

Sometimes, the numerals are referred to as *Arabic* numerals.

Worksheet 3. Tell the child to complete the worksheet. The solutions are as follows.

16: **XVI**
59: **LVIIII**
290: **CCLXXXX**
44: **XXXXIIII**
103: **CIII**
377: **CCCLXXVII**

XXII: **22**
CXI: **111**
CC: **200**
LXVI: **66**
CXX: **120**
CCCXXXX: **340**
LXXXXVII: **97**
CLXXXII: **182**
CCCCXXXV: **435**

In conclusion. Ask the child to write today's date and year in Roman numerals.

Lesson 17: Roman Numerals from 1 to 4999

OBJECTIVES:

1. To review entering quantities on side 2 of the AL Abacus
2. To work with the Roman numeral for 500, D, and for 1000, M
3. To learn the later Roman numerals

MATERIALS:

1. AL Abacus
2. Math journal
3. Worksheet 4, Roman Numerals from 1 to 4999

ACTIVITIES FOR TEACHING:

Warm-up. Ask the child to say the multiples of 5 to 100 [5, 10, 15, . . . , 100] and 10 to 200. [10, 20, 30, . . . , 200]

Then ask: Is 10 a multiple of 5? [yes] Is 20 a multiple of 10? [yes] Is 17 a multiple of 2? [no] Is 17 a multiple of 5? [no]

Ask the child to say the multiples of 3 to 30 as she enters them on the abacus. [3, 6, 9, . . . , 30] Also ask her to say the even numbers to 20 and the odd numbers to 19.

Play the Comes Before game and ask: What even number comes before 12? [10] Before 4? [2] Before 10? [8] Before 2? [0] Before 8? [6] Then ask: What odd number comes before 11? [9] Before 7? [5] Before 3? [1] Before 9? [7] Before 5? [3]

Comparing 2, 20, 200, and 2000. Ask the child to turn her abacus to side 2. Ask: Where are the 1s? [in the ones columns] Where are the 10s? [in the tens columns] Continue for hundreds and thousands.

Have the child take out her math journal and write H-A and Roman as headings for two columns. Tell her that H-A stands for Hindu-Arabic numerals. Ask the child to enter 2 on side 2 of her abacus and to write the number in Hindu-Arabic numerals [2] and in Roman numerals [II] as shown. Continue with 20 and 200. See figures below.

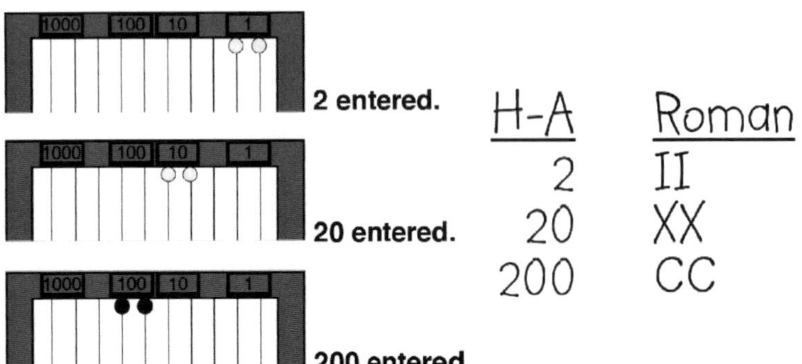

Tell the child that the Romans wrote 1000 as M. Ask the child to enter 2000 on the abacus and write the numerals. See figure at the top of the next page

EXPLANATIONS:

The child who used RightStart™ Mathematics Level B will be familiar with side 2 of the AL Abacus.

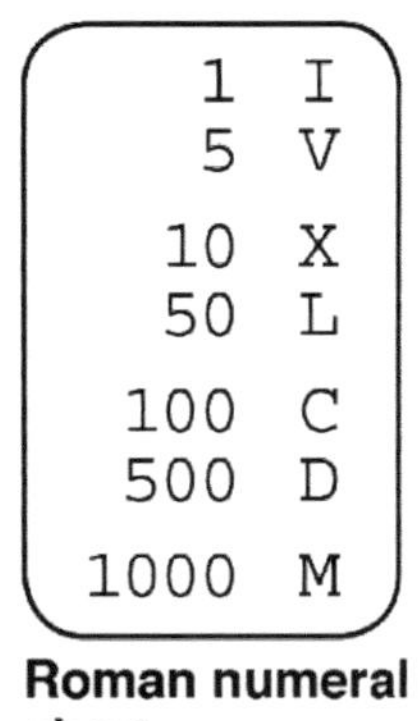

Roman numeral chart.

ACTIVITIES FOR TEACHING:

H-A	Roman
2	II
20	XX
200	CC
2000	MM

Ask her to add all the numbers in the chart and enter it on her abacus. [2222] Then tell her to write both numbers in the chart. See below.

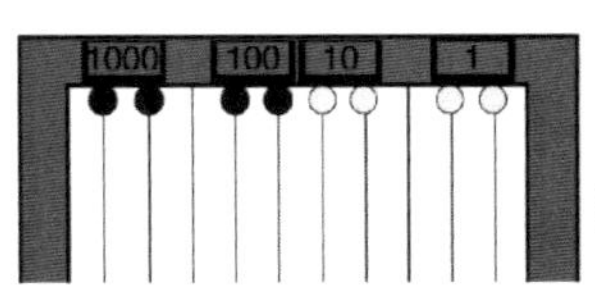

2222 entered.

H-A	Roman
2	II
20	XX
200	CC
2000	MM
2222	MMCCXXII

Later Roman numerals. Tell her that hundreds of years later, the Roman numerals were changed to save space and write less. So instead of writing the number 4 as IIII, they thought that since 4 is 1 less than 5, they could write it as IV. Ask: Why do you think they also wrote IX for 9? [1 less than 10] How do you think they wrote 40 and why? [XL, 10 less than 50] How do you think they wrote 90 and why? [XC, 10 less than 100]

Tell her to enter 3544 on her abacus. Then tell her to write the number using Hindu-Arabic numerals, [3544] early Roman numerals, [MMMDXXXXIIII] and the later Roman numerals. [MMMDXLIV]

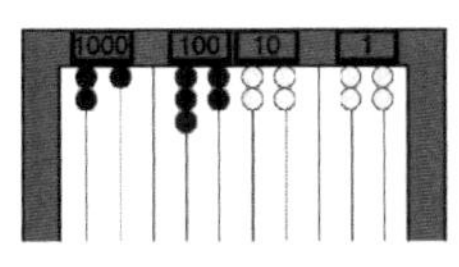

Repeat for 1399. [MCCCLXXXXVIIII, MCCCXCIX]

Worksheet 4. Give the child the worksheet. The solutions are below.

H-A	Early	Later
2014	**MMXIIII**	**MMXIV**
3129	**MMMCXXVIIII**	**MMMCXXIX**
572	DLXXII	**DLXXII**
1346	**MCCCXXXXVI**	MCCCXLVI

In conclusion. Ask: Do you think it is easier to use the early Roman numerals or the later Roman numerals?

EXPLANATIONS:

The Romans used M for 1000 because they had the word millennium which starts with M and means 1000 years, like C stands for century which is 100 years.

H-A	Early	Later
4	IIII	IV
9	VIIII	IX
40	XXXX	XL
90	LXXXX	XC

Many clocks using Roman numerals use the early 4, IIII, and the later 9, IX.

The late Roman numerals are introduced especially for the curious child who sees them in everyday life.

Mastery is not expected.

Lesson 18: Trading on Side 2 of the AL Abacus

OBJECTIVES:

1. To trade on side 2 of the AL Abacus
2. To play the Corners™ game

MATERIALS:

1. AL Abacus
2. *Math Card Games* book, A9
3. Math journal

ACTIVITIES FOR TEACHING:

Warm-up. Ask the child to answer: What is 10 + 6, [16] 10 + 2, [12] 10 + 3, [13] 20 + 9, [29] 40 + 7, [47] 90 + 5, [95] and 10 + 1? [11]

Ask her to say the multiples of 10 backward, starting at 100. [100, 90, 80, . . . , 10] Ask the child to say the multiples of 3 to 30. [3, 6, 9, . . . , 30]

Trading ones on side 2. Write:

28 + 6 = ____ [34]

Enter 28 on side 2 of the abacus. Tell the child to add 6. See the left figure below. Demonstrate trading with the words, "ready, set, trade." The right hand gets ready to move 10 beads down, the left thumb gets set to move 1 ten-bead up, and the hands move simultaneously in opposite directions to trade. See the right figure below.

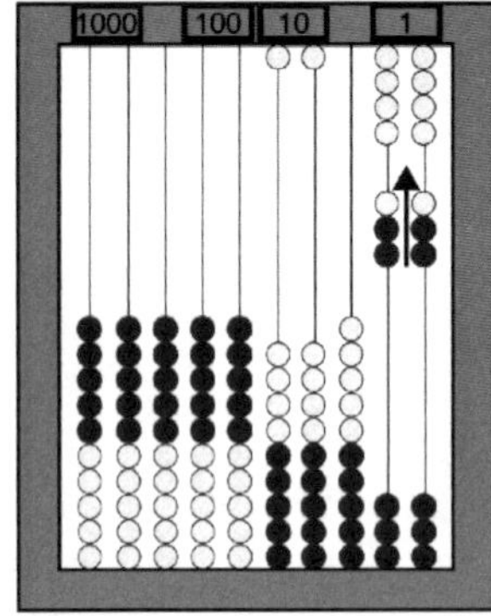

28 + 6.

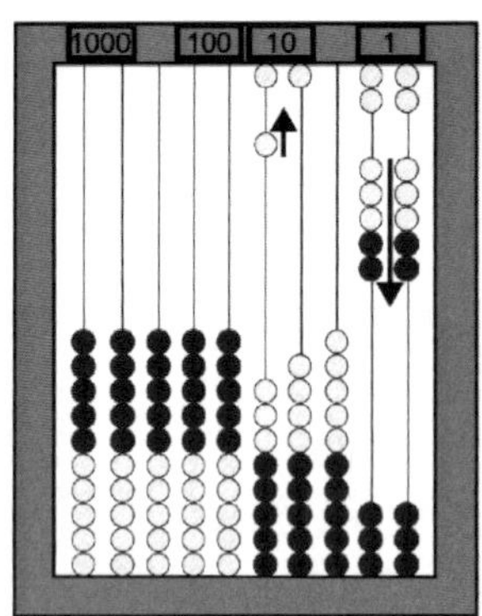

Trading 10 ones for 1 ten.

Ask the child to enter 28 + 6 on her abacus. Ask: How can you tell what the sum is before you trade? [2 tens in the tens column and another ten in the ones column plus 4, giving 34] See figure above.

Ask her to trade and then read the sum. [34]

Repeat for 49 + 7 [56] and 82 + 8. [90]

EXPLANATIONS:

The right hand can feel the ten by placing the thumb under and two fingers on top of the ten, giving tactile affirmation of the quantity.

Some children benefit from moving the ten beads half way down and the one ten bead half way up, pausing to verify they have a correct trade, then finishing the trade.

It is important to keep the two wires as even as possible to make trading easier. See the figures below, both showing 12 ones entered. The right figure is clearly easier for trading.

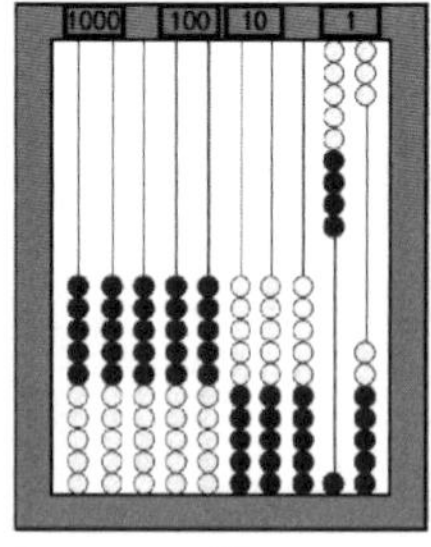

Incorrectly entering 12.

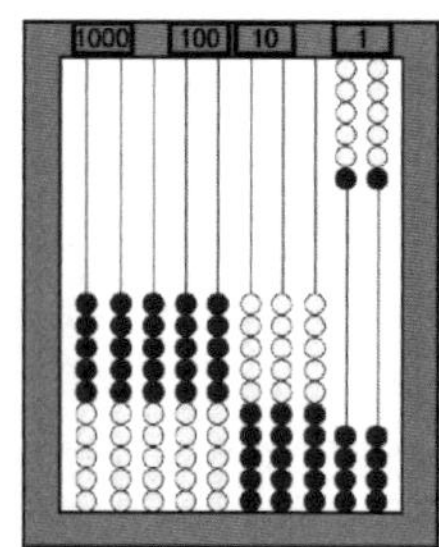

Correctly entering 12.

Quantities are entered from left to right for several reasons. We read from left to right, do mental arithmetic from left to right, and enter quantities on a calculator from left to right. It also is the way we say numbers (except the teens).

ACTIVITIES FOR TEACHING:

Trading tens on side 2. Write:

$$79 + 60 = \_\_\_\_ \ [139]$$

Ask the child to enter both quantities on her abacus. See the left figure below. Tell her to trade as needed.

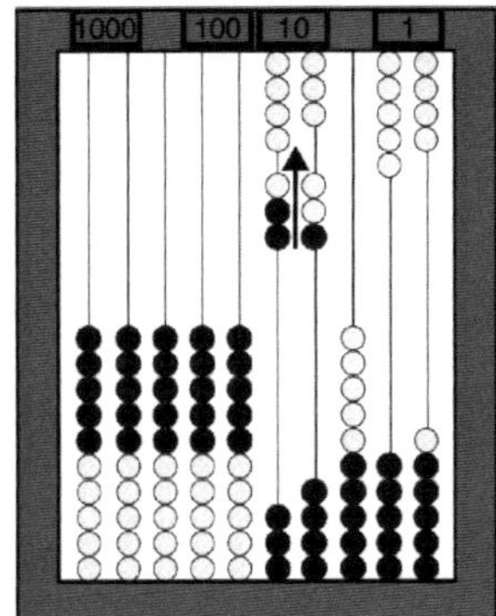

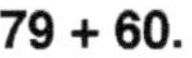
79 + 60.

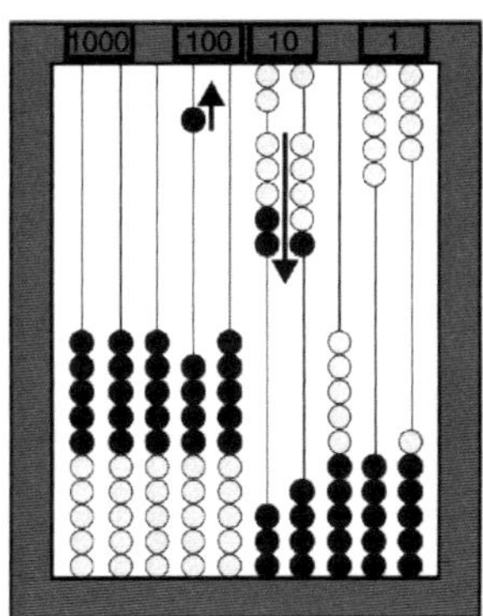

Trading 10 tens for 1 hundred.

Repeat for 96 + 30 [126] and 64 + 80. [144]

Corners™ game. Play the Corners™ game found in the *Math Card Games* book, A9.

Have the child write down her score after each turn in her math journal. She writes down only the result of the latest addition, no intermediate steps. An example of scoring is shown below.

10
15
25
30
45
55
70
90

Sample scoring for Corners™ game.

In conclusion. Ask: In the Corners™ game, what three numbers can you join with 9? [1, 6, and 9] How many points would a 1 give you? [10] How many points would a 6 give you? [15] How many points would a 9 give you? [0]

EXPLANATIONS:

Instructions for the Corners™ game can also be found on the DVD inside the back cover of the *Math Card Games* book or at RightStartMath.com.

Note that the numbers touching must either be the same or have a sum of 5, 10, 15, or 20. However, only the sums that are a multiple of 5 are added to the score. In other words, matching numbers that are not a multiple of 5 are valid plays, but result in no points.

Lesson 19: Adding on Side 2 of the AL Abacus

OBJECTIVES:

1. To review adding a 2-digit number and a 1-digit number
2. To review adding a 2-digit number and a multiple of 10

MATERIALS:

1. AL Abacus
2. *Math Card Games* book, A57

ACTIVITIES FOR TEACHING:

Warm-up. Ask the child to answer the following questions: What is 10 + 7, [17] 10 + 1, [11] 10 + 4, [14] 20 + 8, [28] 40 + 6, [46] 90 + 3, [93] and 10 + 9? [19]

Ask: Is 11 a multiple of 2? [no] Is 11 a multiple of 5? [no] Is 6 a multiple of 2? [yes] Is 10 a multiple of 2? [yes] Is 10 a multiple of 5? [yes]

Ask her to say the multiples of 10 backward, starting at 100. [100, 90, 80, . . . , 10]

Play the Comes Before game and ask: What odd number comes before 11? [9] Before 7? [5] Before 3? [1] Before 9? [7] Before 5? [3] Then ask: What even number comes before 12? [10] Before 4? [2] Before 10? [8] Before 2? [0] Before 8? [6]

Adding 2-digit plus 1-digit numbers. Write and ask the child to solve:

36 + 6 = ____ [42]

Ask her how she did it. One way is to use side 1 of the abacus as shown below.

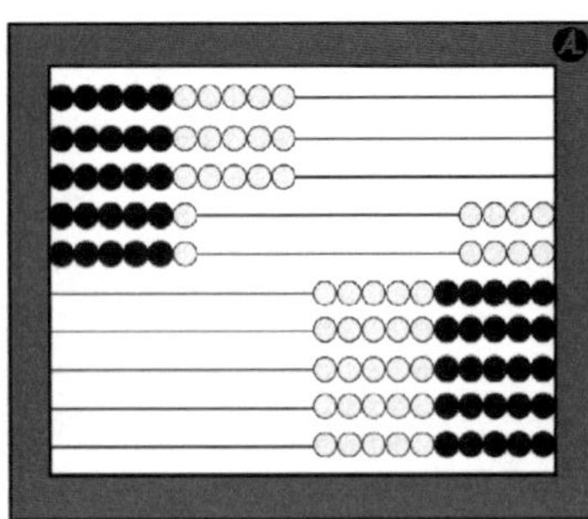

Finding 36 + 6.

A second way is using side 2 without trading, where the sum can be seen at once. See the left figure on the next page.

A third way is to trade on side 2 as in the right figure on the next page. Ask her to explain.

Repeat for 28 + 7, [35] 49 + 8, [57] and 86 + 7. [93]

EXPLANATIONS:

Research has shown that most people who need to add 2-digit numbers do not reach for paper and pencil or a calculator, but do it mentally. The child in RightStart™ Mathematics Level B also learned to add mentally.

Most math standards today call for a greater emphasis on mental computation.

ACTIVITIES FOR TEACHING:

EXPLANATIONS:

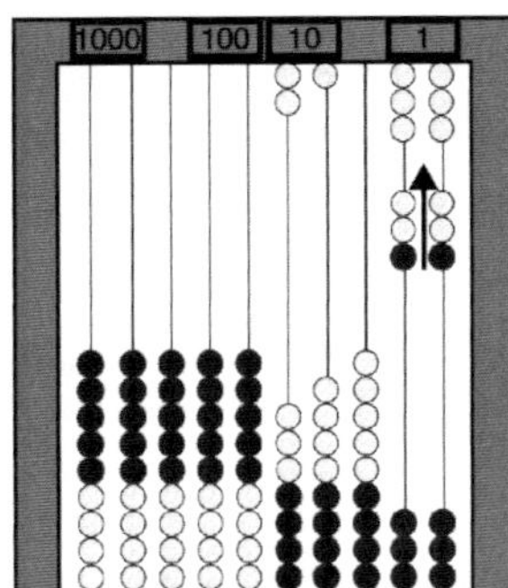

36 + 6 before trading.

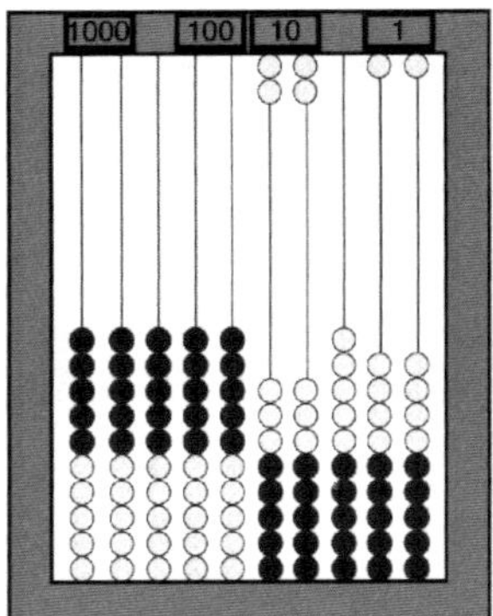

36 + 6 after trading.

Adding 2-digit numbers plus tens. Write and ask the child to solve:

66 + 70 =____ [136]

A solution is to see the 6 tens and add 7 tens, giving 13 tens, which is 1 hundred thirty. Adding the 6 ones gives a sum of 136. This can be seen on side 2 of the abacus with or without physically trading as shown below.

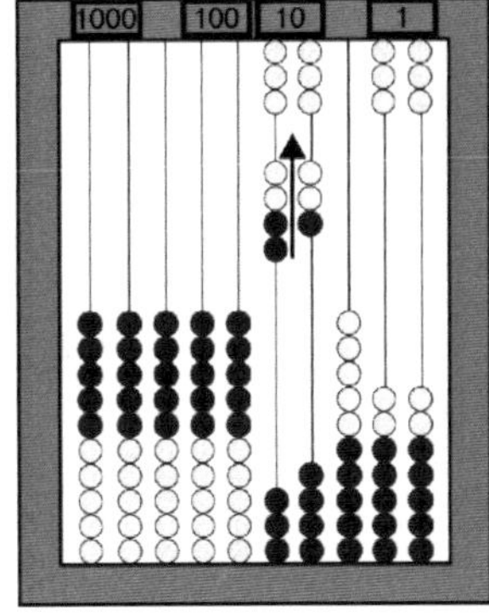

66 + 70 before trading.

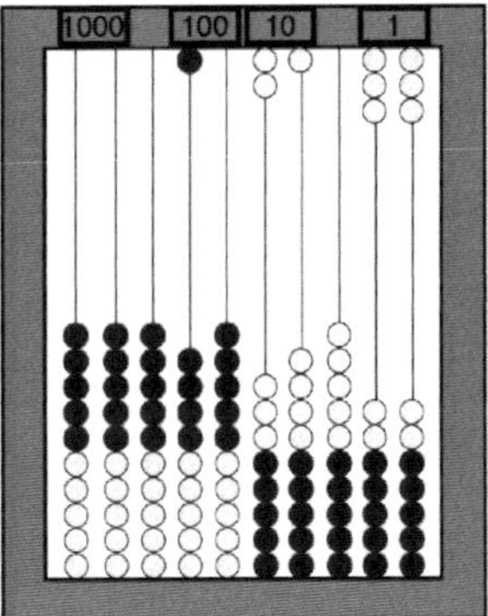

66 + 70 after trading.

Repeat for 25 + 90, [115] 96 + 40, [136] and 78 + 60. [138]

Mental Addition game. Play the Mental Addition game found in the *Math Card Games* book, A57. Use six of each basic number card from 0–9 and the multiplication cards from the 7s, 8s, and 9s envelopes. At the end of game, tell the child to put the cards back into the correct envelopes.

Included with the multiplication cards are 10 envelopes, each printed with the multiples of a number from 1–10. Insert into each envelope 10 multiplication cards matching the numbers listed on the front of the envelope. A new deck of multiplication cards is collated to make this task easy: the first 10 cards go into the 1s envelope; the next 10 cards go into the 2s envelope; and so forth.

In conclusion. Ask the child to answer without writing anything down: How much is 23 + 7? [30] How much is 55 + 8? [63] How much is 55 + 70? [125]

It is also important that the child be able to calculate without seeing the numbers written down. If necessary, let the child use her abacus.

LESSON 20: ADDING 2-DIGIT NUMBERS

OBJECTIVES:

1. To find several ways to add 2-digit numbers together

MATERIALS:

1. AL Abacus
2. Worksheet 5, Adding 2-Digit Numbers

ACTIVITIES FOR TEACHING:

Warm-up. Ask the child to answer without writing anything down: How much is 33 + 7? [40] How much is 45 + 8? [53] How much is 65 + 70? [135]

Ask the child to answer: What is 10 + 6, [16] 10 + 2, [12] 10 + 3, [13] 20 + 9, [29] 40 + 7, [47] 90 + 5, [95] and 10 + 1? [11]

Problem 1. Write:

49 + 23 = ____ [72]

Ask her to add the numbers and explain how she did it. There are several ways to solve this problem. One way is to complete the 10. Take 1 from the 23 and give it to the 49, which makes 50. Next add 20 from 22, making 70. Finally, add 70 and 2 to get 72.

A second way is to add the tens, 40 and 20, getting 60. Then add the ones, 9 and 3, which makes 12. Finally, add 60 and 12 to get 72.

A third way is to add the tens, 40 and 20, resulting in 60, and then add each of the ones. So, 60 plus 9 is 69; 69 plus 3 is 72.

Ask the child to show one of these strategies on side 2 of the abacus. Ask her to explain her strategy.

In the first strategy for adding 49 + 23, the problem was changed to 50 + 22. The left figure on the top of the next page shows adding 50 and 22.

In the second strategy, the tens were combined giving 60, which is entered on the abacus, followed by the combining the ones, 12. See the second figure on the next page.

EXPLANATIONS:

Children are not likely to start with the ones as is done for the formal algorithm. It is more efficient and natural to start at the left.

ACTIVITIES FOR TEACHING:

EXPLANATIONS:

50 + 22 **60 + 12** **60 + 9 + 3** **49 + 20 + 3**

If only one bead is moved, it can be moved to either of the two columns.

In the third strategy, 40 and 20 are combined and then 9 and 3 added separately. See the third figure above.

There is a fourth strategy. Start with 49 and add the 20, which is 69, followed by the 3. See the fourth figure above.

Problem 2. Give her a harder problem:

87 + 39 = ____ [126]

Ask the child to explain her solution. The same strategies used previously apply here. For example, change the numbers to 86 + 40. Or, add 80 + 30 to get 110 and then add 7 + 9 to get 126. Or, 87 + 30 = 117 and 117 + 9 = 126. The strategies are shown below:

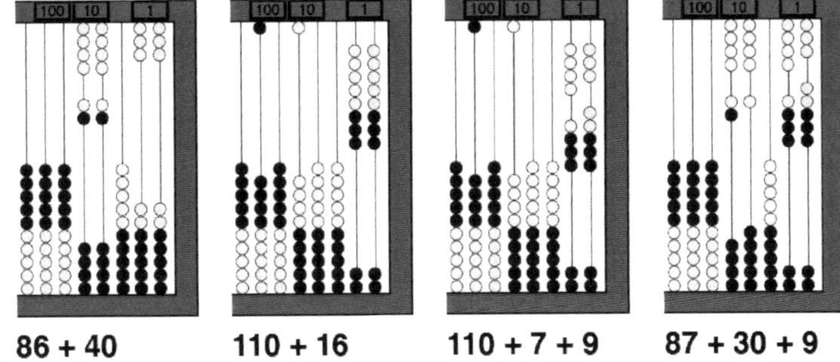

86 + 40 **110 + 16** **110 + 7 + 9** **87 + 30 + 9**

Worksheet 5. Give the child the worksheet and tell her to complete the equations. Solutions are as follows.

65 + 16 = **81** 29 + 43 = **72** 34 + 58 = **92**
55 + 55 = **110** 79 + 62 = **141** 99 + 87 = **186**
18 + 15 = **33** 59 + 61 = **120** 47 + 67 = **114**
73 + 27 = **100** 98 + 37 = **135** 88 + 88 = **176**
18 + 74 = **92**

In conclusion. Ask: What is your favorite strategy?

Lesson 21: Mental Addition

OBJECTIVES:

1. To add 2-digit numbers without seeing them written down

MATERIALS:

1. AL Abacus
2. Dry erase board
3. *Math Card Games* book, A9
4. Math journal

ACTIVITIES FOR TEACHING:

EXPLANATIONS:

Warm-up. Ask the child: What is 20 + 7, [27] 30 + 2, [32] 10 + 8, [18] 30 + 9, [39] 80 + 5, [85] 70 + 2, [72] and 50 + 1? [51]

Ask her to say the multiples of 10 backward, starting at 200 going back to 100. [200, 190, 180, . . . , 100]

Ask the child to say the multiples of 3 to 30 as she enters them on the abacus. [3, 6, 9, . . . , 30]

Play the Comes Before game and ask: What odd number comes before 9? [7] Before 7? [5] Before 11? [9] Before 3? [1] Before 5? [3] Then ask: What even number comes before 14? [12] Before 6? [4] Before 12? [10] Before 2? [0] Before 8? [6]

Adding mentally. Say: Today you will be adding numbers that are not written down. Say the number to yourself to help you remember it and add it on side 2 of the abacus. Then write the sum on your dry erase board.

How much is 29 + 2? [31]

How much is 44 + 9? [53]

How much is 57 + 20? [77]

How much is 57 + 21? [78]

How much is 76 + 30? [106]

How much is 76 + 39? [115]

Say: The children in the Netherlands do problems like this by starting with 76, then adding 30 and then 9. It is the same order they hear the numbers. They use this strategy because they can remember the numbers better.

Continue with:

How much is 27 + 37? [64]

How much is 54 + 48? [102]

How much is 92 + 38? [130]

ACTIVITIES FOR TEACHING:	EXPLANATIONS:

Tell her to do the next problems by entering only the first number on the abacus. Then tell her to add the second number mentally, first the tens and then the ones.

What is 48 + 48? [96]

What is 88 + 67? [155]

What is 17 + 39? [56]

Tell her to do the next problems without the abacus. Say: Add the first number and the tens of the second number and say it out loud. Then add the ones from the second number.

If a child struggles without the abacus, have her enter the first number as before.

How much is 37 + 22? [57, 59]

How much is 48 + 45? [88, 93]

How much is 62 + 39? [92, 101]

Corners™ game. Play the Corners™ game, found in the *Math Card Games* book, A9. Tell her to write her scores in her math journal. If she needs the abacus for scoring, tell her to use side 2. A sample of scoring is shown below.

	10
	15
	25
	30
	45
	55
	70
	90

Sample scoring for Corners™ game.

In conclusion. Ask: If Jamie had 45 points and got 25 more points, what is Jamie's score now? [70] If Andi had 95 points and got 15 more points, what is Andi's new score? [110]

Lesson 22: Adding Several 2-Digit Numbers

OBJECTIVES:

1. To add several 2-digit numbers

MATERIALS:

1. Math journal
2. AL Abacus
3. *Math Card Games* book, A53
4. Worksheet 6, Adding Several 2-Digit Numbers

ACTIVITIES FOR TEACHING:

Warm-up. Draw the Venn diagram with concentric circles as shown below. Write in the name of your city and state.

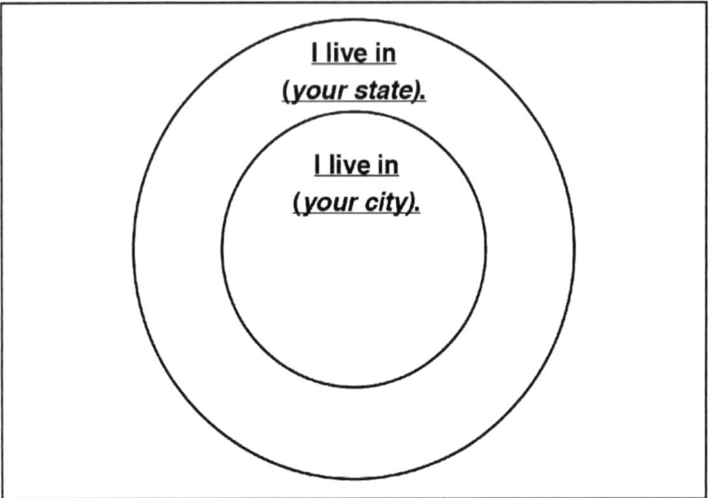

A Venn diagram with one circle inside another.

Ask: Why is the "city" circle completely inside the "state" circle? [The whole city is in the state.]

Say the following aloud and ask the child to write only the answers in her math journal: 48 + 6, [54] 80 + 80, [160] 41 + 44, [85] and 78 + 50. [128] Use side 2 of the abacus if necessary.

Ask the child to say the multiples of 5 to 50 while entering them on the abacus. [5, 10, 15, . . . , 50]

Play the Comes Before game and ask: What even number comes before 16? [14] Before 8? [6] Before 10? [8] Before 4? [2] Before 6? [4] Then ask: What odd number comes before 5? [3] Before 9? [7] Before 11? [9] Before 3? [1] Before 7? [5]

Rows and Columns game. Play the Rows and Columns game found in the *Math Card Games* book, A53. Tell the child that she can play for about 10 minutes.

EXPLANATIONS:

ACTIVITIES FOR TEACHING:

Adding several numbers. Write:

14 + 3 + 6 + 1 = ____ [24]

Tell the child to find the sum in two different ways. Ask her to explain one strategy she used. She might add the numbers in the order written: 14 + 3 = 17, 17 + 6 = 23, and 23 + 1 = 24. Another way might be 14 + 6 = 20 and 20 + 3 + 1 = 24. Another might be 3 + 6 + 1 = 10 and 14 + 10 = 24.

Write:

27 + 3 + 17 + 20 = ____ [67]

Tell the child to find the amount in two ways. Again ask for her method. She might see 27 + 3 = 30, 30 + 20 = 50, and 50 + 17 = 67. Another possibility is adding all the tens to get 50, then adding the ones to get 17, and finally adding 50 + 17 to get 67. There are more possibilities.

Ask the child to decide which methods she likes best and why.

Repeat for:

78 + 39 + 22 + 54 = ____ [193]

Worksheet 6. Give the child the worksheet and have her complete the equations. The problems and solutions are below.

35 + 26 + 9 + 31 = **101**	2 + 73 + 98 + 6 = **179**
16 + 12 + 2 + 93 = **123**	86 + 2 + 29 + 22 = **139**
13 + 1 + 37 + 15 = **66**	54 + 37 + 8 + 25 = **124**
71 + 52 + 70 + 32 = **225**	23 + 70 + 53 + 6 = **152**

In conclusion. Say: Alex was adding several numbers together in different ways. But Alex did not get the same answer. What should Alex do? [Try a third way or recheck the other ways.]

EXPLANATIONS:

Performing calculations a second way is a good check on correctness.

You might remind the child that it is important to keep trying. By working hard, skills can be improved.

Children who know that their IQs can increase do better than children who think their IQs are fixed.

LESSON 23: REVIEW AND GAMES 1

OBJECTIVES:

1. To review recent topics
2. To continue to develop skills through playing math card games

MATERIALS:

1. Worksheet 7-A or 7-B, Review 1
2. *Math Card Games* book, A51 and A9

ACTIVITIES FOR TEACHING:

Worksheet 7-A. Give the child the worksheet. Tell her to listen to the problems and write only the answers on the worksheet. Read each problem twice.

8 + 9　　　　40 + 60　　　　72 + 9

Tell her to complete the worksheet. Solutions are below:

Write only the answers.

17

100

81

Add.

38 + 6 = 44

99 + 64 = 163

36 + 14 + 50 + 47 = 147

Explain how to add 39 and 41 two different ways.

Take 1 from 41 and give it to 39. Then you have 40 and 40, which makes 80.

Add 30 and 40, which makes 70. The 9 and 1 = 10, so 70 plus 10 = 80.

Add 39 + 40 to get 79. Then add 1 more to get 80.

Write the number of squares with Hindu-Arabic numerals and with Roman numerals.

1	I
5	V
10	X

□□□□□ □□□□□
□□□□□ □□□□□
□□□□□ □□□□□
□□□□□ □□

37

XXXVII

Addition Array game. Play the Addition Array game, found in the *Math Card Games* book, A51.

Corners™ game. Play the Corners™ game found in the *Math Card Games* book, A9.

EXPLANATIONS:

The Review worksheets each have two versions. The second version can be used in various ways: as a quiz, as a test, as a check after tutoring, and so forth.

ACTIVITIES FOR TEACHING:

Worksheet 7-B. Give the child the worksheet. Tell her to listen to the problems and write only the answers on the worksheet. Read each problem twice.

6 + 9 20 + 80 63 + 9

Tell her to complete the worksheet. Solutions are below:

Write only the answers.

15

100

72

Add.

47 + 8 = 55

99 + 56 = 155

22 + 18 + 60 + 75 = 175

Explain how to add 21 and 19 two different ways.

Take 1 from 21 and give it to 19. Then you have 20 and 20, which makes 40.

Add 20 and 10, which makes 30. The 1 and 9 = 10, so 30 plus 10 = 40.

Add 21 + 10 to get 31. Then add 9 more to get 40.

Write the number of squares with Hindu-Arabic numerals and with Roman numerals.

1	I
5	V
10	X

28

XXVIII

EXPLANATIONS:

Lesson 24: Composing Numbers in the Thousands

OBJECTIVES:

1. To compose numbers through the thousands with several models
2. To learn the terms, *base-10, expanded form,* and *standard form*

MATERIALS:

1. Math journal
2. AL Abacus
3. Place-value cards
4. Base-10 picture cards
5. Worksheet 8, Composing Numbers in the Thousands

ACTIVITIES FOR TEACHING:

Warm-up. Ask the child to name the ways to make 10. [9 & 1, 8 & 2, 7 & 3, 6 & 4, 5 & 5, 4 & 6, 3 & 7, 2 & 8, 1 & 9, 0 & 10]

Ask the child: What is 10 + 5, [15] 10 + 1, [11] 10 + 2, [12] 20 + 8, [28] 40 + 6, [46] 90 + 4, [94] and 10 + 6? [16]

Say the following aloud and ask the child to write only the answers in her math journal: 58 + 6, [64] 60 + 80, [140] 51 + 44, [95] and 68 + 50. [118]

Ask the child to say the multiples of 2 to 30. [2, 4, 6, . . . , 30]

Reviewing thousands. Give the child the abacus, place-value cards, and base-10 picture cards.

Tell her to find the base-10 cards for 1, 10, 100, and 1000. Tell her to lay the base-10 cards out in a row from greatest to least. Then ask her to name each picture. [thousand, hundred, ten, one] Ask her to lay the corresponding place-value cards below the picture. See the figures below.

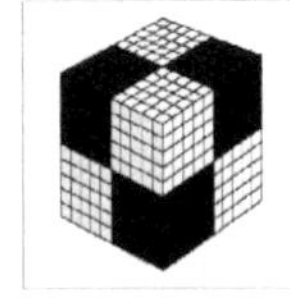

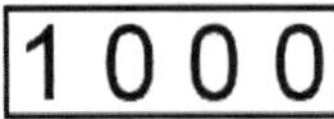

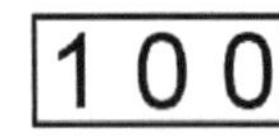

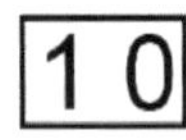

Matching the base-10 cards with place-value cards.

Tell her to look at the pictures to answer the following:

How many ones do you need to make 10? [10]
How many tens do you need to make 100? [10]
How many hundreds do you need to make 1000? [10]

Ask: What is our special number? [10] Tell her we call our number system *base-10* because it is based on tens.

EXPLANATIONS:

ACTIVITIES FOR TEACHING:

Ask the child to take the corresponding place-value cards and stack them into the *standard form,* as shown at right. Also ask her to enter the number on side 2 of her abacus. See figure.

1111 in standard form.

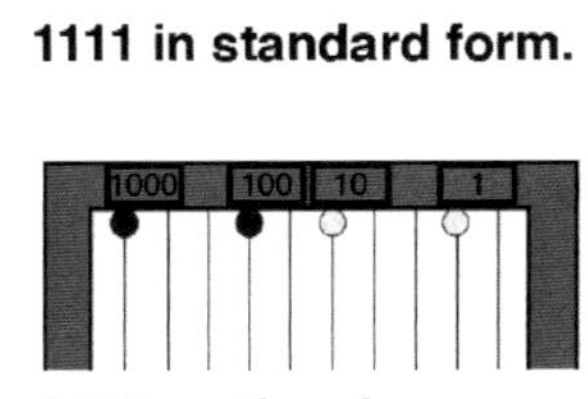

1111 on the abacus.

Composing 2468. Tell the child to make the number 2468 with the base-10 cards, grouping in twos, as shown below. Tell her to spread the corresponding place-value cards out below the base-10 cards as shown. Tell her this is called the *expanded form.* Ask her to make the number in standard form with her place-value cards as shown. Also ask her to enter the number on her abacus.

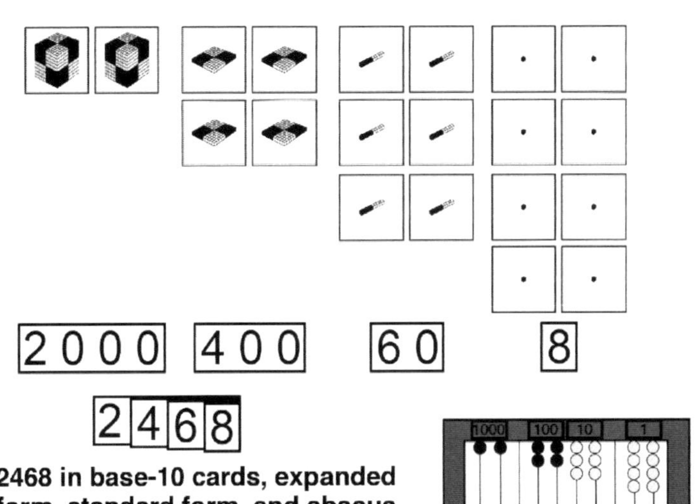

2468 in base-10 cards, expanded form, standard form, and abacus.

Worksheet 8. Give the child the worksheet where she will show quantities in all four forms. Explain that she is to circle the base-10 cards she needs, to write the missing numbers on the place-value cards, and to draw missing beads. Solutions are below:

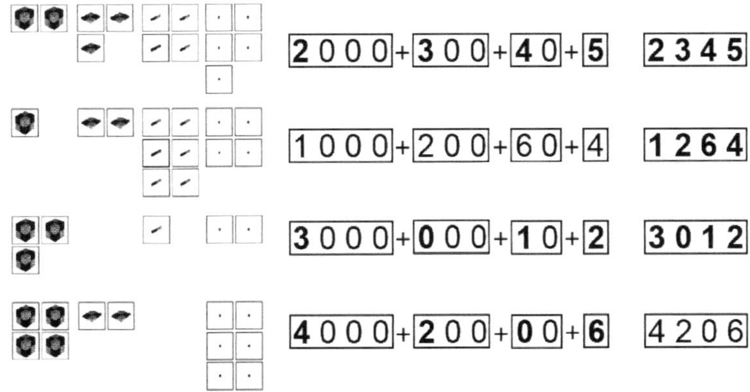

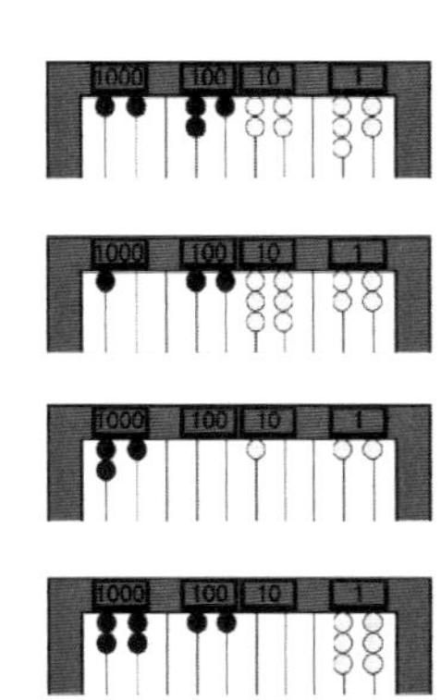

In conclusion. Ask: Which is more, one hundred or one thousand? [one thousand] Which is more, ten hundreds or one thousand? [same]

EXPLANATIONS:

To ensure proper alignment of the place-value cards, overlap them up as shown below and lightly tap the cards on the right side.

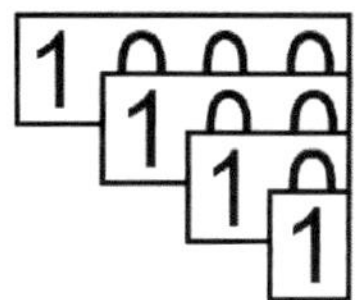

Lesson 25: Adding 1, 10, and 100 to Numbers

OBJECTIVES:

1. To add 1, 10, and 100 to numbers up to 1000

MATERIALS:

1. Dry erase board
2. AL Abacus
3. Place-value cards
4. Base-10 picture cards
5. *Math Card Games* book, N43 and A9

ACTIVITIES FOR TEACHING:

Warm-up. Write 4000 + 300 + 50 + 2. Ask the child to write her answer on the dry erase board. [4352] Repeat for 6000 + 000 + 70 + 9. [6079]

Ask: Which is more, one hundred or one thousand? [one thousand] Which is more, ten hundreds or one thousand? [same]

Ask the child to name the ways to make 10. [9 & 1, 8 & 2, 7 & 3, 6 & 4, 5 & 5, 4 & 6, 3 & 7, 2 & 8, 1 & 9, 0 & 10]

Reviewing numbers to 99. Give the child the abacus, place-value cards, and base-10 picture cards.

Tell the child to enter 86 on side 2 of the abacus. Then have her compose 86 with place-value cards in the expanded form then in standard form. Finally have her compose 86 with the base-10 picture cards. See below.

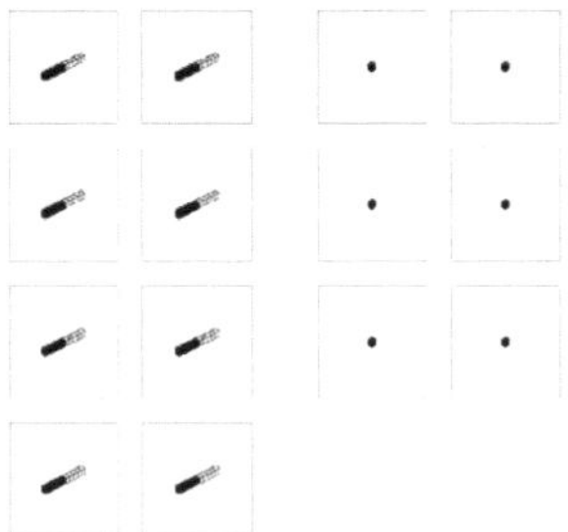

86 composed with base-10 picture cards.

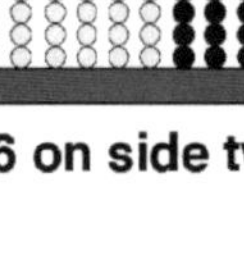

86 on side two.

80 6

86 composed with place-value cards in expanded form.

86

86 composed with place-value cards in standard form.

Adding 1. Say: Look at your three models. If you add 1, how much will you have? [87] Tell her to change all three models to show 87.

EXPLANATIONS:

ACTIVITIES FOR TEACHING:

Adding 10. Tell her to change her models back to 86. Tell her to think about what she would need to do to add 10 to each model. Ask: When you add 10, what will each model show? [96] Which models need you to add one piece representing 10? [abacus and base-10 cards] Which model needs something changed? [place-value cards] Tell her to make the changes.

Adding 100. Tell her to change her models back to 86 again. Say: This time you are to add 100 to each model. Ask: What will the new number be? [186] See below.

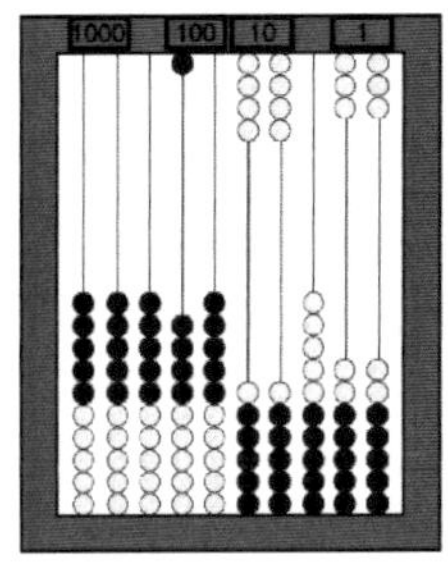

186 entered on side 2.

186 with base-10 cards.

100 80 6 186 **186 with place value cards.**

Can You Find Plus game. This harder version of Can You Find from the *Math Card Games* book, N43, asks the child to find the sum of the numbers you say. Include the place-value cards for the hundreds. Below are numbers to ask so all the cards will be picked up at the conclusion of the game.

1. Can you find 3 + 10? [10 & 3]
2. Can you find 12 + 10? [20 & 2]
3. Can you find 350 + 100? [400 & 50]
4. Can you find 877 + 10? [800 & 80 & 7]
5. Can you find 529 + 1? [500 & 30]
6. Can you find 644 + 100? [700 & 40 & 4]
7. Can you find 590 + 100? [600 & 90]
8. Can you find 199 + 10? [200 & 9]
9. Can you find 90 + 10 + 1? [100 & 1]
10. Can you find 266 + 100? [300 & 60 & 6]
11. Can you find 68 + 10? [70 & 8]
12. Can you find 895 + 10? [900 & 5]

Corners™ Plus game. In this variation of Corners™, from the *Math Card Games* book, A9, players receive one extra point for every Corner they play.

In conclusion. Ask: What did you learn about hundreds today?

EXPLANATIONS:

The extra point awarded for playing to a corner will require players to add to numbers that are not multiples of 5.

Lesson 26: Comparing Numbers

OBJECTIVES:

1. To compare numbers using =, <, and > symbols

MATERIALS:

1. Dry erase board
2. Worksheet 9, Comparing Numbers

ACTIVITIES FOR TEACHING:

Warm-up. Ask the child: What is 34 plus 10? [44] What is 36 plus 10? [46] What is 72 plus 10? [82] What is 89 plus 10? [99]

Write 1000 + 800 + 30 + 1. Ask the child to write her answer on the dry erase board. [1831] Repeat for 8000 + 100 + 40 + 5. [8145]

Ask: Which is more, ten hundreds or one thousand? [same] Which is more, one hundred or one thousand? [one thousand]

Comparing numbers. Write:

9 ___ 6 + 3

Ask: Is 9 equal to 6 plus 3? [yes] What do we write on the line? [an equal sign] Tell the child to write an equal sign.

Below the first equation, write:

10 ___ 6 + 3

Ask: Is 10 equal to 6 plus 3? [no] Is 10 greater than or less than 6 + 3? [greater]

The > symbol. Show her how to write the greater than symbol by starting at the top of the larger number, draw a line to the middle of the smaller number, and finish by drawing to the bottom of the larger number. See below.

10 > 6 + 3   10 > 6 + 3

The < symbol. Tell the child suppose the equation changed and written as:

6 + 3 ___ 10

Write the equation below the first two equations. Ask: What symbol do we need now? [less than] Tell her we can write it the same way by starting at the larger number. See below.

6 + 3 < 10   6 + 3 < 10

EXPLANATIONS:

The > and < symbols were taught in Level B by drawing two dots at the greater number and one dot at the lesser number, and then connecting the dots.

10 > 6 + 3

ACTIVITIES FOR TEACHING:

EXPLANATIONS:

Reading the > and < symbols. Show the child how to tell the difference when reading the greater than and less than symbols. Write >, cover it, and slowly uncover it from left to right as shown below on the left. Ask: How many points do you see? [2] Say: Two points mean greater than. Repeat for the < symbol, uncovering it from left to right as shown below on the right. Ask: How many points do you see? [1] Say: One point means less than.

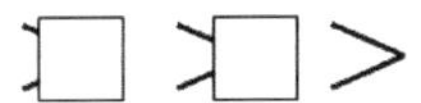

Reading the > symbol.

Reading the < symbol.

Write the three equations and ask the child to read them.

9 = 6 + 3 [Nine equals six plus three.]
10 > 6 + 3 [Ten is greater than six plus three.]
6 + 3 < 10 [Six plus three is less than ten.]

More comparisons. Write the following:

48 __ 40 + 7

Ask: Which symbol do we need? [>] Ask the child to explain her answer. [48 is 40 plus 8, which is more than 40 plus 7.]

Write another example:

201 + 10 __ 211

Ask: Which symbol do we need? [=] Ask the child to explain her answer. [1 plus 10 = 11; 200 plus 11 does equal 211.]

Write a third example:

863 + 1 __ 861 + 10

Ask: Which symbol do we need? [<] Ask the child to explain her answer. [863 plus 1 equals 864; 861 plus 10 equals 871, which is more than 864.]

Worksheet 9. Give the child the worksheet and have her complete the equations. The solutions are below.

38 + 6 **>** 30 + 6
506 **<** 560
99 + 10 **=** 109
250 + 10 **=** 251 + 9
700 + 80 **>** 708
1000 **=** 300 + 700
611 + 100 **>** 611 + 10
95 + 10 + 5 **=** 110
455 + 10 + 1 **>** 100 + 365

99 + 64 **<** 100 + 64
211 **>** 200 + 10
99 + 100 **>** 190
89 + 63 **<** 100 + 73
38 **=** 30 + 8
461 **>** 400 + 60

In conclusion. Ask: What is the mathematical word for more? [greater] What is the opposite of greater? [less] Name all numbers greater than 5 and less than 9. [6, 7, and 8]

Lesson 27: Adding with Base-10 Picture Cards

OBJECTIVES:

1. To add 4-digit numbers with the base-10 picture cards

MATERIALS:

1. Base-10 picture cards
2. Place-value cards
3. *Math Card Games* book, A44 or A45
4. **The following numbers on separate slips of paper, 1549, 2735, and 3817**
5. Math journal

ACTIVITIES FOR TEACHING:

Warm-up. Show a 10 from the base-10 picture cards and say: Suppose I had 80 of these cards. Ask: How much would it show? [800] Have the child explain her answer. [Each group of ten cards is 100, so 8 groups of 10 would be 800.] Show the 800 place-value card and ask: Is it the same? [yes] Why? [it shows 80-ten or 8 hundred]

Ask: Which is more, 2 thousand or 6 hundred? [2 thousand] Which is greater, 1 thousand or 10 hundred? [same] Which is less, 1 hundred or 11? [11]

Ask: How much is 1000 plus 5000? [6000] How much is 6000 plus 2000? [8000] How much is 2000 plus 5000? [7000]

Addition War game. Play the Addition War game, found in the *Math Card Games* book, A44. If a game for three players is needed, use game A45.

Preparation for adding with base-10 cards. Tell the child the following story:

> There were three shepherds, named Abe, Amy, and Adrian. Abe had 1549 sheep, Amy had 2735 sheep, and Adrian had 3817 sheep (point to the numbers on the three slips of paper as you say them). The shepherds called a meeting and decided they wanted to know how many sheep they had altogether.

Give the child the slips of paper with the shepherd's numbers. You will be the banker.

Tell the child to construct the numbers with her place-value cards and then collect the corresponding base-10 cards. Collect the remaining base-10 cards.

Adding. Ask the child to add her base-10 cards together, combining denominations. She lays the three sets of place-value cards in columns as shown on the next page.

EXPLANATIONS:

This lesson is not intended to teach the paper and pencil algorithm for adding numbers, but only to extend the concept of trading to a more abstract form.

To keep track of the shepherds, note that the number of syllables in the name is the same as the number of thousands.

ACTIVITIES FOR TEACHING:

1549
2735
3817

6 thousands, 20 hundreds, 8 tens, and 21 ones.

Tell the child to do the trading for one of the denominations by starting at the bottom of the column to gather ten. She then takes ten cards to the banker who makes the appropriate trade. For example, if trading hundreds, she gives 10 hundreds to the banker who returns 1 thousand. The child then places the thousand at the end of the thousands columns and checks to see if there is another group of 10 to be traded.

Tell the child to do the remaining denominations. At the conclusion of the trading, the child composes the sum with her place-value cards.

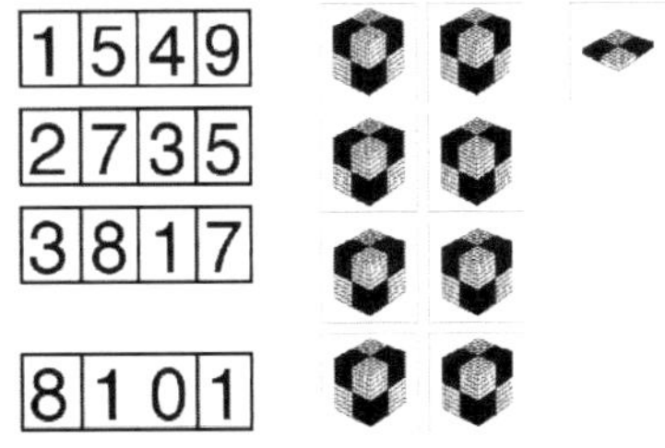

The sum after trading.

Summarize. Ask: How many sheep did the three shepherds have altogether? [8101]

Tell the child to write the numbers in a column in her math journal. If necessary, remind her to draw a line below the third number to separate the parts from the whole and to write the plus sign.

In conclusion. Ask: When do you need to trade? [when you have 10 or more of the same card]

EXPLANATIONS:

The order of the trading is not important. Calculating mentally or on a calculator is easier to do when starting at the left; only on paper is it easier to start at the right.

Counting from the bottom is more orderly and will be done later on side 2 of the abacus.

Lesson 28: More Adding with Base-10 Picture Cards

OBJECTIVES:

1. To practice adding 4-digit numbers with the base-10 picture cards

MATERIALS:

1. Base-10 picture cards
2. Place-value cards
3. Worksheet 10, More Adding with Base-10 Cards

ACTIVITIES FOR TEACHING:

Warm-up. Show a 10 from the base-10 picture cards and say: Suppose I had 50 of these cards. Ask: How much would it show? [500] Have the child explain her answer. [Each group of ten cards is 100, so 5 groups of 10 would be 500.] Show the 500 place-value card and ask: Is it the same? [yes] Why? [it shows 50-ten or 5 hundred]

Ask: When do you need to trade base-10 cards? [when you have 10 or more of the same card]

Ask: Which is more, 3 thousand or 4 hundred? [3 thousand] Which is greater, 1 thousand or 10 hundred? [same] Which is less, 2 hundred or 222? [2 hundred]

Ask: How much is 2000 plus 5000? [7000] How much is 6000 plus 3000? [9000] How much is 1000 plus 5000? [6000]

Ask: How many ones are in 10? [10] How many tens are in 100? [10] How many one hundreds in 1000? [10]

Worksheet 10. Give the place-value cards, base-10 cards, and the worksheet to the child. Then ask her to read the first problem:

> Planners are building a swimming pool and need to know how many children live in the towns of Addie, Hammer, and Preston. Addie has 2697 children. Hammer has 3986 children and Preston has 1449 children.

Tell the child to construct the numbers with her place-value cards and collect the corresponding base-10 cards.

Adding. Have the child add her base-10 cards together, combining denominations. She lays the three sets of place-value cards in columns as shown on the next page.

EXPLANATIONS:

These three towns are actually ghost towns in South Dakota.

ACTIVITIES FOR TEACHING:

EXPLANATIONS:

2697

3986

1449

6 thousands, 19 hundreds, 21 tens, and 22 ones.

The child trades whenever she has ten cards of the same denomination, taking the 10 cards to the banker who makes the appropriate trade. Have her do the remaining denominations. At the conclusion of the trading, she composes the sum with her place-value cards. The results are shown below.

The sum after trading.

Written work. Ask: How many children were in the three towns? [8132] Tell the child to write the numbers in the grid on her worksheet. Then tell to write how she found the answer.

Tell her to read the second problem and solve it the same way. [7984 birds]

In conclusion. Ask: Does it matter which numbers you add first? [no]

The act of explaining something is another step in the learning process. A child may know the answer to an equation, but explaining how they found the answer adds an additional layer to their understanding. Therefore, it really doesn't matter what they write; rather, it's the act of expressing their thoughts that is important.

LESSON 29: ADDING 4-DIGIT NUMBERS ON THE AL ABACUS

OBJECTIVES:

1. To add 4-digit numbers on the AL Abacus

MATERIALS:

1. AL Abacus
2. Abacus Tiles
3. Place-value cards
4. Worksheet 11, Adding 4-Digit Numbers

ACTIVITIES FOR TEACHING:

Warm-up. Play the Comes Before game for counting by 5s. Ask: What comes before 15, [10] 25, [20] 40, [35] 50, [45] and 100. [95]

Ask: How many ones are in 10? [10] How many tens are in 100? [10] How many one hundreds in 1000? [10]

Ask the following: What is ten 1s the same as? [one 10] What is ten 10s the same as? [one 100] What is ten 100s the same as? [one 1000]

Ask the child to show 1, 10, and 100 using side 1 of the abacus. To show 1000, have the child lay out 9 abacus tiles and the abacus with a 100 beads entered.

Adding on the abacus. Tell her: Today you are going to learn a way to add large numbers. Write the following problem for her to see:

$$\begin{array}{r} 4817 \\ \underline{+2639} \end{array}$$

Ask the child to compose the numbers with the place-value cards. Tell her to enter the first number on side 2 of the abacus. See the left figure below.

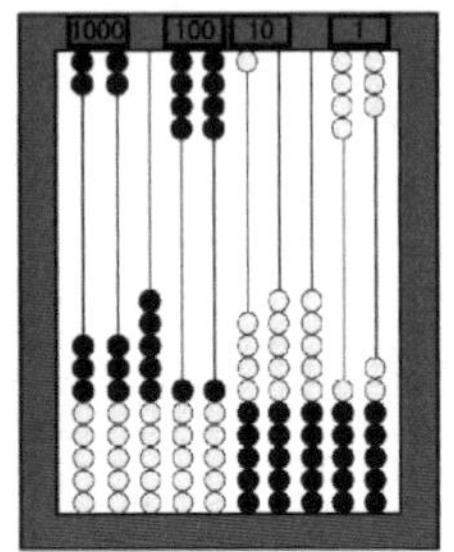

4817 entered.

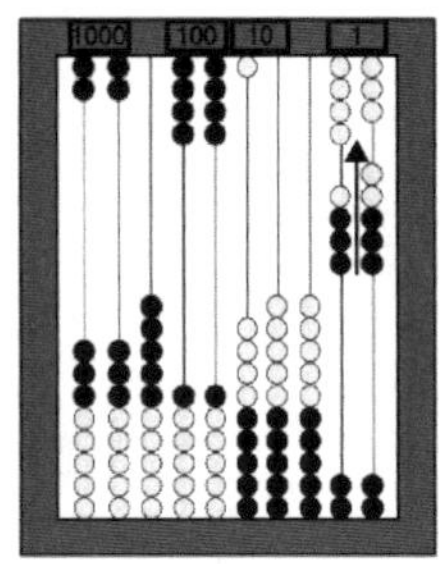

9 added.

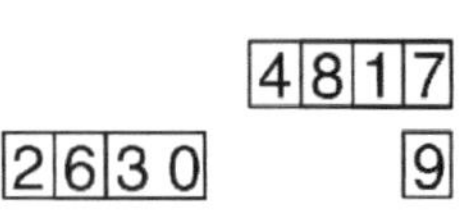

Say: Remove the top place-value card, 9, from the second number, 2639, and move it to the right. Add the quantity on the abacus. See the right figure above.

EXPLANATIONS:

The place-value cards for 2639 will be separated for adding, which emphasizes each digit's place value.

ACTIVITIES FOR TEACHING:

EXPLANATIONS:

Ask: Do you need to trade? [yes] Tell her to trade. See left figure below. Tell her to write what happened by asking: How many ones do we have? [6] Write 6. Did anything else happen? [yes, another 10 was added] Explain that we will show the extra ten by writing 1 above the other tens. See below.

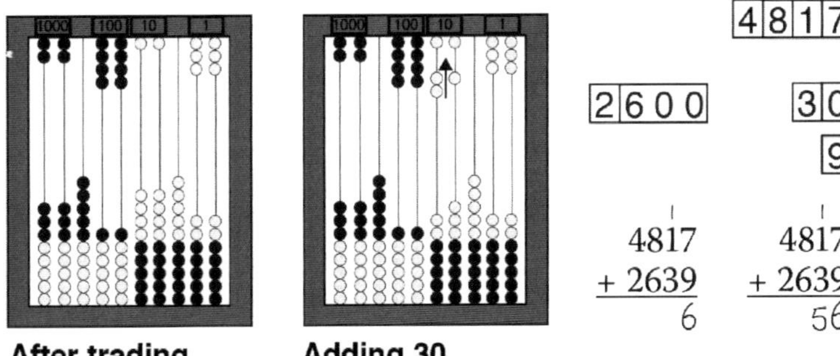

After trading. Adding 30.

Slide the most recent place-value card down.

Tell the child: Continue with the next place-value card, 30, and add the quantity on the abacus. See the right figure above. Record what happened. See above.

Tell her: Remove the next place-value card, 600, and add it on the abacus. See the left figure below. Ask the child to trade and record. See below on the right.

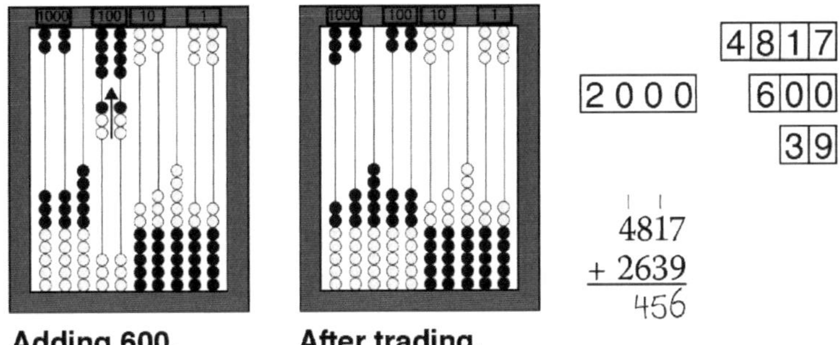

Adding 600. After trading.

Tell her: Add the last place-value card, 2000, on the abacus. See the left figure above. Record what happened.

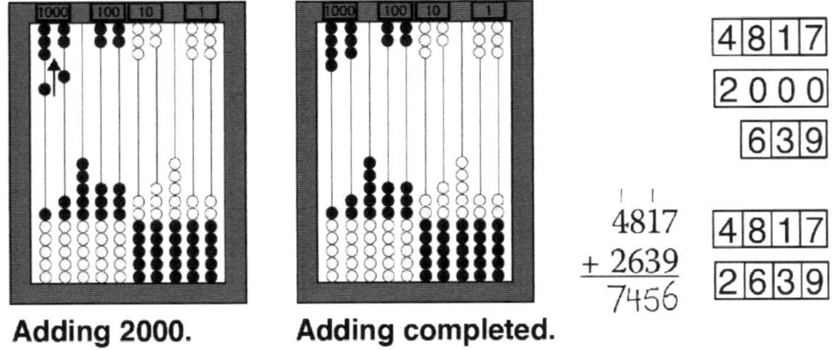

Adding 2000. Adding completed.

Worksheet 11. Give the child the worksheet and tell her to do only the top row using her abacus and place-value cards. The solutions are: **7456, 6213, 9430.**

The first problem is the same as the one demonstrated here.

The second half of this worksheet will be completed in the next lesson.

In conclusion. Ask: What is the biggest difference between adding this way and other ways? [start at right]

LESSON 30: ADDING 4-DIGIT NUMBERS ON PAPER

OBJECTIVES:

1. To add 4-digit numbers on paper
2. To write 4-digit numbers in words

MATERIALS:

1. AL Abacus
2. Abacus Tiles
3. Worksheet 11, Adding 4-Digit Numbers
4. Dry erase board
5. *Math Card Games* book, A9

ACTIVITIES FOR TEACHING:

Warm-up. Ask the following: What is ten 1s the same as? [one 10] What is ten 10s the same as? [one 100] What is ten 100s the same as? [one 1000]

Ask the child to show 1, 10, and 100 using side 1 of the abacus. To show 1000, have the child lay out 9 abacus tiles and the abacus with a 100 beads entered.

Ask: How much is 2000 plus 5000? [7000] How much is 4000 plus 3000? [7000] How much is 4000 plus 5000? [9000]

Play the Comes Before game for counting by 2s. Ask: What comes before 8, [6] 12, [10] 40, [38] 20, [18] and 38? [36]

Worksheet 11. Give the child the worksheet from the previous lesson and ask her to add the first problem in the second row as shown below. Say: Try adding without your abacus, but use the abacus if you need it.

$$\begin{array}{r} 2482 \\ \underline{+5613} \\ [8095] \end{array}$$

When she has finished, ask her to read the answer [8 thousand ninety-five] and explain how to solve the problem.

Repeat for the second problem in the row:

$$\begin{array}{r} 2934 \\ \underline{+6373} \\ [9307] \end{array}$$

Ask the child to read the answer [9 thousand 3 hundred seven] and to write the number in words on her dry erase board.

9 thousand 3 hundred seven

EXPLANATIONS:

ACTIVITIES FOR TEACHING:	**EXPLANATIONS:**

Copy the equation onto the dry erase board. Change the 2 in the top number to 3 and add. See below.

```
  3934
 +6373
[10307]
```

Explain that the sum is read as 10 thousand 3 hundred seven. Ask the child to change the previously written answer.

10 thousand 3 hundred seven

Ask the child to do the last problem in the row and to read the answer.

```
  6879
 +4217
[11096]
```

Tell the child that the sum is read as 11 thousand ninety-six.

Adding on paper. Ask the child to complete the worksheet. The problems and solutions, starting from the second row, are given below.

```
  2482      2934      6879
+ 5613    + 6373    + 4217
  8095      9307     11096
```

```
  4258
+ 3166
  7424     7 thousand 4 hundred twenty-four

  7582
 + 939
  8521     8 thousand 5 hundred twenty-one

  6058
+ 6273
 12331     12 thousand 3 hundred thirty-one

  2525
+ 2525
  5050     5 thousand fifty
```

Corners™ Plus game. Have the child play Corners™ Plus from the *Math Card Games* book, A9. In this Corners™ variation, players receive one extra point for every Corner that is played.

In conclusion. Ask the child to count by hundreds to one thousand. [100, 200, 300, . . . , 1000]

Lesson 31: Review and Games 2

OBJECTIVES:

1. To review recent topics
2. To continue to develop skills through playing math card games

MATERIALS:

1. Worksheet 12-A or 12-B, Review 2
2. *Math Card Games* book, A64 and A9

ACTIVITIES FOR TEACHING:

Worksheet 12-A. Give the child the worksheet. Tell her to listen to the problems and write only the answers on the worksheet. Read each problem twice.

7 + 9   42 + 60   83 + 20

Tell her to complete the worksheet. Solutions are below.

Write only the answers.

16

102

103

Add.

75 + 27 = 102

6 + 109 = 115

27 + 13 + 100 + 34 = 174

Write the number shown by the pictures.

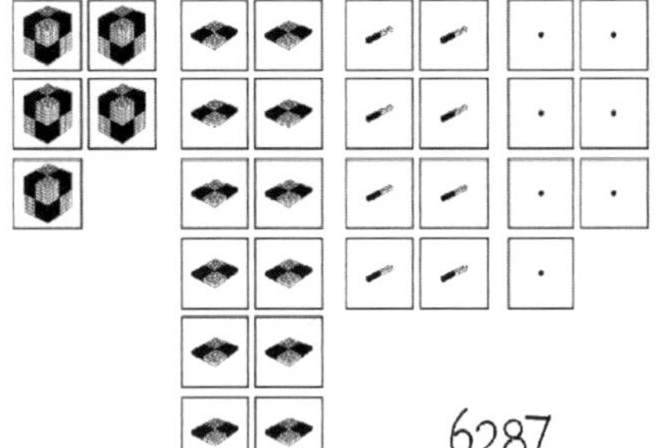

6287

Add.

	3	8	4	7
+	5	0	8	5
	8	9	3	2

Write >, <, or = on the lines.

138 > 30 + 80   101 + 11 < 122

Write this number in expanded form.

2017 2000 + 10 + 7

Write this number in standard form.

4 thousand 8 hundred thirty-seven 4837

EXPLANATIONS:

The Review worksheets each have two versions. The second version can be used in various ways: as a quiz, as a test, as a check after tutoring, and so forth.

Although the child has not previously answered a question like the one on the left, it follows from her work with the base-10 cards.

ACTIVITIES FOR TEACHING:

Column Addition game. Play a simpler version of Column Addition game, found in the *Math Card Games* book, A64. Use only two cards, not three, in each of the nine groups. Or, use three cards in a group, but have only four groups—two horizontal and two vertical.

Corners™ Plus Two game. Have the child play Corners™ Plus Two from the *Math Card Games* book, A9. In this Corners™ variation, players receive two extra points for every Corner played.

Worksheet 12-B. Give the child the worksheet. Tell her to listen to the problems and write only the answers on the worksheet. Read each problem twice.

9 + 8 34 + 70 76 + 30

Tell her to complete the worksheet. Solutions are below.

Write only the answers.

17

104

106

Add.

35 + 88 = 123

7 + 106 = 113

42 + 18 + 100 + 24 = 184

Write the number shown by the pictures.

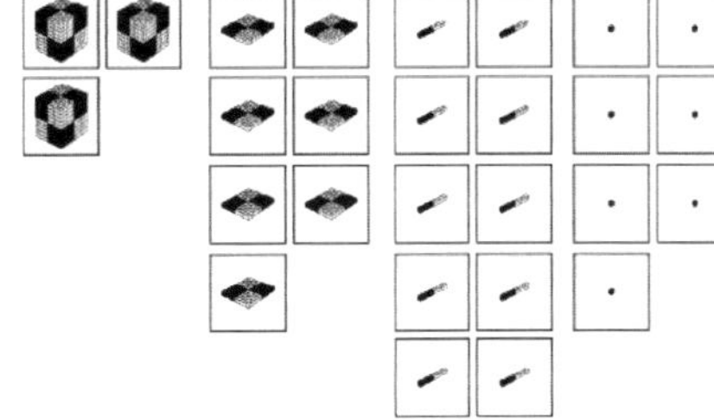

3827

Add.

	4	9	3	7
+	3	5	4	8
	8	4	8	5

Write >, <, or = on the lines.

127 < 40 + 90 101 + 16 = 117

Write this number in expanded form.

3560 3000 + 500 + 60

Write this number in standard form.

3 thousand 9 hundred twenty-four 3924

EXPLANATIONS:

Lesson 32: Introducing Arrays

OBJECTIVES:

1. To introduce *arrays*
2. To learn the term *by* to describe an array as in 4 by 2
3. To learn ways to find the value of an array

MATERIALS:

1. AL Abacus
2. Abacus Tiles
3. Tiles
4. Worksheet 13, Introducing Arrays

ACTIVITIES FOR TEACHING:

Warm-up. Ask the child: What is ten 1s the same as? [one 10] What is ten 10s the same as? [one 100] What is ten 100s the same as? [one 1000]

Ask the child to show 1, 10, and 100 using side 1 of the abacus. To show 1000, have the child lay out 9 abacus tiles and the abacus with a 100 beads entered.

Ask: How much is 3000 plus 5000? [8000] How much is 2000 plus 3000? [5000] How much is 1000 plus 6000? [7000]

Play the Comes Before game for counting by 3s. Ask: What comes before 6, [3] 9, [6] 12, [9] 15, [12] and 18? [15]

Building a 4 by 3 array. Distribute about 25 tiles to the child. Ask her to build a row with four tiles. Then ask her to build two more rows with four tiles directly below the first row. See below.

4 by 3 array.

Say: This is an *array.* In math, an array is things arranged in rows and columns. We name this array 4 *by* 3 and write it like this:

4 by 3

Ask: How many tiles are in this array? [12] Say: There are several ways we can write an equation to show how many tiles are in the array. Write the following:

4 + 4 + 4 = ___

Ask: What is the total amount? [12] How did you add it? Can you think of another way to write the equation? Write:

3 + 3 + 3 + 3 = ___ [12]

Ask: How can you add it? Which equation is easier to add?

EXPLANATIONS:

Naming arrays with the word *by* helps children connect arrays with multiplication and area.

ACTIVITIES FOR TEACHING:

Building a 5 by 2 array. Tell the child to make another array, this time a 5 by 2 array. See below.

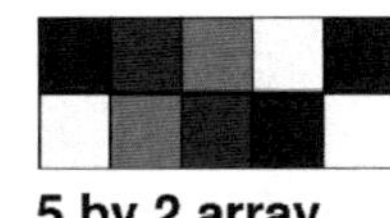

5 by 2 array.

Ask the child to write the name and the equations.

5 by 2

$5 + 5 = 10$

$2 + 2 + 2 + 2 + 2 = 10$

Ask: Which group of numbers is easier to add?

Worksheet 13. Give the child the worksheet. The solutions are:

5 by 3 **5 + 5 + 5 = 15** or **3 + 3 + 3 + 3 + 3 = 15**

2 by 4 **4 + 4 = 8** or **2 + 2 + 2 + 2 = 8**

4 by 4 4 + 4 + 4 + 4 = **16**

3 by 2 **3 + 3 = 6** or **2 + 2 + 2 = 6**

4 by 5 **5 + 5 + 5 + 5 = 20** or **4 + 4 + 4 + 4 + 4 = 20**

In conclusion. Remind the child that an array can be things like an egg carton. Ask her to find arrays around the room.

EXPLANATIONS:

Lesson 33: Multiplication through Arrays

OBJECTIVES:

1. To build arrays on the AL Abacus
2. To understand multiplication as arrays
3. To review (or learn) the symbol for multiplication, ×
4. To learn different ways to find the value of an array

MATERIALS:

1. Tiles
2. AL Abacus
3. Dry erase board
4. Worksheet 14, Multiplication through Arrays

ACTIVITIES FOR TEACHING:

Warm-up. Ask the child: What arrays in the room do you see?

Ask: How much is 2000 plus 4000? [6000] How much is 6000 plus 3000? [9000] How much is 2000 plus 5000? [7000]

Play the Comes Before game for counting by 5s. Ask: What comes before 10, [5] 15, [10] 40, [35] 20, [15] and 30? [25]

Arrays on the abacus. Give the child tiles and an abacus. Ask her to build a 6 by 3 array with her tiles, using two colors to group by fives, as shown below on the left. Tell her to make the same array on her abacus as shown below on the right.

6 by 3 array.

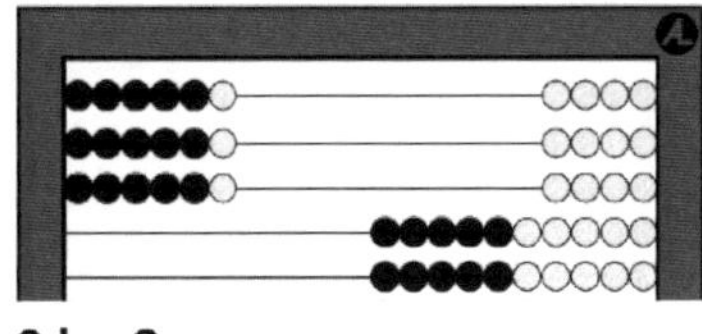

6 by 3 array.

Ask: How many tiles are in your array? [18] How many beads are in your array? [18] Ask the child to write the array name and the equation on the dry erase board.

6 by 3

6 + 6 + 6 = 18

The multiplication symbol. Ask: Are you getting tired of writing all the 6s? Say: There is a simpler way to write the amount of the array. Write:

6 by 3 = 18

Say: Now we will use a math sign for the word *by*. Write:

6 × 3 = 18

Say: We can read it as 6 *multiplied by* 3 equals 18. Some people say it is 6 taken 3 times. Some other people say 6 times 3. It is still the 6 by 3 array.

EXPLANATIONS:

Sometimes 6 × 3 is thought of as "6 groups of 3." However, consistency with the other arithmetic operations requires a second look. When adding 6 + 3, we start with 6 and transform it by adding 3. When subtracting 6 – 3, we start with 6 and transform it by removing 3. When dividing 6 ÷ 3, we start with 6 and transform it by dividing it into 3 groups or into groups of 3s. Likewise, 6 × 3 means we start with 6 and transform it by duplicating it 3 times.

In the array (an arrangement of quantities in rows and columns) model, 6 × 3, 6 represents the horizontal quantity and 3 the vertical quantity. This is also consistent with the coordinate system; in (6, 3), the first number, 6, indicates the horizontal number and 3, the vertical number.

ACTIVITIES FOR TEACHING:

Explain that the multiplication sign is made like the diagonals in a square, as shown below.

Finding 9 × 4. Tell the child to enter the 9 by 4 array on the abacus. See below.

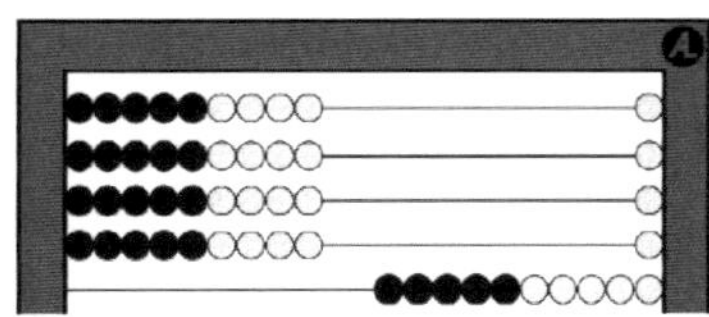

9 multiplied by 4.

Ask her to think of as many ways as possible to find the amount. [36] Some possibilities include:

1. The dark-colored beads are 2 tens, or 20, and the light-colored beads are 8 + 8 = 16; 20 + 16 is 36.
2. The first two rows are 18; 18 + 18 is 36.
3. Four 10s is 40; 40 – 4 is 36.
4. Take and Give, shown below, ends up with 36.

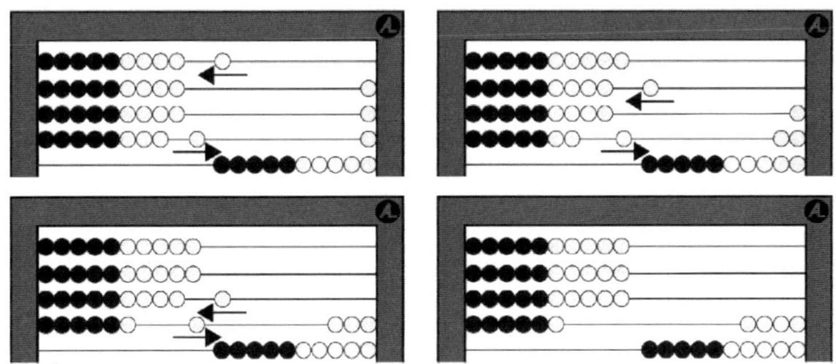

Using Take and Give to find 9 × 4 = 36

Worksheet 14. Give the child the worksheet and ask her to complete only the top half of the worksheet using an abacus as needed. The solutions are shown.

5 × 2 = **10**	8 × 2 = **16**
4 × 10 = **40**	9 × 3 = **27**
5 × 5 = **25**	6 × 4 = **24**
2 × 7 = **14**	3 × 8 = **24**
5 × 10 = **50**	7 × 3 = **21**
7 × 7 = **49**	10 × 10 = **100**
3 × 4 = **12**	4 × 4 = **16**

In conclusion. Ask: How much is 10 + 3? [13] How much is 10 multiplied by 3? [30] How much is 10 + 4? [14] How much is 10 multiplied by 4? [40]

EXPLANATIONS:

Note that the multiplication sign, ×, is not an "x," which is an unknown or a variable in algebra. A good model for writing the multiplication sign is the diagonals in a square as discussed in the lesson.

In Take and Give, beads from one row are "moved" to another row. Simultaneously, one hand "takes" while the other hand "gives." Several beads may be traded during a Take and Give operation.

When 5-year-olds were introduced to multiplication, they said, "Don't give us easy ones like 2 × 4, but give us hard ones like 9 × 9." They greatly enjoyed using Take and Give to find the answers.

The second half of this worksheet will be completed in the next lesson.

Lesson 34: Comparing Addition and Multiplication

OBJECTIVES:

1. To introduce the term *product*
2. To compare adding and multiplying

MATERIALS:

1. AL Abacus
2. *Math Card Games* book, P3
3. Math journal
4. Worksheet 14, Multiplication through Arrays

ACTIVITIES FOR TEACHING:

Warm-up. Ask the child: How much is 10 + 4? [14] How much is 10 multiplied by 4? [40] How much is 10 + 5? [15] How much is 10 multiplied by 5? [50] Use the abacus as needed.

Ask: What is ten 1s the same as? [one 10] What is ten 10s the same as? [one 100] What is ten 100s the same as? [one 1000]

Ask: How much is 1000 plus 4000? [5000] How much is 6000 plus 2000? [8000] How much is 2000 plus 7000? [9000]

Play the Comes Before game for counting by 5s. Ask: What comes before 10, [5] 15, [10] 40, [35] 20, [15] and 30? [25]

Sum Rummy game. Show the child how to play the Sum Rummy game, found in the *Math Card Games* book, P3. The point of the game is determining her score, that is, the value of her cards at the end of the game. Let her decide how to do this for her first game; be sure an abacus is available. Tell her to write her work in her math journal.

One multiplied by a number. Tell the child: Enter 1 multiplied by 5. See below on the left. Ask: How much is it? [5] Tell her the answer in multiplication is called the *product.* Ask: What is the product of 1 multiplied by 7? [7] See the right figure below. Ask: What is 1 multiplied by 10? [10]

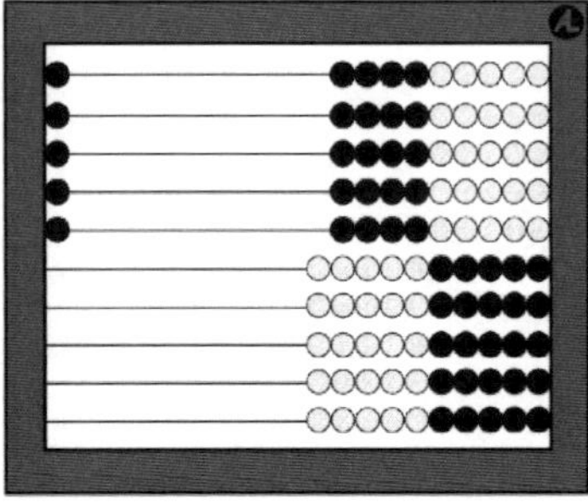

1 multiplied by 5.

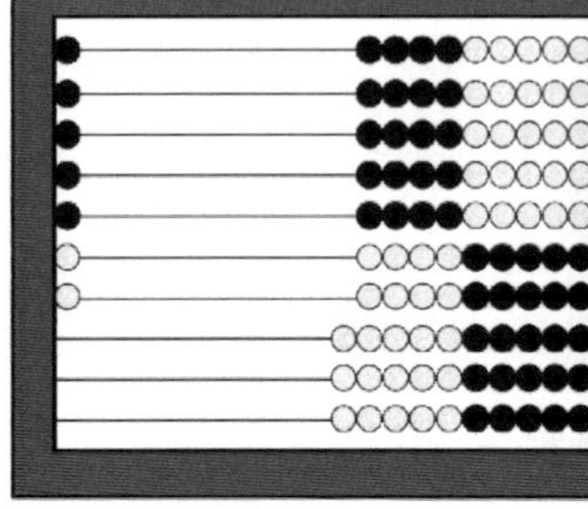

1 multiplied by 7.

EXPLANATIONS:

Sum Rummy will be played again during the next lesson.

The child should not be taught any rules about 1 multiplied by a number or a number multiplied by 1. A mental image is far superior.

ACTIVITIES FOR TEACHING:

EXPLANATIONS:

Multiplying by 1. Tell the child: Enter 5 multiplied by 2. See below. Ask: How much is it? [10] What is the product? [10]

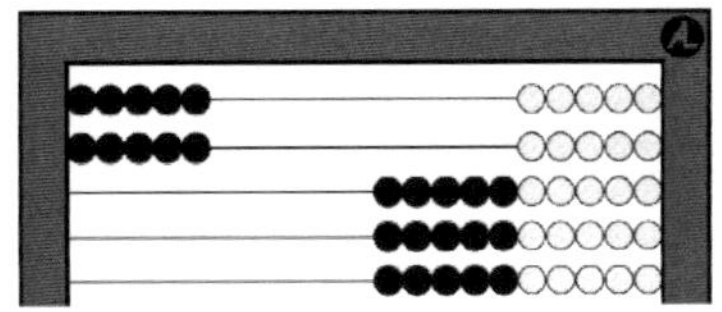
5 multiplied by 2.

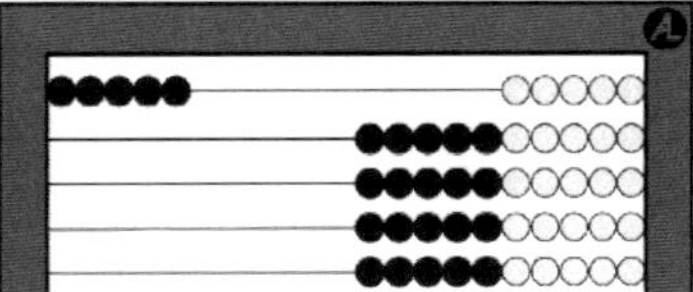
5 multiplied by 1.

Tell her: Now enter 5 multiplied by 1. It must be an array with only one row. See the right figure above. Write the equation:

$$5 \times 1 = 5$$

Tell her to enter 8 multiplied by 1. Ask: What is the product? [8] What is 6 multiplied by 1? [6]

Comparing. Write the following:

$$5 \times 2 \_\_\_ 5 + 2$$

Ask: Is the product of 5 and 2 equal to the sum of 5 and 2? [no] Why not? [The product is 10 and sum is 7.] What symbol do we need? [>, is greater than] Write it on the line:

$$5 \times 2 \underline{\ >\ } 5 + 2$$

Repeat for:

$$6 \times 1 \_\_\_ 6 + 1 \ [<]$$

Worksheet 14. Give the child Worksheet 14, used in the previous lesson. Tell the child to complete the bottom half of the worksheet using her abacus as needed. The solutions are as follows.

$2 \times 1 < 2 + 1$	$8 \times 1 < 8 + 1$
$2 \times 2 = 2 + 2$	$2 \times 3 > 2 + 3$
$1 \times 4 < 1 + 4$	$2 \times 4 = 2 + 1 + 5$
$5 \times 1 = 5 + 1 - 1$	$3 \times 3 = 3 + 3 + 3$
$3 \times 4 = 4 + 4 + 4$	$10 \times 10 > 10 + 10$

Some children may benefit from writing down the results of each side of the equation before deciding on the correct symbol.

In conclusion. Ask: How much is 1 + 3? [4] How much is 1 multiplied by 3? [3] How much is 1 + 4? [5] How much is 1 multiplied by 4? [4]

LESSON 35: MULTIPLICATION EQUATIONS

OBJECTIVES:

1. To write equations using repeated addition
2. To write multiplication equations

MATERIALS:

1. AL Abacus
2. Math journal
3. *Math Card Games* book, P3

ACTIVITIES FOR TEACHING:

Warm-up. Ask: How much is 1 + 6? [7] How much is 1 multiplied by 6? [6] How much is 1 + 7? [8] How much is 1 multiplied by 7? [7]

Ask: How much is 10 + 2? [12] How much is 10 multiplied by 2? [20] How much is 10 + 3? [13] How much is 10 multiplied by 3? [30]

Ask: What is ten 1s the same as? [one 10] What is ten 10s the same as? [one 100] What is ten 100s the same as? [one 1000]

Play the Comes Before game for counting by 3s. Ask: What comes before 9, [6] 3, [0] 12, [9] 15, [12] and 30? [27]

Repeated addition equations. Write the following:

1 1 1 1 1 1

3 3 3 3

6 6 6

8 8 8 8 8

Explain to the child that these numbers represent cards a player collected while playing the Sum Rummy game. Ask: How could we write equations to find the total value? Ask the child to write each equation using the long way in her math journal. See below. Use an abacus as needed.

$1 + 1 + 1 + 1 + 1 + 1 = 6$

$3 + 3 + 3 + 3 = 12$

$6 + 6 + 6 = 18$

$8 + 8 + 8 + 8 + 8 = 40$

Ask her: What is the total of all the cards? [76]

EXPLANATIONS:

ACTIVITIES FOR TEACHING:

Multiplication equations. Using the same numbers as before, ask the child to write the equations in her math journal using multiplication. Remind the child that the multiplication sign is made like the diagonals in a square, as shown below.

The equations are:

$1 \times 6 = 6$

$3 \times 4 = 12$

$6 \times 3 = 18$

$8 \times 5 = 40$

Sum Rummy game. Ask the child to play the Sum Rummy game, found in the *Math Card Games* book, P3. Tell her to play it twice. Remind her to use the abacus when she needs it. The first time she is to use addition equations. The second time she is to use multiplication equations. Tell her to write her work in her math journal.

In conclusion. Ask: Which equations would you rather write? Why?

EXPLANATIONS:

Remember that the multiplication sign, ×, is not an "x," which is often the unknown in algebra.

Lesson 36: Multiples of 2 to 5

OBJECTIVES:

1. To find multiples for 2, 3, 4, and 5

MATERIALS:

1. Worksheet 15, Multiples of 2 to 5
2. AL Abacus
3. *Math Card Games* book, P2

ACTIVITIES FOR TEACHING:

Warm-up. Ask the child: How much is 1 + 3? [4] How much is 1 multiplied by 3? [3] How much is 1 + 4? [5] How much is 1 multiplied by 4? [4]

Ask: How much is 10 + 6? [16] How much is 10 multiplied by 6? [60] How much is 10 + 8? [18] How much is 10 multiplied by 8? [80]

Ask: How much is ten ones? [one 10] How much is 10 tens? [one 100] How much is 10 hundreds? [one 1000]

Play the Comes Before game for counting by 2s. Ask: What comes before 8, [6] 6, [4] 12, [10] 16, [14] and 20? [18]

Worksheet 15. Give the child the worksheet and tell her to complete the first column using her abacus to enter the multiples. Then ask her to read her answers. See the first column below.

2 × 1 = **2**
2 × 2 = **4**
2 × 3 = **6**
2 × 4 = **8**
2 × 5 = **10**
2 × 6 = **12**
2 × 7 = **14**
2 × 8 = **16**
2 × 9 = **18**
2 × 10 = **20**

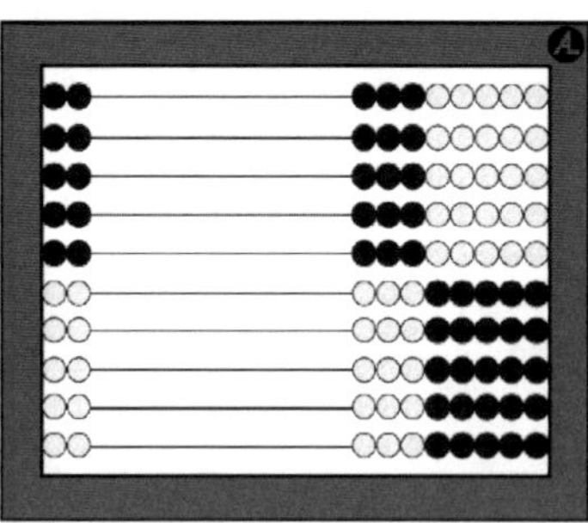

Multiples of 2.

Ask: What did that sound like? [counting by twos] Tell her to keep the multiples of two on her abacus as shown above. Then tell her to point and name the multiples as you ask: What is 2 multiplied by 3? [6] What is 2 multiplied by 5? [10] What is 2 multiplied by 7? [14] Continue if needed.

Multiples of 5. Tell the child to use her abacus and find the multiples of 5 for the second column on her worksheet. See the top of the next page.

EXPLANATIONS:

ACTIVITIES FOR TEACHING:

5 × 1 = **5**
5 × 2 = **10**
5 × 3 = **15**
5 × 4 = **20**
5 × 5 = **25**
5 × 6 = **30**
5 × 7 = **35**
5 × 8 = **40**
5 × 9 = **45**
5 × 10 = **50**

Multiples of 5.

Ask her to read the products. Ask: What does it sound like? [counting by 5s]

With 5 × 10 on her abacus, as shown above, ask the child to point to and find: What is 5 multiplied by 2? [10] What is 5 multiplied by 4? [20] What is 5 multiplied by 6? [30] What is 5 multiplied by 8? [40] What is 5 multiplied by 10? [50]

Multiples of 3 and 4. Tell the child to use her abacus and find the multiples of 3 and 4 and write the sums on her worksheet. See the answers below.

3 × 1 = **3**	4 × 1 = **4**
3 × 2 = **6**	4 × 2 = **8**
3 × 3 = **9**	4 × 3 = **12**
3 × 4 = **12**	4 × 4 = **16**
3 × 5 = **15**	4 × 5 = **20**
3 × 6 = **18**	4 × 6 = **24**
3 × 7 = **21**	4 × 7 = **28**
3 × 8 = **24**	4 × 8 = **32**
3 × 9 = **27**	4 × 9 = **36**
3 × 10 = **30**	4 × 10 = **40**

Multiples Memory game. Have the child use the product envelopes with 2s, 3s, 4s, and 5s to play the Multiples Memory game found in the *Math Card Games* book, P2.

In conclusion. Ask: When you played the Multiples Memory game, did both players ever need the same card? [yes] Ask: Do you know why? [For example, using 2s and 3s, 2 × 3 = 3 × 2.]

EXPLANATIONS:

Learning the multiples is necessary for fractions and algebra. Do not teach children to recite them in order to find a multiplication fact.

Lesson 37: Area

OBJECTIVES:

1. To learn the term *area*
2. To relate area to arrays
3. To find area of rectangles
4. To find distances around rectangles

MATERIALS:

1. Dry erase board
2. Centimeter cubes
3. Worksheet 16, Area

ACTIVITIES FOR TEACHING:

Warm-up. Play the Comes Before game for counting by 5s. Ask: What comes before 15, [10] 25, [20] 40, [35] 50, [45] and 100? [95] Repeat using the 2s.

Ask the child to write only the answers on the dry erase board for the following as the problems are read aloud: 27 + 3, [30] 43 + 7, [50] 66 + 4, [70] 22 + 8, [30] 35 + 5, [40] and 81 + 9. [90]

Ask: How much is 10 + 2? [12] How much is 10 multiplied by 2? [20] How much is 10 + 7? [17] How much is 10 multiplied by 7? [70]

Ask: How much is ten ones? [one 10] How much is 10 tens? [one 100] How much is 10 hundreds? [one 1000]

Area. Give the child the centimeter cubes. Tell her to use the cubes to make a 3 by 3 array and a 4 by 2 array. See below.

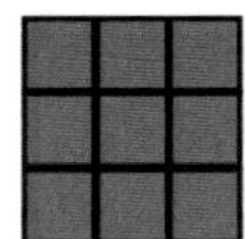

3 by 3 array

4 by 2 array

Ask: Which takes up more space, a baby's footprint or your footprint? [the child] Which array uses more cubes, the 3 by 3 or the 4 by 2 array? [3 by 3] Which array takes more space? [3 by 3] How do you know? [The 3 by 3 needs 9 cubes, but the 4 by 2 needs only 8.] Say: Yes, the 3 by 3 array takes up more space; it has more *area*.

Explain: The amount of space something takes up is called *area*. Can you think of other areas? [play area, parking area, and so forth]

Worksheet 16, problem 1. Give the child the worksheet and tell her to read the first problem on the worksheet. Give her time to solve it by making arrays to cover the rectangles. See the figures on the next page. Ask her to explain her solutions.

EXPLANATIONS:

ACTIVITIES FOR TEACHING:

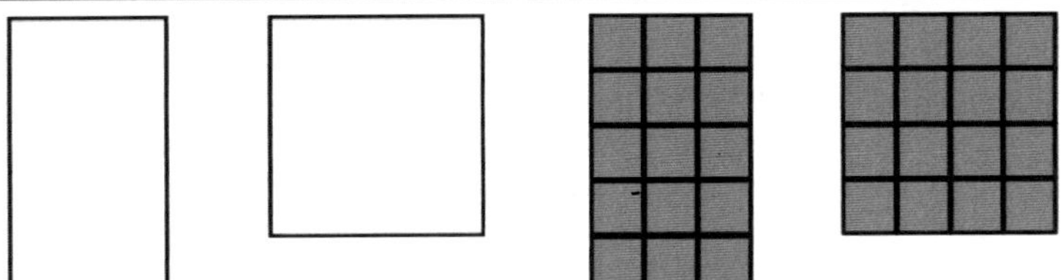

Rectangle A. **Rectangle B.** **Rectangle A.** **Rectangle B.**

Ask: Which array is larger? [rectangle B] How do you know? [Rectangle A needs 15 centimeter cubes and rectangle B needs 16 centimeter cubes.] Which rectangle takes up the greater space? [rectangle B] Which rectangle has less area? [rectangle A]

Centimeters. Tell the child to look at one of the centimeter cubes. Remind her that each edge of the centimeter cube is 1 centimeter long. Ask: If you drew a line all around the cube, how long would your line be? [4 cm] See below. Tell her we can write centimeter as *cm.*

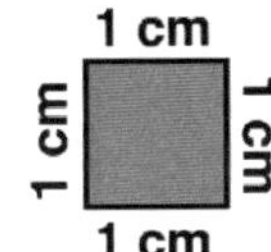

Distance around: 4 cm

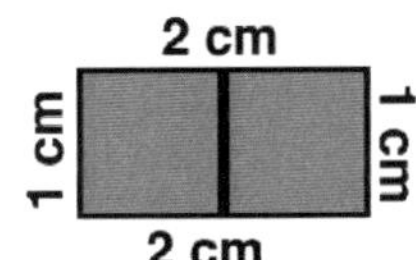

Distance around: 6 cm

Problem 2. Now tell her to read and solve problem 2 on the worksheet. Tell her to use the same arrays. Then ask the child to write the equation for rectangle A.

5 + 3 + 5 + 3 = 16 cm

Ask the child to write the equation for rectangle B.

4 + 4 + 4 + 4 = 16 cm

Ask: Which rectangle has the greatest distance around it? [same] Are you surprised at the answer?

Problems 3–5. Ask her to complete the worksheet. The solutions are as follows.

Area: **5 by 1 = 5**	Distance: **1 + 5 + 1 + 5 = 12 cm**
Area: **4 by 3 = 12**	Distance: **4 + 3 + 4 + 3 = 14 cm**
Area: **2 by 5 = 10**	Distance: **2 + 5 + 2 + 5 = 14 cm**

In conclusion. Ask: What is area? [the space that something takes up]

EXPLANATIONS:

The term *perimeter* will be introduced in the next lesson.

Lesson 38: Area and Perimeter

OBJECTIVES:

1. To introduce the term *perimeter*
2. To learn about square inches
3. To learn about square cm

MATERIALS:

1. AL Abacus
2. Tiles
3. Centimeter cubes
4. Worksheet 17, Area and Perimeter

ACTIVITIES FOR TEACHING:

Warm-up. Ask: What is area? [the space that something takes up]

Ask the child to say the multiples of 4 as she moves over groups of 4s on the abacus to 40. [4, 8, 12, . . . , 40] Ask her to say the multiples of 3 to 30. [3, 6, 9, . . . , 30]

Play the Comes Before game for counting by 2s. Ask: What comes before 8, [6] 12, [10] 40, [38] 20, [18] and 38? [36] Repeat using 5s.

Ask the child to say the months of the year. Then play the Comes After game. Ask: What month comes after March? [April] After August? [September] After October? [November]

Inches. Give the tiles and centimeter cubes to the child. Tell her to look at one tile. See the left figure below. Remind her that the distance along one edge is 1 inch. Ask: What is the distance around the whole square? [4 inches]

1 tile

2 tiles

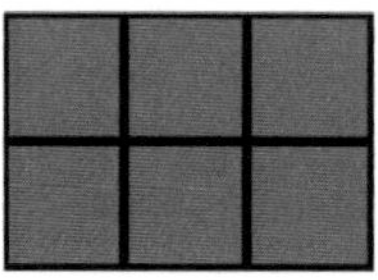
3 by 2 array

Tell her the math word for distance around a shape is *perimeter.* Ask: What is the perimeter of one tile? [4 inches] Show her how to write it:

4 inches

Tell her to place another tile next to the first tile as shown above in the second figure. Ask: What is the perimeter now? [6 inches] Ask the child to write it.

6 inches

Worksheet 17, problems 1 and 2. Give the child the worksheet. Tell her to solve the first two problems. Remind her to write the word inches. See the figures on the next page.

EXPLANATIONS:

To remember the basic meaning of the word *perimeter,* some children might find it helpful to point to each side of a rectangle while saying "pe-rim-e-ter" as shown below:

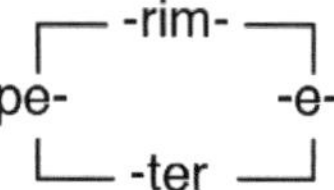

ACTIVITIES FOR TEACHING:

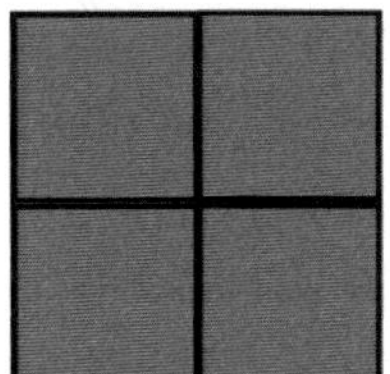
Rectangle F.

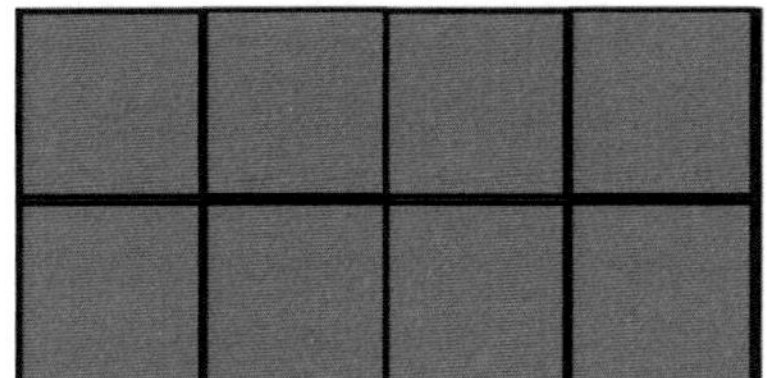
Rectangle G.

1. **2 + 2 + 2 + 2 = 8 inches**
2. **4 + 2 + 4 + 2 = 12 inches**

Ask for explanations on how to solve the problems.

Square inches. Tell her to look again at one tile. Say: We can measure area with these tiles. The area of one tile is 1 square inch. Ask: What is the area of 2 tiles? [2 square inches]

Problems 3 and 4. Tell the child to solve problems 3 and 4. Remind her to write the words *square inches*. See the same figures above.

Ask for an explanation. The areas are:

3. **2 by 2 = 4 square inches**
4. **4 by 2 = 8 square inches**

Ask: Do you think rectangle G is twice as large as rectangle F? [Yes, rectangle F is 4 square inches and rectangle G is 8 square inches, which is twice as much.]

Ask: Is the perimeter twice as much? [no] Ask the child to explain.

Square centimeters. Tell the child to look at one centimeter cube. Say: We measured area with these cubes in the last lesson. Ask: What do you think we call the area of one cube? [square centimeter]

Problems 5–8. Ask the child to finish the worksheet. Tell her that she does not have to fill in the whole rectangles with the cubes if she can figure out the answers without all of them. The solutions are below.

5. **5 + 5 + 5 + 5 = 20 cm**
6. **10 + 5 + 10 + 5 = 30 cm**
7. **5 by 5 = 25 sq cm**
8. **10 by 5 = 50 sq cm**

In conclusion. Ask: What is perimeter? [the distance around] What is area? [the amount of space something takes up]

EXPLANATIONS:

The term *sq cm* is used only temporarily. The standard cm^2 will be introduced later.

Lesson 39: Assessment Review 1

OBJECTIVES:

1. To review recent topics

MATERIALS:

1. Worksheet 18, Assessment Review 1
2. Centimeter cubes

ACTIVITIES FOR TEACHING:

Worksheet 18. Give the child the worksheet and some centimeter cubes.

Addition. Tell her to listen to the following problems and write only the answers on the worksheet. Read each problem twice.

6 + 9　　　53 + 9　　　87 + 30

Complete the equations. Tell the child to complete the following problems on the worksheet. Answers shown on next page.

87 + 25 + 3 =

5 by 2 =

6 × 1 =

4529 + 5385 =

Perimeter and area. Have the child find the perimeter and area using the centimeter cubes. Answers shown on next page.

Place-value. Tell her to fill in the missing place-value card numbers. Answers shown in bold.

Greater than and less than. Tell the child to use the <, >, or = sign to complete the equations. Answers shown on next page.

Drawing arrays. Have the child draw a 4 by 3 array and write the answers on the line provided.

Writing numerals. Tell the child to complete the rest of the worksheet. Answers are shown.

EXPLANATIONS:

ACTIVITIES FOR TEACHING:

Write only the answers.

15   87 + 25 + 3 = 115

62   5 by 2 = 10

117   6 × 1 = 6

	4	5	2	9
+	5	3	8	5
	9	9	1	4

Find the perimeter in cm and the area in square cm.

5 + 3 + 5 + 3 = 16 cm

5 × 3 = 15 square cm

Fill in the missing place-value card numbers.

2 0 0 0 + **3 0 0** + **4 0** + **5**   **2 3 4 5**

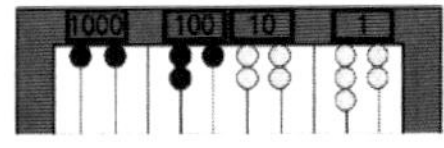

1 0 0 0 + **2 0 0** + **6 0** + **4**   **1 2 6 4**

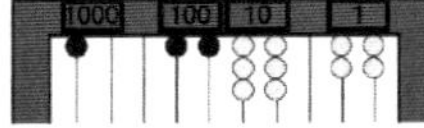

Write >, <, or = on the lines.

3 × 1 < 3 + 1

1 inch > 1 cm

Draw a 4 × 3 array. How much is it?

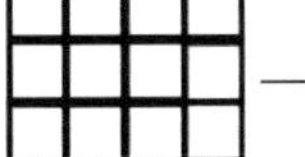

12

Write this number in standard form.

seven thousand one hundred thirteen 7113

Write this number in words.

4807 four thousand eight hundred seven

EXPLANATIONS:

Lesson 40: Review Games

OBJECTIVES:

1. To review recent topics through playing math card games

MATERIALS:

1. *Math Card Games* book, A64, A9, P2, and P3
2. AL Abacus
3. Math journal

ACTIVITIES FOR TEACHING:

Review with games. Tell the child that today we will be playing games for practice and review.

Column Addition game. Play a simpler version of Column Addition game, found in the Math Card Games book, A64. Use only two cards, not three, in each of the nine groups. Or, use three cards in a group, but have only four groups—two horizontal and two vertical.

Corners™ Plus game. Have the child play Corners™ Plus from the Math Card Games book, A9. In this Corners™ variation, players receive one extra point for every Corner played.

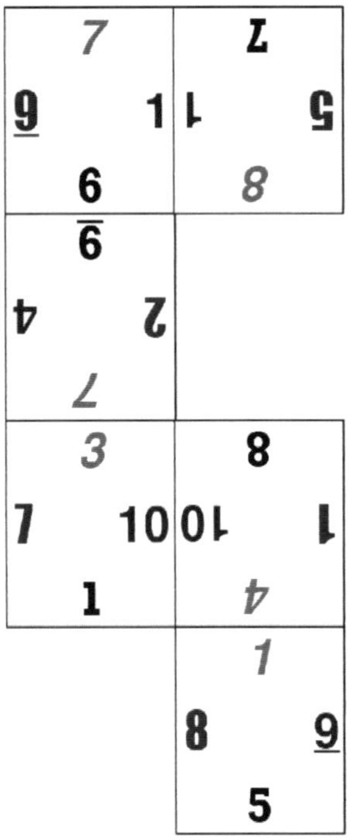

EXPLANATIONS:

ACTIVITIES FOR TEACHING:

Multiples Memory game. Have the child use the product envelopes with 2s, 3s, 4s, and 5s to play the Multiples Memory game found in the Math Card Games book, P2.

Sum Rummy game. Ask the child to play the Sum Rummy game, found in the Math Card Games book, P3. Tell her to play it twice. Remind her to use the abacus when she needs it. The first time she is to use adding equations. The second time she is to use multiplication equations. Tell her to record her score in her math journal.

EXPLANATIONS:

Lesson 41: Assessment 1

OBJECTIVES:

1. To assess recent topics

MATERIALS:

1. Worksheet 19, Assessment 1
2. Centimeter cubes

ACTIVITIES FOR TEACHING:

Worksheet 19. Give the child the worksheet and some centimeter cubes.

Addition. Tell her to listen to the problems and write only the answers on the worksheet. Read each problem twice.

8 + 9 52 + 9 83 + 50

Complete the equations. Tell the child to complete the following problems on the worksheet. Answers shown on next page.

79 + 37 + 1 =

5 by 3 =

1 × 4 =

3538 + 4775 =

Perimeter and area. Have the child find the perimeter and area using the centimeter cubes. Answers shown on next page.

Place-value. Tell her to fill in the missing place-value card numbers. Answers shown in bold.

Greater than and less than. Tell the child to use the <, >, or = sign to complete the equations. Answers shown on next page.

Drawing arrays. Have the child draw a 3 by 4 array and write the answer on the line provided.

Writing numerals. Tell her to complete the rest of the worksheet. Answers shown.

EXPLANATIONS:

ACTIVITIES FOR TEACHING:

Write only the answers.

17 ______ 79 + 37 + 1 = 117

61 ______ 5 by 3 = 15

133 ______ 1 × 4 = 4

	3	5	3	8
+	4	7	7	5
	8	3	1	3

Find the perimeter in cm and the area in square cm.

6 + 2 + 6 + 2 = 16 cm

6 x 2 = 12 square cm

Fill in the missing place-value card numbers.

3 0 0 0 + **0** 0 0 + **1** 0 + **2** **3 0 1 2**

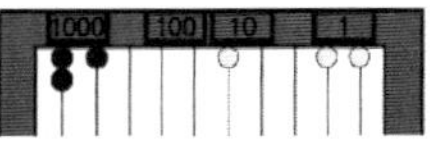

4 0 0 0 + **2** 0 0 + **0** 0 + **6** **4 2 0 6**

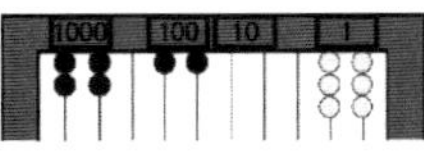

Write >, <, or = on the lines.

2 × 2 = 2 + 2

1 cm < 1 inch

Draw a 3 × 4 array. How much is it?

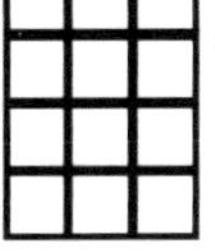

12

Write this number in standard form.

eight thousand four hundred fifteen 8415

Write this number in words.

3260 three thousand two hundred sixty

EXPLANATIONS:

Lesson 42: Solving Missing Addend Problems

OBJECTIVES:

1. To solve missing addend problems
2. To introduce the Going Up Strategy
3. To write missing addend and subtraction equations

MATERIALS:

1. AL Abacus
2. Worksheet 20, Solving Missing Addend Problems

ACTIVITIES FOR TEACHING:

Warm-up. Ask the child: What is perimeter? [the distance around] What is area? [the amount of space something takes up]

Ask the child to say the multiples of 5 as she moves over groups of 5s on the abacus to 50. [5, 10, 15, . . . , 50] Ask her to say the multiples of 2 to 20 by merely looking at an abacus. [2, 4, 6, . . . , 20]

Ask the child to say the multiples of 3 to 30. [3, 6, 9, . . . , 30] Then play the Comes After game. Ask: What multiple of 3 comes after 6, [9] 12, [15] and 21? [24] Also ask: What is 6 + 3, [9] 12 + 3, [15] and 21 + 3? [24]

Ask her to say the months of the year. Then play the Comes After game. Ask: What month comes after June? [July] After September? [October] After April? [May]

Worksheet 20, problem 1. Give the child the worksheet. Ask her to read the first problem.

> There are 17 boys and 14 girls in a chorus. How many children are in the chorus? [31 children]

This problem is a simple combine addition problem, but it presents a difficulty because combining is done conceptually. It also reviews part-whole thinking.

Tell her to use the part-whole circle set to solve the problem and to write the equation. Ask the child to discuss the problem and explain her solutions. See the figure below.

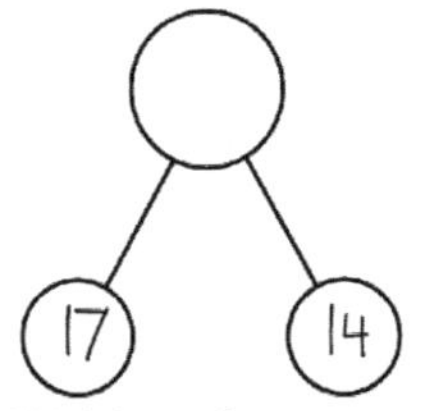

Writing the parts.

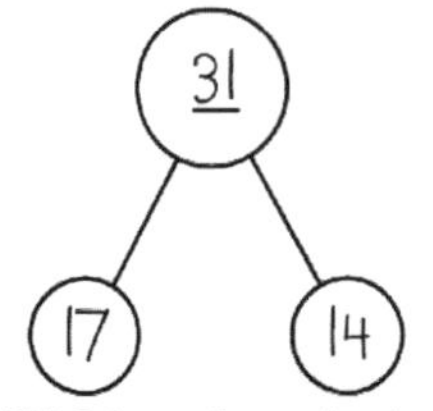

Writing the whole.

17 + 14 = <u>31</u>

Ask: What is the whole? [31 children] What are the parts? [17 boys and 14 girls] Then ask her to write the equation. [17 + 14 = 31] Tell her to underline the answer.

EXPLANATIONS:

Underlining the answer helps identify the solution portion of the problem.

ACTIVITIES FOR TEACHING:

Problem 2. Ask the child to read the next problem, which is a missing addend problem.

> Jack wants to buy a gift that costs one dollar. A dollar is 100 cents. Jack already has 85¢. How much more money does he need? [15¢]

Ask her to write the numbers in her part-whole circle set. Tell her to underline her answer and to write the equation. Ask her how she solved the problem. Refer to the strategy of starting with 85 and going up to 100 as the Going Up Strategy. See the figures below.

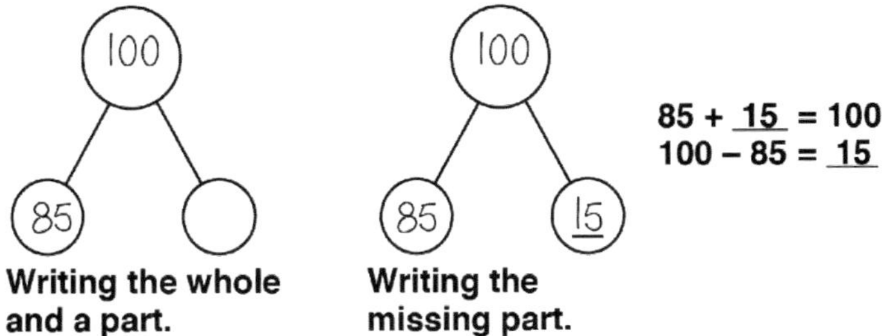

Problems 3–5. Tell the child to solve these problems by herself, then explain.

> 3. Jill is packing 24 bagels in a bag. She has 9 bagels in the bag already. How many more bagels must she put into the bag? [15]
>
> 4. On Monday Kerry read 11 pages in a book. Now Kerry is on page 34. What page did Kerry start on? [23]
>
> 5. Some children were lined up. Fourteen more children join the line. Now there are 21 children. How many children were in line at the start? [7]

The solutions are shown below.

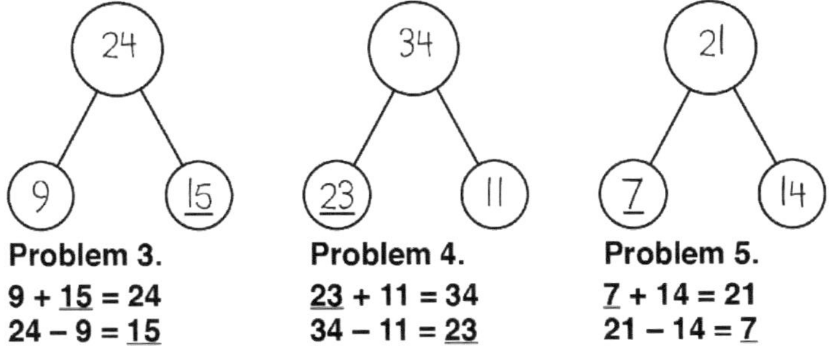

In conclusion. Ask: Which subtraction strategy is easier, Going Up or Going Down?

EXPLANATIONS:

It is extremely important that children view questioning as part of the learning process.

The numbers in these problems are chosen to encourage the child to think going up, not going down. Research shows going up to be easier.

Writing equations does not help children solve problems. That is why children should write the equations after solving the problem.

It is best to avoid the term "take away" when referring to subtraction. It is not listed in the dictionary. The term emphasizes the going back aspect of subtraction, ignoring other meanings such as going up and differences, making it difficult for children to develop a complete understanding of subtraction.

Lesson 43: Ones and Twos Subtraction Strategies

OBJECTIVES:

1. To learn the term *difference*
2. To begin recording subtraction facts on the subtraction table
3. To focus on the strategies for subtracting 1 and 2

MATERIALS:

1. AL Abacus
2. Worksheet 21, Subtraction Tables 1
3. *Math Card Games* book, S6

ACTIVITIES FOR TEACHING:

EXPLANATIONS:

Warm-up. Ask: What is perimeter? [the distance around] What is area? [the amount of space something takes up]

Ask the child to say the multiples of 2 to 20 as she moves over groups of 2s on the abacus. [2, 4, 6, . . . , 20] Ask her to say the multiples of 3 to 30 [3, 6, 9, . . . , 30] by merely looking at an abacus.

Ask the child to say the multiples of 5 to 50. [5, 10, 15, 20, . . . , 50] Then play the Comes After game. Ask: What multiple of 5 comes after 5, [10] 20, [25] and 25? [30]

Also ask: What is 5 + 2, [7] 5 + 3, [8] and 5 + 20? [25]

Play the Comes Before game using evens and odds. Ask: What even number comes before 8, [6] 12, [10] 40, [38] 20, [18] and 38? [36] Repeat using odd numbers.

Worksheet 21. Give the child the worksheet. Explain: These subtraction tables will show subtraction facts.

Subtracting 1. Tell the child: The answer after subtracting is called the *difference*. What is the difference for 3 – 1? [2] Demonstrate writing it in the first subtraction table, Ones and Twos Strategies, as you say: Go across the top row until you come to 3. Then go down in that column to the minus 1 row along the side. That is the square where you write 2. See the figure below.

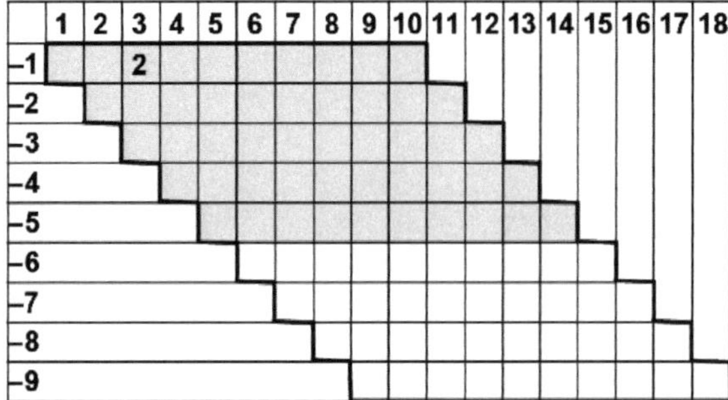

	1	2	3	4	5	6	7	8	9	10	11	12	13	14	15	16	17	18
–1			2															
–2																		
–3																		
–4																		
–5																		
–6																		
–7																		
–8																		
–9																		

Subtraction table showing 3 – 1 = 2.

Ask: How did you know the difference was 2? [the number right before] What is 8 – 1? [7] What is

ACTIVITIES FOR TEACHING:

5 – 1? [4] What is 1 – 1? [0] Tell her to fill in the whole minus 1 row as shown below.

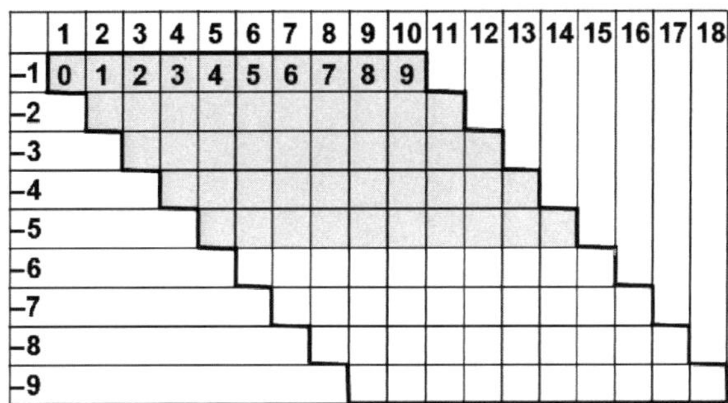

	1	2	3	4	5	6	7	8	9	10	11	12	13	14	15	16	17	18
–1	0	1	2	3	4	5	6	7	8	9								
–2																		
–3																		
–4																		
–5																		
–6																		
–7																		
–8																		
–9																		

Subtraction table subtracting 1 from a number.

Subtracting 2 from an even number. Next ask how the child could find 8 – 2 and 6 – 2. [the previous even number] Remind her that zero is an even number. Tell her to write the even numbers minus 2 on the table Ones and Twos Strategies. See the figure.

	1	2	3	4	5	6	7	8	9	10	11	12	13	14	15	16	17	18
–1	0	1	2	3	4	5	6	7	8	9								
–2		**0**		**2**		**4**		**6**		**8**								
–3																		
–4																		
–5																		
–6																		

Subtracting 2 from even numbers.

Subtracting 2 from an odd number. Ask for examples of odd numbers minus 2. [3 – 2, 5 – 2, 7 – 2, and 9 – 2] Ask: How could you remember them? [the previous odd number] Ask her to write the answers on the table. See below.

	1	2	3	4	5	6	7	8	9	10	11	12	13	14	15	16	17	18
–1	0	1	2	3	4	5	6	7	8	9								
–2		0	**1**	2	**3**	4	**5**	6	**7**	8	**9**							
–3																		
–4																		
–5																		
–6																		

Subtracting 2 from even and odd numbers.

Subtraction Memory game. To provide practice for the facts involving subtracting 2, have the child play Subtraction Memory, found in the *Math Card Games* book, S6. Use 2 as the subtrahend, that is, the number being subtracted.

In conclusion. Ask: What is 13 – 1, [12] 36 – 2, [34] 45 – 2, [43] 99 – 1, [98] and 60 – 2? [58]

EXPLANATIONS:

If the child is uncertain about the results of the subtraction, she should use the abacus to verify the differences.

The new entries to the subtraction table are shown in boldface.

A sticky note with "– 2" can be used for the subtrahend instead of another card.

Lesson 44: Consecutive Numbers Subtraction Strategies

OBJECTIVES:

1. To focus on subtracting the same numbers
2. To learn the term *consecutive numbers*
3. To focus on subtracting consecutive numbers
4. To focus on subtracting consecutive even and consecutive odd numbers

MATERIALS:

1. Dry erase board
2. Worksheet 21, Subtraction Tables 1
3. AL Abacus

ACTIVITIES FOR TEACHING:

Warm-up. Ask: What is 12 – 1, [11] 38 – 2, [36] 55 – 2, [53] 99 – 1, [98] and 40 – 2? [38]

Ask the child to write the answers to the following written problems on her dry erase board: 58 + 26, [84] 49 + 49, [98] 85 – 10, [75] and 130 – 15. [115]

Ask her to say the months of the year, then play the Comes After game. Ask: What month comes after January? [February] After July? [August] After December? [January]

Subtracting the same number. Give the child the worksheet from the previous lesson. Ask: What happens when you subtract the same number, such as 9 – 9 or 3 – 3? [0] Then ask her to find the nine places for such facts on the second subtraction table, Consecutive and Same Numbers Strategies, on the worksheet and to write the differences. See below.

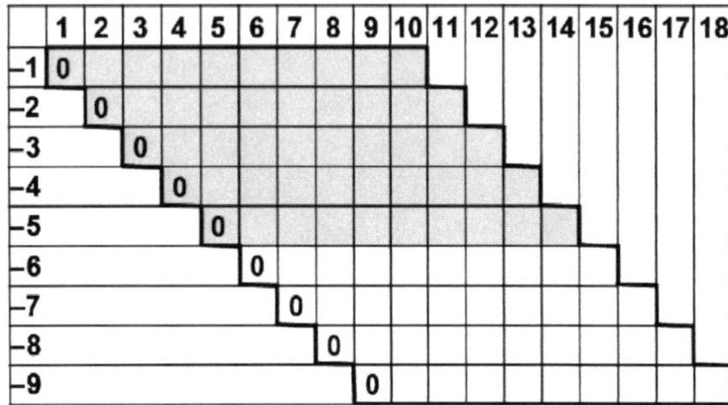

	1	2	3	4	5	6	7	8	9	10	11	12	13	14	15	16	17	18
–1	0																	
–2		0																
–3			0															
–4				0														
–5					0													
–6						0												
–7							0											
–8								0										
–9									0									

Subtracting the same numbers.

Subtracting consecutive numbers. Tell the child: Two numbers that follow in order are called *consecutive numbers*, for example, 3 and 4, or 8 and 7. Ask: What happens when you subtract consecutive numbers, the smaller from the larger, such as 8 – 7 or 5 – 4? [The difference is 1.] Then ask her to find such facts on her subtraction table and write them. See the figure on the next page.

EXPLANATIONS:

If the child is uncertain about the results of the subtraction, she should use the abacus to verify the differences.

ACTIVITIES FOR TEACHING:

	1	2	3	4	5	6	7	8	9	10	11	12	13	14	15	16	17	18
–1	0	**1**																
–2		0	**1**															
–3			0	**1**														
–4				0	**1**													
–5					0	**1**												
–6						0	**1**											
–7							0	**1**										
–8								0	**1**									
–9									0	**1**								

Subtracting consecutive numbers.

Subtracting consecutive even numbers. Tell the child to write the even numbers to 10 in a row.

2 4 6 8 10

Ask: What happens when you subtract two consecutive even numbers, the smaller from the larger? [The difference is 2.]

Ask her to find these facts on the subtraction table and write them. See the figure below.

Subtracting consecutive odd numbers. Ask the child to write the odd numbers to 11 in a row.

1 3 5 7 9 11

Ask: What happens when you subtract two consecutive odd numbers, the smaller from the larger? [The difference is 2.]

Ask her to find these facts on the subtraction table and write them. See the figure below.

	1	2	3	4	5	6	7	8	9	10	11	12	13	14	15	16	17	18
–1	0	1	**2**															
–2		0	1	**2**														
–3			0	1	**2**													
–4				0	1	**2**												
–5					0	1	**2**											
–6						0	1	**2**										
–7							0	1	**2**									
–8								0	1	**2**								
–9									0	1	**2**							

Subtracting even and odd consecutive numbers.

Practice. Ask the child a few facts from the table and have her verify if the answers are correct.

In conclusion. Ask: Subtracting what kind of numbers gives a difference of zero? [same numbers] What kind of numbers gives a difference of one? [consecutive numbers] What kind of numbers gives the difference of two? [consecutive evens or odds]

EXPLANATIONS:

The new entries to the subtraction table are shown in boldface.

Lesson 45: Tens and Near Tens Subtraction Strategies

OBJECTIVES:

1. To focus on subtracting from 10
2. To focus on subtracting from 11 and 9, compared to subtracting from 10

MATERIALS:

1. Dry erase board
2. *Math Card Games* book, S1
3. Worksheet 22, Subtraction Tables 2

ACTIVITIES FOR TEACHING:

Warm-up. Ask the child: Subtracting what kind of numbers gives a difference of zero? [same numbers] What kind of numbers gives a difference of one? [consecutive numbers] What kind of numbers gives the difference of two? [consecutive evens or odds]

Ask: What is 11 – 1, [10] 48 – 2, [46] 45 – 2, [43] 99 – 1, [98] and 50 – 2? [48]

Ask: What is perimeter? [the distance around] What is area? [the amount of space something takes up]

Also ask the child to write the answers to the following written problems on her dry erase board: 68 + 26, [94] 39 + 39, [78] 65 – 10, [55] and 130 – 25. [105]

Ten Minus game. Have the child play a quick game of Ten Minus, found in the *Math Card Games* book, S1. Tell her that the pairs are the card and 10 minus the number on the card.

Worksheet 22. Give the child the worksheet and ask her to find and enter the subtraction facts for ten minus a number in the top subtraction table, Tens and Near Tens Strategies. Fill in the column. See the table below.

	1	2	3	4	5	6	7	8	9	10	11	12	13	14	15	16	17	18
–1										9								
–2										8								
–3										7								
–4										6								
–5										5								
–6										4								
–7										3								
–8										2								
–9										1								

Subtracting from ten.

EXPLANATIONS:

If needed, make the game quicker by using fewer cards.

ACTIVITIES FOR TEACHING:

Eleven Minus game. Ask: What is 10 – 6? [4] So, what is 11 – 6? [5] How do you know? [It will be one more.] Repeat for 10 – 3 [7] and 11 – 3. [8]

Tell her to play the Eleven Minus game, a variation of the Ten Minus game. To play, either remove the cards with 1s or add cards with 10s. Players need to calculate what they need for 11 minus the card in their hands.

After the game, tell her to enter the 11 minus facts in the same table as the 10 minus facts. See the figure below.

	1	2	3	4	5	6	7	8	9	10	11	12	13	14	15	16	17	18
–1										9								
–2										8	9							
–3										7	8							
–4										6	7							
–5										5	6							
–6										4	5							
–7										3	4							
–8										2	3							
–9										1	2							

Subtracting from eleven.

Nine Minus game. This is another variation of the Ten Minus game. Use cards with numbers from 0 to 9. The players need to calculate what they need for 9 minus the card in their hands.

After the game, tell the child to enter the 9 minus facts in the same table as the 10 minus and 11 minus facts. See the figure below.

	1	2	3	4	5	6	7	8	9	10	11	12	13	14	15	16	17	18
–1									8	9								
–2									7	8	9							
–3									6	7	8							
–4									5	6	7							
–5									4	5	6							
–6									3	4	5							
–7									2	3	4							
–8									1	2	3							
–9									0	1	2							

Subtracting from nine.

In conclusion. Ask: What is 9 – 5? [4] What is 10 – 5? [5] What is 11 – 5? [6] Tell her to find those facts on her subtraction table. Ask: What is 9 – 3? [6] What is 10 – 3? [7] What is 11 – 3? [8] Tell her to find those facts on her subtraction table.

EXPLANATIONS:

Lesson 46: Subtracting from Five Strategy

OBJECTIVES:

1. To focus on subtracting numbers up to 10 by Subtracting from Five Strategy

MATERIALS:

1. AL Abacus
2. Dry erase board
3. Worksheet 22, Subtraction Tables 2
4. *Math Card Games* book, S12

ACTIVITIES FOR TEACHING:

EXPLANATIONS:

Warm-up. Ask: What is 9 – 4, [5] 10 – 5, [5] 11 – 5, [6] 9 – 6, [3] 10 – 7, [3] and 11 – 8? [3]

Ask: Subtracting what kind of numbers gives a difference of zero? [same numbers] What kind of numbers gives a difference of one? [consecutive numbers] What kind of numbers gives the difference of two? [consecutive evens or odds]

Ask: What is 21 – 1, [20] 38 – 2, [36] 55 – 2, [53] 89 – 1, [88] and 60 – 2? [58]

Ask the child to say the months of the year. Then play the Comes After game. Ask: What month comes after April? [May] After August? [September] After January? [February] After December? [January]

Finding differences up to 5 on the abacus. Ask the child how she could find the *difference* between 7 and 4 on her abacus. Suggest entering the quantities on two different wires. See the figure below. The difference is easily seen between the quantities on the two wires.

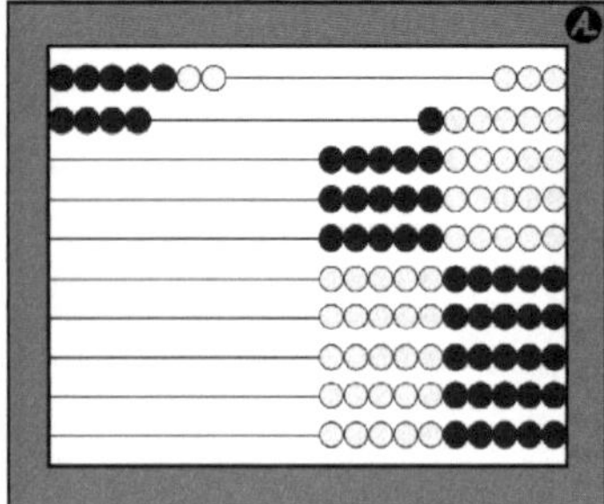

7 – 4 = 3.

Ask the child to write the subtraction equation on her dry erase board.

7 – 4 = 3

ACTIVITIES FOR TEACHING:

EXPLANATIONS:

Finding differences on an imaginary abacus. While looking at her abacus, ask the child to move an imaginary 7 by moving her finger from right to left. Then ask her move an imaginary 4 below the imaginary 7. To see the difference, tell her to notice that it takes 1 to reach 5 and 2 more to reach 7. Since 1 and 2 is 3, the difference is 3. Now ask the child to actually enter the 7 and 4 on the abacus and see if it is like she imagined. See figure below on the left.

Repeat for the difference between 9 and 2. See the figure below. Notice it takes 3 to reach 5 and 4 more to reach 9. Since 3 and 4 is 7, the difference is 7. Again, ask the child to enter it on her abacus. See below on right.

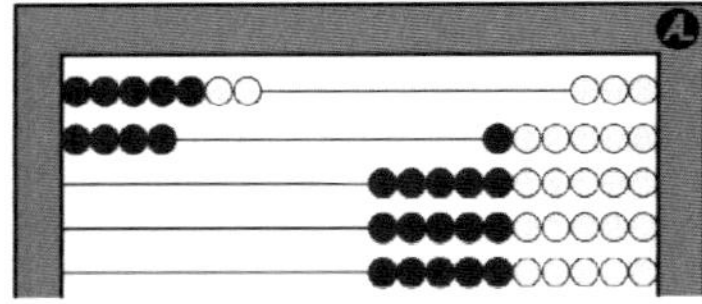

7 – 4 = 3.

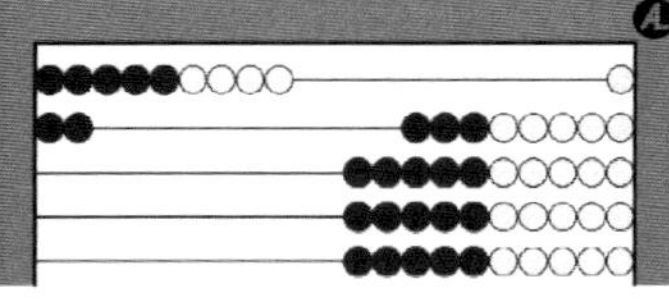

9 – 2 = 7.

Tell her: Since you can find the difference by first going up to five we can call this the Take from Five Strategy.

Worksheet 22. Give the child the worksheet and tell her to write the differences on the second subtraction table, Take from Five Strategies, shown below as she plays the Difference War game.

Difference War game. Have the child play the Difference War game, found in the *Math Card Games* book, S12. Each time the child picks up her two cards, she enters the differences in her subtraction table, unless it is already entered.

	1	2	3	4	5	6	7	8	9	10	11	12	13	14	15	16	17	18
–1	0	1	2	3	4	5	6	7	8	9								
–2		0	1	2	3	4	5	6	7	8								
–3			0	1	2	3	4	5	6	7								
–4				0	1	2	3	4	5	6								
–5					0	1	2	3	4	5								
–6																		
–7																		
–8																		
–9																		

Subtraction facts for subtracting from five.

In conclusion. Ask the child to use her imaginary abacus to find the following: 9 – 5, [4] 8 – 4, [4] 7 – 3, [4] 6 – 3, [3] 9 – 3, [6] and 8 – 3. [5]

Lesson 47: Subtracting from Ten Strategies

OBJECTIVES:

1. To subtract with the Subtracting All from Ten Strategy
2. To subtract with the Subtracting Part from Ten Strategy

MATERIALS:

1. AL Abacus
2. Worksheet 23, Subtraction Tables 3
3. *Math Card Games* book, S12

ACTIVITIES FOR TEACHING:

Warm-up. Ask the child to use her imaginary abacus to solve the following: 8 – 5, [3] 9 – 4, [5] 7 – 4, [3] 6 – 3, [3] 4 – 3, [1] and 8 – 3. [5] Use the abacus as needed.

Ask: Subtracting what kind of numbers gives a difference of zero? [same numbers] What kind of numbers gives a difference of one? [consecutive numbers] What kind of numbers gives the difference of two? [consecutive evens or odds]

Ask: What is 31 – 1, [30] 48 – 2, [46] 65 – 2, [63] 99 – 1, [98] and 70 – 2? [68]

Subtracting All from Ten Strategy. Tell the child: We practiced subtracting from numbers up to 10. Today we will practice subtraction facts for numbers from 11 to 18. Enter 15 on the abacus. Tell the child to subtract 7 from the 10, as shown in the figures below.

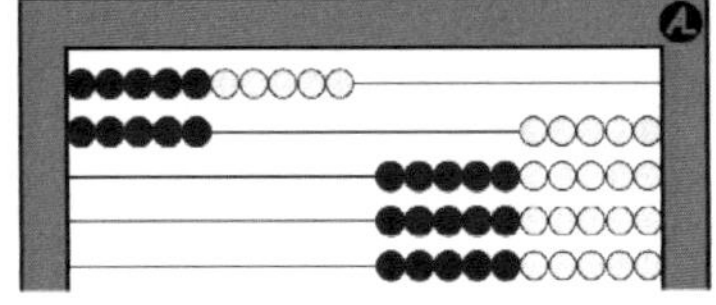

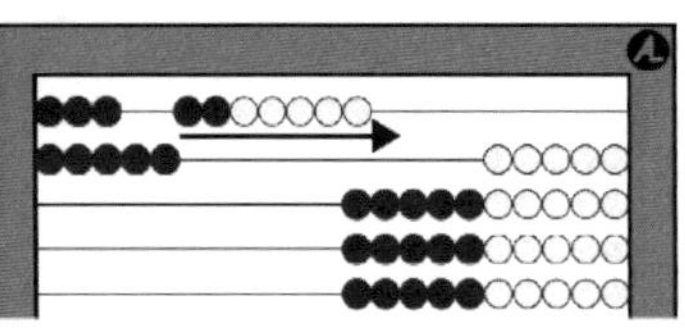

15 – 7 by subtracting 7 from the 10 and adding 5 + 3 = 8.

Then ask: What is left? [8, 3 plus 5] Say: This is the subtracting by Subtracting All from Ten Strategy. Repeat for 14 – 8, [6] and 18 – 9. [9]

Subtracting Part from Ten Strategy. Ask the child how she could subtract part from ten to find 15 – 7. [Subtract the 5 from the second row and 2 from the 10 on the top row leaving 8.] Tell the child to show 15 – 7 on her abacus. Then ask: What is left? [8] See the figures below.

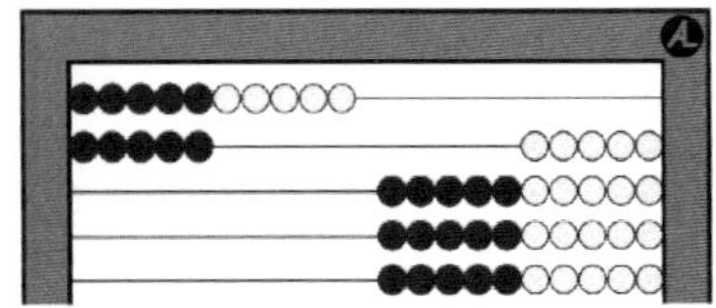

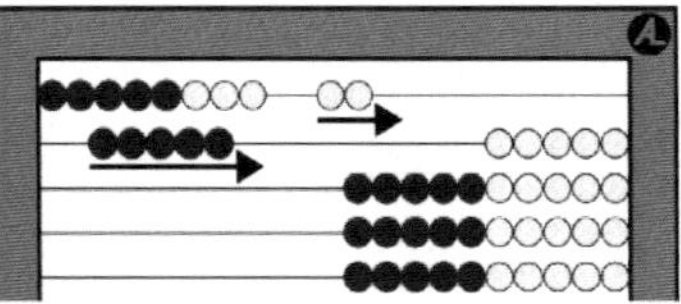

Subtracting 15 – 7 [8] by subtracting 5 from 5 and 2 from 10.

EXPLANATIONS:

In the Middle Ages, people did not bother to memorize addition or subtraction facts past 10 because they used the Subtracting All from Ten Strategy.

ACTIVITIES FOR TEACHING:

Say: This is the subtracting by Subtracting Part from Ten Strategy. Repeat for 14 – 8, [6] and 18 – 9, [9] which is shown below.

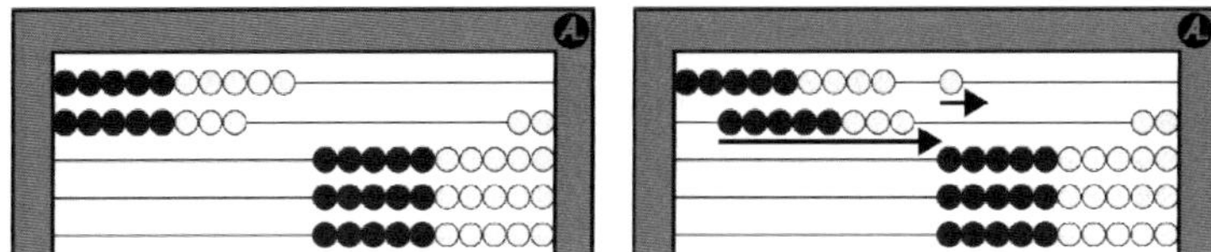

Subtracting 18 – 9 [9] by subtracting 8 from 8 and 1 from 10.

Worksheet 23. Give the child the worksheet and tell her to write the differences on the first subtraction table, Subtracting from Ten Strategies, see below, as she plays the Difference War game variation.

Difference War game variation. This game is a variation of Difference War, found in the *Math Card Games* book, S12. When players turn over two cards, they add 10 to the lower number and subtract the higher number. For example, if the cards are 2 and 4, adding 10 to the 2 gives 12, and 12 – 4 = 8. Then the child enters the differences on her subtraction table, unless it is already entered.

	1	2	3	4	5	6	7	8	9	10	11	12	13	14	15	16	17	18
–1																		
–2											9							
–3											8	9						
–4											7	8	9					
–5											6	7	8	9				
–6											5	6	7	8	9			
–7											4	5	6	7	8	9		
–8											3	4	5	6	7	8	9	
–9											2	3	4	5	6	7	8	9

Subtraction facts for subtracting from ten.

In conclusion. Ask: What are two ways to find 13 – 4? [Subtract 4 from 10, then add 6 and 3 to get 9 or subtract 3 from 3 and 1 from 10 to get 9.] Which way do you like better?

EXPLANATIONS:

There are other ways to subtract from the teens besides the two methods given here. Although not addressed, some children might discover other methods.

Lesson 48: Subtraction Facts Practice

OBJECTIVES:

1. To learn the term *subtrahend*
2. To practice subtraction facts through recitation and subtraction games

MATERIALS:

1. Worksheet 23, Subtraction Tables 3
2. *Math Card Games* book, S6 and S25

ACTIVITIES FOR TEACHING:

EXPLANATIONS:

Warm-up. Ask: What are two ways to find 13 – 4? [Subtract 4 from 10, then add 6 and 3 to get 9 or subtract 3 from 3 and 1 from 10 to get 9.]

Ask her to use her imaginary abacus to find the following: 8 – 5, [3] 9 – 4, [5] 7 – 4, [3] 6 – 3, [3] 4 – 3, [1] and 8 – 3. [5]

Ask: Subtracting what kind of numbers gives a difference of zero? [same numbers] What kind of numbers gives a difference of one? [consecutive numbers] What kind of numbers gives the difference of two? [consecutive evens or odds]

Worksheet 23. Give the child the worksheet and tell her that she will fill in the first row of the second subtraction table as she says the equations aloud. Start by saying: 1 minus 1 is . . . . [0] Tell her to write the 0 in the first row. Tell her to join in as you continue with: 2 minus 1 is 1 (write 1). See below.

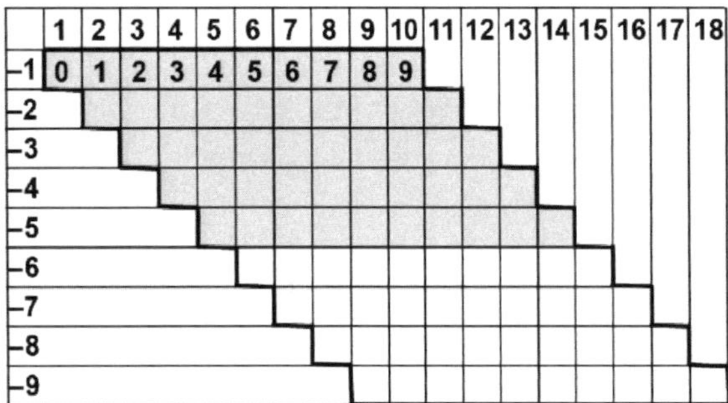

	1	2	3	4	5	6	7	8	9	10	11	12	13	14	15	16	17	18
–1	0	1	2	3	4	5	6	7	8	9								
–2																		
–3																		
–4																		
–5																		
–6																		
–7																		
–8																		
–9																		

First row of the subtraction table.

Continue with the second row: 2 minus 2 is 0, 3 minus 2 is 1, 4 minus 2 is 2, and so forth. Complete the first three rows as shown on the next page.

ACTIVITIES FOR TEACHING:

	1	2	3	4	5	6	7	8	9	10	11	12	13	14	15	16	17	18
–1	0	1	2	3	4	5	6	7	8	9								
–2		0	1	2	3	4	5	6	7	8	9							
–3			0	1	2	3	4	5	6	7	8	9						
–4																		
–5																		
–6																		
–7																		
–8																		
–9																		

First three rows of the subtraction table.

The term subtrahend. Write the following subtraction equation:

$$11 - 3 = 8$$

Ask: What do we call the 8? [difference] Say: The 3, the number being subtracted, is called the *subtrahend.* Write out the word so she can see how it is spelled.

Subtraction Memory game. To provide practice for the facts involving subtracting 3, have the child play Subtraction Memory, found in the *Math Card Games* book, S6. Use 3 as the subtrahend.

On the Number Ten game. Another game for the child to play is On the Number Ten, found in the *Math Card Games* book, S25.

In conclusion. Write the following equation:

$$10 - 3 = 7$$

Ask: Which number is the difference? [7] Which number is the subtrahend? [3] What happens to the difference if the subtrahend is increased by one? [10 – 4 = 6, difference is decreased by one.] What happens to the difference if the subtrahend is decreased by one? [10 – 2 = 8, difference is increased by one.]

EXPLANATIONS:

Lesson 49: More Subtraction Facts Practice

OBJECTIVES:

1. To practice subtraction facts through recitation and subtraction games

MATERIALS:

1. Worksheet 23, Subtraction Tables 3
2. *Math Card Games* book, S18 and S19

ACTIVITIES FOR TEACHING:

EXPLANATIONS:

Warm-up. Write the following equation:

10 – 6 = 4

Ask: Which number is the difference? [4] Which number is the subtrahend? [6] What happens to the difference if the subtrahend is increased by one? [10 – 7 = 3, difference is decreased by one] What happens to the difference if the subtrahend is decreased by one? [10 – 5 = 5, difference is increased by one]

Ask: What are two ways to find 13 – 5? [Subtract 5 from 10, then add 5 and 3 to get 8 or subtract 3 from 3 and 2 from 10 to get 8.]

Ask the child to use her imaginary abacus to find the following: 7 – 5, [2] 10 – 4, [6] 8 – 4, [4] 5 – 3, [2] 9 – 3, [6] and 8 – 3. [5]

Ask: Subtracting what kind of numbers gives a difference of zero? [same numbers] What kind of numbers gives a difference of one? [consecutive numbers] What kind of numbers gives the difference of two? [consecutive evens or odds]

Worksheet 23. Give the child the worksheet and tell her that today she will do more writing in her subtraction table as she says the equations aloud. Ask her to join you as you say: 4 minus 4 is 0, 5 minus 4 is 1, 6 minus 4 is 2, and so forth. Complete three more rows the same way. See the subtraction table shown below.

	1	2	3	4	5	6	7	8	9	10	11	12	13	14	15	16	17	18
–1	0	1	2	3	4	5	6	7	8	9								
–2		0	1	2	3	4	5	6	7	8	9							
–3			0	1	2	3	4	5	6	7	8	9						
–4				0	1	2	3	4	5	6	7	8	9					
–5					0	1	2	3	4	5	6	7	8	9				
–6						0	1	2	3	4	5	6	7	8	9			
–7																		
–8																		
–9																		

First six rows of the subtraction table.

ACTIVITIES FOR TEACHING:

EXPLANATIONS:

Practice. Ask the child a few facts from the table and have her verify if the answers are correct.

Short Chain Subtraction game. This Short Chain Subtraction game, found in the *Math Card Games* book, S18, can be played by two or three players. In this game, the same 12 subtraction facts are needed three times.

Either or both of the Short Chain Subtraction games may be played. The subtraction chain games are similar to the addition chain games, played in RightStart™ Mathematics Level B.

Short Chain Subtraction Solitaire game. Have the child play Short Chain Subtraction Solitaire, found in the *Math Card Games* book, S19. Although this game is a solitaire game, several people can play together. The goal is to "beat the cards" by completing the solitaire. The cards and the subtraction facts required are the same as the previous game.

In conclusion. Ask: What patterns do you see in the rows on subtraction table? [Each row goes from zero to nine.] Which fact in the second row has the greatest difference? [11 – 2 = 9] Which fact in the second row has the least difference? [2 – 2 = 0]

Lesson 50: Completing the Subtraction Table

OBJECTIVES:

1. To practice subtraction facts while completing the subtraction table
2. To practice subtraction facts through recitation and games

MATERIALS:

1. Worksheet 23, Subtraction Tables 3
2. *Math Card Games* book, S22 and S23

ACTIVITIES FOR TEACHING:

Warm-up. Write the following equation:

$$10 - 2 = 8$$

Ask: Which number is the difference? [8] Which number is the subtrahend? [2] What happens to the difference if the subtrahend is increased by one? [10 – 3 = 7, difference is decreased by one] What happens to the difference if the subtrahend is decreased by one? [10 – 1 = 9, difference is increased by one]

Ask: What are two ways to find 14 – 5? [Subtract 5 from 10, then add 5 and 4 to get 9 or subtract 4 from 4 and 1 from 10 to get 9.]

Ask: Subtracting what kind of numbers gives a difference of zero? [same numbers] What kind of numbers gives a difference of one? [consecutive numbers] What kind of numbers gives the difference of two? [consecutive evens or odds]

Worksheet 23. Give the child the worksheet and tell her that today she will finish writing in her subtraction table as she says the equations aloud. Ask her to join you as you say: 7 minus 7 is 0, 8 minus 7 is 1, 9 minus 7 is 2, and so forth. Complete the last three rows the same way. See the completed subtraction table shown below.

	1	2	3	4	5	6	7	8	9	10	11	12	13	14	15	16	17	18
–1	0	1	2	3	4	5	6	7	8	9								
–2		0	1	2	3	4	5	6	7	8	9							
–3			0	1	2	3	4	5	6	7	8	9						
–4				0	1	2	3	4	5	6	7	8	9					
–5					0	1	2	3	4	5	6	7	8	9				
–6						0	1	2	3	4	5	6	7	8	9			
–7							0	1	2	3	4	5	6	7	8	9		
–8								0	1	2	3	4	5	6	7	8	9	
–9									0	1	2	3	4	5	6	7	8	9

The completed subtraction table.

EXPLANATIONS:

This worksheet will be used as reference in future lessons.

ACTIVITIES FOR TEACHING:

Practice. Ask the child a few facts from the table and have her verify if the answers are correct.

Long Chain Subtraction game. This Long Chain Subtraction game, found in the *Math Card Games* book, S22, can be played by two or three players. In this game, 60 subtraction facts are needed.

Long Chain Subtraction Solitaire game. Have the child play Long Chain Subtraction Solitaire, found in the *Math Card Games* book, S23. Although this game is a solitaire game, several people can play together. The goal is to "beat the cards" by completing the solitaire. The cards and the subtraction facts are the same as in the previous game.

In conclusion. Ask: What patterns do you see in the columns on the subtraction table? [Up to 10, each column counts down one number at a time. For numbers over 10 each column starts with 9 and counts down.] Why do the numbers decrease in a column? [As you go down, each time you are subtracting a greater number.]

EXPLANATIONS:

Play either or both of the Long Chain Subtraction games.

LESSON 51: REVIEW AND GAMES 4

OBJECTIVES:

1. To review recent topics
2. To continue to develop skills through playing math card games

MATERIALS:

1. Worksheet 24-A or 24-B, Review 4
2. Centimeter cubes
3. *Math Card Games* book, S24
4. Worksheet 23, Subtraction Tables 3, as needed

ACTIVITIES FOR TEACHING:

Worksheet 24-A. Give the child the worksheet and some centimeter cubes. Tell her to listen to the problems and write only the answers on the worksheet. Read each problem twice.

9 – 2 61 + 9 91 + 20

Tell her to complete the worksheet. Solutions are below.

Write only the answers.

7

70

111

Write the answers.

67 + 25 – 7 = 85

4 by 3 = 12

13 – 4 = 9

Find the perimeter in cm and the area in square cm.

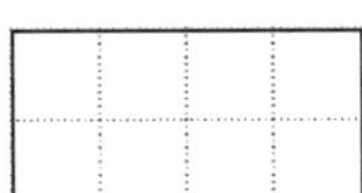

4 + 2 + 4 + 2 = 12 cm

4 x 2 = 8 square cm

Add.

	5	6	8	3
+	3	3	5	6
	9	0	3	9

Fill in the subtraction table.

	9	10	11	12
–4	5	6	7	8
–5	4	5	6	7
–6	3	4	5	6
–7	2	3	4	5

Write >, <, or = on the lines.

4 – 1 < 4 + 1

9 – 6 = 10 – 7

13 – 5 > 13 – 6

3 inches > 3 cm

8 – 6 = 7 – 5

9 – 8 < 0 + 6

Explain two ways how to find 14 – 5.

Subtract 5 from 10 to get 5 and add to 4 to get 9.

Subtract 4 from 4 and 1 from 10 to get 9.

EXPLANATIONS:

ACTIVITIES FOR TEACHING:

Subtraction Bingo game. Ask the child to play the Subtraction Bingo game, found in the *Math Card Games* book, S24. Use the subtraction table as needed.

Worksheet 24-B. Give the child the worksheet and some centimeter cubes. Tell her to listen to the problems and write only the answers on the worksheet. Read each problem twice.

11 – 2   72 + 8   89 + 20

Tell her to complete the worksheet. Solutions are below.

Write only the answers.

9

80

109

Write the answers.

74 + 15 – 4 = 85

3 by 4 = 12

16 – 7 = 9

Find the perimeter in cm and the area in square cm.

3 + 3 + 3 + 3 = 12 cm

3 x 3 = 9 square cm

Add.

	4	2	7	3
+	2	7	8	7
	7	0	6	0

Fill in the subtraction table.

	10	11	12	13
–5	5	6	7	8
–6	4	5	6	7
–7	3	4	5	6
–8	2	3	4	5

Write >, <, or = on the lines.

5 + 2 > 5 – 2

8 – 5 = 11 – 8

14 – 6 < 14 – 5

2 inches > 2 cm

10 – 8 = 5 – 3

9 + 7 > 8 – 0

Explain two ways how to find 11 – 6.

Subtract 6 from 10 to get 4 and add to 1 to get 5.

Subtract 1 from 1 and 5 from 10 to get 5.

EXPLANATIONS:

Lesson 52: Subtracting Fives and Tens

OBJECTIVES:

1. To learn the term *minuend*
2. To practice subtracting fives and tens

MATERIALS:

1. Worksheet 23, Subtraction Tables 3
2. Math journal
3. *Math Card Games* book, S9

ACTIVITIES FOR TEACHING:

Warm-up. Tell the child to take out Worksheet 23, Subtraction Tables 3, from a prior lesson. Ask: What patterns do you see in the columns on the subtraction table? [Up to 10, each column counts down one number at a time. For numbers over 10 each column starts with 9 and counts down.] Why do the numbers decrease in a column? [As you go down, each time you are subtracting a greater number.]

Ask: What patterns do you see in the rows on subtraction table? [Each row goes from zero to nine.] Which fact in the fifth row has the greatest difference? [14 – 5 = 9] Which fact in the fifth row has the least difference? [5 – 5 = 0]

Ask: Subtracting what kind of numbers gives a difference of zero? [same numbers] What kind of numbers gives a difference of one? [consecutive numbers] What kind of numbers gives the difference of two? [consecutive evens or odds]

Minuend. Tell the child: The number we start with when we subtract is called the *minuend*. Write it as:

minuend – subtrahend = difference

Worksheet 23. Tell the child to look at her subtraction table, shown on the next page, to answer the following questions:

What do you call the numbers across the top on the table? [minuends]

What do you call the numbers along the left side of the table? [subtrahends]

What do you call the numbers inside the table? [differences]

What are the two subtraction facts with a minuend of 17? [17 – 8 = 9 and 17 – 9 = 8]

Where are the differences of 5? [in a diagonal]

How many subtraction facts have 5 as a difference? [9]

EXPLANATIONS:

It seems curious that the word "subtrahend" is longer than the word "minuend," even though in basic subtraction, the subtrahend is a smaller number than the minuend. It does help that "minuend" precedes "subtrahend" alphabetically.

ACTIVITIES FOR TEACHING:

	1	2	3	4	5	6	7	8	9	10	11	12	13	14	15	16	17	18
–1	0	1	2	3	4	5	6	7	8	9								
–2		0	1	2	3	4	5	6	7	8	9							
–3			0	1	2	3	4	5	6	7	8	9						
–4				0	1	2	3	4	5	6	7	8	9					
–5					0	1	2	3	4	5	6	7	8	9				
–6						0	1	2	3	4	5	6	7	8	9			
–7							0	1	2	3	4	5	6	7	8	9		
–8								0	1	2	3	4	5	6	7	8	9	
–9									0	1	2	3	4	5	6	7	8	9

The completed subtraction table.

Tell the child to write the first four subtraction facts that have five as a difference in her math journal.

6 – 1 = 5
7 – 2 = 5
8 – 3 = 5
9 – 4 = 5

Ask: What pattern do you see? [Both the minuends and the subtrahends increase by one.] What are the four facts with 15 as a minuend? Tell the child to write them.

15 – 6 = 9
15 – 7 = 8
15 – 8 = 7
15 – 9 = 6

Ask: Which pairs seem related? [15 – 6 = 9 and 15 – 9 = 6; also, 15 – 7 = 8 and 15 – 8 = 7] What game have you played that needed these facts? [Corners™ game] What other facts did the Corners™ game need? [facts making 10] Where are they in the table? [in the column under 10]

Ask: Are there any other facts needed to play the Corners™ game? [facts equaling five] How many of them are there? [five] Which one cannot be used? [5 – 0 = 5] Why not? [There are no Corners™ cards with zeroes.]

Zero Corners™ game. Have the child play the Zero Corners game, found in the *Math Card Games* book, S9. Tell her to start with a score of 200 and write the differences in her math journal.

In conclusion. Ask: Do you think the Zero Corners™ game is any harder to score than the regular Corners™ game?

EXPLANATIONS:

Lesson 53: Subtracting 1-Digit Numbers

OBJECTIVES:

1. To practice subtracting 1-digit from 2-digit numbers
2. To practice subtraction

MATERIALS:

1. Worksheet 23, Subtraction Tables 3
2. AL Abacuses
3. *Math Card Games* book, S27
4. Worksheet 25, Subtraction Puzzle

ACTIVITIES FOR TEACHING:

Warm-up. Review with the child: The number we start with when we subtract is called the minuend. Write it as:

minuend – subtrahend = difference

Tell the child to take out Worksheet 23, Subtraction Tables 3, from a prior lesson. Ask: What patterns do you see in the columns on the subtraction table? [Up to 10, each column counts down one number at a time. For numbers over 10 each column starts with 9 and counts down.] Why do the numbers decrease in a column? [As you go down, each time you are subtracting a greater number.]

Ask: What patterns do you see in the rows on subtraction table? [Each row goes from zero to nine.] Which fact in the ninth row has the greatest difference? [18 – 9 = 9] Which fact in the ninth row has the least difference? [9 – 9 = 0]

Subtracting 1-digit numbers. Write and ask the child to subtract the following:

64 – 3 = ___ [61]

64 – 5 = ___ [59]

Ask her how she solved the second equation. She might take 5 from 60 getting 55 and then adding 4 to get 59. Or, she might take 4 from 5 and 1 more from 60 to get 59. Or, the child might notice that since 64 – 3 is 61, 64 – 5 is 2 less, which is 59. Sometimes the child will benefit from seeing it on the abacus. See the figures below.

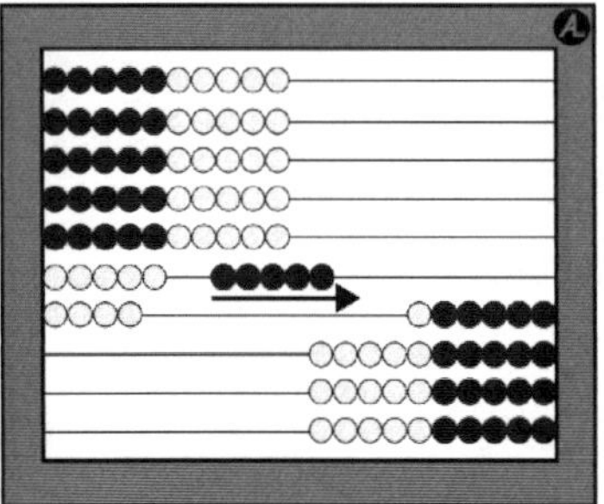

64 – 5 by taking 5 from a 10.

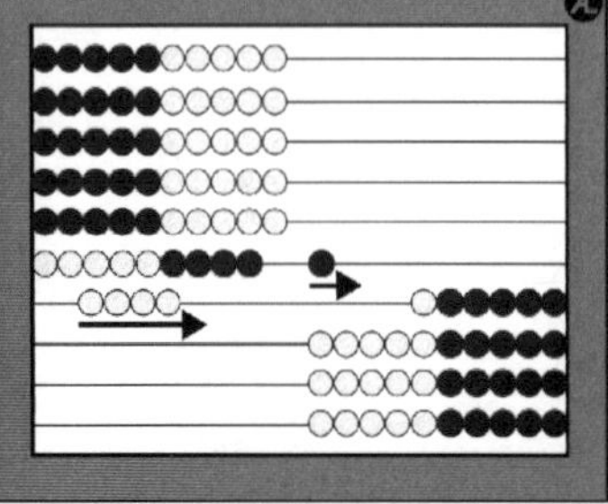

64 – 5 by taking 1 from 10.

EXPLANATIONS:

Counting backward is the most difficult strategy and should be discouraged.

ACTIVITIES FOR TEACHING:

EXPLANATIONS:

Now write:

42 – 8 = ___ [34]

Ask: What is the difference? [34] Did you need to take some of the 8 from a 10? [yes] How did you know? [2 ones in the 42 are not enough for the 8 ones.]

Repeat for:

25 – 7 = ___ [18]

63 – 2 = ___ [61]

97 – 8 = ___ [89]

Subtracting a Single-Digit Number game. Have the child play the Subtracting a Single-Digit Number game, found in the *Math Card Games* book, S27.

Worksheet 25. Give the child the worksheet and tell her to only solve the first 10 problems of the puzzle. She is to complete the subtraction equations using the following 15 numbers: 18, 20, 21, 24, 27, 30, 32, 35, 40, 45, 49, 50, 56, 60, and 64. Explain that to find the answers, she needs to try some numbers and check to see if they work, just like putting a puzzle together.

The remainder of the puzzle will be done in the next lesson.

Solutions are shown below.

1 = **21 – 20** or **50 – 49**
2 = **20 – 18**
3 = **27 – 24** or **35 – 32**
4 = **24 – 20** or **64 – 60**
5 = **50 – 45** or **40 – 35**
6 = **56 – 50** or **30 – 24**
7 = **27 – 20** or **56 – 49**
8 = **32 – 24** or **64 – 56**
9 = **49 – 40** or **30 – 21**
10 = **30 – 20**

There are additional solutions not given here.

This activity helps the child connect subtraction and addition. Also, the form of the equations emphasizes the mathematical meaning of the equal sign, that the two sides of an equation must be equal.

In conclusion. Give the child the following problem:

A book has 35 pages. Alex is on page 9 in the book. How many more pages will Alex need to read to finish the book? [26]

Lesson 54: Subtracting 2-Digit Numbers

OBJECTIVES:

1. To practice subtraction facts with a calculator
2. To practice subtracting 2-digit numbers
3. To use a calculator to check answers

MATERIALS:

1. Worksheet 23, Subtraction Tables 3
2. Casio SL-450S calculator
3. Worksheet 25, Subtraction Puzzle

ACTIVITIES FOR TEACHING:

Warm-up. Read the following problem to the child:

> A bus has 35 seats. There are 9 children seated on the bus. How many more children can be seated on the bus to make it full? [26]

Review with the child: The number we start with when we subtract is called the minuend. Write it as:

minuend – subtrahend = difference

Tell the child to take out Worksheet 23, Subtraction Tables 3, from a prior lesson. Ask: Which fact in the seventh row has the greatest difference? [16 – 7 = 9] Which fact in the seventh row has the least difference? [7 – 7 = 0]

Introducing calculators. Give the child the calculator. If necessary, show her how to remove the cover from the front of the calculator and put it on the back. Tell her that when she puts the calculator away, the cover needs to be put back on the front of the calculator.

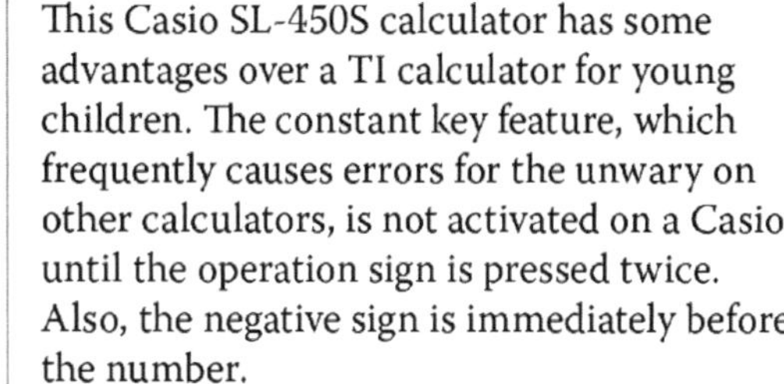

Casio SL-450S calculator.

Tell the child to press AC to turn the calculator on.

Simple adding. Ask the child to figure out 6 + 9 + 17 for herself. [32] Then ask her to explain how she did it. If necessary, demonstrate it as follows:

> Press 6 + 9 + 17 =.
>
> The answer shows as 32.

Tell her: If you need to start over, the AC key clears everything. AC means "all clear." Ask her to add some numbers of her own.

EXPLANATIONS:

This Casio SL-450S calculator has some advantages over a TI calculator for young children. The constant key feature, which frequently causes errors for the unwary on other calculators, is not activated on a Casio until the operation sign is pressed twice. Also, the negative sign is immediately before the number.

The Casio SL-450S calculator replaces the previous Casio SL-450L model. This newer model includes a battery as well as a solar cell allowing it to work in low-light conditions. It shuts off after six minutes of inactivity. However, whatever is in memory is retained after shutdown. To clear memory, press MRC MRC.

ACTIVITIES FOR TEACHING:

Simple subtracting. Ask the child to figure out 13 – 8 by herself [5] After a few minutes, ask her to explain how she did it. If necessary, demonstrate as follows:

Press 13 (–) 8 (=).

The answer shows as 5.

Subtraction practice with a calculator. Say a subtraction fact for the child to enter on her calculator. Tell her to think of the difference while she presses the (=) key and try to get the answer before the calculator does.

Worksheet 25. Give the child the worksheet from the previous lesson and tell her to finish the puzzle. She is to complete the subtraction equations using only the following 15 numbers: 18, 20, 21, 24, 27, 30, 32, 35, 40, 45, 49, 50, 56, 60, and 64.

Solutions for the completed worksheet are as shown below.

1 = **21 – 20** or **50 – 49**	21 = **45 – 24** or **56 – 35**
2 = **20 – 18**	22 = **49 – 27**
3 = **27 – 24** or **35 – 32**	23 = **50 – 27**
4 = **24 – 20** or **64 – 60**	24 = **56 – 32**
5 = **50 – 45** or **40 – 35**	25 = **60 – 35**
6 = **56 – 50** or **30 – 24**	26 = **56 – 30**
7 = **27 – 20** or **56 – 49**	27 = **45 – 18**
8 = **32 – 24** or **64 – 56**	28 = **60 – 32**
9 = **49 – 40** or **30 – 21**	29 = **64 – 35**
10 = **30 – 20**	30 = **60 – 30** or **50 – 20**
11 = **35 – 24**	31 = **49 – 18**
12 = **32 – 20**	32 = **64 – 32**
13 = **40 – 27**	33 = **60 – 27**
14 = **49 – 35** or **64 – 50**	34 = **64 – 30**
15 = **35 – 20**	35 = **56 – 21**
16 = **56 – 40**	36 = **56 – 20**
17 = **49 – 32**	37 = **64 – 27**
18 = **50 – 32**	38 = **56 – 18**
19 = **40 – 21** or **49 – 30**	39 = **60 – 21**
20 = **40 – 20**	40 = **60 – 20** or **64 – 24**

When she has finished, tell her to check her answers with the calculator. She should make any needed corrections.

In conclusion. Ask: 11 – what = 6? [5] 12 – what = 9? [3] 15 – what = 7? [8] 14 – what = 9? [5]

EXPLANATIONS:

Encourage the child to learn about the calculator intuitively.

Intuition is a method of learning that is becoming increasingly more important in our technological world. To learn intuitively is to try new procedures by combining common sense with a willingness to take a risk. It implies the hope that what is learned is worth the inevitable frustration.

This might seem improbable, but it truly does work.

There are additional solutions not given here.

Lesson 55: Finding and Correcting Errors

OBJECTIVES:

1. To find errors
2. To correct errors

MATERIALS:

1. Worksheet 23, Subtraction Tables 3
2. Worksheet 26, Finding and Correcting Errors

ACTIVITIES FOR TEACHING:

Warm-up. Ask the child: 12 – what = 5? [7]
13 – what = 9? [4] 15 – what = 8? [7] 14 – what = 5? [9]

Give her the following problem:

> Carrie's deck of cards has 45 cards in it. She lost some of the cards. Now she has 32 cards. How many cards did she lose? [13]

Tell the child to take out Worksheet 23, Subtraction Tables 3, from a prior lesson. Ask: What patterns do you see in the columns on the subtraction table? [Up to 10, each column counts down one number at a time. For numbers over 10 each column starts with 9 and counts down.] Why do the numbers decrease in a column? [As you go down, each time you are subtracting a greater number.]

Finding an error. Draw the following part-whole circle set, as shown at the right. Ask the child: Is this part-whole circle correct, or does it have an error? [It has an error, since 6 + 8 ≠ 13.]

13
6 8

Part-whole circle set with an error.

Tell the child to fix the error, crossing out a wrong number and writing the correct number. Draw two more identical part-whole circle sets. Ask: Is there another way to fix it? [yes] Have the child correct the error in a different way. See the three figures below showing the corrections.

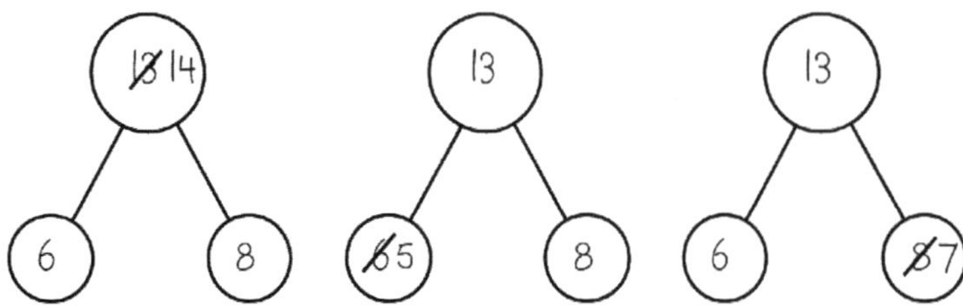

The three ways to make corrections.

Worksheet 26. Give the child the worksheet and ask her to correct the part-whole circle sets as shown on the next page.

EXPLANATIONS:

This is the last lesson referencing Worksheet 23, Subtraction Tables 3.

ACTIVITIES FOR TEACHING:

~~14~~ 15, 6, 9   14, ~~6~~ 5, 9   14, 6, ~~9~~ 8

The three ways to make corrections.

Next ask the child to find and fix the three errors in the subtraction table. See the left figure below. Ask her how she found the errors. She might have performed the subtractions or noticed the patterns.

If she does not notice, tell her she could also check by adding a subtrahend from the left column to a difference in the same row, giving the minuend along the top. For example, in the first row, 6 + 5 = 11, but in the third row, 7 + 8 ≠ 13.

	11	12	13	14	15
–6	5	6	7	8	9
–7	4	5	~~8~~ 6	7	8
–8	3	4	5	6	~~8~~ 7
–9	2	~~4~~ 3	4	5	6

+	4	5	6	7	8
~~6~~ 5	9	10	11	12	13
6	10	11	12	13	14
7	11	12	13	14	~~4~~ 15
8	12	13	~~4~~ 14	15	16

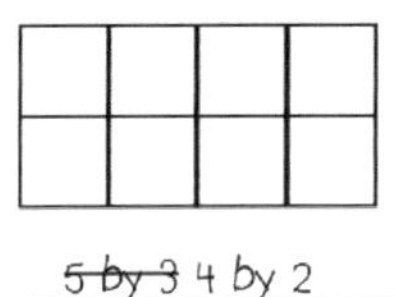

~~5 by 3~~ 4 by 2

Next tell the child to find and fix the three errors in the addition table. See the middle figure above. Ask her how she found the errors. This is harder because many people see the five sums in the first row as wrong, rather than noticing the column of addends.

For the array problem, ask: How could someone think the answer was 5 by 3? [counting lines instead of squares]

Ask her to do the next three problems on the worksheet.

Help the child discuss why the answers are wrong. In the first problem, no trading was recorded. In the second problem, trading was recorded when there was no reason to. In the third problem, wrong operations were performed.

Continue with the last three problems. The solutions are:

5015, three thousand two hundred six, 2410

Error practice. Write similar problems and ask the child to find the errors.

In conclusion. Ask: Who makes errors in math? [everybody] How can we find errors? [looking carefully and checking]

EXPLANATIONS:

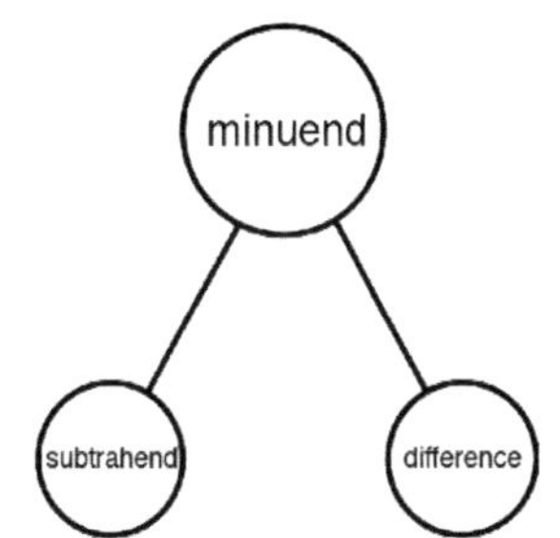

Minuend – subtrahend = difference

Lesson 56: Subtracting from One Hundred

OBJECTIVES:

1. To practice subtracting from 100

MATERIALS:

1. AL Abacus
2. *Math Card Games* book, S33

ACTIVITIES FOR TEACHING:

Warm-up. Ask: Who makes errors in math? [everybody] How can we find errors? [looking carefully and checking]

Play the Comes Before game for counting by 2s. Ask: What comes before 8, [6] 12, [10] 40, [38] 20, [18] and 38? [36] Repeat using 5s.

Ask the child to say the months of the year. Then play the Comes After game. Ask: What month comes after March? [April] After August? [September] After October? [November]

Subtracting from 100 on the abacus. Write:

100 – 37 = ___ [63]

Ask: How can you find the difference on your abacus? Explain that sometimes it is easier to solve a problem by first solving the same problem with simpler numbers.

Write:

10 – 3 = ___ [7]

Ask the child to find the answer with the abacus. The usual way is shown below on the left. Then ask: Is there another way? Tell her to enter 3 as shown below on the right and ask: Can you see the answer? [7, on the right]

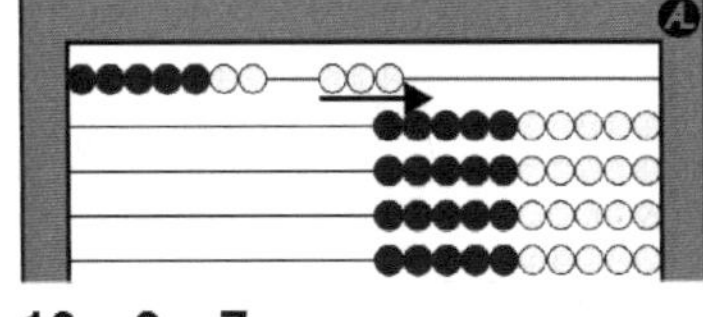

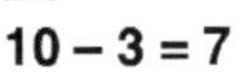

10 – 3 = 7

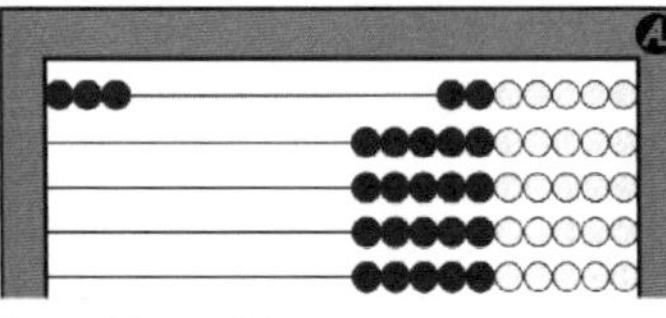

3 + _7_ = 10

Draw a part-whole circle set as shown on the next page. Ask the child to fill in the blank.

Then ask her to write subtraction and addition equations based on the part-whole circle set.

EXPLANATIONS:

Subtracting from 100 is helpful for making change, subtracting some 2-digit numbers, calculating percentages, and finding probabilities.

Using simpler numbers is a good problem-solving strategy.

ACTIVITIES FOR TEACHING:

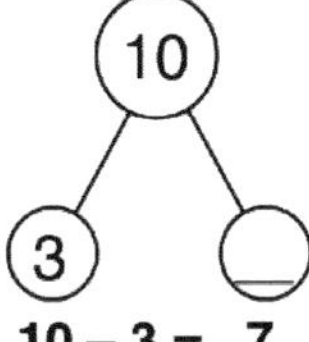

10 – 3 = 7

10
3 7

3 + 7 = 10

10 – 3 = 7

3 + 7 = 10

Subtracting from 100 on the abacus. Refer to the previously written equation:

100 – 37 = ___ [63]

Ask: How can you find the difference using both ways on the abacus? See the figures below.

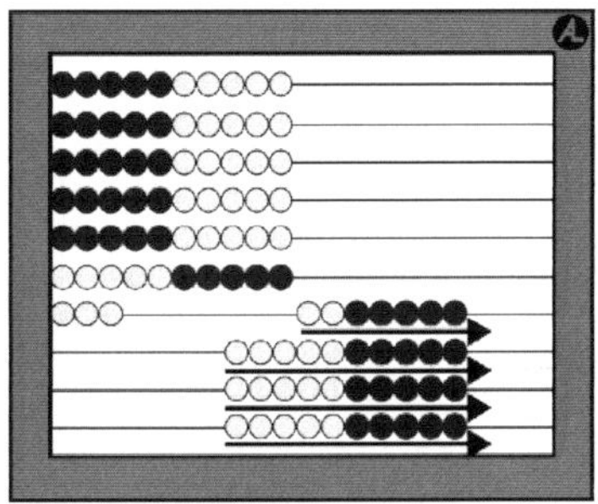

100 – 37 = 63

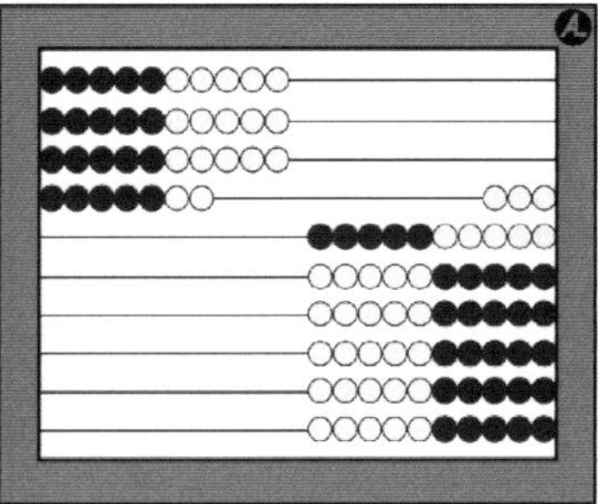

37 + 63 = 100

Ask the child to explain why entering 37 on the abacus gives the difference for 100 – 37. [37 + 63 = 100]

Ask her to find the following:

100 – 88 = ___ [12]

100 – 45 = ___ [55]

100 – 61 = ___ [39]

Subtracting from One Hundred game. Have the child play Subtracting from One Hundred found in the *Math Card Games* book, S33. Tell her to use the abacus.

In conclusion. Ask: How many equations are there for subtracting from 10? [11] How many equations are there for subtracting from 100? [101]

EXPLANATIONS:

Repeated practice with the abacus will lead to developing a mental abacus.

Lesson 57: More Subtracting 2-Digit Numbers

OBJECTIVES:

1. To understand several methods to subtract 2-digit numbers
2. To practice subtracting 2-digit numbers

MATERIALS:

1. Dry erase board
2. AL Abacuses
3. *Math Card Games* book, S34

ACTIVITIES FOR TEACHING:

Warm-up. Ask: How many equations are there for subtracting from 10? [11] How many equations are there for subtracting from 100? [101]

Draw a part-whole circle set on the dry erase board as shown below on the left. Ask the child to fill in the blank, as shown.

Then ask the child to write subtraction and addition equations.

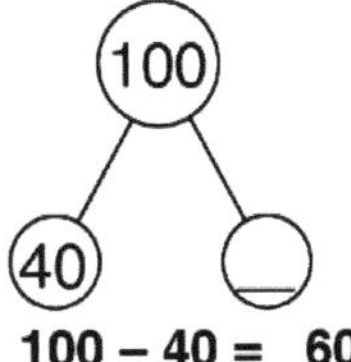

100
40 60
40 + 60 = 100

100 – 40 = 60
40 + 60 = 100

Subtracting 2-digit numbers. Write the following:

64 – 23 = ___ [41]

Ask the child to find the difference using any method. Ask her to explain.

Possibilities are: 60 – 20 = 40, and 4 – 3 = 1, 40 + 1 = 41.

Or, add up by starting with 23, needing 7 to reach 30, 30 to 60 takes 30, 30 + 7 is 37. Then 4 more is need to reach 64; so the difference is 37 + 4 = 41.

Or, 64 – 24 = 40, so 64 – 23 must be 1 more, or 41.

Or, it may have been solved on the abacus as shown on the next page.

EXPLANATIONS:

ACTIVITIES FOR TEACHING:

EXPLANATIONS:

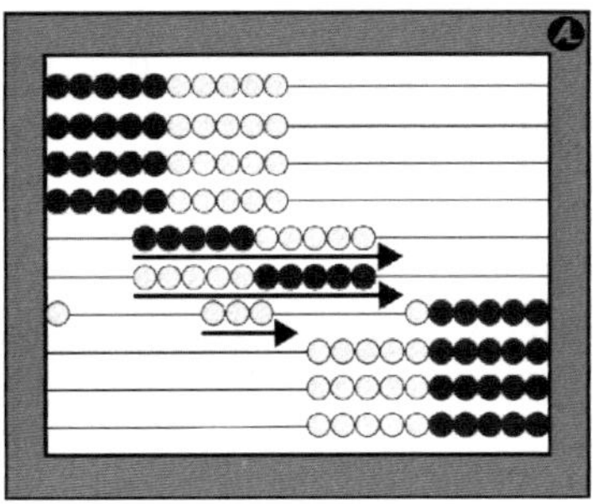

64 – 23 = ___ **64 – 23 = 41**

Example 2. Write the following:

41 – 29 = ___ [12]

Ask the child to find the difference. Ask her to explain her method. Ask her to think of other ways to find the difference.

Encourage the child to solve problems two ways as a check on the answer.

One way is to go up. It takes 1 to get to 30, 10 more to get to 40 and 1 more to 41, giving the answer 1 + 10 + 1 = 12.

Another way is to add 1 to 29 and 1 to 41, so the problem becomes 42 – 30 = 12.

Still another way is to think that since there is not enough ones in the ones of 41 to subtract 9, change 41 into 30 and 11. Then 30 – 20 = 10 and 11 – 9 = 2, and 10 + 2 = 12.

An abacus solution using the Taking All from Ten Strategy is shown below.

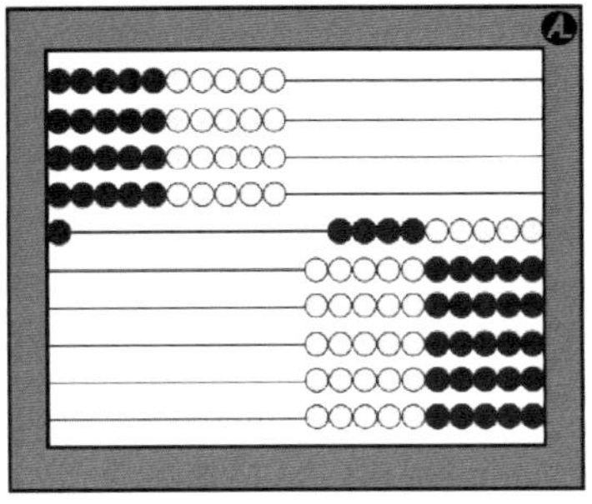

41 – 29 = ___

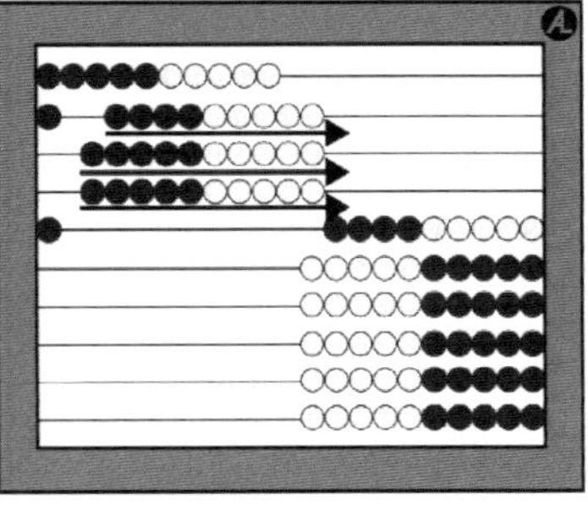

41 – 29 = 12

Subtracting Two-Digit Numbers game. Have the child play the Subtracting Two-Digit Numbers game, found in the *Math Card Games* book, S34.

In conclusion. Ask: Is there only one way to subtract? [no, there are many]

LESSON 58: TENS & SUBTRACTING 2-DIGIT NUMBERS

OBJECTIVES:

1. To find the number of tens in numbers such as 240
2. To practice subtracting 2-digit numbers

MATERIALS:

1. AL Abacuses
2. Abacus Tiles
3. Base-10 picture cards
4. Place-value cards
5. Worksheet 27, Subtracting 2-Digit Numbers

ACTIVITIES FOR TEACHING:

Warm-up. Ask: Is there only one way to subtract? [no, there are many]

Ask: Who makes errors in math? [everybody] How can we find errors? [looking carefully and checking]

Also ask the child to say the answers to the following problems: 95 – 15, [80] 75 – 20, [55] 170 – 15, [155] and 150 – 15. [135]

Tens in 240. Give the child the following problem:

> Kim has 240 balloons. Kim's job is to put 10 balloons in a package. How many packages can Kim fill? [24]

Suggest she use whatever manipulatives she needs to solve the problem. Give her several minutes to think about the problem. Then ask her to explain her solution.

There are many different ways to solve the problem. One way is to find the number of tens in each hundred [10 tens] and add that to the number of tens in 40. [4 tens] That can be done with two abacus tiles and the abacus as shown below.

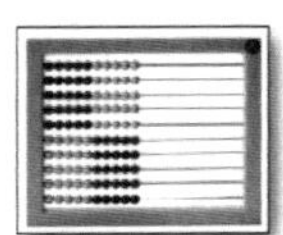

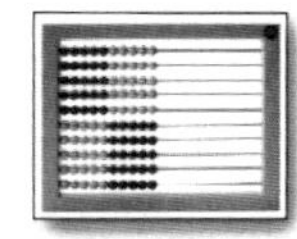

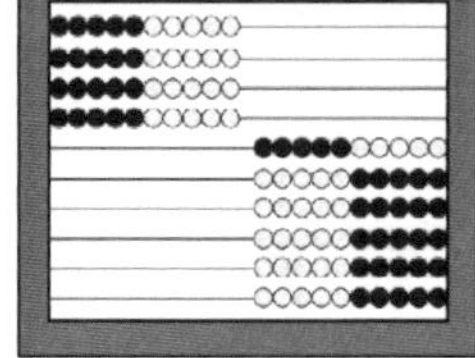

10 tens in 100. **10 tens in 100.** **4 tens in 40.**

Suggest using the base-10 cards. Tell the child to use them to make 240 as shown below. Then ask: How many tens are there? [10 in each hundred and 4 more]

240 represented with base-10 cards.

EXPLANATIONS:

The question, "How many tens are in 240," is not the same question as "In the number 240, how many tens are in the tens place." The first question has the answer of 24 while the second answer is 4.

ACTIVITIES FOR TEACHING:

EXPLANATIONS:

Tens in 960. Now extend the problem by saying:

The next day Kim gets a friend, Miguel, to help. Now they have 960 balloons to put in packages of ten each. How many packages can they fill? [96]

Practice. Write the following numbers:

90 [9]	540 [54]	870 [87]
610 [61]	100 [10]	1000 [100]

Have the child find the quantity of tens in each number using the abacus tiles, abacus, and base-10 cards.

Pointing to ones place.

Show her 380 made with place-value cards as shown on the right. Say: If you put your finger on the number in the ones place and look to the left, you will see the number of tens. Do you agree? [yes]

Subtracting from hundreds. Write:

140 – 83 = ___ [57]

Ask her to solve it and to explain. One way to do this problem is to think 14 tens minus 8 tens is 6 tens, or 60, and 60 minus 3 is 57.

Another way is to go up from 83; 17 to 100, then 40 to 140, so 17 + 40 = 57.

Worksheet 27. Give the child the worksheet and ask her to complete the equations. Use the abacus when necessary. Solutions are shown below.

68 – 42 = **26**	170 – 134 = **36**
87 – 39 = **48**	141 – 36 = **105**
93 – 79 = **14**	122 – 96 = **26**
193 – 114 = **79**	66 – 42 = **24**
56 – 31 = **25**	105 – 69 = **36**
100 – 47 = **53**	100 – 18 = **82**
100 – 85 = **15**	100 – 36 = **64**

36 animals were fed.

53 – 24 = **29**

In conclusion. Ask: What is 100 – 50, [50] 200 – 150, [50] 300 – 250, [50] and 250 – 150? [100]

Lesson 59: Review and Games 5

OBJECTIVES:

1. To review recent topics
2. To continue to develop skills through playing math card games

MATERIALS:

1. Worksheet 28-A or 28-B, Review 5
2. Centimeter cubes
3. *Math Card Games* book, S13

ACTIVITIES FOR TEACHING:

EXPLANATIONS:

Worksheet 28-A. Give the child the worksheet and some centimeter cubes. Tell her to listen to the problems and write only the answers on the worksheet. Read each problem twice.

11 – 2   61 – 9   61 + 9

Tell her to complete the worksheet. Solutions are below.

Write only the answers.

9

52

70

Write the answers.

67 + 25 + 13 = 105

5 by 4 = 20

47 – 9 = 38

Find the perimeter in cm and the area in square cm.

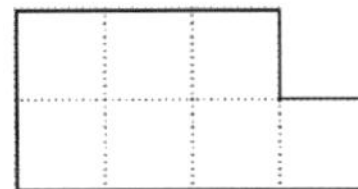

3 + 1 + 1 + 1 + 4 + 2 = 12 cm

3 x 2 + 1 = 7 square cm

Fix the answer.

	4	7	5	2
+	1	9	8	5
	6	~~6~~ 7	3	7

Find the differences.

42 – 28 = 14

100 – 63 = 37

123 – 49 = 74

Write >, <, or = on the lines.

10 – 2 = 11 – 3

9 – 6 < 10 – 6

15 – 6 > 15 – 7

1 cm < 2 cm

18 + 6 = 19 + 5

9 – 8 < 9 – 1

Explain two ways how to find 87 – 39.

Add 1 to both numbers. Then 88 – 40 = 48.

Go up: 1 to 40, 40 to 80, 7 to 87. 1 + 40 + 7 = 48.

ACTIVITIES FOR TEACHING:

Harder Difference War. Ask the child to play Harder Difference War found in the *Math Card Games* book, S13.

Worksheet 28-B. Give the child the worksheet and some centimeter cubes. Tell her to listen to the problems and write only the answers on the worksheet. Read each problem twice.

13 – 9 76 – 7 76 + 7

Tell her to complete the worksheet. Solutions are below.

Write only the answers.

4

69

83

Write the answers.

74 + 15 + 16 = 105

3 by 5 = 15

56 – 7 = 49

Find the perimeter in cm and the area in square cm.

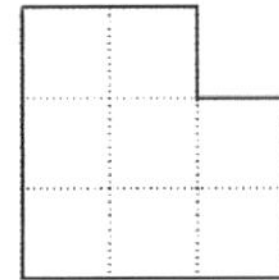

2 + 1 + 1 + 2 + 3 + 3 = 12 cm

2 x 3 + 2 = 8 square cm

Fix the answer.

	4	2	7	3
+	2	7	8	7
	~~6~~ 7	0	6	0

Find the differences.

63 – 25 = 38

100 – 74 = 26

137 – 59 = 78

Write >, <, or = on the lines.

5 – 2 = 7 – 4

8 – 7 < 11 – 7

14 – 6 < 14 – 5

2 cm < 3 cm

13 – 8 > 13 – 9

9 + 17 = 8 + 18

Explain two ways how to find 46 – 18.

Add 2 to both numbers. Then 48 – 20 = 28.

Go up: 2 to 20, 20 to 40, 6 to 46. 2 + 20 + 6 = 28.

EXPLANATIONS:

Lesson 60: Drawing Five-Sided Stars

OBJECTIVES:

1. To learn the term *polygon*
2. To learn terms *vertex, diagonal,* and *pentagon*
3. To learn the term *angle*
4. To draw lines using a triangle
5. To construct stars from pentagons

MATERIALS:

1. Dry erase board
2. Worksheet 29, Drawing Five-Sided Stars
3. 30-60 triangle*

ACTIVITIES FOR TEACHING:

EXPLANATIONS:

Warm-up. Ask: What is 200 – 50? [150] What is 300 – 150? [150] What is 300 – 250? [50] What is 350 – 150? [200]

The triangles provided by RightStart™ Mathematics do not have inking, or beveled, edges. Inking edges will slide over the T-square and can be very frustrating.

Ask the child to solve the following problem on the dry erase board:

> 6897 people are at a concert in a stadium. There is room for 2710 more people. How many people will fill the stadium? [9607 people]

Then ask the child to write the equations and answers to the following problems: 58 + 26, [84] 49 + 49, [98] 85 – 10, [75] and 130 – 15. [115]

Introducing polygons. Draw a rectangle, triangle, and pentagon as shown below. Tell the child that closed figures with straight sides are called *polygons.*

4 vertices.

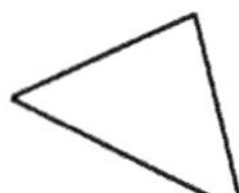

3 vertices.

5 vertices.

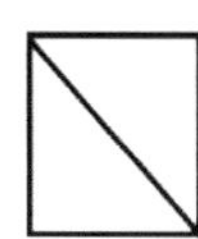

Diagonal.

Vertices. Point to a vertex, or corner, and tell her: The mathematical name for the point where two lines meet is called a *vertex.* Ask: How many vertices does a rectangle have? [4] How many vertices does a triangle have? [3] How many vertices does the third figure have? [5]

The plural of vertex is usually *vertices*, but vertexes is also correct.

Diagonals. Draw a diagonal in the rectangle as shown above on the right. Say: A line drawn between two vertices is a *diagonal.* Tell her to draw a rectangle with a diagonal on her dry erase board. Tell her to rotate her board until the diagonal is horizontal, then to rotate it until the diagonal is vertical.

In everyday usage, a diagonal is a slanted line, one that is neither horizontal nor vertical, for example, a street that does not run true north and south or east and west is referred to as a diagonal street. In geometry, on the other hand, a diagonal is a line in a polygon joining two non-adjacent vertices.

A horizontal diagonal.

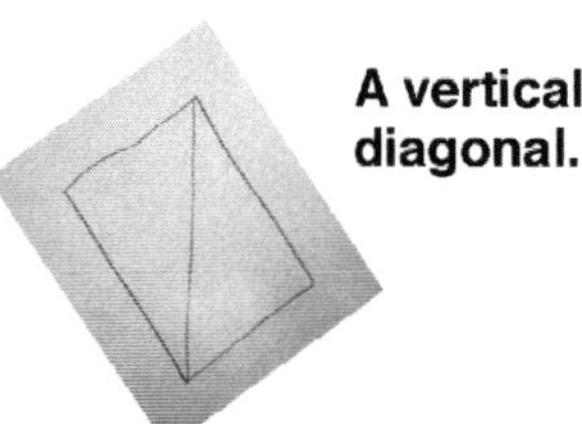

A vertical diagonal.

ACTIVITIES FOR TEACHING:

Worksheet 29. Give the child the worksheet. Ask: How many sides do the figures have? [5] Say: They are *pentagons.*

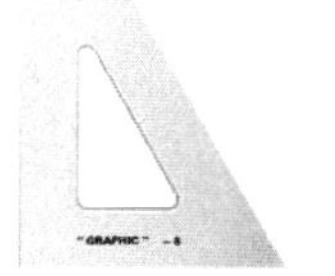
30-60 triangle.

Next show her a 30-60 triangle as shown on the right. Tell her: It is called a *30-60 triangle.* One angle is 90°, also called a right angle; the sharper point is a 30° angle; and the other angle is a 60° angle. An *angle* is the measure of space between two intersecting lines.

Demonstrate drawing a line between two points as shown below. Emphasize placing the triangle a little ways away, the same amount, from both dots and holding the triangle firmly while drawing the line.

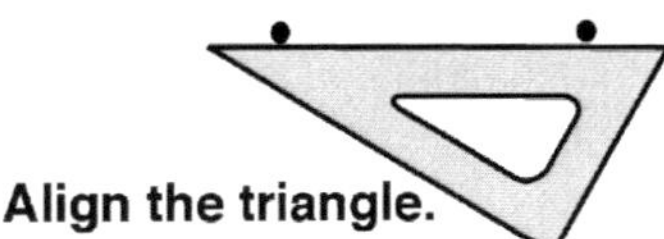
Align the triangle.

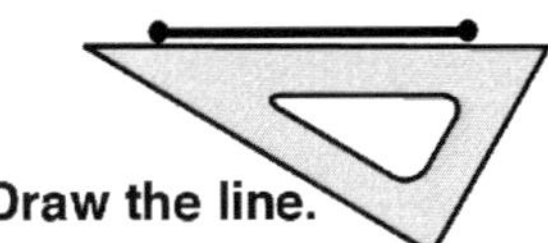
Draw the line.

Drawing the diagonals. Tell the child to draw all the diagonals in the left pentagon on her worksheet with her 30-60 triangle. Let her appreciate her star, shown on the right, before asking: How many diagonals did you draw? [5] What is in the center of the pentagon? [another pentagon]

Diagonals.

Extending the sides. Demonstrate what extend means by placing your hands on your shoulders and then extending your arms out in a straight line.

Then demonstrate extending lines by first aligning the triangle near, but not touching the line, and then making the line longer. See the figures below.

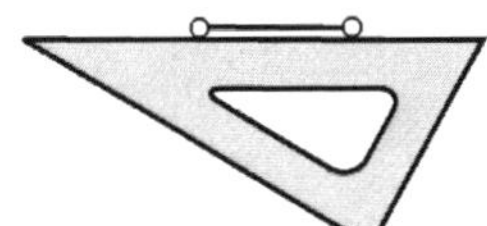
Align triangle to the line.

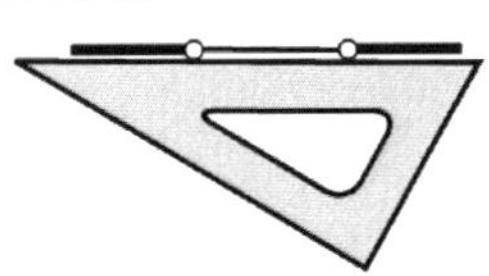
Draw the extended line.

Ask the child to extend the lines of the right pentagon on the worksheet to the edge of the circle. See the figure.

After she has drawn the star, ask: What figure would you have if you connected the vertices of the star? [a pentagon]

Extended sides.

In conclusion. Ask: What do we call a closed figure with straight sides? [polygon] What polygon has five sides and five angles? [pentagon] What is the point where two sides meet called? [vertex] What do we call a line between two vertices in a pentagon? [diagonal]

EXPLANATIONS:

Tell the child to remove this worksheet from her workbook before starting.

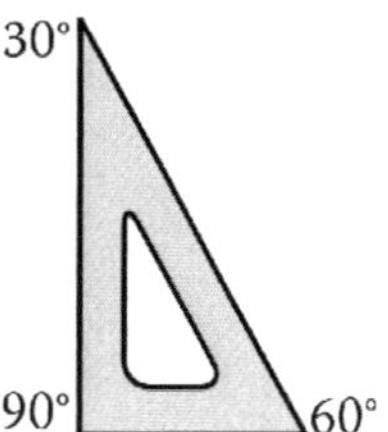

The goniometer, shown below, may be a useful tool in showing the measure of the space between two vertices. We label this measurement as a degree.

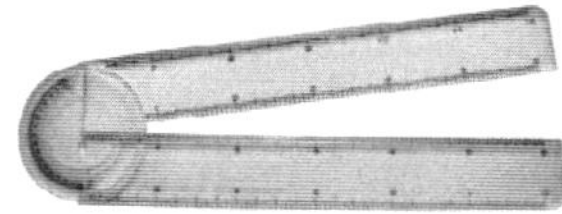

This star may be colored and displayed.

The little white dots indicate where to align the triangle.

You might tell the child that there is a government building shaped like a pentagon near Washington, D.C.

Some children may like to draw stars inside the pentagon.

Lesson 61: Drawing Horizontal Lines

OBJECTIVES:

1. To learn to use the T-square
2. To learn to draw horizontal lines with a T-square
3. To review halves

MATERIALS:

1. Worksheet 30, Drawing Horizontal Lines
2. Tape*
3. T-square
4. Drawing board**
5. **Sharp pencil (preferably mechanical) and eraser**

ACTIVITIES FOR TEACHING:

Warm-up. Ask: What do we call a closed figure with straight sides? [polygon] What polygon has five sides and five angles? [pentagon] What do we call the point where two sides meet? [vertex] What do we call a line between two vertices in a pentagon? [diagonal]

Ask: What is 250 – 50? [200] What is 350 – 150? [200] What is 300 – 150? [150] What is 400 – 150? [250]

Ask the child to say the answers to the following problems: 68 + 25, [93] 39 + 39, [78] 73 – 10, [63] and 150 – 15. [135]

Preparation. Tape the worksheet to the drawing board before giving it to the child. To do this, place the T-square along a side of the board. Then position a horizontal line on the paper so it is aligns with the top edge of the T-square and tape the top two corners. See the figure below.

T-square.

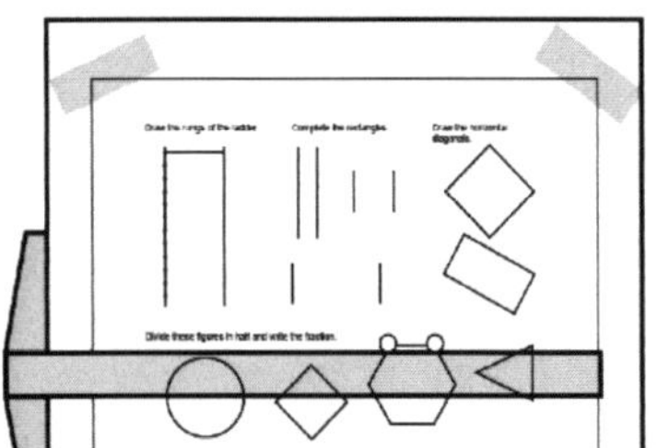

Aligning and taping the worksheet to the drawing board.

Introducing the drawing tools. Show the child the dry erase board with the worksheet attached and tell her it is now a drawing board. Next show her the T-square and tell her it is called a T-square. Ask: Why do you think it is called a T-square? [looks like the letter T] Is this the same reason a certain shirt is called a T-shirt? [yes]

EXPLANATIONS:

*The best tape is "removable" tape, which can be reused several times.

The dry erase board is also the drawing board. **See preparation instructions for preparing the worksheet in advance.

Teaching geometry with a drawing board, T-square, triangles, and compass helps the child learn the informal, practical side of geometry. It also helps develop coordination, which improves with practice.

Tape is not used at the bottom corners because it interferes with moving the T-square.

ACTIVITIES FOR TEACHING:

Drawing horizontal lines. Give the child the drawing board with the worksheet attached and T-square. For a right-handed user, the T-square is placed along the left side. A left-handed user places the T-square along the right side. See the figures below.

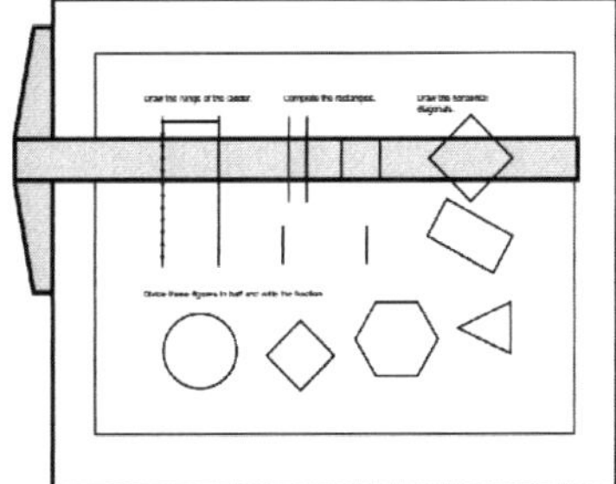

T-square position for right-handed user.

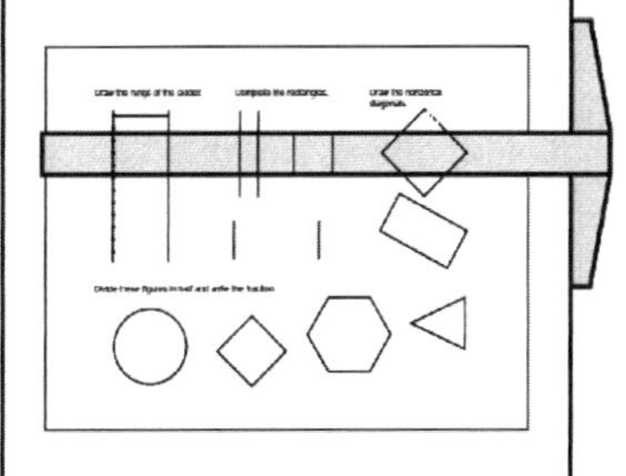

T-square position for left-handed user.

Say: Use the T-square to draw horizontal lines. It slides up and down the side of the board. Hold it tight against the board with one hand while you draw the line with your writing hand along the top of the T-square.

Tell the child to check to be sure the T-square is hugging the board before drawing each line.

Worksheet 30. For the first problem on the worksheet, tell the child to draw horizontal lines to make the rungs on a ladder. Tell her that all lines must be drawn with the T-square. Tell her to read the remaining instructions and complete the worksheet.

Solutions are shown below.

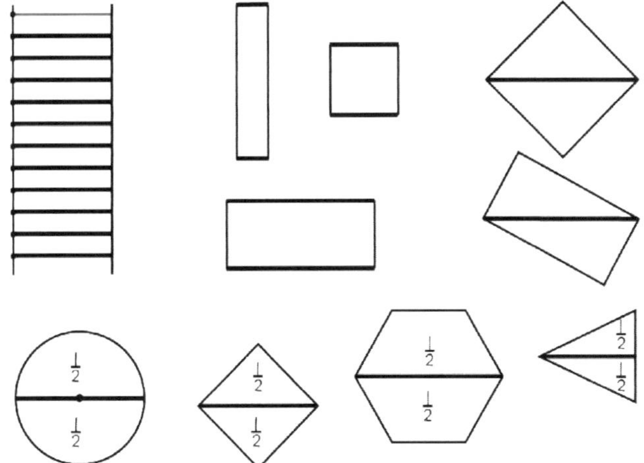

Ask: Where do you see congruent, or identical, shapes? [two squares, rectangle, circle, hexagon, and triangle] In the bottom row, which shape is not a polygon? [circle]

In conclusion. Ask: What is the name of the drawing tool that you use to draw horizontal lines? [T-square] What is one half plus one half? [whole, or 1]

EXPLANATIONS:

Congruent means that the figures exactly fit on top of each other, sometimes requiring rotation or reflection.

At the end of the lesson, you might ask the child to leave the tape on the board; it can frequently be reused.

Lesson 62: Drawing Vertical Lines

OBJECTIVES:

1. To learn to use the T-square and triangle together
2. To learn to draw vertical lines
3. To learn the term *rhombus*
4. To review fourths

MATERIALS:

1. Math journal
2. Drawing board
3. T-square and 30-60 triangle
4. Worksheet 31, Drawing Vertical Lines

ACTIVITIES FOR TEACHING:

Warm-up. Ask: What is the name of the drawing tool that you use to draw horizontal lines? [T-square] What is one half plus one half? [whole, or 1]

Ask: What do we call a closed figure with straight sides? [polygon] What polygon has five sides and five angles? [pentagon] What is the point where two sides meet called? [vertex] What do we call a line between two vertices in a pentagon? [diagonal]

Tell the child to solve the following problem in her math journal:

> There are 4007 people attending a rodeo. There is room for 2906 more people in the arena. How many people can attend the rodeo altogether? [6913 people]

Drawing vertical lines. Give the child the drawing board with worksheet sattached, and drawing tools. Tell the child that today she will draw vertical lines using both her T-square and 30-60 triangle. To draw vertical lines, the triangle needs to touch the T-square while the T-square hugs the board. The T-square needs to be at least a centimeter or quarter inch below the lower starting point.

To hold the tools in place, demonstrate the following procedure for a right-handed child:

1. The left hand moves the T-square below the starting point and holds it in place. See the left figure below.

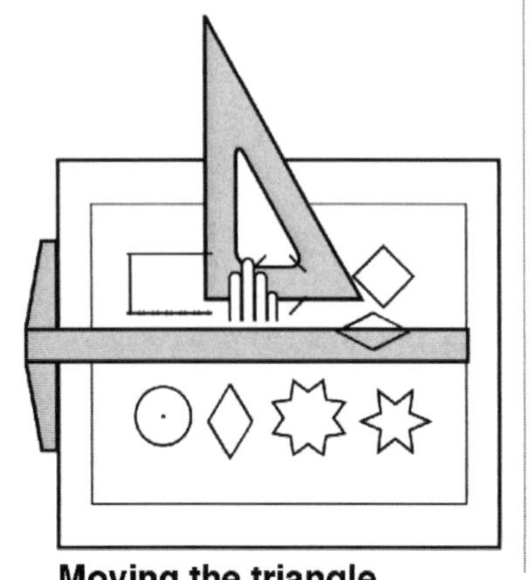

Holding the T-square. **Moving the triangle.**

EXPLANATIONS:

The T-square needs to be below the starting point in order to draw a precise line.

Left handed children will do the mirror image of the instructions listed.

ACTIVITIES FOR TEACHING:

2. The right hand moves the triangle toward the correct place on the T-square. See right figure.

3. Both hands hold the tools momentarily. See the left figure below.

4. The left hand takes over holding both tools, see the right figure below.

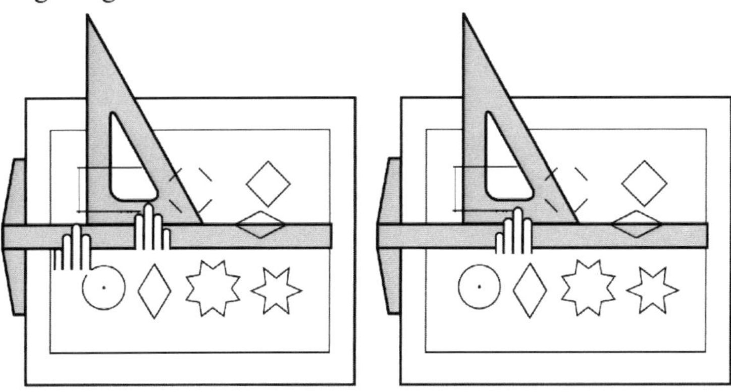

Each hand holds a tool. **One hand holds both tools.**

Worksheet 31. For the first problem on the worksheet, tell the child to draw vertical lines to make slats for the fence. Remind her that all lines must be made with her T-square and the 90° of her 30-60 triangle. Lines are generally drawn from bottom to top.

Tell her to read the remaining instructions and complete the worksheet. Solutions are shown below.

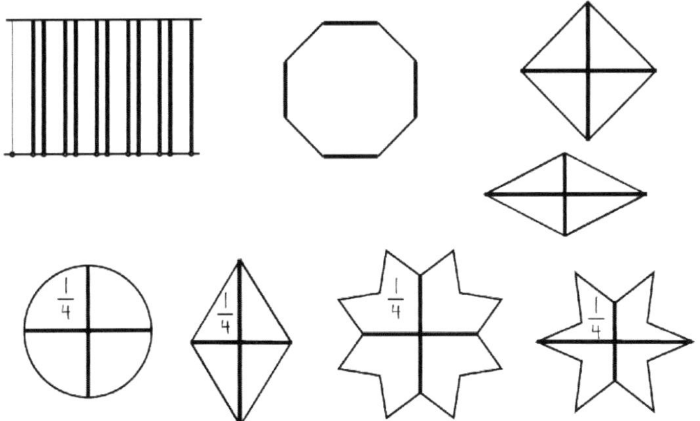

Are the four parts in each figure congruent? **yes**

Rhombuses. Say: A parallelogram has four sides. Ask: How many parallelograms do you see on the worksheet, excluding the fence? [3] How many are squares? [1] Say: All three are *rhombuses* because their sides are equal. A rhombus is an equilateral parallelogram.

In conclusion. Ask: Did you draw any parallel lines? [yes, the fence] Did you draw any perpendicular lines? [yes, in several figures] How many halves in a whole? [2] How many fourths are in a whole? [4]

EXPLANATIONS:

The word lateral means side. So, equilateral means equal sides, or all the sides are congruent.

Lesson 63: Drawing Diagonals in a Hexagon

OBJECTIVES:

1. To review term *hexagon*
2. To draw 60° and 30° lines with the 30-60 triangle
3. To draw all the diagonals in a hexagon
4. To identify figures within a hexagon with diagonals

MATERIALS:

1. Math journal
2. Worksheet 32, Drawing Diagonals in a Hexagon
3. Drawing board
4. T-square and 30-60 triangle

ACTIVITIES FOR TEACHING:

Warm-up. Ask: How many halves in a whole? [2] How many fourths are in a whole? [4]

Ask: What do we call a closed figure with straight sides? [polygon] What polygon has five sides and five angles? [pentagon] What is the point where two sides meet called? [vertex] What do we call a line between two vertices in a pentagon? [diagonal]

Tell the child to solve the following problem in her math journal:

> There are 5403 people running a marathon. There is room for 2709 more people to run. How many people can run the marathon altogether? [8112 people]

Worksheet 32. Give the child the drawing board with the worksheet attached, T-square, and 30-60 triangle. Ask: What is the name of the figure on the worksheet? [hexagon]

Drawing the horizontal diagonal. Tell the child to read the directions on the worksheet. Explain that all the diagonals are to be done with the T-square and triangle. Ask: Do you see where to draw a horizontal diagonal? See below. Tell her to draw it. Remind her to slide her T-square slightly below the bottom of the hexagon.

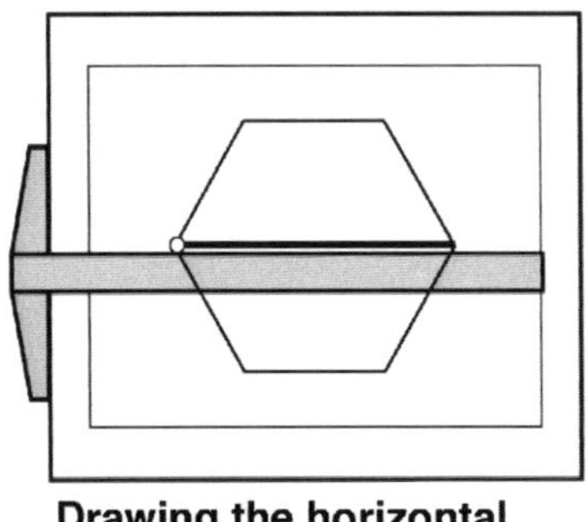

Drawing the horizontal diagonal with the T-square.

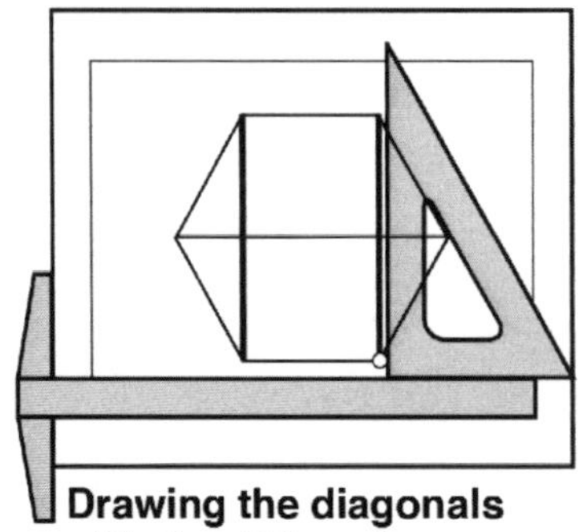

Drawing the diagonals with the 90° angle.

Drawing the vertical diagonals. Ask: Do you see where to draw vertical diagonals? See the right figure above. Tell her to draw them.

EXPLANATIONS:

To help in remembering that hexagons have six sides, think that the words "hexagon" and "six" both have an "x."

ACTIVITIES FOR TEACHING:

Drawing the 60° diagonals. Now point to the 60° on the triangle and ask: Do you see any diagonals that you could draw with this edge? See the left figure below.

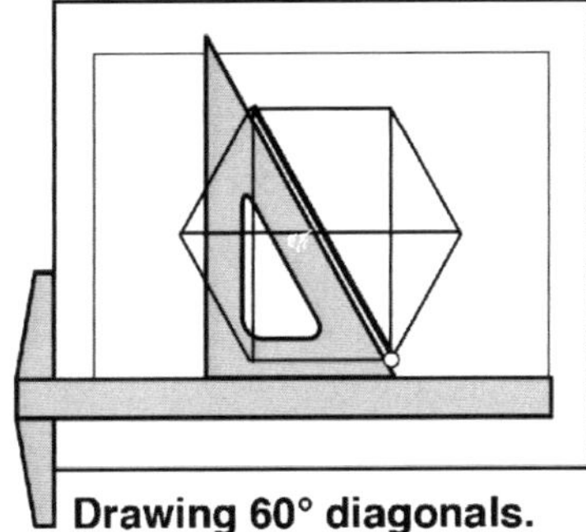

Drawing 60° diagonals.

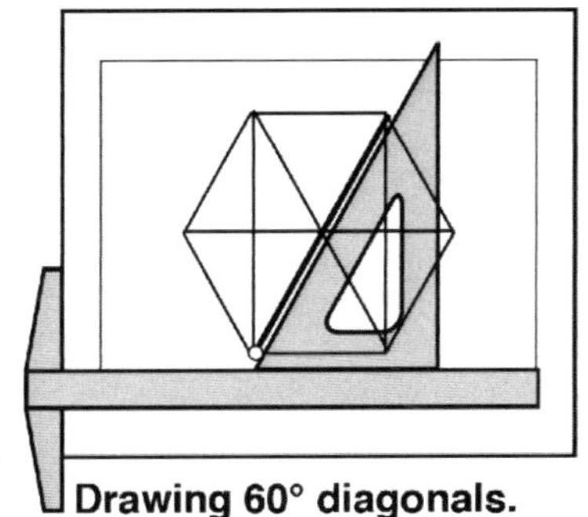

Drawing 60° diagonals.

Ask: Do you see the other diagonal to draw at that angle? Suggest she flip her triangle over and draw it. See the right figure above.

Drawing the 30° diagonals. Say: There are four diagonals to draw with the 30° angle on your triangle. Show her how to orient her triangle, as shown below on the left. Tell her to draw the four diagonals. If necessary, remind her to flip her triangle over to draw the last two diagonals. See the right figure below.

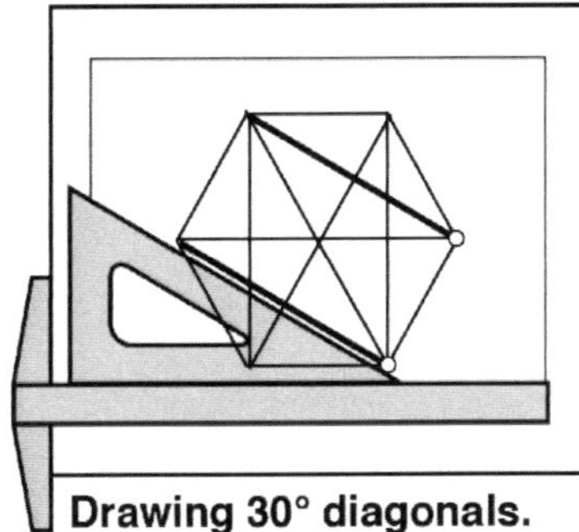

Drawing 30° diagonals.

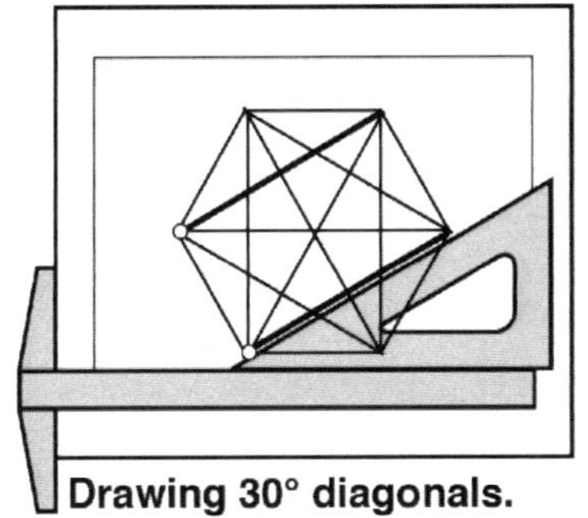

Drawing 30° diagonals.

Figures in the hexagon. Ask the child if she can find the figures on the worksheet:

1. Rectangles [3 large and 6 small]
2. Hexagons [1 large and 1 small]
3. Equilateral triangles [2 large, 6 medium, and 6 small]
4. Other triangles [too many to count]
5. Rhombuses [6 large]

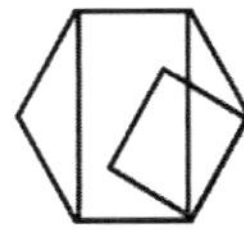

Rectangles

Hexagons

Equilateral triangles

Other triangles

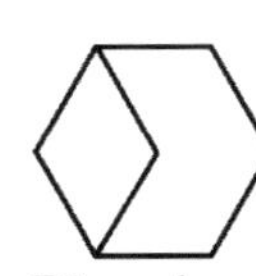

Rhombus

In conclusion. Ask: How many sides does a hexagon have? [6] How many vertices? [6] How many sides does a rhombus have? [4] How many vertices? [4]

EXPLANATIONS:

Either vertex could be a starting point.

Lesson 64: Dividing Equilateral Triangles into Halves

OBJECTIVES:

1. To review *equilateral* triangles
2. To learn the term *congruent*
3. To learn to draw equilateral triangles
4. To draw halves

MATERIALS:

1. Worksheet 33, Dividing Equilateral Triangles into Halves
2. Drawing board
3. T-square and 30-60 triangle

ACTIVITIES FOR TEACHING:

Warm-up. Ask: How many sides does a hexagon have? [6] How many vertices? [6] How many sides does a rhombus have? [4] How many vertices? [4]

Ask: How many halves in a whole? [2] How many fourths are in a whole? [4]

Ask: What do we call a closed figure with straight sides? [polygon] What polygon has five sides and five angles? [pentagon] What is the point where two sides meet called? [vertex] What do we call a line between two vertices in a pentagon? [diagonal]

Reviewing triangles. Draw the following:

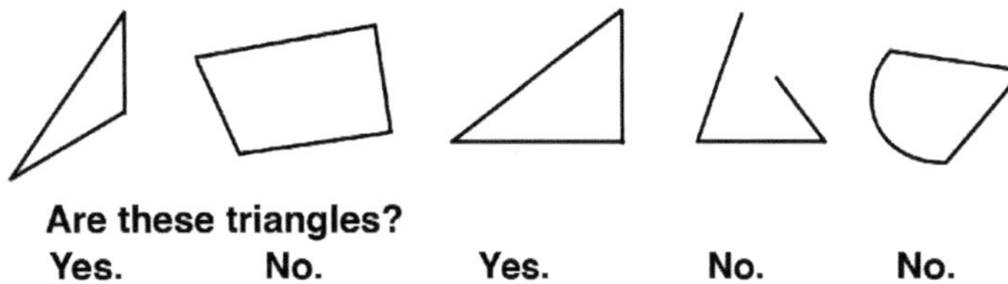

Are these triangles?
Yes. No. Yes. No. No.

Ask: How many triangles so you see? [2] Why are the other figures not triangles? [The second figure has four sides. The fourth figure is not closed. The fifth figure does not have straight lines.]

Draw the following equilateral triangles:

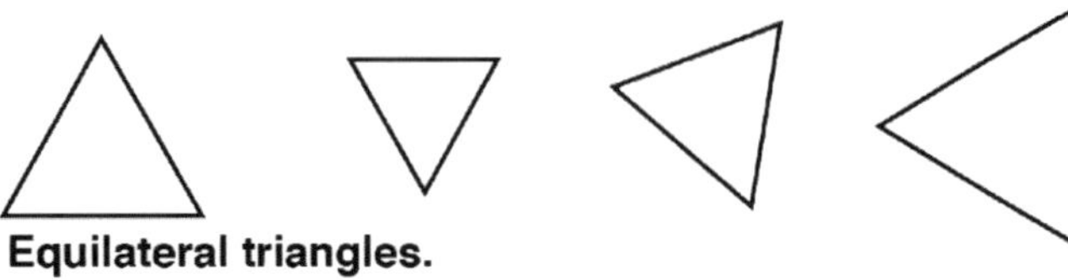

Equilateral triangles.

Ask: What is special about the sides in these triangles? [same length] Explain: Because their sides are the same length, these are *equilateral* triangles. The word *lateral* means side. So, equilateral means equal sides, or all the sides are *congruent*. Congruent means that the figures exactly fit on top of each other.

EXPLANATIONS:

Sometimes examples are clearer than a definition.

Football fans will know that a lateral pass is a pass to the *side*.

ACTIVITIES FOR TEACHING:

Worksheet 33. Give the child the drawing board with the worksheet attached, T-square, and 30-60 triangle. Tell her that today she will draw equilateral triangles with the drawing tools and divide them into halves.

Demonstrate drawing the left side of the triangle with the 60° angle of the triangle. Explain that since we do not know how long to make the line, we will draw it extra long. Then flip the triangle over and draw the other side. See the figures below. The extra part of the line can now be erased.

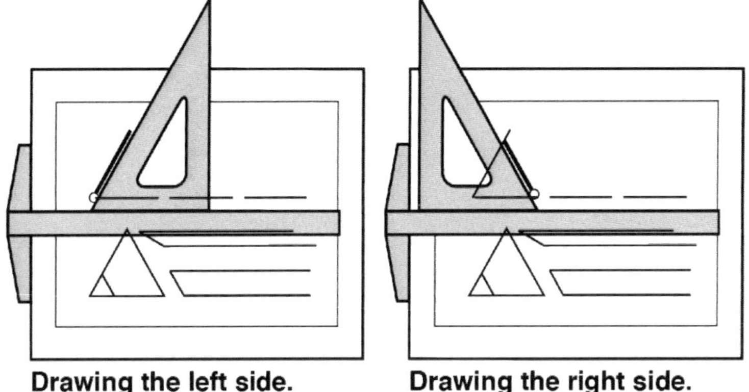

Drawing the left side. **Drawing the right side.**

Tell the child to divide her triangles into halves; she needs to use the 30° angle on her triangle. See solutions below.

Problem 1.

Problems 2 and 3. Say: Each line you draw needs a starting point and the angle. Tell her to complete the worksheet. See below.

Ask: How many triangles do you see in the "pyramid" of triangles? [9 small triangles, 3 middle-size, and 1 large = 13 triangles] Also ask: How many small triangles are in each row? [1, 3, 5] How many would be in the next row? [7] How do you know? [next odd number]

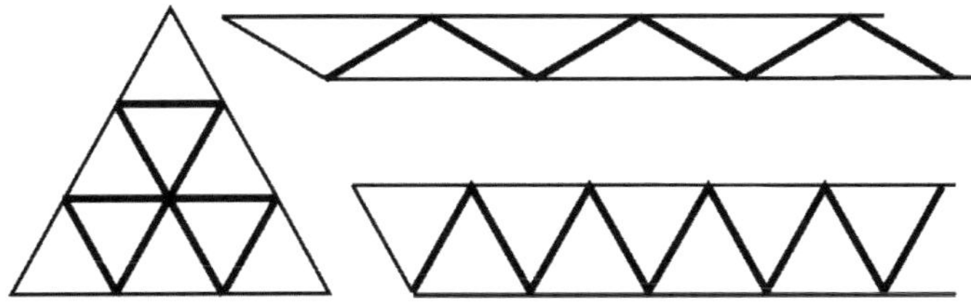

How many triangles are there altogether? **13**

In conclusion. Ask: What does equilateral mean? [equal sides] What is another name for an equilateral parallelogram? [rhombus]

EXPLANATIONS:

Erasing is a necessary and natural part of drawing. This may cause a problem initially for a child who is a perfectionist.

Lesson 65: Dividing Equilateral Triangles into Thirds

OBJECTIVES:

1. To review thirds
2. To learn to dividing equilateral triangles in thirds

MATERIALS:

1. Worksheet 34, Dividing Equilateral Triangles into Thirds
2. Drawing board
3. T-square and 30-60 triangle

ACTIVITIES FOR TEACHING:

EXPLANATIONS:

Warm-up. Ask: What does equilateral mean? [equal sides] What is another name for an equilateral parallelogram? [rhombus] How many sides does a hexagon have? [6] How many vertices? [6] How many sides does a rhombus have? [4] How many vertices? [4]

Ask: How many halves in a whole? [2] How many fourths are in a whole? [4]

Ask: What do we call a closed figure with straight sides? [polygon] What polygon has five sides and five angles? [pentagon] What is the point where two sides meet called? [vertex] What do we call a line between two vertices in a pentagon? [diagonal]

Reviewing fractions. Ask: If you divide something into two equal parts, what do you call each part? [a half] If you divide it into four parts, what do you call each part? [a fourth] If you divide it into three parts, what do you call each part? [a third] If you divide it into six parts, what do you call each part? [a sixth]

Dividing the equilateral triangle into thirds. Draw two equilateral triangles freehand and ask the child to divide both triangles into halves the three different ways, creating sixths. See the left figure below. Ask: Now what is the triangle divided into? [sixths]

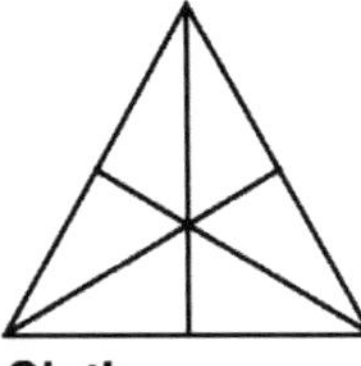

Sixths.

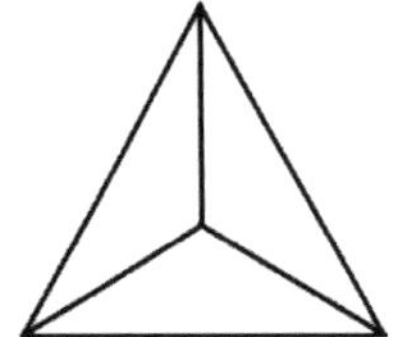

Thirds.

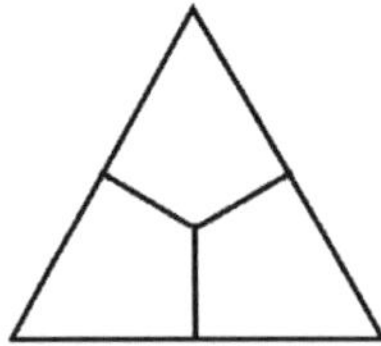

Thirds.

Ask: Which lines could you partly erase so we could have thirds? Ask her to find another way with the other triangle. The solutions are shown above on the right.

ACTIVITIES FOR TEACHING:

Worksheet 34. Give the child the drawing board with the worksheet attached, T-square, and 30-60 triangle. Tell her that today she will divide equilateral triangles into thirds with the drawing tools.

Demonstrate drawing the left side of the triangle with the 30° angle. See the left figure below. Remind her that we do not know how long to make the line, so we draw it extra long. Then flip the triangle over and draw the other side. See the right figure below. The extra part of the line can be erased now or after the third line is drawn.

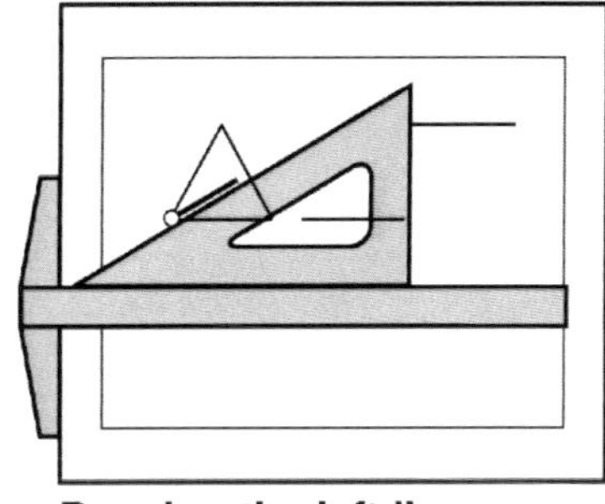

Drawing the left line.

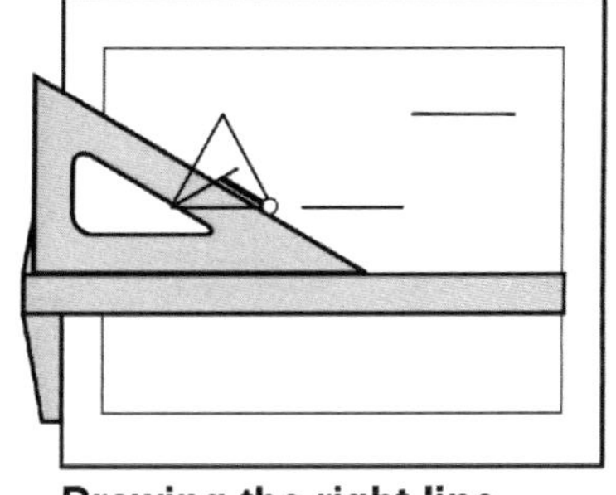

Drawing the right line.

Ask: What line do you draw next? [vertical line] See below.

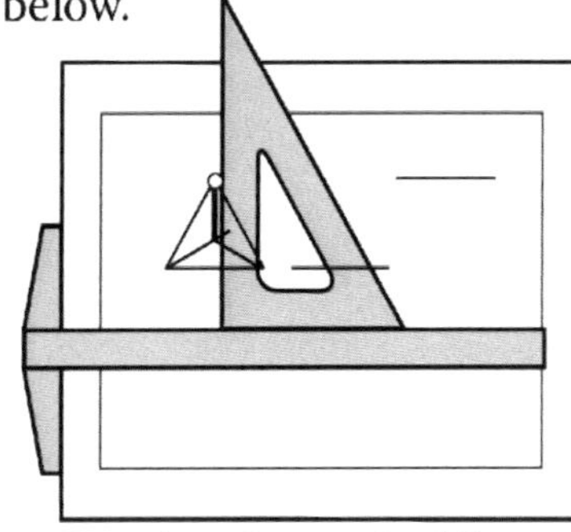

Drawing the vertical line.

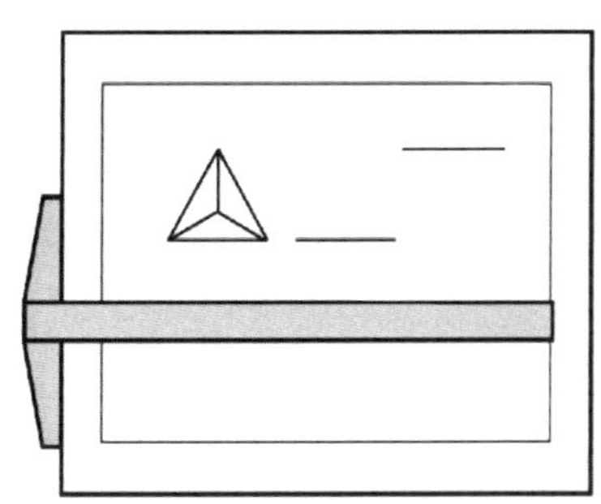

Completed thirds.

Ask her to finish the worksheet completing the circle and star like the triangles. Some figures can be done in more than one way. Some possible solutions are below.

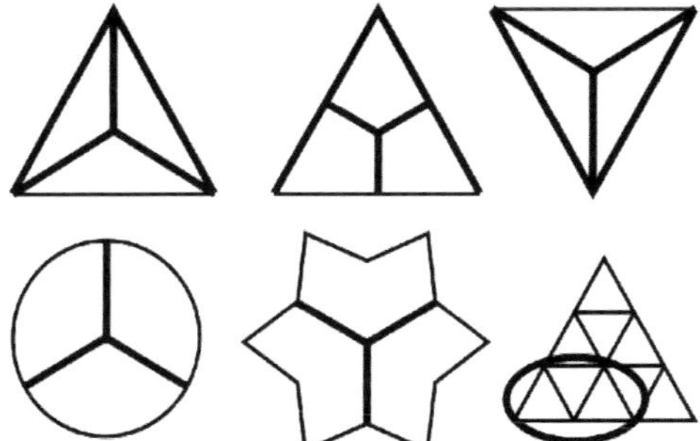

In conclusion. Ask: What does one third mean? [something divided into three equal parts] What is one third of six? [two]

EXPLANATIONS:

These three lines can be drawn in any order.

The triangle slides over the "ears" of the T-square.

There are other solutions for all but the first two figures. One is shown below.

Lesson 66: Dividing Equilateral Triangles into Fourths

OBJECTIVES:

1. To learn to dividing equilateral triangles in fourths and eighths
2. To review fourths and eighths
3. Comparing fractions

MATERIALS:

1. Worksheet 35, Dividing Equilateral Triangles into Fourths
2. Drawing board
3. T-square and 30-60 triangle

ACTIVITIES FOR TEACHING:

Warm-up. Ask: What does one third mean? [something divided into three equal parts] What is one third of six? [2] How many halves in a whole? [2] How many fourths are in a whole? [4]

Ask: What does equilateral mean? [equal sides] What is another name for an equilateral parallelogram? [rhombus] How many sides does a hexagon have? [6] How many vertices? [6] How many sides does a rhombus have? [4] How many vertices? [4]

Worksheet 35. Give the child the drawing board with the worksheet attached, T-square, and 30-60 triangle. Tell her that today she will draw equilateral triangles and divide them in fourths and eighths.

Triangle 1. Draw an equilateral triangle freehand. Divide it into fourths as shown on the right. Ask: What do you notice about where the two 60° angle lines start at the bottom? [in the center] To find that point with the drawing tools, pretend to divide the triangle in half and draw a small line at the bottom, called a *tick mark*. See the left figure below.

Divided into fourths.

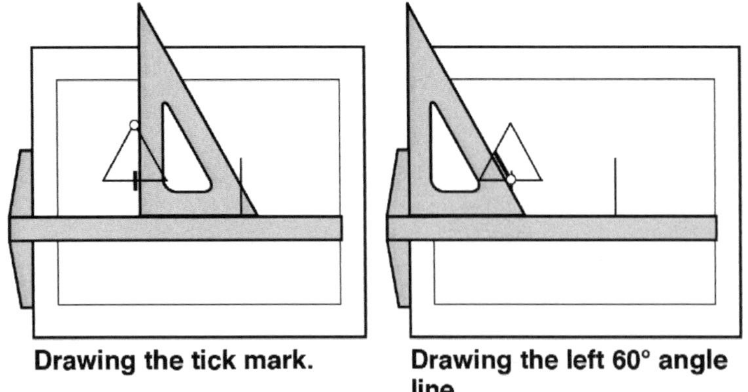

Drawing the tick mark. **Drawing the left 60° angle line.**

Now use the tick mark as the starting point for the 60° line. See the right figure. Ask: How can you draw the other 60° line? [Flip the triangle over and do it again.] See the left figure on the top of the next page.

EXPLANATIONS:

ACTIVITIES FOR TEACHING:

EXPLANATIONS:

Drawing the right 60° line. **Drawing the last line.**

Many people are puzzled by drawing the horizontal line; they try to use their triangle, but only the T-square is needed.

Ask: How could you draw the last line? [with the T-square] See the right figure above. Ask: Are the four triangles congruent? [yes] How could you draw eighths? [Divide each fourth in half.]

Tell the child to complete her worksheet. Triangles 2 and 3 and the fraction chart are shown below.

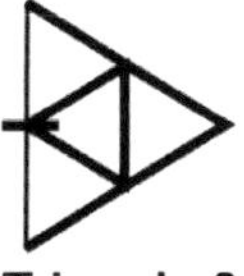
Triangle 2.

Triangle 3.

Triangle 3.

There are other solutions for Triangle 3.

1							
$\frac{1}{2}$				$\frac{1}{2}$			
$\frac{1}{4}$		$\frac{1}{4}$		$\frac{1}{4}$		$\frac{1}{4}$	
$\frac{1}{8}$	$\frac{1}{8}$	$\frac{1}{8}$	$\frac{1}{8}$	$\frac{1}{8}$	$\frac{1}{8}$	$\frac{1}{8}$	$\frac{1}{8}$

Comparing fractions. Remind the child another name for fourth is *quarter.* Ask the following questions using the fraction chart from the worksheet:

1. How many halves do you need to make a whole? [2]
2. How many quarters do you need to make a whole? [4]
3. How many eighths do you need to make one? [8]
4. What is the same as 2 one fourths? [one half]
5. Which is greater, one quarter or one eighth? [one fourth or one quarter]
6. What is equal to two eighths? [one fourth]
7. What is a half of one half? [one fourth]
8. What is a half of one quarter? [one eighth]

In conclusion. Ask: What does one quarter mean? [something divided into four equal parts] What is one divided by eight? [one eighth]

Lesson 67: Making Pyramids

OBJECTIVES:

1. To learn about tetrahedrons and square pyramids
2. To learn the terms, *face*, *edge*, and *vertex*
3. To draw the nets for the tetrahedron and square pyramid and to create them

MATERIALS:

1. Geometry panels: 8 equilateral triangles and 7 squares*
2. Worksheet 36, Making Pyramids
3. Drawing board
4. T-square and 30-60 triangle
5. **Scissors**

ACTIVITIES FOR TEACHING:

Warm-up. Ask: How many halves do you need to make a whole? [2] How many fourths do you need to make a whole? [4] How many eighths do you need to make one? [8] What is the same as two one quarters? [one half]

Ask: What does one quarter mean? [something divided into four equal parts] What is one divided by eight? [one eighth]

Ask: Which is greater, one quarter or one eighth? [one fourth or one quarter] What is equal to two eighths? [one fourth] What is a half of one half? [one fourth] What is a half of one quarter? [one eighth]

Ask: What does one third mean? [something divided into three equal parts] What is one third of six? [two]

Preparation. Using the geometry panels, make a tetrahedron from four equilateral triangles. Also make a square pyramid from the square and four equilateral triangles. Next make a cube with six squares. See the figures below.

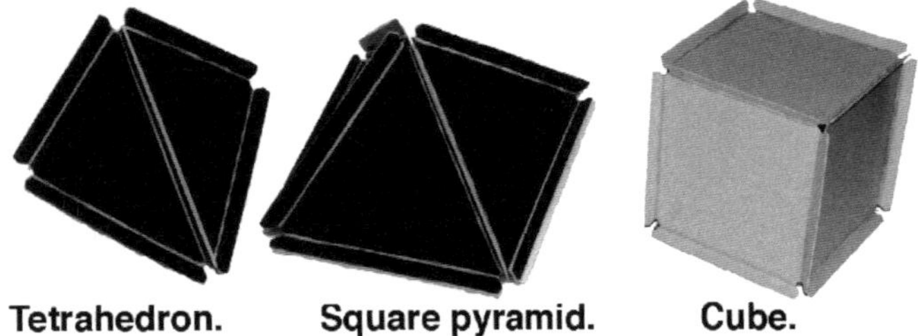

Tetrahedron. **Square pyramid.** **Cube.**

Reviewing faces and edges. Say: The math word for surfaces of a three-dimensional shape is *face*. Show her an edge of one of the shapes and say: The line where two faces meet is called an *edge*.

EXPLANATIONS:

*If the panels have not been used, the edges will need to be creased. Bend the perforated lines near each edge of the panels toward the colored side. Place the edge on a hard surface and bend gently. Bending two at a time works well.

While we might refer to a surface of a cube as a side, the mathematical term is *face*, with the word *side* reserved for lines in a polygon.

ACTIVITIES FOR TEACHING:	EXPLANATIONS:

Reviewing pyramids. Show the child the two pyramids. Say: These are both pyramids because they have a polygon at the base, or bottom, and triangular faces that meet at a vertex. Show her the cube and ask: Is a cube a pyramid? [no] Why not? [no triangular faces]

Ask: What is the difference between the two pyramids? [One has a triangular base; the other has a square base.] Say: The pyramid with the square base is called a *square pyramid*. The pyramid with the triangular base is called a *tetrahedron*.

Ask: How many faces does the tetrahedron have? [4] How many faces does the square pyramid have? [5] How many faces does the cube have? [6]

Ask: How many edges does the tetrahedron have? [6] How many edges does the square pyramid have? [8] How many edges does the cube have? [12]

Worksheet 36. Give the child the drawing board with the worksheet attached, T-square, and 30-60 triangle. Tell the child that today she will draw two special figures, which she will cut out, and fold up to make pyramids. Complete the problems in order, even though the numbers are scattered about.

The solutions to Problem 5 are shown below.

	Faces	Edges	Vertices
Tetrahedron	**4**	**6**	**4**
Square Pyramid	**5**	**8**	**5**

In conclusion. Ask: Which pyramid that you made has four congruent faces? [They both do.] Which pyramid has all faces congruent? [tetrahedron]

Lesson 68: Dividing Equilateral Triangles into Twelfths

OBJECTIVES:

1. To review measuring centimeters with a ruler
2. To divide an equilateral triangle into twelfths
3. To find perimeters

MATERIALS:

1. Worksheet 37, Dividing Equilateral Triangles into Twelfths
2. Drawing board
3. T-square and 30-60 triangle
4. Centimeter cubes
5. 4-in-1 ruler

ACTIVITIES FOR TEACHING:

Warm-up. Ask: When looking at a tetrahedron and a square pyramid, which pyramid has four congruent faces? [They both do.] Which pyramid has all faces congruent? [tetrahedron]

Ask: How many halves do you need to make a whole? [2] How many fourths do you need to make a whole? [4] How many eighths do you need to make one? [8]

Ask: What does one quarter mean? [something divided into four equal parts] What is one divided by eight? [one eighth] How many eighths are the same as one fourth? [2] What is the same as 2 one quarters? [one half or four one eighths]

Worksheet 37. Give the child the drawing board with the worksheet attached, T-square, 30-60 triangle, centimeter cubes, and 4-in-1 ruler.

Reviewing centimeters. Show the child a centimeter cube and ask: How long is the edge of this cube? [1 cm] Ask her to use her cubes and measure the four lines at the top of her worksheet as shown.

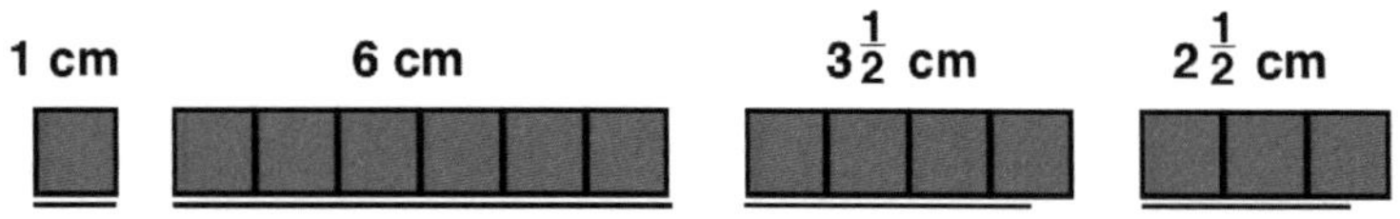

Measuring the lines on the top of the worksheet.

Tell her to take the 4-in-1 ruler and find the centimeter side marked with the little "CM." Tell her to measure the row of 6 centimeter cubes. Ask: What measurement does the ruler show? [6 cm] See below.

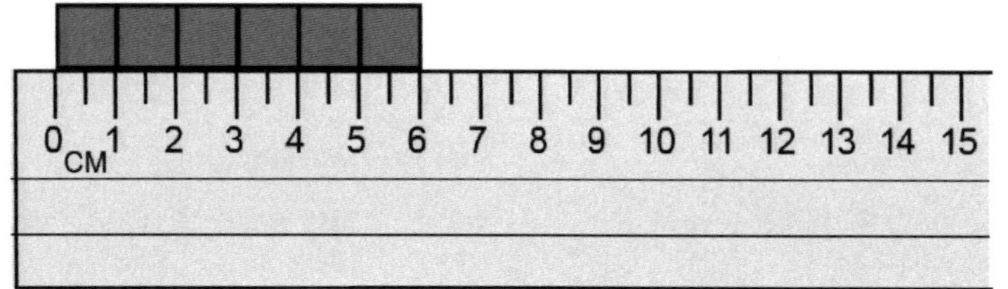

EXPLANATIONS:

Although fractions are not common within the metric system, they are permissible.

ACTIVITIES FOR TEACHING:	EXPLANATIONS:

Ask her to measure each of the four lines with her ruler. See below. Ask: Did you get the same answers that you got with the cubes? [yes]

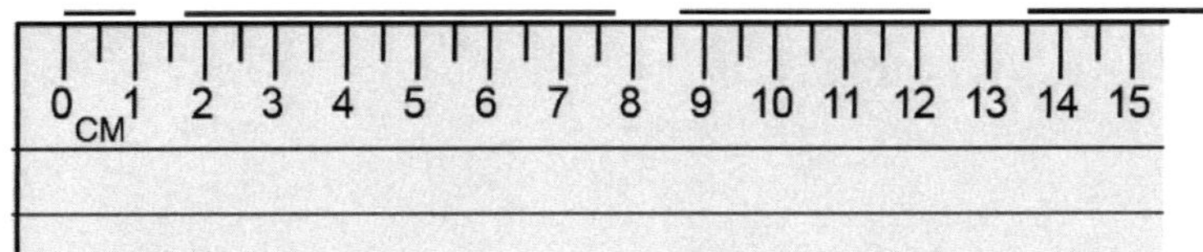

Measuring the first and third lines with the 4-in-1 ruler.

Write and ask the child to add:

$$3\text{ cm} + 2\text{ cm} = \_\_\_\_ \quad [5\text{ cm}]$$
$$3\text{ cm} + 2\tfrac{1}{2}\text{ cm} = \_\_\_\_ \quad [5\tfrac{1}{2}\text{ cm}]$$
$$3\tfrac{1}{2}\text{ cm} + 2\tfrac{1}{2}\text{ cm} = \_\_\_\_ \quad [6\text{ cm}]$$
$$5\tfrac{1}{2}\text{ cm} + 5\tfrac{1}{2}\text{ cm} = \_\_\_\_ \quad [11\text{ cm}]$$

Dividing the equilateral triangle into twelfths. Tell the child to follow the instructions to divide the equilateral triangle into twelfths. See right figure. Tell her she will see a surprise when she is finished. [the cube in the middle]

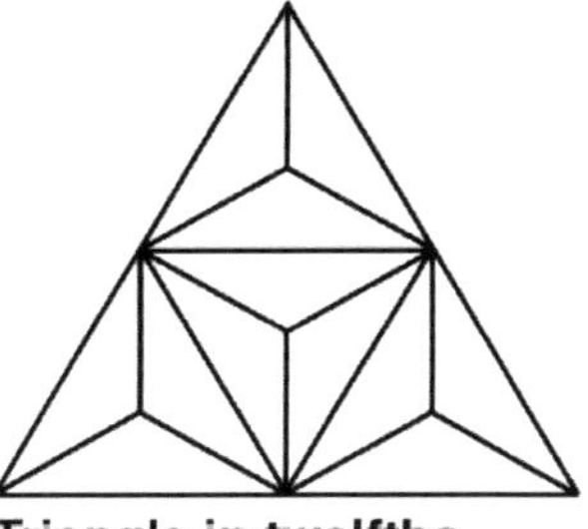

Triangle in twelfths.

Perimeter. Tell her to complete the worksheet. The perimeter solutions are shown below.

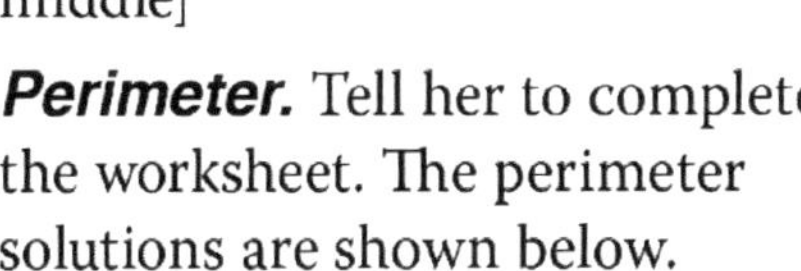

Large equilateral triangle	**$P = 16 + 16 + 16 = 48$**	**$P = 48$ cm**
Small equilateral triangle	**$P = 8 + 8 + 8 = 24$**	**$P = 24$ cm**
Small rhombus	**$P = 4\frac{1}{2} + 4\frac{1}{2} + 4\frac{1}{2} + 4\frac{1}{2} = 18$**	**$P = 18$ cm**
Hexagon	**$P = 4\frac{1}{2} + 4\frac{1}{2} + 4\frac{1}{2} + 4\frac{1}{2} + 4\frac{1}{2} + 4\frac{1}{2} = 27$**	**$P = 27$ cm**

The equations might also be written as follows:

$$P = 16 \times 3 = 48\text{ cm}$$
$$P = 8 \times 3 = 24\text{ cm}$$
$$P = 4\tfrac{1}{2} \times 4 = 18\text{ cm}$$
$$P = 4\tfrac{1}{2} \times 6 = 27\text{ cm}$$

When she has finished, ask her to explain how she found the perimeters.

For the rhombus, she might add two 4s and two halves to get 9 and then double that to get the answer of 18 cm. Or, she might add the four 4s to get 16 and then the four halves to get 2 to get the answer of 16 + 2 = 18 cm.

In conclusion. Ask: What does a centimeter ruler do? [It measures the length of something in centimeters.]

Lesson 69: Dividing Equilateral Triangles into Sixths

OBJECTIVES:

1. To realize that two sixths is the same as one third
2. To divide an equilateral triangle into sixths
3. To understand that the same fraction of identical figures, even though a different shape, are equal

MATERIALS:

1. Fraction pieces
2. Worksheet 38, Dividing Equilateral Triangles into Sixths
3. Drawing board
4. T-square and 30-60 triangle
5. **Crayons**

ACTIVITIES FOR TEACHING:

EXPLANATIONS:

Warm-up. Ask: What does a centimeter ruler do? [It measures the length of something in centimeters.] What is perimeter? [the length around the outside of a shape]

Ask: When looking at a tetrahedron and a square pyramid, which pyramid has four congruent faces? [They both do.] Which pyramid has all its faces congruent? [tetrahedron]

Ask: How many thirds do you need to make a whole? [3] How many sixths do you need to make a whole? [6] How many sevenths do you need to make one? [7] What is the same as 2 one quarters? [one half or four one eighths]

Fraction charts. Give the child the fraction pieces. Ask her to assemble the chart. See figure below.

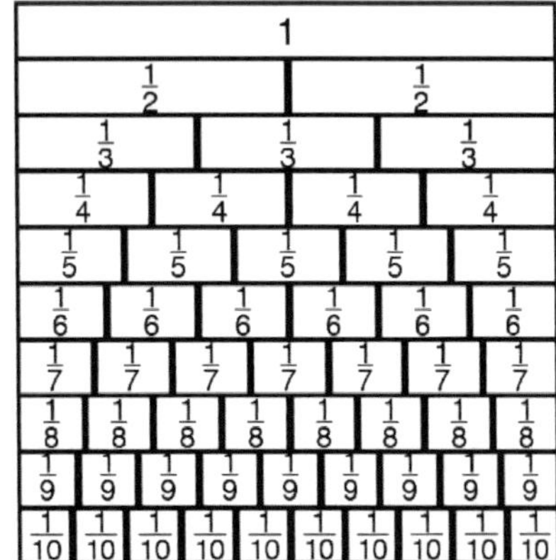

The fraction chart assembled.

Comparing fractions. With the assembled chart in view of the child, ask the following questions:

1. How many thirds do you need to make a whole? [3]
2. How many sixths do you need to make a whole? [6]
3. How many halves do you need to make a whole? [2]
4. How many sixths do you need to make a half? [3]
5. What is a half of one third? [one sixth]
6. What is the same as two sixths? [one third]

ACTIVITIES FOR TEACHING:

Tell the child to look away from the assembled fraction chart for the next two questions.

7. Which is more, a sixth or a third? [third]

8. Which is more, a half or a third? [a half]

The next questions include fractions that are not unit fractions, that is, fractions that have a number other than 1 for the numerator. Ask the child to look at her fraction chart and ask:

9. Which is more, three sixths or one third? [three sixths]

10. Which is more, three sixths or two thirds? [two thirds]

Ask the child similar questions if needed.

Worksheet 38. Give the child the drawing board with the worksheet attached, T-square, and 30-60 triangle. Tell her to complete the worksheet. The solutions are shown below.

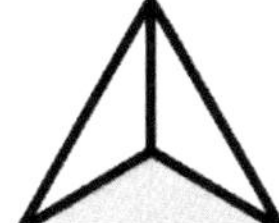

Which third of a triangle that you colored is largest? **same**

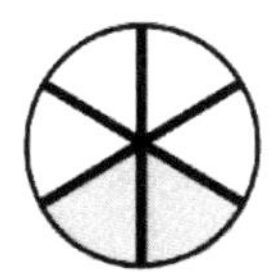

Which is more, $\frac{1}{3}$ or $\frac{2}{6}$?
same

Ask: Can you explain why the thirds are the same in the top row? [The two sixths would fit into the thirds.]

Fractions of a square. Draw two squares freehand. Ask the child to divide one square into halves using a vertical line. Then ask her to divide the other square into halves using a diagonal line. See the left figures below. Ask: If these are sandwiches, which half is larger? [They are equal.]

Repeat for fourths. See the right figures below.

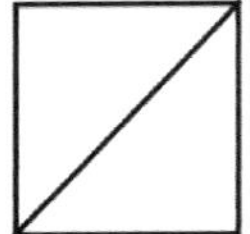
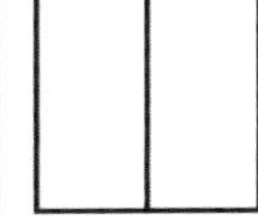

Halves

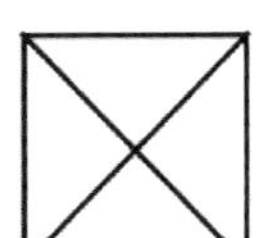
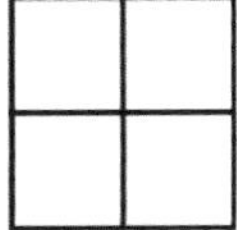

Fourths or quarters

In conclusion. Ask: What is another word for fourth? [quarter] What is half of 16? [8] What is a quarter of 16? [4] What is one fourth of 16? [4]

EXPLANATIONS:

Enrichment Lesson 70: More Dividing Triangles

OBJECTIVES:

1. To divide an equilateral triangle into two other arrangements

MATERIALS:

1. Fraction chart
2. Worksheet 39, More Dividing Triangles
3. Drawing board
4. T-square and 30-60 triangle
5. 4-in-1 ruler
6. **Extra paper and colored pencils or crayons**

ACTIVITIES FOR TEACHING:

Warm-up. With the fraction chart in view of the child, ask: How many thirds do you need to make a whole? [3] How many sixths do you need to make a whole? [6] How many halves do you need to make a whole? [2] How many sixths do you need to make a half? [3]

Ask: What is another word for fourth? [quarter] What is half of 12? [6] What is a quarter of 12? [3] What is one fourth of 12? [3]

Ask: What does a centimeter ruler do? [It measures the length of something in centimeters.] What is perimeter? [the length around the outside of a shape]

Ask: When looking at a tetrahedron and a square pyramid ask: Which pyramid has all faces congruent? [tetrahedron] Which pyramid has four congruent faces? [They both do.]

Worksheet 39. Give the child the drawing board with the worksheet attached, T-square, 30-60 triangle, and 4-in-1 ruler.

Tell the child to follow the instructions and complete the worksheet. The solutions are shown on the next page.

Tell her that both figures start out as equilateral triangles divided into fourths. Ask: What is each fourth in the first figure divided into? [sixths] What is each fourth in the second figure divided into? [fourths]

EXPLANATIONS:

This the first of several enrichment lessons designed to bring the world of math into everyday life. If necessary because of time restraints, the lesson may be omitted without loss of continuity.

ACTIVITIES FOR TEACHING:

EXPLANATIONS:

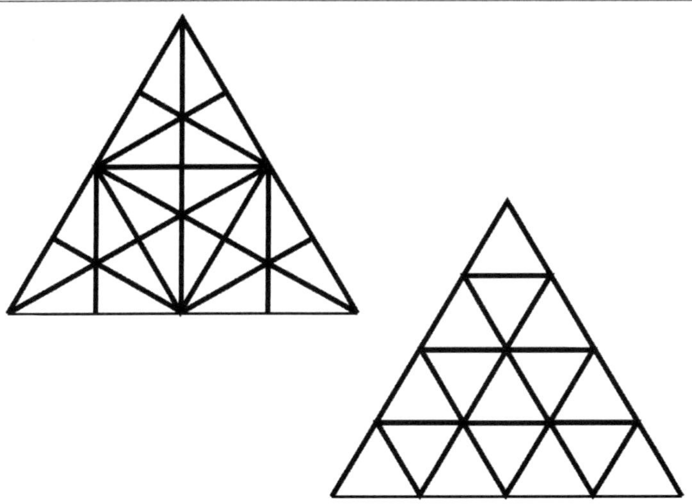

How many small congruent triangles are in the triangle above? __24__

How many small congruent triangles are in the triangle at the right? __16__

Original design. Give the child extra paper and suggest that she make her own design using the drawing tools and colored pencils or crayons.

In conclusion. Ask: After dividing the triangles into equal parts, which triangle do you like better?

Lesson 71: Drawing a Star in a Hexagon

OBJECTIVES:

1. To practice following picture directions
2. To enjoy geometry through drawing stars

MATERIALS:

1. Fraction chart
2. Worksheet 40, Drawing a Star in a Hexagon
3. Drawing board
4. T-square and 30-60 triangle

ACTIVITIES FOR TEACHING:

Warm-up. With the fraction chart in view of the child, ask: How many thirds do you need to make a whole? [3] How many sixths do you need to make a whole? [6] How many halves do you need to make a whole? [2] How many sixths do you need to make a half? [3]

Ask: What is another word for fourth? [quarter] What is half of 12? [6] What is a quarter of 12? [3] What is one fourth of 12? [3]

Ask: What is perimeter? [the length around the outside of a shape]

Worksheet 40. Give the child the drawing board with the worksheet attached, T-square, and 30-60 triangle.

Constructing the star. Explain to the child that the small figures along the left side on the worksheet show him how to make a star in a hexagon. More detailed instructions are given below.

Start by drawing a horizontal line through the hexagon as shown in the left figure below. Then draw the two 60° angle lines as shown below on the right. The triangle is flipped over to draw the second line.

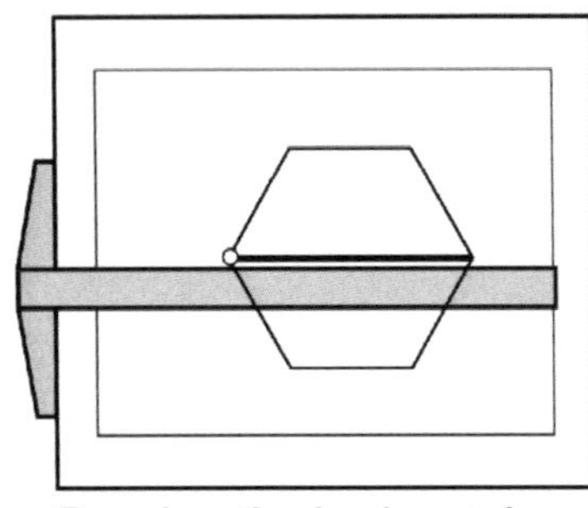

Drawing the horizontal diagonal.

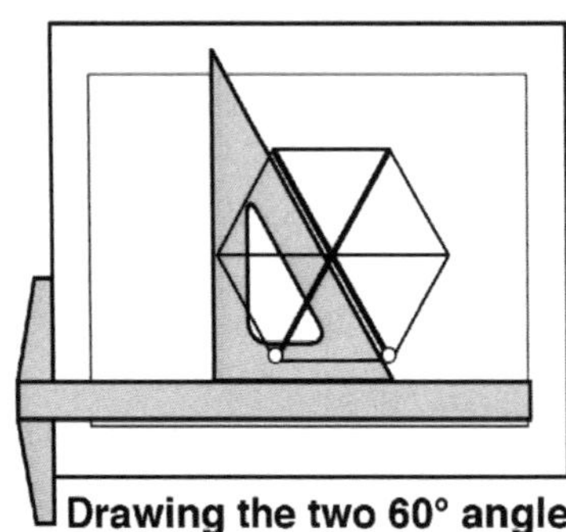

Drawing the two 60° angle diagonals.

EXPLANATIONS:

The first half of these RightStart™ Mathematics lessons referred to the child as a female and the second half refers to the child as a male.

ACTIVITIES FOR TEACHING:

Next draw a vertical diagonal as shown below on the left.

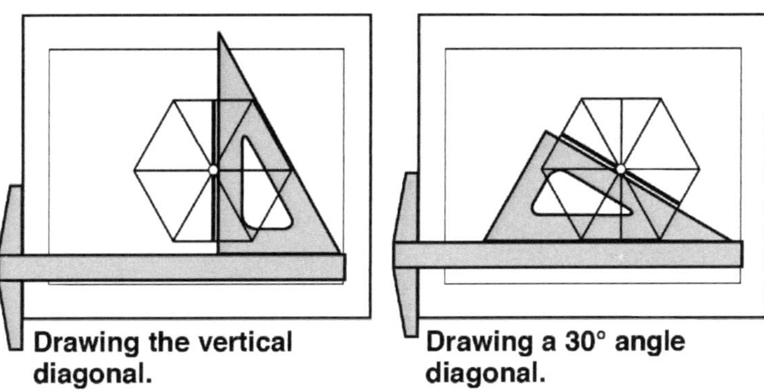

Drawing the vertical diagonal.

Drawing a 30° angle diagonal.

Draw a 30° diagonal as shown above on the right. Flip the triangle over and draw the other 30° diagonal as shown below on the left.

Next draw some of the short 30° lines for the sides of the star. See the figure below on the right.

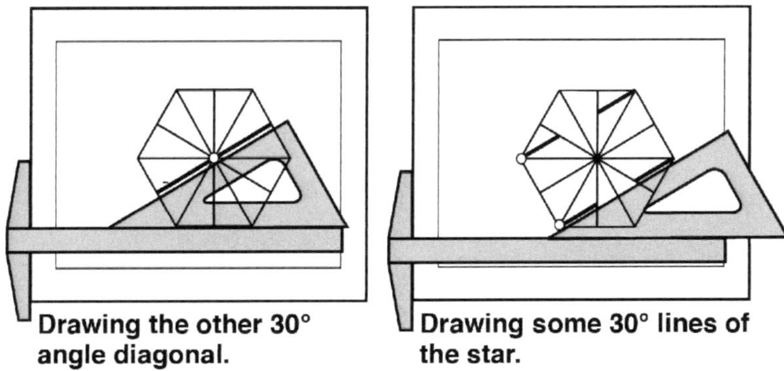

Drawing the other 30° angle diagonal.

Drawing some 30° lines of the star.

Flip the triangle over and draw the other four 30° sides. See the figure below on the left. Draw the four vertical lines with the 90° angle of the triangle. See the right figure below.

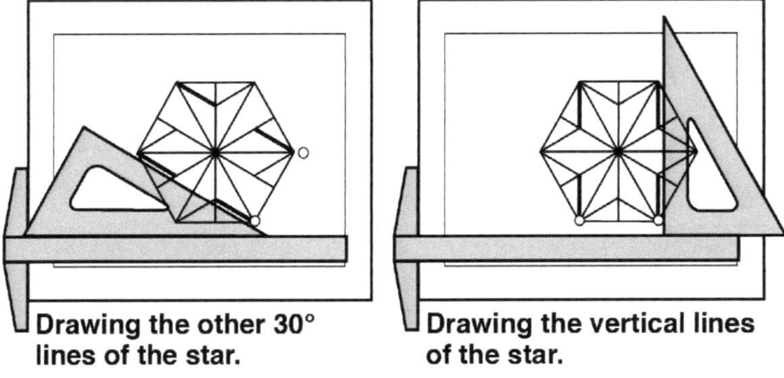

Drawing the other 30° lines of the star.

Drawing the vertical lines of the star.

In conclusion. Ask: Which lines are easier to draw, those with just the T-square or those with the T-square and triangle?

EXPLANATIONS:

This star will be used in the next lesson.

Lesson 72: Drawing Another Star in a Hexagon

OBJECTIVES:

1. To review measuring inches with a ruler
2. To practice following picture directions
3. To enjoy geometry through drawing stars

MATERIALS:

1. Worksheet 41, Drawing Another Star in a Hexagon
2. Drawing board, T-square, and 30-60 triangle
3. 4-in-1 ruler and Tiles
4. Math journal
5. Worksheet 40, Drawing a Star in a Hexagon

ACTIVITIES FOR TEACHING:

Warm-up. Ask: How many fifths do you need to make a whole? [5] How many ninths do you need to make a whole? [9] How many halves do you need to make a whole? [2] How many tenths do you need to make a half? [5]

Ask: What is another word for fourth? [quarter] What is half of 16? [8] What is a quarter of 20? [5] What is one fourth of 20? [5]

Worksheet 41. Give the child the drawing board with the worksheet attached, T-square, 30-60 triangle, 4-in-1 ruler and tiles.

Reviewing inches. Show the child a tile and say: An edge of a tile is 1 inch. Tell him to use his tiles to measure one or more sides of the hexagon on his worksheet. See the figure below.

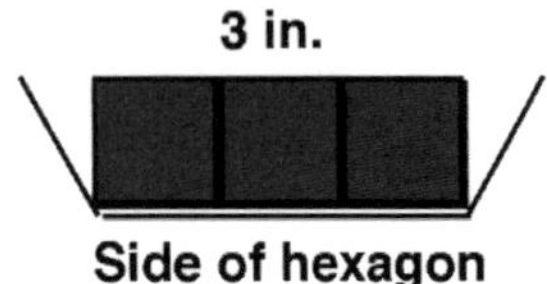

Tell him to take his 4-in-1 ruler and find the inch side with the word "INCH" in the corner. Tell him to measure the row of 3 tiles. Ask: What measurement does the ruler show? [3 inches] See below.

Ask him to measure each of the sides of the hexagon on the worksheet with his ruler. See top of next page. Ask: Did you get the same answers as you got with the tiles? [yes]

EXPLANATIONS:

Even if you do not use inches (or centimeters) in everyday life, they can help children realize that the size of a unit used for measuring is important.

ACTIVITIES FOR TEACHING:

EXPLANATIONS:

0 1 2 3 4 5 6 7 8 9 10
INCH

Writing equations. Write the following fractions and tell the child to write and solve the equations in his math journal.

9 in. and $8\frac{1}{2}$ in. [$9 + 8\frac{1}{2} = 17\frac{1}{2}$ in.]

$6\frac{1}{2}$ in. and $6\frac{1}{2}$ in. and $6\frac{1}{2}$ in. [$6\frac{1}{2} + 6\frac{1}{2} + 6\frac{1}{2} = 19\frac{1}{2}$ in.]

Then ask him to write the next problems as multiplication equations.

In writing multiplication equations, the subject being duplicated is written first, followed by the number of times.

3 pieces each $6\frac{1}{2}$ in. [$6\frac{1}{2} \times 3 = 19\frac{1}{2}$ in.]

3 pieces each $1\frac{1}{2}$ in. [$1\frac{1}{2} \times 3 = 4\frac{1}{2}$ in.]

4 pieces each $5\frac{1}{2}$ in. [$5\frac{1}{2} \times 4 = 22$ in.]

Drawing another star in a hexagon. Tell the child to follow the picture directions on the worksheet to draw another star in a hexagon. See the figure.

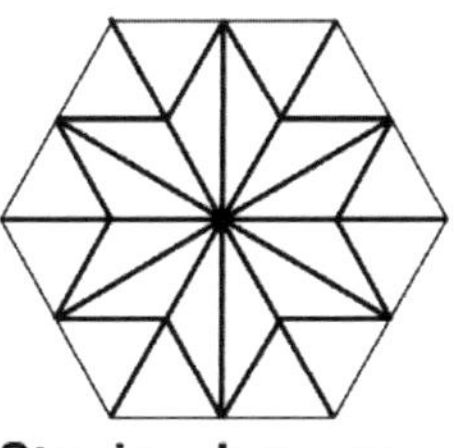

Star in a hexagon.

Tell him to complete the questions on the worksheet. The solutions are shown below.

Perimeter of hexagon.	$P = 3 \times 6 = 18$ in.
Perimeter of star.	$P = 1\frac{1}{2} \times 12 = 18$ in.

Ask: Why do you think the perimeters are the same? [The sides of each vertex of the star is the same a side of the hexagon.]

Tell him to compare this star with the star he made on Worksheet 40. Ask: Which is larger? [first star] How do you know? [measuring a side]

This star and that of the last lesson will be used for comparison and a review of symmetry in upcoming lessons.

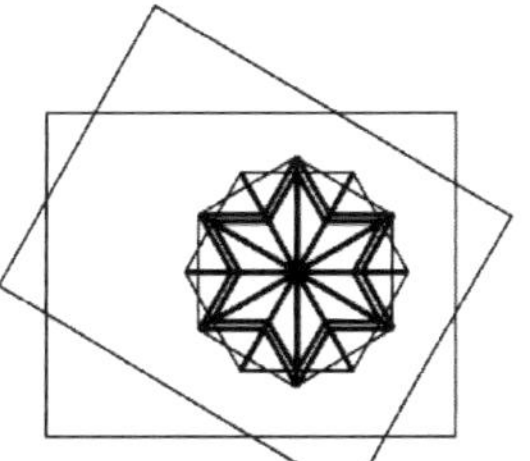

The two stars superimposed.

Tell him to put the first star on top of the second star as shown and hold them up to the light so he can see it superimposed.

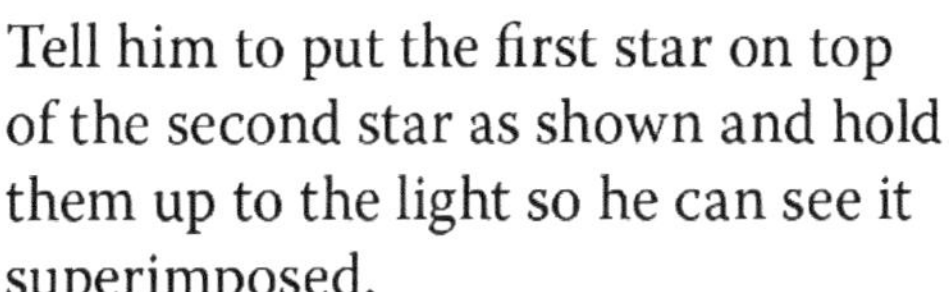

In conclusion. Ask: If you had measured the hexagons in centimeters rather than inches, would the perimeter be different? [The number of centimeters would be greater.]

Lesson 73: Tessellating

OBJECTIVES:

1. To learn the term *regular polygon*
2. To learn the terms *tessellating* and *tessellate*
3. To discover that some figures tessellate
4. To review line of symmetry

MATERIALS:

1. Geometry panels
2. Geometry reflector
3. Worksheet 42, Tessellating
4. **Colored pencils or crayons**

ACTIVITIES FOR TEACHING:

Warm-up. Ask: If you measure a hexagon in centimeters rather than inches, would the perimeter be different? [The number of centimeters would be greater.]

Ask: How many halves do you need to make a whole? [2] How many fourths do you need to make a whole? [4] How many eighths do you need to make one? [8] What is the same as 2 one quarters? [one half]

Ask: What does equilateral mean? [equal sides] What is another name for an equilateral parallelogram? [rhombus]

Ask: How many sides does a hexagon have? [6] How many vertices? [6] How many sides does a rhombus have? [4] How many vertices? [4]

Geometry panels. Give the child the geometry panels. Tell him to look at the triangles. Ask: Are the sides equal? [yes] Are the angles equal? [yes] Say: A *regular polygon* means that all the sides and angles are equal. Repeat for the square, pentagon, and hexagon. Ask: Which of the geometry panels are regular polygons? [all of them]

Tessellating with squares. Tell him that today he will discover which of these polygons could be used to cover an area without overlapping or leaving gaps. Tell him that this is called *tessellating.*

Tell him to use his squares to cover an area. Ask him to find more than one way. See the figures below. Ask: Did the squares *tessellate*? [yes]

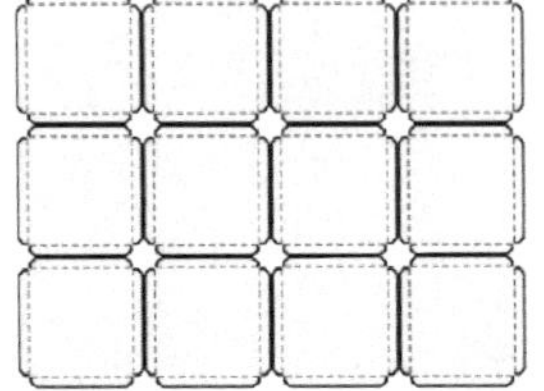

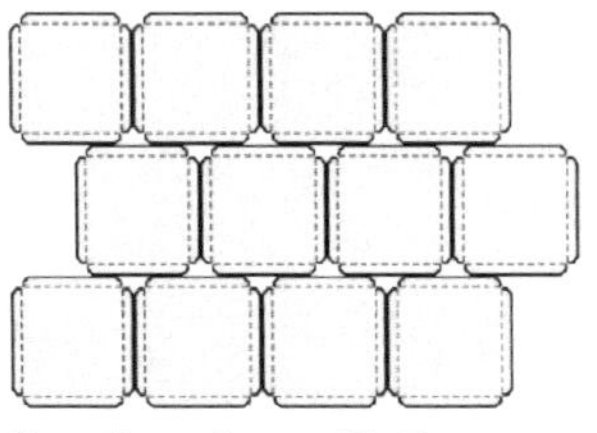

Tessellating with squares. **Another tessellation.**

EXPLANATIONS:

Remind the child that an angle is the measure of space between two vertices.

The goniometer may be a useful tool in showing the measure of the space between two vertices. This measurement is labeled as a *degree.*

ACTIVITIES FOR TEACHING:

EXPLANATIONS:

Tessellating with triangles. Tell him to use his equilateral triangles to cover an area. See the figure at the right. Ask: Do the triangles tessellate? [yes] Did they all fit facing the same way? [No, some were up side down.]

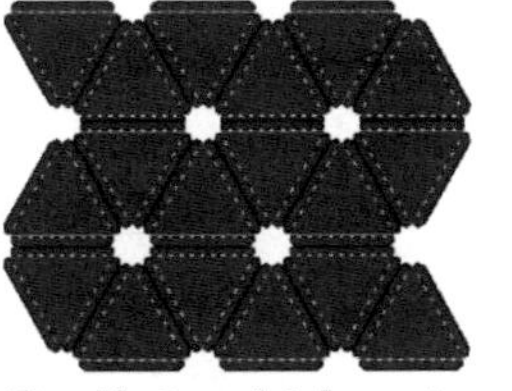

Equilateral triangles do tessellate.

Tessellating with pentagons. Tell the child to tessellate with the pentagons. Ask him to explain what happened. See left figure below for an attempt. Ask: Do these pentagons tessellate? [no]

There are some special pentagons that do tessellate.

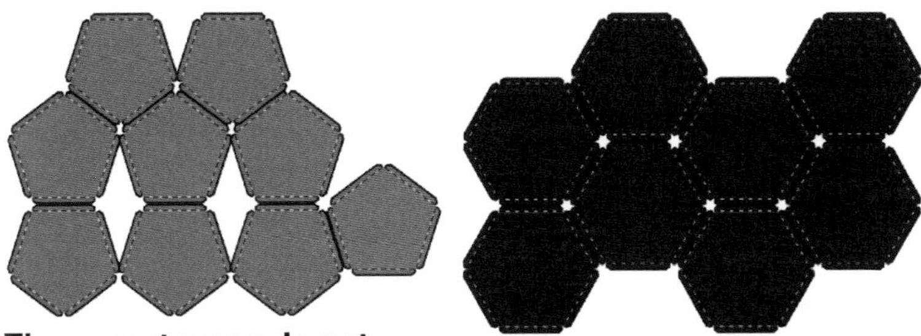

These pentagons do not tessellate. **Hexagons do tessellate.**

Tessellating with hexagons. Repeat for hexagons. See the right figure above. Tell the child that bees tessellate the cells they use to store honey. They are called honeycombs.

Geometry reflectors. Give the child the geometry reflector. Review that a line of symmetry is a line of reflection, the line that acts as a mirror. Tell him to find lines of symmetry on the geometry panels.

Worksheet 42. Give the child the worksheet and ask: What does the drawing on the worksheet look like? [a hexagon star tessellated] Tell him to draw outlines of the figures listed on the worksheet without using drawing tools. He can use colored pencils or crayons.

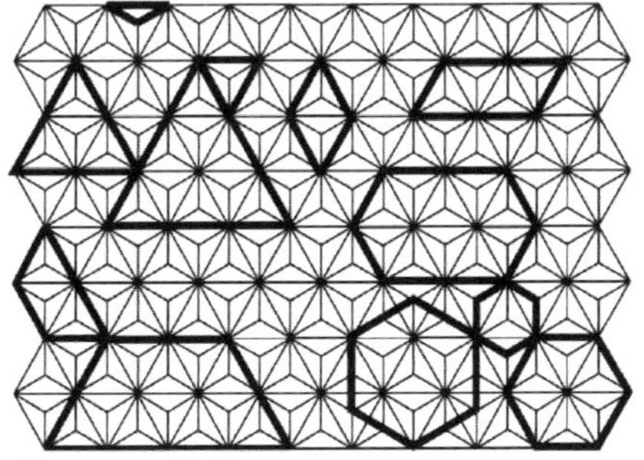

Some solutions.

Some solutions are shown above on the right.

In conclusion. Ask: Can you find tessellations in the room or building? Will sheets of paper tessellate? [yes] Ask the child to name some figures that will tessellate. [squares, rectangles, triangles, hexagons]

Lesson 74: Geometry Terms and Symmetry

OBJECTIVES:

1. To review the terms *right angle* and *right triangle*
2. To review the terms *quadrilateral, trapezoid,* and other geometry terms
3. To organize polygons in a Venn diagram
4. To record polygon characteristics

MATERIALS:

1. Paper 30-60 Triangle Replicas (Appendix p. 3)*
2. Worksheet 43, Geometry Terms and Symmetry
3. Geometry reflector

ACTIVITIES FOR TEACHING:

Warm-up. Ask: If you measure a hexagon in inches rather than centimeters, would the perimeter be different? [The number of inches would be less.]

Ask: What does equilateral mean? [equal sides] How many sides does a hexagon have? [6] How many angles? [6] How many sides does a rhombus have? [4] How many angles? [4] What does regular polygon mean? [all sides and angles are equal]

Geometry terms. Tell the child that today we will discuss geometry words. Show the paper replica 30-60 triangles and ask: What is this called? [30-60 triangle] How many sides does it have? [3] How many angles does it have? [3] Point to each angle and ask for its name. [30°, 60°, 90°]

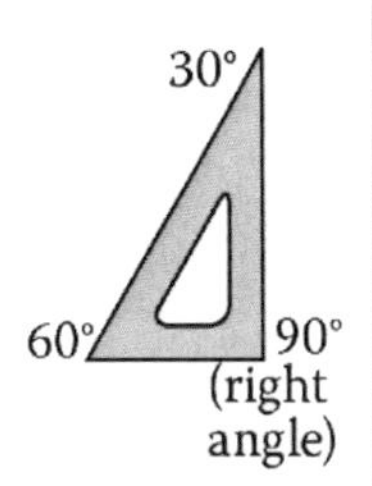

Tell him to show a 90° angle with his elbows or with thumb and hand. Remind him that a 90° angle is also called a *right angle.* Tell him that a triangle with a right angle is called a *right triangle.*

Tell the child to combine the two right triangles to make an equilateral triangle. See figure at right. Say: Name the angles the new triangle created. [60°, 60°, 60°] Ask: How do you know the third angle is 60°? [30° and 30° is 60°]

Equilateral triangle

Tell the child to make a rectangle with the two triangles. See the figure on the right. Ask: How many sides does the rectangle have? [4] How many angles? [4] What are the angles? [all 90°] Have him show parallel lines with his arms. Ask: Do you see any parallel sides in the rectangle? [two pairs]

Rectangle

Tell him to put the two triangles together to make a parallelogram. Ask: Are these angles all equal? [no] Does the parallelogram have parallel lines? [two pairs]

Parallelogram

EXPLANATIONS:

*Cut apart the triangles on the appendix page.

ACTIVITIES FOR TEACHING:

Tell the child to use the two triangles to make a polygon with four sides. See the figure at the right. Tell him that polygons with four sides are called *quadrilaterals.*

Quadrilateral

Draw the trapezoids shown on the right and tell him they are *trapezoids.* Explain: Trapezoids have only one pair of parallel sides.

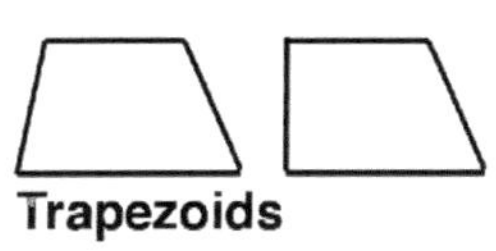

Trapezoids

Venn diagram. Draw the Venn diagram with the underlined words, shown below. Read the list of polygons from the chart and ask the child to write them in the correct places.

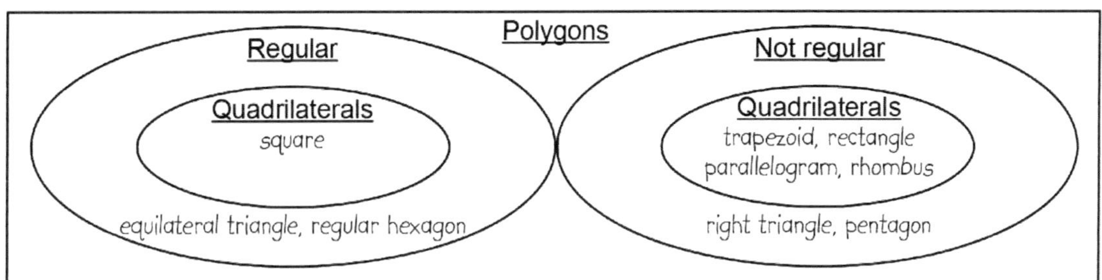

Venn diagram for polygons.

Worksheet 43. Give the child the worksheet and geometry reflector. Complete the first row together. Ask: What polygon are we looking for? [rectangle] What letter is the rectangle? [G] Write G in the box. Are all sides equal? [no] Write "no" in the next box. Are all angles equal? [yes] Write "yes" in the next box. Tell him to use his reflector to check for symmetry. Continue the row and tell him to complete the worksheet. The completed chart is shown below.

Polygon	Letter	= sides	= angles	Regular	Symmetry	ll lines
Rectangle	**G**	**no**	**yes**	**no**	**yes**	**2**
Rhombus	**F**	**yes**	**no**	**no**	**yes**	**2**
Regular hexagon	**D**	**yes**	**yes**	**yes**	**yes**	**3**
Pentagon	**A**	**no**	**no**	**no**	**yes**	**0**
Right triangle	**H**	**no**	**no**	**no**	**no**	**0**
Equilateral triangle	**C**	**yes**	**yes**	**yes**	**yes**	**0**
Parallelogram	**I**	**no**	**no**	**no**	**no**	**2**
Square	**B**	**yes**	**yes**	**yes**	**yes**	**2**
Trapezoid	**E**	**no**	**no**	**no**	**no**	**1**

Answers to the other questions: **4, 4, 3, regular hexagon, 5, 4.**

In conclusion. Say: Name some quadrilaterals. [square, trapezoid, rhombus, rectangle] Name some regular polygons. [square, equilateral triangle, regular hexagon]

EXPLANATIONS:

There is another parallelogram that can be made with the two triangles.

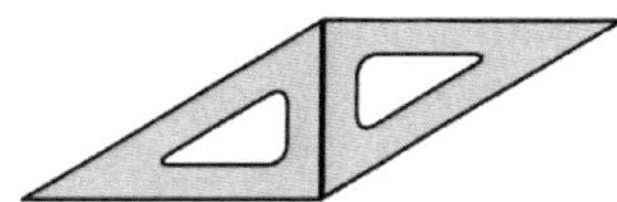

Terms trapezoid (trapezium in British English) and quadrilateral were introduced in earlier levels.

Some pentagons are regular, however not all pentagons are regular.

Some children might benefit by placing a plain sheet of paper below the row they are working on.

Lesson 75: Assessment Review 2

OBJECTIVES:

1. To review recent topics

MATERIALS:

1. Worksheet 44, Assessment Review 2

ACTIVITIES FOR TEACHING:

Worksheet 44. Give the child the worksheet.

Oral problems. Tell him to listen to the problems and write only the answers on the worksheet. Read each problem twice. Answers shown on the next page.

$47 + 15 =$

$110 - 11 =$

$61 + 39 =$

Written problems. Have the child solve the following problems on the worksheet. Answers shown on the next page.

$4\frac{1}{2} + 2\frac{1}{2} =$

$5 \times 4 =$

$1 - \frac{1}{2} =$

Geometry. Tell the child to draw a line to match the drawing to the words on the worksheet. Answers shown on the next page.

Word problem. Read the following story problem to the child:

> Sam had 5729 trees and planted 367 more trees. How many trees does Sam have now?

Tell him to write the equation in the grid provide and solve. Write the answer on the line. Solutions shown on the next page.

Dividing rectangles. Have him divide the rectangles on the worksheet into equal quarters, three different ways. Some possible solutions are shown.

EXPLANATIONS:

ACTIVITIES FOR TEACHING:

Write only the answers.

62

99

100

Write the answers.

$4\frac{1}{2} + 2\frac{1}{2} =$ 7

$5 \times 4 =$ 20

$1 - \frac{1}{2} =$ $\frac{1}{2}$

Draw lines to match each drawing to the words.

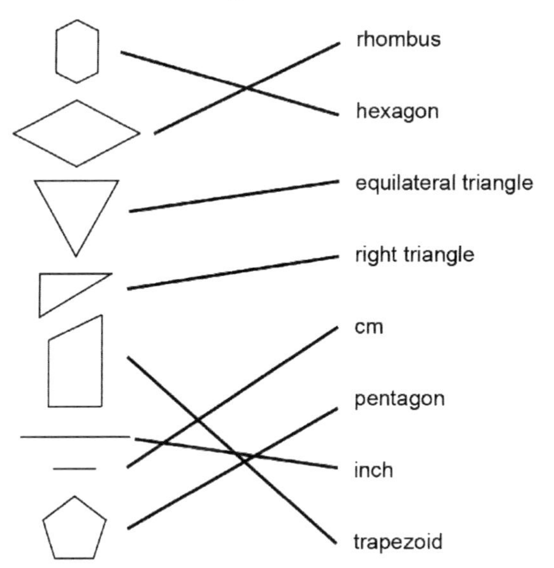

Sam had 5729 trees and planted 367 more trees. How many trees does Sam have now? 6096 trees

$$\begin{array}{r} 5729 \\ +\ 367 \\ \hline 6096 \end{array}$$

Divide the rectangle into equal quarters three different ways.

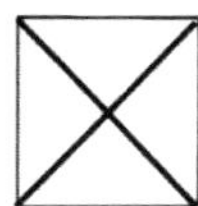 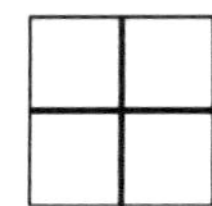 

EXPLANATIONS:

There are many more solutions for the last problem.

Lesson 76: Tessellation Art and Game Day

OBJECTIVES:

1. To enjoy geometry through tessellations
2. To continue to develop skills through playing math card games

MATERIALS:

1. Worksheet 45, Tessellation Art
2. **Colored pencils or crayons**
3. *Math Card Games* book, S6, S9, and S33
4. Math journal

ACTIVITIES FOR TEACHING:

Worksheet 45. Give the child the worksheet. Ask: Can you find 3 equilateral triangles of different sizes? A triangle that is not equilateral? A rhombus? A parallelogram that is not a rhombus? Two trapezoids of different sizes? Three regular hexagons of different sizes? One hexagon that is not regular? See below for possible solutions.

Tell the child he can create his own designs on the tessellation using colored pencils or crayons.

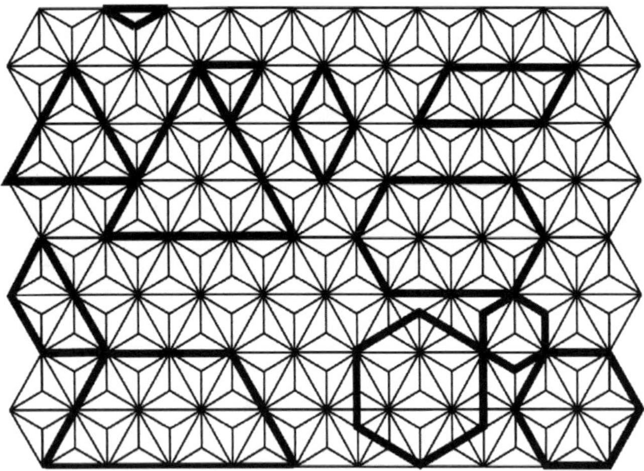

Some solutions for the oral questions.

EXPLANATIONS:

ACTIVITIES FOR TEACHING:	EXPLANATIONS:

Subtraction Memory game. To provide practice for the facts involving subtracting 2, have the child play the Subtraction Memory game, found in the *Math Card Games* book, S6. Use 2 as the subtrahend, the number being subtracted.

Zero Corners™ game. Have the child play the Zero Corners game, found in the *Math Card Games* book, S9. Tell him to start with a score of 200 and write the differences in his math journal.

Subtracting from One Hundred game. Have the child play Subtracting from One Hundred, found in the *Math Card Games* book, S33.

Lesson 77: Assessment 2

OBJECTIVES:

1. To assess recent topics

MATERIALS:

1. Worksheet 46, Assessment 2

ACTIVITIES FOR TEACHING:

Worksheet 46. Give the child the worksheet.

Oral problems. Tell him to listen to the problems and write only the answers on the worksheet. Read each problem twice. Answers shown on the next page.

$53 + 18 =$

$120 - 21 =$

$52 + 28 =$

Written problems. Have the child solve the following problems on the worksheet. Answers shown on the next page.

$3\frac{1}{2} + 4\frac{1}{2} =$

$4 \times 3 =$

$1\frac{1}{2} - \frac{1}{2} =$

Geometry. Tell the child to draw a line to match the drawing to the words on the worksheet. Answers shown on the next page.

Word problem. Read the following story problem to the child:

> The library received 256 new books. They already had 7692. How many books does the library have now?

Tell him to write the equation in the grid provide and solve. Write the answer on the line. Solutions shown on the next page.

Dividing rectangles. Have him divide the square on the worksheet into equal fourths, three different ways. Some possible solutions are shown.

EXPLANATIONS:

ACTIVITIES FOR TEACHING:

Write only the answers.

71

99

80

Write the answers.

$3\frac{1}{2} + 4\frac{1}{2} =$ 8

$4 \times 3 =$ 12

$1\frac{1}{2} - \frac{1}{2} =$ 1

Draw lines to match each drawing to the words.

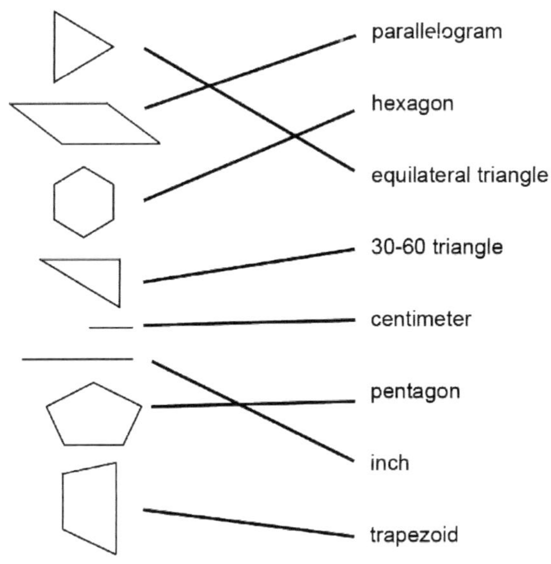

The library received 256 new books. They already had 7692. How many books does the library have now? 7948 books

	7	6	9	2
+		2	5	6
	7	9	4	8

Divide the square into equal fourths three different ways.

  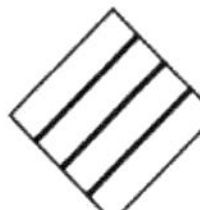

EXPLANATIONS:

There are many more solutions for the last problem.

Lesson 78: Reading Scales

OBJECTIVES:

1. To learn to read scales

MATERIALS:

1. Tally sticks
2. Worksheet 47, Reading Scales
3. **A thermometer,** optional

ACTIVITIES FOR TEACHING:

EXPLANATIONS:

Warm-up. Ask the child to count by 10s to 200 [10, 20, 30, . . . , 200] and by 5s to 100. [5, 10, 15, . . . , 100]

Ask: If you measure a square in centimeters rather than inches, would the perimeter be different? [The number of centimeters would be greater.]

Ask: How many sides does a rhombus have? [4] How many angles? [4] How many sides does a hexagon have? [6] How many angles? [6]

Ask: What does equilateral mean? [equal sides] What is another name for an equilateral parallelogram? [rhombus]

Scale with one mark at each number. Draw the following curved scale:

First draw arc, center dot; write 40, 50, 60.

Then draw marks between numbers; write 45, 55.

Finally draw four evenly-spaced marks between numbers.

Point to the scale and ask the child: Where have you seen such a scale? [speedometer or thermostat] Why do you think some numbers are missing? [not enough space] Is there a mark for every missing number? [yes]

Show him how such a scale works. Place one end of a tally stick at 40 and the other end at the center. See the figure at the right. Repeat for 45 and 50.

Scale showing 40.

Tell the child to set the tally stick at 55. Ask: Could you show 57?

Ask the child to show 43, 59, and 48. Set the scale at various numbers and ask him to name them.

Scale with marks at even numbers. Draw the scale shown at the right:

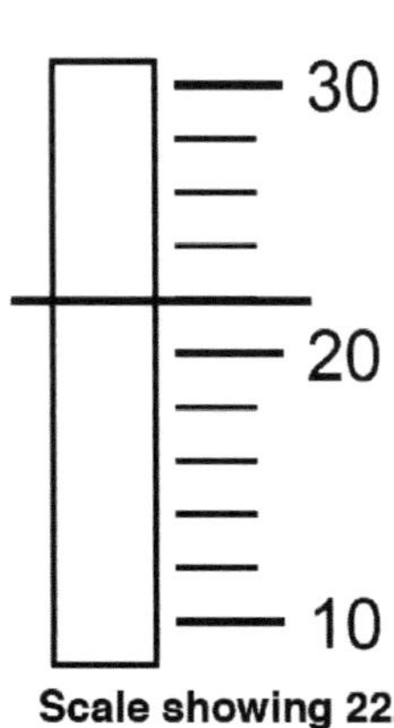

Scale showing 22.

ACTIVITIES FOR TEACHING:

Ask: Is there a mark for every missing number? [no] Which numbers have marks? [even numbers] Tell the child to place the tally stick at the number 22 as shown. Repeat for 12 and 28. Place the tally stick at 14 and ask the child to read it. Repeat for 26 and 18.

Scale with marks at multiples of five. Draw the scale shown below:

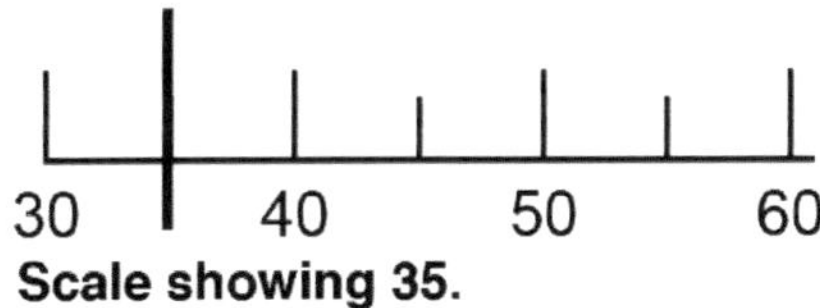

Scale showing 35.

Ask: What numbers have marks on this scale? [multiples of five, or counting by fives] How can anyone know what kind of counting to do when they see a scale? Explain that most people guess what kind of counting they need to do and then try it out. If that method does not work, they try other methods until one is found that works.

Place a tally stick at 35, as shown, and ask the child to read it. Repeat for 45 and 30. Then ask him to find 55 and 40.

Worksheet 47. Give the child the worksheet. Remind him that when drawing lines in the curved scales, start at the number and draw toward the center point. Then draw the arrow. The solutions are shown below.

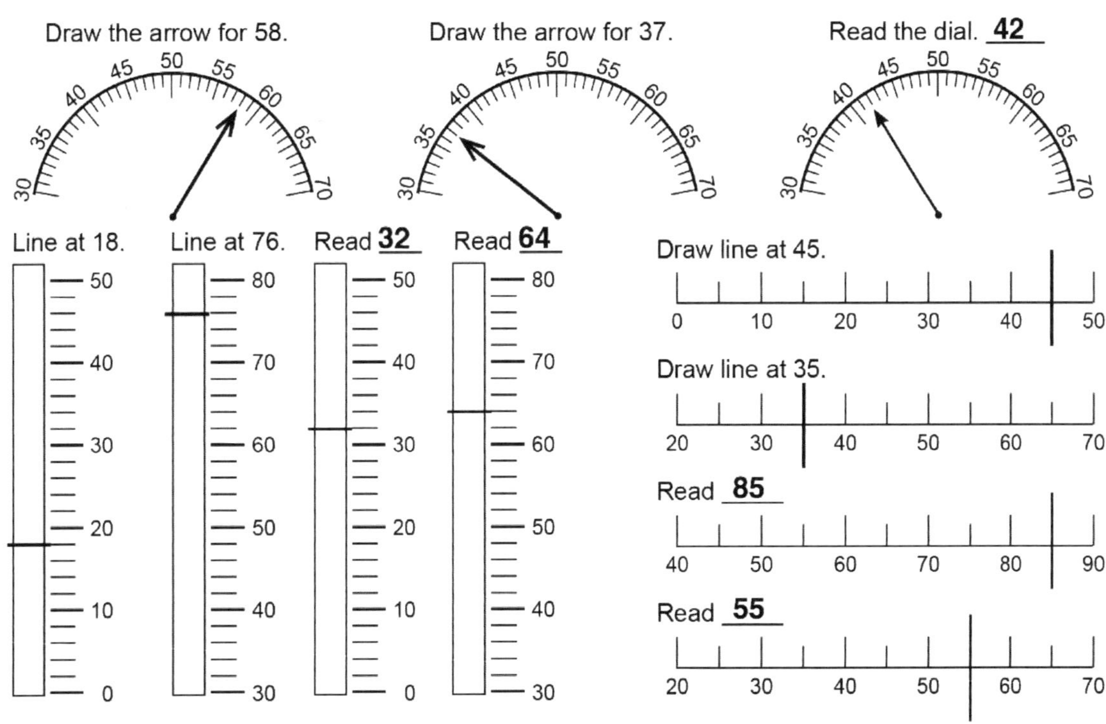

In conclusion. Ask: In a scale that counts by twos, where would you find 75? [halfway between two marks; 74 and 76]

EXPLANATIONS:

If possible, ask the child to read a thermometer several times during the day.

You might explain that as the temperature goes up, the liquid in a thermometer expands and moves up. If a thermometer is available, demonstrate this phenomenon by immersing it in hot and cold water.

Lesson 79: Drawing a Clock

OBJECTIVES:

1. To review the term *octagon*
2. To make a clock with hour marks

MATERIALS:

1. Geared clock
2. Worksheet 48, Drawing a Clock
3. Drawing board*
4. T-square and 30-60 triangle

ACTIVITIES FOR TEACHING:

Warm-up. Ask: In a scale that counts by fives, where would you find 73? [about halfway between two marks; 70 and 75]

Ask the child to count by 10s to 300 starting at 100 [100, 110, 120, . . . , 300] and by 5s to 200 starting at 100. [100, 105, 110, . . . , 200]

Ask: How many sides does a rhombus have? [4] How many angles? [4] How many sides does a pentagon have? [5] How many angles? [5]

Ask: What does equilateral mean? [equal sides] What is another name for an equilateral parallelogram? [rhombus]

Reviewing time telling. Set the hands of the geared clock to various o'clock positions and ask the child to name the times. Then ask: What o'clock would it be when the hands form a right angle? [3:00 and 9:00]

Ask: What number is at the top of the clock? [12] What number is at the bottom? [6] Tell him to move his arms to show these positions as you say the numbers.

Worksheet 48. Give the child the drawing board with the worksheet attached, T-square, and 30-60 triangle. Tell the child that clocks sometimes have an *octagon* around them. Ask: How many sides does an octagon have? [8] How many angles does an octagon have? [8] Is this octagon a regular octagon? [yes] Can you think of a street sign that is an octagon? [stop signs]

Tell the child that today he will draw the hour marks on the clock on the worksheet using the drawing tools. He will also write the numbers for the hours and the numbers for the minutes.

EXPLANATIONS:

*The drawing board will be used in the "portrait" view. See the figures on the next page.

ACTIVITIES FOR TEACHING:

Tell him to draw first the hour marks for the 9 and the 3 as shown below on the left. Then he can draw the hour marks for the 12 and 6. See the right figure below.

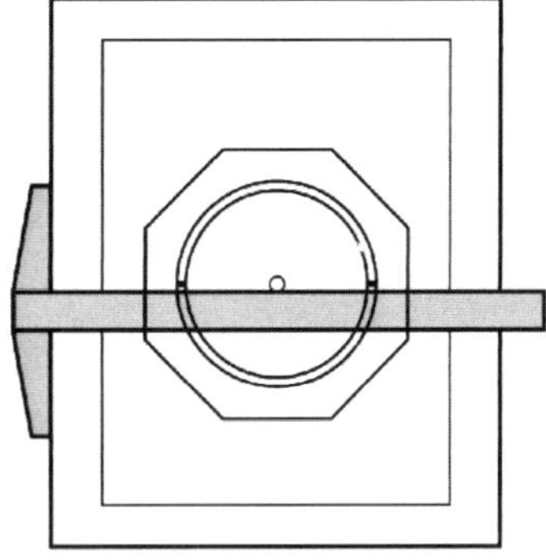

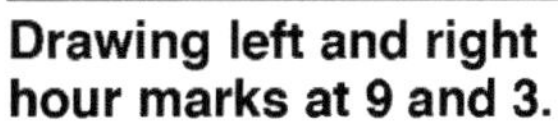

Drawing left and right hour marks at 9 and 3.

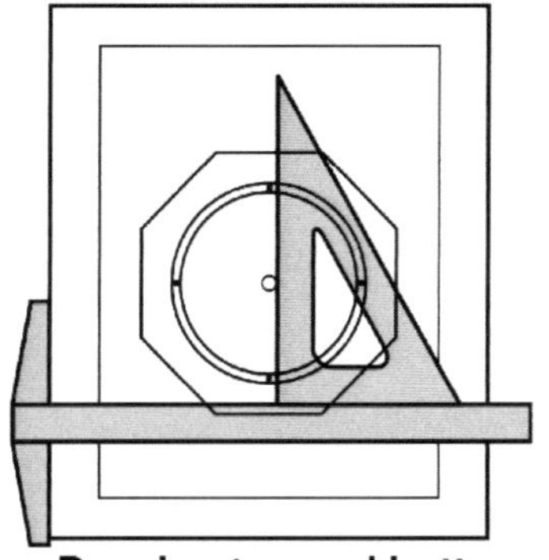

Drawing top and bottom hour marks at 12 and 6.

Ask: Where do you need to draw the marks with the 60° angle? [at 11 and 5 and at 1 and 7] See the left figure below. Ask: Where do you draw the marks with the 30° angle? [at 10 and 4 and at 8 and 2] See the right figure below.

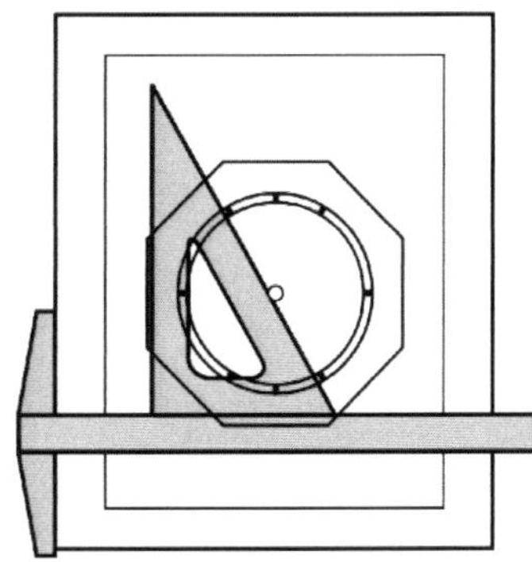

Draw the marks at 60°: 11 and 5 and at 1 and 7.

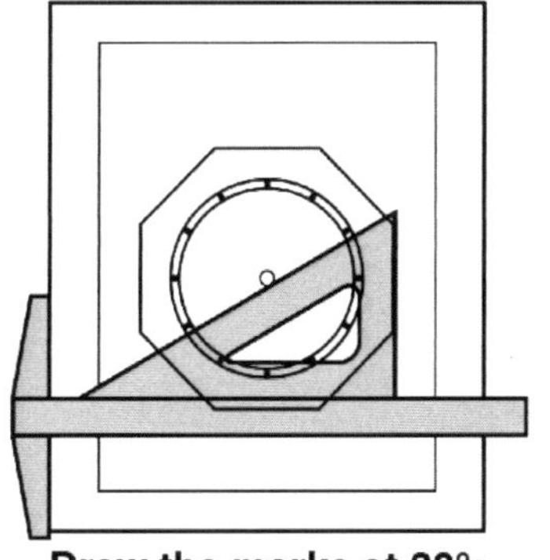

Draw the marks at 30°: 10 and 4 and at 8 and 2.

Writing the numbers on the clock. Tell the child that the clock starts at the top with an invisible zero. So write the number 1 at the first hour mark to the right of the invisible zero, inside the circle. Tell him to write all the hour numbers 1 to 12 around his clock. See the figure on the right.

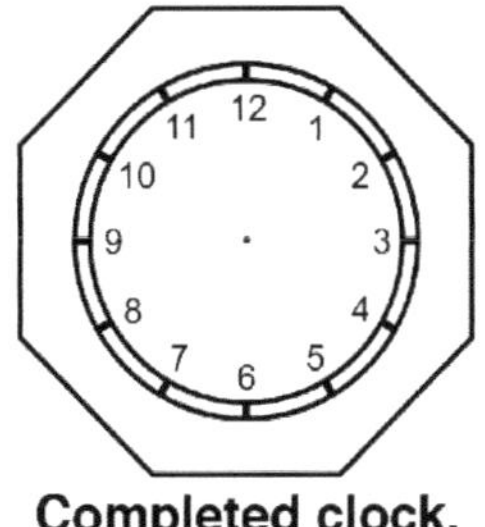

Completed clock.

In conclusion. Ask: How many hour numbers does a clock show? [12] How many hours are in a day? [24]

EXPLANATIONS:

This clock will be used in the next few lessons.

Lesson 80: Hours in a Day

OBJECTIVES:

1. To learn the terms *a.m.* and *p.m.*
2. To associate activities to times during the day

MATERIALS:

1. Worksheet 48, Drawing a Clock
2. **Paper with direction words, North, East, South, and West***
3. Worksheet 49, Hours in a Day

ACTIVITIES FOR TEACHING:

Warm-up. Ask: How many hour numbers does a clock show? [12]

Ask: In a scale that counts by twos, where would you find 47? [about halfway between two marks; 46 and 48]

Ask: If you measure a octagon in inches rather than centimeters, would the perimeter be different? [The number of inches would be less.]

Ask: How many sides does a octagon have? [8] How many angles? [8] How many sides does a hexagon have? [6] How many angles? [6]

Hour numbers. Tell the child to look at the clock he made in the previous lesson as shown on the right. Ask: How many hour numbers, or numbers inside the circles, does the clock have? [12] What kind of pattern did you use to write the hour numbers? [around in order] What number is at the top? [12] The bottom? [6]

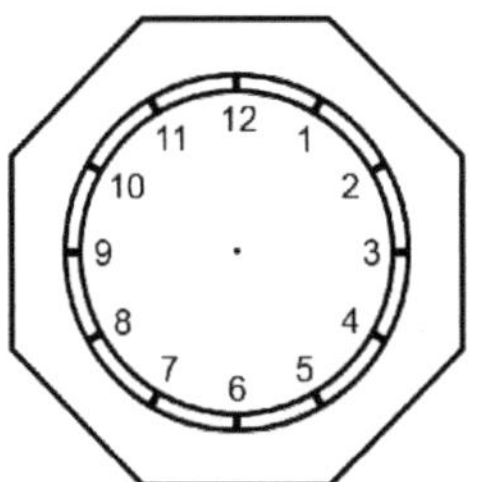

Clock from last lesson.

Ask: What do the numbers 1 to 12 on your clock tell us? [hours] How long is an hour? [They will probably relate it to the length of a TV program.]

Hours in a day. Tell him: Clocks show 12 hours, but they only show half a day. Ask: How many hours are in a whole day? [24] Give him a little history:

> A long time ago before there were any electric lights, the Egyptians wanted some way to measure time. They knew the sun moved in the sky during the day. And they knew the stars moved in the sky at night. To measure time during the day they observed the shadow of a stick, or pointer. In the early morning when the sun rises in the east, the pole's shadow points to the opposite direction, to the west.

EXPLANATIONS:

*Attach paper to the appropriate walls in the room.

ACTIVITIES FOR TEACHING:

EXPLANATIONS:

At noon the shadow points to the north. In the evening at sunset the shadow points to the east. The day was divided into 12 parts, which we call hours.

To measure time at night, the Egyptians observed the motion of the stars. They divided the night into parts. After a while they also divided the night into 12 hours. Midnight is the "middle of the night" because it is generally halfway between sunset and sunrise.

Tell the child that midnight is the beginning of each day and is shown with a 12 at the top of the clock.

Noon is the second most important time on a clock. Noon is generally halfway between sunrise and sunset. It is also shown with a 12 at the top of the clock.

Write a.m. and p.m. Say: So that we can tell whether we talking about day hours or night hours, we use *a.m.* for time between midnight and noon and *p.m.* for time after noon.

Directions. Point out the direction paper on the wall and ask the child to point to the north. Tell the child to point to the direction where the sun rises. [east] Then have him point to the direction where his shadow points at sunrise. [west] Point to where his shadow is at noon. [north] Point to the direction where his shadow points at sunset. [east]

If possible, do these activities at a place in the sunlight where the child can see his shadow.

Daily routine. Tell the child that Grandma eats breakfast at 6 a.m. Ask: Where is that hour on your paper clock? [at 6] Belle eats breakfast at 7 a.m. Where is that hour? [at 7] Colin eats at 6:30. Remind them: Six-thirty is halfway between 6 o'clock and 7 o'clock. Point to the time that Colin eats breakfast. [halfway between 6 and 7] Repeat for 7:30 and 8:00 using familiar names.

Worksheet 49. Give the child the worksheet. Explain to the child that this worksheet shows a day spread out in a line. See below. Ask him: Where is 6 a.m.? [first 6] Where is 6 p.m.? [second 6] Tell him to draw a line from each activity to the time, an example and solutions are shown below.

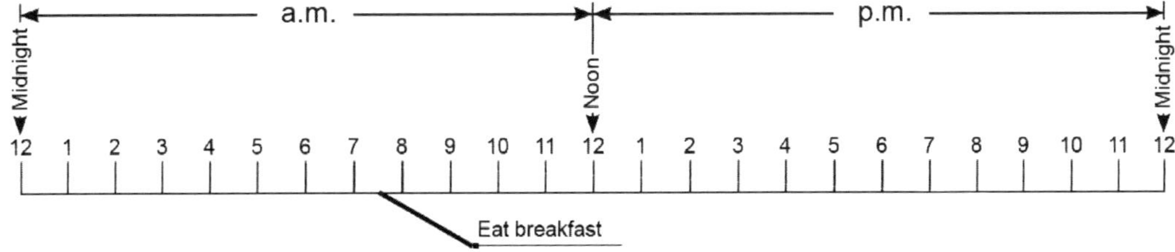

midnight, middle of day, 24, before noon, after noon, 1 hour

In conclusion. Ask: If you were to sleep 10 hours a day, how many hours would you be awake? [14 hours]

Lesson 81: Hours and Minutes on a Clock

OBJECTIVES:

1. To learn the terms *clockwise* and *counterclockwise*
2. To review reading clock set to the hour
3. To learn the placement of the minute numbers

MATERIALS:

1. Worksheet 48, Drawing a Clock
2. Geared clock
3. Set of minute cards, :00 to :55
4. *Math Card Games* book, C11 and C12

ACTIVITIES FOR TEACHING:

Warm-up. Ask: If you were to sleep 10 hours a day, how many hours would you be awake? [14 hours]

Ask: How many hour numbers does a clock show? [12] How many hours are in a day? [24]

Ask: On a scale that counts by twos, where would you find 35? [about halfway between two marks; 34 and 36]

Tell him to count by 2s to 30. [2, 4, 6, . . . , 30]

Tell him to count by 5s to 60. [5, 10, 15, . . . , 60]

Numbers around a clock. Tell the child to look at the clock he made previously on Worksheet 48 as shown below. Tell him to show with his finger how the hour hand would move on his clock during the whole day starting at midnight. Ask: Where did you start? [at 12] What number was next? [1] How many times did your finger go around the clock? [2]

Clock from earlier lesson.

Say: When something goes around in the same direction as the hands on a clock we call it *clockwise.* If something goes in the opposite direction we call it *counterclockwise.* Sometimes the word *counter* means opposite. We turn a lid on a jar clockwise to close it. Ask: What direction would we turn the lid to open it? [counterclockwise]

Reviewing o'clock. Give the child the geared clock and ask: What color are the hour numbers and hour hand?

Finding the hours. Tell the child to point to the hour numbers on the clock as quickly as possible, as you say numbers from 1 to 12 in random order.

Set the clock to 1:00 and ask: What time does it say? [one o'clock] Write 1:00. Explain: The two digits that follow the two dots, or colon, are the minute numbers. When they are both zeroes, we read it as *o'clock.* Repeat for 2:00 and 5:00.

EXPLANATIONS:

ACTIVITIES FOR TEACHING:

EXPLANATIONS:

Ask the child to set the clock to 4:00 and to 6:00. Write 8:00 and 10:00. Ask him to show these on the clock.

The minute hand. Say: Because an hour is quite a long time, each hour was divided into 60 minutes. In the 1500s, a Swiss man, Jost Bürgi, invented the minute hand. He put it on top of the hour hand.

Tell the child that the minute hand uses the same marks on the clock as the hour hand, but there are five minutes between each hour mark. Some clocks show all the minute marks and some do not. The minute hand starts at the top of the clock and takes an hour to go all the way around.

Tell him to move the minute hand on the clock to 12. Now move the minute hand all the way around the clock and watch what happens to the hour hand. [It moves to the next number.] Try it again. Move the minute hand halfway around. What happens to the hour hand? [halfway between two numbers]

The minute clock cards. Give the child a set of minute cards. Tell him to find the o'clock card [:00] and put it at the top of his worksheet clock. Then find the card with a zero and a five and put it at the 1. Say: We read it as *oh five*. Continue with the remaining cards. See the figure at the right.

For the minute number at 1, the child's geared clock might show 5, rather than :05.

When all the cards are in place, ask the child to read them in order. [o'clock, oh 5, 10, 15, . . . , 55]

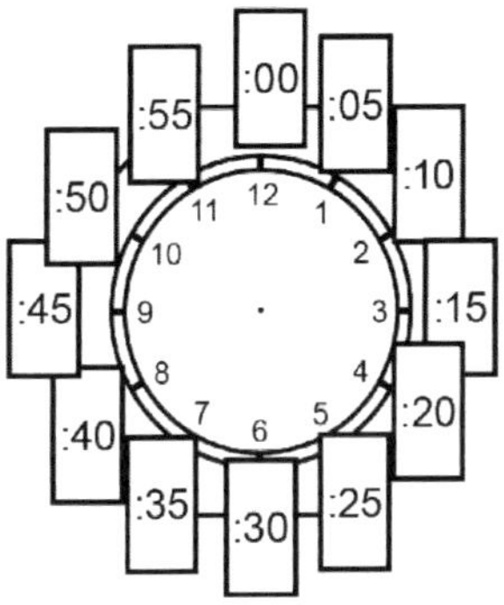

Minute cards around the clock.

Minute Memory game. Tell the child to play Minute Memory, found in the *Math Card Games* book, C11. Tell him to use his own paper clock and the second player can use Clock B found in the *Math Card Games* book, Appendix p. 14. Suggest that he uses the geared clock for reference.

Minute Solitaire. He can also play Minute Solitaire, found in the *Math Card Games* book, C12.

A person learns the minutes' place easier by using a reference rather than counting by 5s each time.

In conclusion. Ask: How many hours in a day? [24] Is 10:00 a.m. in the morning or evening? [morning] How many minutes in an hour? [60] Where is the minute hand at the beginning of an hour? [at the top] In what direction does the minute hand go around a clock? [clockwise]

Lesson 82: Telling Time to Five Minutes

OBJECTIVES:

1. To practice reading clock in five-minute intervals
2. To learn the terms *digital clock* and *analog clock*

MATERIALS:

1. Worksheet 48, Drawing a Clock
2. Set of minute cards
3. Geared clock
4. **A digital clock**
5. Worksheet 50, Telling Time to Five Minutes

ACTIVITIES FOR TEACHING:

Warm-up. Ask: How many hours in one day? [24] Is 7:00 p.m. in the morning or evening? [evening] How many minutes in an hour? [60] Where is the minute hand at the beginning of an hour? [at the top] In what direction do the minute numbers go around a clock? [clockwise]

Ask: How many hour numbers does a clock show? [12] How many hours are in a day? [24]

Ask: If you were to sleep 8 hours a day, how many hours would you be awake? [16 hours]

Tell him to count by 2s to 30. [2, 4, 6, . . . , 30]

Tell him to count by 5s to 60. [5, 10, 15, . . . , 60]

Seeing the tens. Using Worksheet 48, have the child lay out the minute cards around the clock. Then tell him to remove the minute cards from the odd hour numbers. Tell the child to read the remaining minute cards. [o'clock, 10, 20, 30, 40, and 50] Ask: What pattern do you see? [The 1 in the 10 is half of 2; the 2 in 20 is half of 4, and so forth.] Could this help you remember where the minute numbers go? [yes]

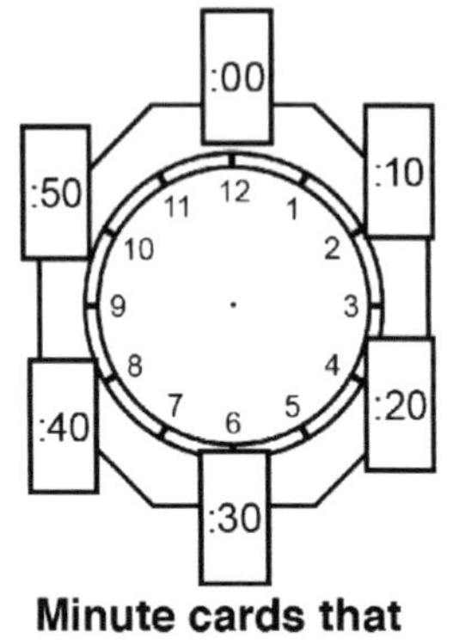

Minute cards that are multiples of 10.

Tell the child to take the six minute cards he removed previously and to place them at the correct positions.

Telling time. Give the child the geared clock. Remind the child that the hour hand tells the hour numbers and the minute hand tells the minute numbers. Set the hands of the clock to 3:00 and ask him to read the time. [three o'clock] Change the time to 3:05 and ask him to read it. [three oh five] Continue moving the hands in five-minute increments to 4:00.

EXPLANATIONS:

Unfortunately, we cannot say the hour can be determined by the smaller of the two numbers near the hour hand. While it works for 2 and 3, it does not for 12 and 1.

These activities help the child to learn the location of the minute numbers.

ACTIVITIES FOR TEACHING:	EXPLANATIONS:

Tell the child to set the clock to 4:00 and say the time. [4:00] Tell him to move the minute hand to the next number and say the time. [4:05] Continue to 5:00.

Ask him to set the clock to 4:15, 4:40, 5:10, 5:30, and so forth.

Digital clock. Show the child a digital clock. Tell him that this clock is called a *digital clock* because it shows the time with digits, not hands. A clock with hands is an *analog clock.* Ask: Which clock tells you whether it is a.m. or p.m.? [most digital clock] Which clock lets you see if you are near the next hour? [analog clock]

Worksheet 50. Give the child the worksheet, where he will match the digital clock in the center to the analog clock on the sides. The solutions are shown below.

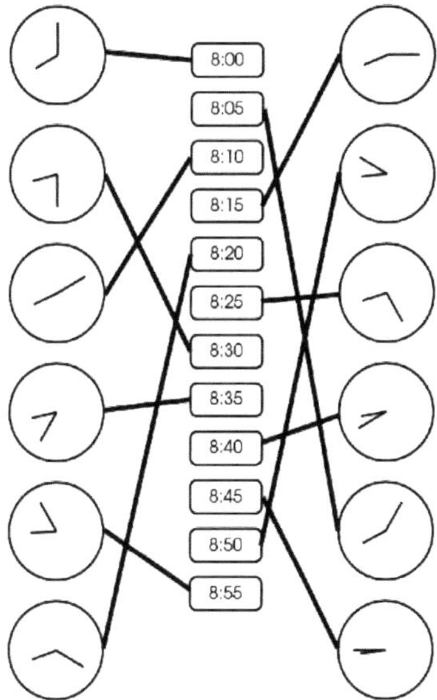

In conclusion. Ask: What do you call a clock that has only numbers? [digital clock] What do you call a clock that has hands? [analog clock] What is the greatest number you will see on a digital clock? [59]

Lesson 83: More Telling Time

OBJECTIVES:

1. To review *quarter hour* and *half hour*
2. To continue practice reading clock in five-minute intervals

MATERIALS:

1. Geared clock
2. Sets of hour cards and minute cards
3. Worksheet 48, Drawing a Clock
4. *Math Card Games* book, C17
5. Worksheet 51, More Telling Time

ACTIVITIES FOR TEACHING:	EXPLANATIONS:

Warm-up. Ask: What do you call a clock that has only numbers? [digital clock] What do you call a clock that has hands? [analog clock] What is the greatest number you will see on a digital clock? [59]

Ask: How many hours in one day? [24] Is 4:00 p.m. in the morning or afternoon? [afternoon] How many minutes in an hour? [60] Where is the minute hand at the beginning of an hour? [at the top] In what direction do the minute numbers go around a clock? [clockwise]

Ask: If you were to sleep 11 hours a day, how many hours would you be awake? [13 hours]

Ask the child to count by 5s to 60. [5, 10, 15, . . . , 60]

Half hours and quarter hours. Give the child the geared clock and tell him to set it to 6:00. Next tell him to move the minute hand halfway to 7:00. Ask: At what number is the minute hand? [6] What time does your clock say? [6:30] Explain that sometimes people call this half past 6 because the hour is half over. Tell him to set the clock to half past 7 and half past 8.

Ask: What are two ways to say half of a half? [quarter and one fourth] Tell the child that with clocks we only use the word quarter. Tell him to set the clock to 8:00. Then to move the minute hand a quarter of the way around. Ask: What number did you stop at? [3] What time does your clock say? [8:15] Say: We call that quarter after 8. Tell him to set the clock to quarter after 9 and then a quarter after 5.

Tell him that sometimes people say a quarter to 10 or a quarter 'til 10. Ask: What do you think that means? [a quarter of a hour before 10:00] Tell the child to set the clock to a quarter to 10. Ask: What would a digital clock say the time is? [9:45]

ACTIVITIES FOR TEACHING:

Minute Mix-ups game. Give the child one set of minute cards and Worksheet 48. Ask the child to place the set of minute cards around the paper clock.

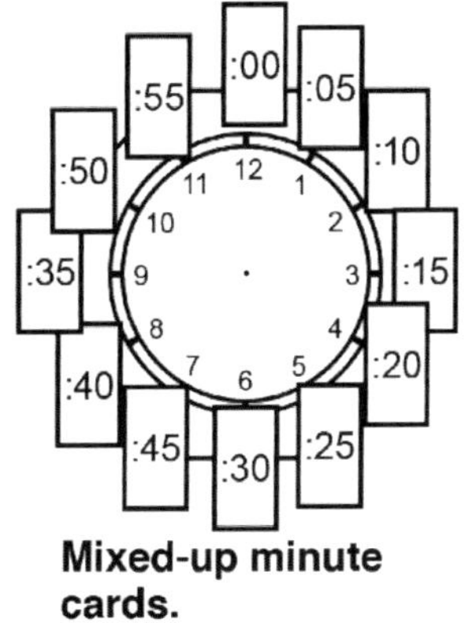

Mixed-up minute cards.

Demonstrate playing the Minute Mix-ups game, found in the *Math Card Games* book, C17. See the figure at the right.

Telling time on the clock. Give the child the hour cards. Set the clock for 7:20. Ask the child to find the matching hour card and minute card and set them aside. See the figures on the right. Continue setting the clock with times listed below. All the cards will be used at the end.

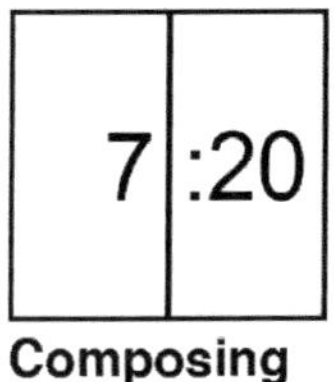

Composing the time.

9:15
10:40
4:00
5:10
6:35
8:05
11:50
12:55
2:30
3:45
1:25

Worksheet 51. Give the child the worksheet where he writes the time or draws the hands. Remind the child to draw a hand by starting near the number and drawing toward the center dot.

A. **5:25**	B. **7:50**	C. **1:35**
D. **2:40**	E. **6:05**	F. **8:15**
G. **12:45**	H. **10:20**	I. **4:00**

L.

The solutions for the three questions are: **F, J, G.**

In conclusion. Ask: Where is the minute hand at half past 3? [at 6] Where is the minute hand at quarter after 11? [at 3] Where is the minute hand at quarter to 7? [at 9]

EXPLANATIONS:

Lesson 84: Telling time to the Minute

OBJECTIVES:

1. To draw a clock
2. To practice reading clock to the minute marks

MATERIALS:

1. Dry erase board
2. Geared clock
3. Worksheet 52, Telling Time to the Minute

ACTIVITIES FOR TEACHING:

Warm-up. Ask: Where is the minute hand at half past 4? [at 6] Where is the minute hand at quarter after 8? [at 3] Where is the minute hand at quarter to 5? [at 9]

Ask: What do you call a clock that has hands? [analog clock] What do you call a clock that has only numbers? [digital clock] What is the greatest number you will see on a digital clock? [59]

Ask: How many hours in one day? [24] Is 8:00 a.m. in the morning or afternoon? [morning] How many minutes in an hour? [60] Where is the minute hand at the beginning of an hour? [at the top] In what direction do the minute numbers go around a clock? [clockwise]

Ask: If you were to sleep 12 hours a day, how many hours would you be awake? [12 hours]

Drawing a clock. Tell the child that today he will draw a clock on his dry erase board. Ask: What do you draw first? [a large circle] Tell him to put a dot in the center. Ask: Which four numbers would you write next? [12, 3, 6, and 9] Now tell him to write the remaining numbers. See the first three figures below.

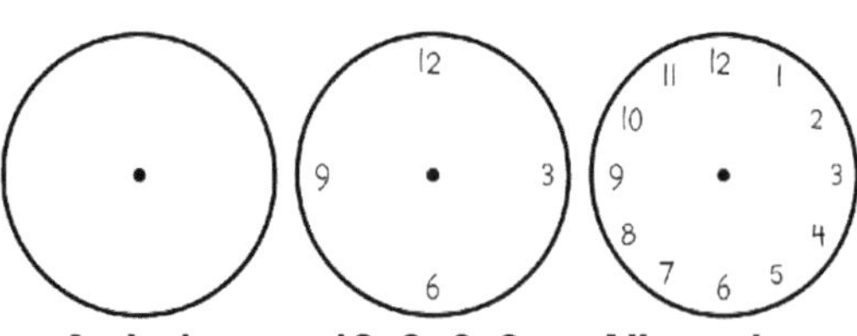

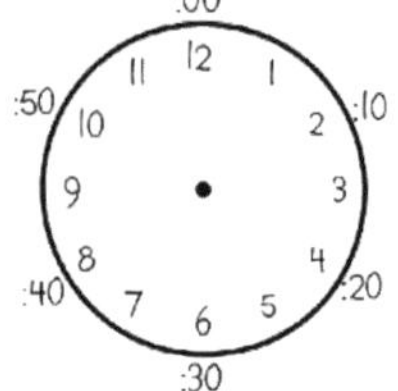

A circle. **12, 3, 6, 9.** **All numbers.** **Minute tens.**

Then tell him to write the tens minute numbers on the outside of the circle. [10, 20, 30, 40, and 50] See the last figure above. Ask him to point to 10 minutes after the hour. [at the number 2] Repeat for 15 minutes after the hour. [at the number 3] Repeat for 25, 45, 35, and 55 minutes. [at numbers 5, 9, 7, and 11]

EXPLANATIONS:

ACTIVITIES FOR TEACHING:

EXPLANATIONS:

Reading any minute on a clock. Tell the child he will learn how to read the minutes between the numbers. Draw a horizontal line similar to a clock, using longer lines for the multiples of 5. See the figure below.

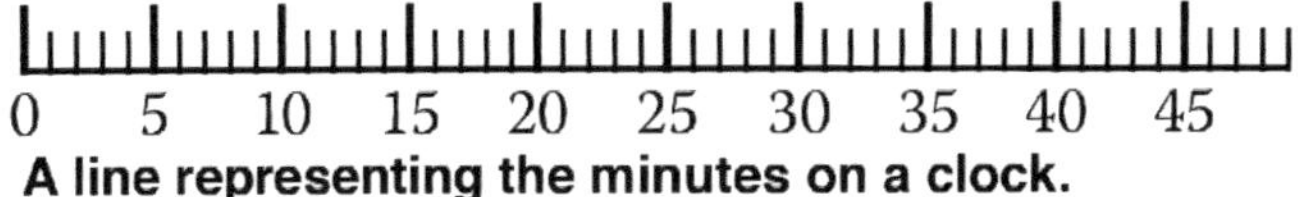

A line representing the minutes on a clock.

Draw an arrow at the 6th mark as shown below and ask: What number does the first arrow point to? [6] Repeat for arrows at other numbers, such as 13, 16, 22, 29, 33, 38, 44, and so forth.

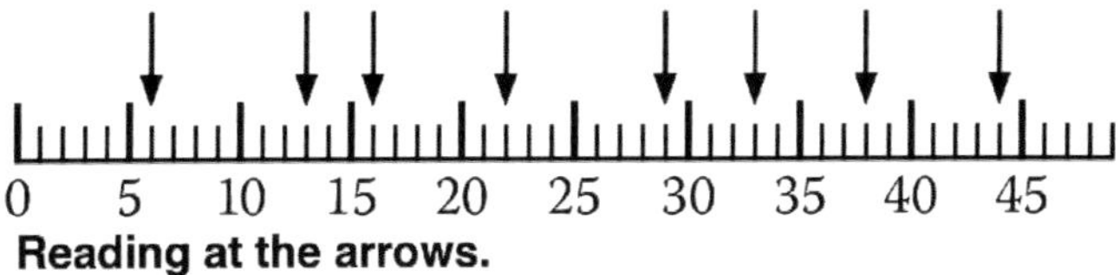

Reading at the arrows.

Note that we are counting spaces, not lines. The line is the landing spot, the space in between is what we count.

Ask the child to draw arrows at specified numbers on the line.

Reading time to the minute. Give the child the geared clock. Tell him to set the time to 1:20. Then tell him to set it to 1:21. Continue with 1:22, 1:23, 1:24, and 1:25. Then tell him to set the clock to various other times.

Set to the Minute game. Tell the child that you will write down times for him to set on the clock. Check to see if you both agree.

After a while exchange roles. Have the child write the time you set the clock, then check if you both agree.

Name the Minute game. In this game, the players take turns setting the clock. Then they both write down the time and compare.

Worksheet 52. Give the child the worksheet, where he matches the digital clock in the center to the analog clock on the sides. The solutions are show at the right.

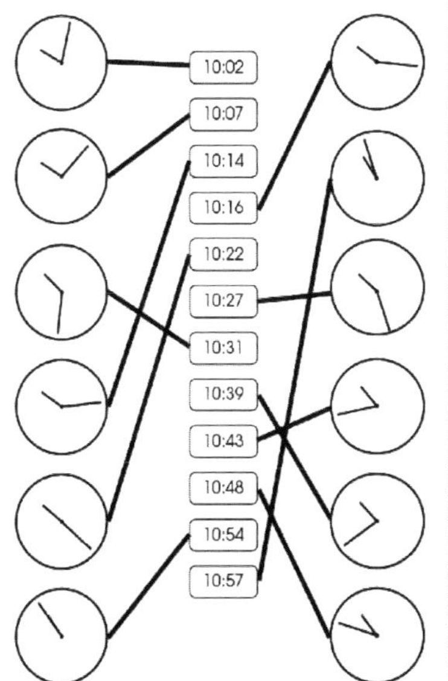

In conclusion. Ask: How many minutes are between each hour mark? [five] How many minutes in an hour? [60]

Lesson 85: Review and Games 7

OBJECTIVES:

1. To review recent topics
2. To continue to develop skills through playing math card games

MATERIALS:

1. Worksheet 53-A or 53-B, Review 7
2. *Math Card Games* book, A9 or S24

ACTIVITIES FOR TEACHING:

Worksheet 53-A. Give the child the worksheet. Tell him to listen to the problems and write only the answers on the worksheet. Read each problem twice.

47 – 20   87 – 85   83 + 28

Tell him to complete the worksheet. Solutions are below.

Write only the answers.

27

2

111

Write the answers.

$\frac{1}{2}$ hour + $\frac{1}{2}$ hour = 1 hour

13 – 4 = 9

11 – 6 = 5

Write the time.

12:30

4:56

8:03

Draw the hands.

7:10

3:22

5:48

Solve the problem.

Alex jumped rope 499 times and Adrian jumped 501 times. Who jumped more and how much more? Adrian jumped 2 more times.

Use > for "is after." Use < for "is before." Use = for "is the same as."

half past 10 > 10:15   11:45 a.m. < 1:10 p.m.

quarter to 1 = 12:45   quarter to 2 < quarter after 2

Write this number in words.

6411 six thousand four hundred eleven

EXPLANATIONS:

Even though this concept was not explicitly taught, time sequencing is an application of what has been taught.

ACTIVITIES FOR TEACHING:	EXPLANATIONS:

Corners™ game. The child can play the Corners™ game found in the *Math Card Games* book, A9.

Subtraction Bingo game. Ask the child to play Subtraction Bingo, found in the *Math Card Games* book, S24.

Worksheet 53-B. Give the child the worksheet. Tell him to listen to the problems and write only the answers on the worksheet. Read each problem twice.

53 – 20 97 – 94 29 + 72

Tell him to complete the worksheet. Solutions are below.

Write only the answers.

33

3

101

Write the answers.

1 hour – $\frac{1}{2}$ hour = $\frac{1}{2}$ hour

14 – 5 = 9

12 – 7 = 5

Write the time.

2:20

6:09

11:41

Draw the hands.

3:45

1:29

9:13

Solve the problem.

Tyler read 400 pages altogether. Val read 390 pages. Who read more pages and how many more? Tyler read 10 more pages.

Use > for "is after." Use < for "is before." Use = for "is the same as."

quarter to 7 = 6:45 3:45 p.m. > 6:50 a.m.

quarter after 9 < 9:45 half past 3 = 3:30

Write this number in words.

4213 four thousand two hundred thirteen

Even though this concept was not explicitly taught, time sequencing is an application of what has been taught.

LESSON 86: COMPARISON PROBLEMS WITH MORE

OBJECTIVES:

1. To solve word problems that compare using the word more

MATERIALS:

1. Base-10 picture cards
2. Place-value cards
3. Worksheet 54, Comparison Problems with More
4. AL Abacus

ACTIVITIES FOR TEACHING:

Warm-up. Show a 10 from the base-10 cards and say: Suppose I had 80 of these cards. Ask: How much would it show? [800] Have the child explain it. [Each group of ten cards is 100, so 8 groups of ten would be 800.] Show the 800 place-value card and ask: Is it the same? [yes] Why? [it shows 80-ten or 8 hundred]

Ask: Which is more, 2 thousand or 6 hundred? [2 thousand] Which is greater, 1 thousand or 10 hundred? [same] Which is less, 1 hundred or 11? [11]

Ask: How much is 1000 plus 5000? [6000] How much is 6000 plus 2000? [8000] How much is 2000 plus 5000? [7000]

Worksheet 54. Give the child the worksheet and abacus. Explain to him that we have done story problems where things were put together or partitioned. The problems for today and in the next lesson are compare problems. This means we will compare two things and think about which is longer, shorter, taller, more, less, fewer, and so on.

Problem 1. Tell the child to read the first problem.

> Mr. Black is 6 feet tall. His son is 4 feet tall. How much taller is the father?

Tell him to show it on his abacus. See the left figure below. Ask: What is the larger amount? [6] Tell the child write the larger amount in the whole-circle on the worksheet. Ask: What is the smaller amount being compared? [4] Tell the child to write it in the left part-circle. Ask: What is the difference? [2] Tell the child to write the difference in the right part-circle. See below. Tell him to write the equation. [6 – 4 = 2 feet]

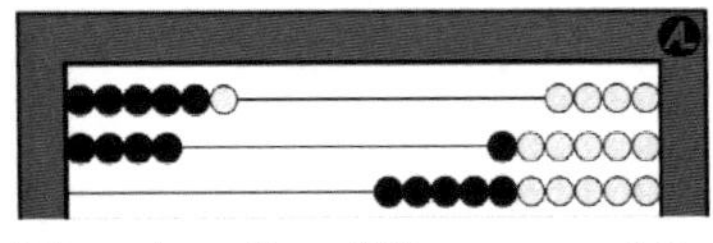

Showing the difference of 2.

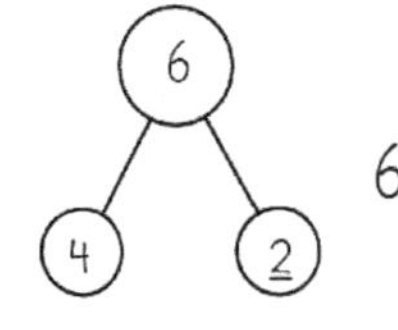

6 – 4 = 2 feet

EXPLANATIONS:

This lesson is a mixture of compare problems to discourage the child from memorizing a particular procedure.

The answer is underlined so that the missing portion of the equation is quickly identified.

ACTIVITIES FOR TEACHING:

Model checking. Draw a part-whole circle set as shown on the right. Tell him it is a math model for solving compare problems.

larger set

smaller set

differ-ence

Part-whole circle set model for compare problems.

Problem 2. Ask the child to read and solve problem 2.

> Mrs. Jackson is 170 cm tall. Her daughter is 119 cm tall. How much taller is the mother? [170 – 119 = 51 cm]

Ask him if the answer makes sense.

Problem 3. Tell the child to read problem 3.

> Jasmine has five pillows. Oliver has four more pillows than Jasmine. How many pillows does Oliver have?

Ask: Who has more pillows, Jasmine or Oliver? [Oliver] How do you know? [Oliver has four more than Jasmine.] Tell him to show it on the abacus. Then ask: Are the five pillows the larger or smaller set? [smaller] Ask: What is the four? [difference] Tell him to solve the problem on his worksheet. See below. Discuss the solutions.

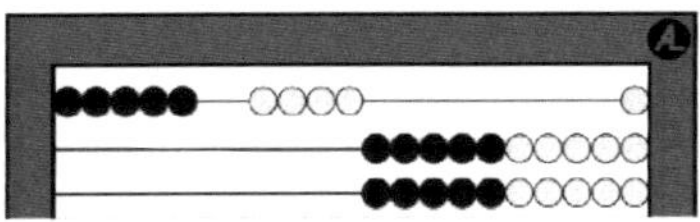

5 pillows and 4 more for Oliver.

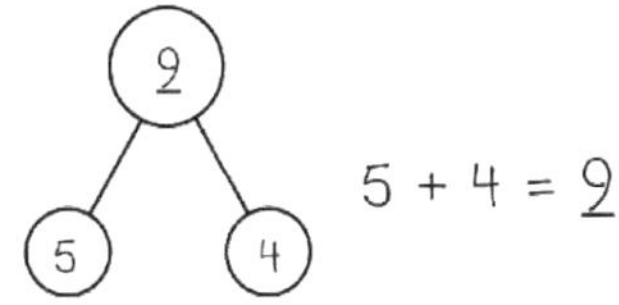

Ask: Does the answer make sense? [Jasmine has 5. Oliver has 9, which is 4 more than Jasmine.]

Problem 4. Tell him to solve problem 4.

> Logan has 12 more cherries than Matt. Matt has 25 cherries. How many cherries does Logan have? [25 + 12 = 37]

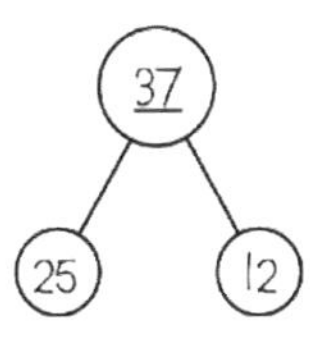

Problem 5. Tell the child to read problem 5.

> Shauna has 3 more flowers than Jacob. Shauna has 5 flowers. How many flowers does Jacob have?

Ask: Are the three flowers a difference or the number of flowers somebody has? [difference] Ask him to solve it on his abacus and on his worksheet. See below.

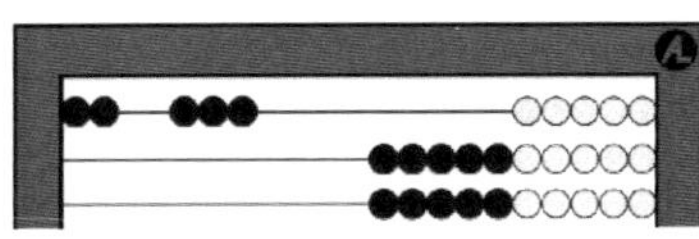

5 flowers; Jacob has 3 more.

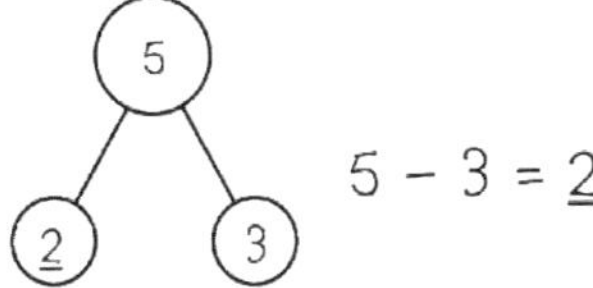

Problem 6. The equation for this problem is 20 – 11 = 9.

In conclusion. Ask: Is the difference a part or a whole? [part]

EXPLANATIONS:

Lesson 87: Comparison Problems with Fewer or Less

OBJECTIVES:

1. To review opposites
2. To solve word problems that compare using the words fewer or less

MATERIALS:

1. Base-10 picture cards
2. Place-value cards
3. Worksheet 55, Comparison Problems with Fewer or Less

ACTIVITIES FOR TEACHING:

Warm-up. Ask: Is the difference in an equation a part or a whole? [part]

Ask: When model checking with a part-whole circle set, where does the larger number go? [whole-circle] Where do we write the smaller set? [left part-circle] Where do we write the difference? [right part-circle] Draw the model at right if necessary.

Show a 10 from the base-10 cards and say: Suppose I had 70 of these cards. Ask: How much would it show? [700] Have the child explain it. [Each group of ten cards is 100, so 7 groups of ten would be 700.] Show the 700 place-value card and ask: Is it the same? [yes] Why? [it shows 70-ten or 7 hundred]

Ask: Which is more, 3 thousand or 5 hundred? [3 thousand] Which is greater, 1 thousand or 10 hundred? [same] Which is less, 2 hundred or 22? [22]

Fewer or less. Ask: What is the opposite of hot? [cold] What is the opposite of black? [white] What is the opposite of short? [long] What is the opposite of subtract? [add] What is the opposite of fewer? [more] What is the opposite of less than? [greater than]

Write: 3 5

Ask: Which number is more? [5] How much more? [2] Which number is less? [3] How much less? [2]

Worksheet 55. Give the child the worksheet. Explain to him that these are more compare problems.

Problem 1. Ask the child to read the first problem.

> Brandon is 2 cm shorter than his twin, Kayla. Brandon is 149 cm tall. How tall is Kayla?

Tell the child to write the numbers in the part-whole circle set on his worksheet. See the figure at the right. Ask: Where did you put the 2 cm and why? [It is the difference in height between them, so it is in the difference circle.] Where did you write the 149 cm and why? [It is the smaller number so in the smaller set circle.]

EXPLANATIONS:

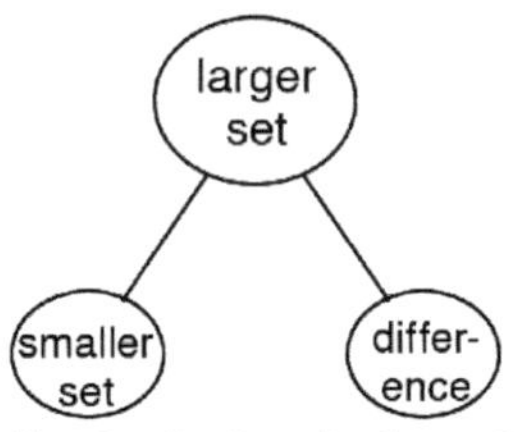

Part-whole circle set model for compare problems.

Grammatically, "fewer" refers to countable (discrete) objects while "less" refers to uncountable quantities and numbers. So, we say, fewer people, less time, less than 50, and less than 4 miles.

ACTIVITIES FOR TEACHING:	EXPLANATIONS:

Ask him to write the equation. [149 + 2 = 151 cm] Ask: Does the answer make sense to say Kayla is 151 cm since Brandon is 149 cm tall? [Yes, the difference is 2 cm.]

Problem 2. Tell the child to solve problem 2.

> Michaela practiced her violin 21 hours last month and 18 hours this month. How much less time did she practice this month? [21 – 18 = 3 hours]

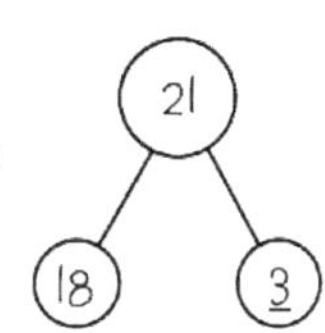

Ask him to explain his results. Ask: Is it correct to say that Michaela practiced 3 more hours last month than this month? [yes]

Problems 3 and 4. Tell the child to solve problems 3 and 4.

Problems 3 and 4 are designed to elicit deep thinking. Children learn much more when they spend time really understanding a problem than solving a plethora of similar problems superficially.

> 3. Joshua's team scored 9 fewer points than Noah's team. Joshua's team scored 43 points. How many points did Noah's team score? [43 + 9 = 52]

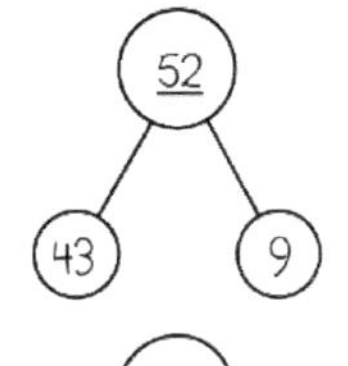

> 4. In the second game, Joshua's team scored 9 fewer points than Noah's team. Noah's team scored 43 points. How many points did Joshua's team score? [43 – 9 = 34]

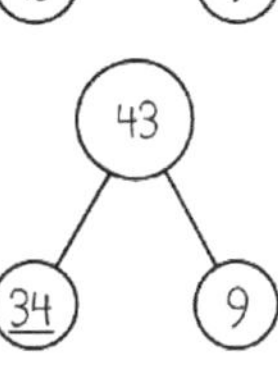

Ask: Whose team was the winner in problem 3? [Noah's] Whose team was the winner in problem 4? [Noah's] What was the highest score in problem 3? [52] What was the highest score in problem 4? [43]

Ask: What makes these two problems different? [The losing team in problem 3 scored 43 points, while the winning team in problem 4 scored 43 points.]

Problem 5. Tell him to solve problem 5.

> Emily's apple weighs 80 grams. Sophie's apple weighs 6 grams less than Emily's apple. How much does Sophie's apple weigh? [80 – 6 = 74]

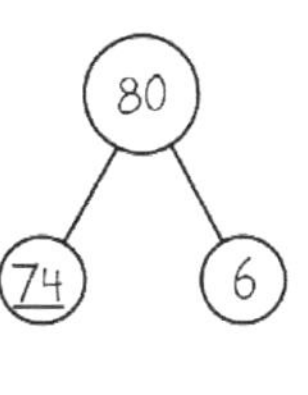

Problem 6. Tell the child to solve problem 6.

> The Wang family traveled 18 miles to a game. The Soto family traveled 27 miles. How many miles less did the Wang family travel? [27 – 18 = 9]

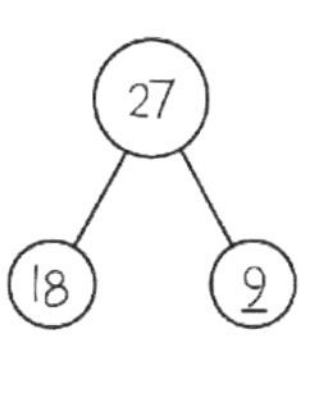

Ask: What are you looking for in this problem? [the difference] How many more miles did the Soto family travel? [9 miles]

In conclusion. Ask: In a compare story problem, can you tell which number will be the larger number without reading the story? [no]

Lesson 88: Subtracting with Base-10 Picture Cards

OBJECTIVES:

1. To experience subtracting with base-10 picture cards
2. To practice trading with base-10 picture cards where necessary

MATERIALS:

1. Math journal
2. Worksheet 56, Subtracting with Base-10 Cards
3. Base-10 picture cards
4. Place-value cards

ACTIVITIES FOR TEACHING:

Warm-up. Ask: How many equations are there for subtracting from 10? [11] How many equations are there for subtracting from 100? [101]

Ask the child to write the answers to the following written problems in his math journal: 95 – 15, [80] 75 – 20, [55] 170 – 15, [155] and 150 – 15. [135]

Ask: Who makes errors in math? [everybody] How can we find errors? [looking carefully and checking]

Ask: How many ones do you need to make 10? [10] How many tens do you need to make 100? [10] How many hundreds do you need to make 1000? [10]

Worksheet 56. Give the child the worksheet, base-10 cards, and place-value cards.

Subtracting without trading. Tell the child to read the first problem and write the equation:

> The city of Logan, Utah is 4534 feet above sea level. The city of Billings, Montana is at 3123 ft. How much higher is Logan than Billings? [4534 – 3123 = 1411 feet]

Tell him to compose the first number with place-value cards and base-10 cards. Then have him compose the number to be subtracted and take the quantity from the base-10 cards laid out, starting with the thousands. See the left figure below. The difference is shown on the right. Ask the child to compose the difference with the place-value cards.

EXPLANATIONS:

Subtraction on paper will also proceed from left to right. Therefore, encourage the child to do so with the base-10 cards.

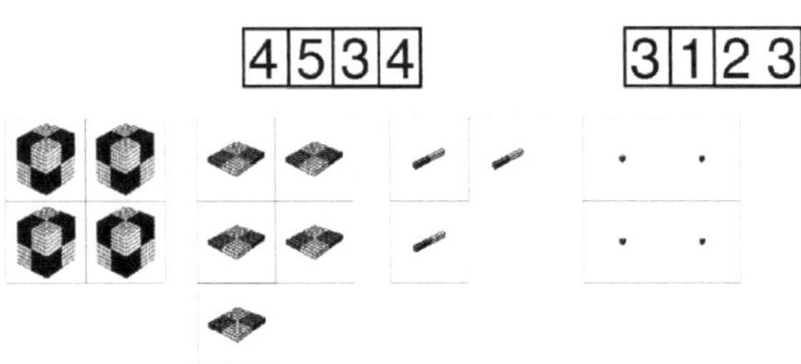

4534 composed with base-10 cards.

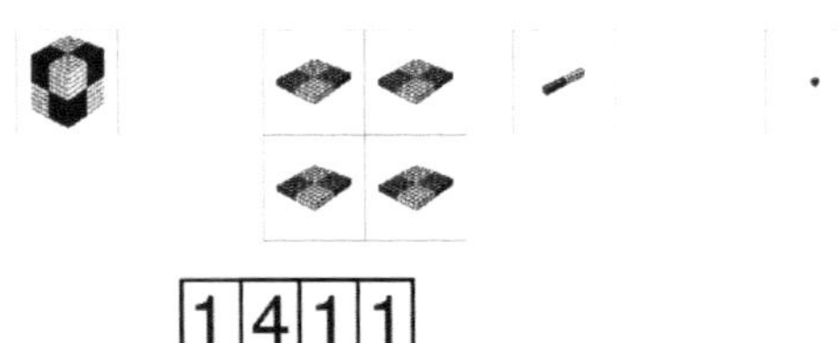

The difference after subtraction.

ACTIVITIES FOR TEACHING:

Problem 2. Ask the child to read and solve the next problem in the same way.

The Appalachian Mountains have a peak of 6684 feet. Sugarloaf Mountain in Maryland is 1283 feet high. How much taller is the Appalachian peak? [5401 feet]

Subtracting with trading. Tell the child to read problem 3.

The distance between New York and Hawaii is 4858 miles. The distance between New York and England is 3296 miles. How much closer is New York to England than to Hawaii? [1562 miles]

Ask the child to set up the place-value cards and base-10 cards as before. See the left figure below. Tell him to subtract the 3 thousand and the 2 hundred and then stop. Ask: How are you going to subtract the 9 tens? [Trade 1 hundred for 10 tens.] See the right figure below.

4858 3296

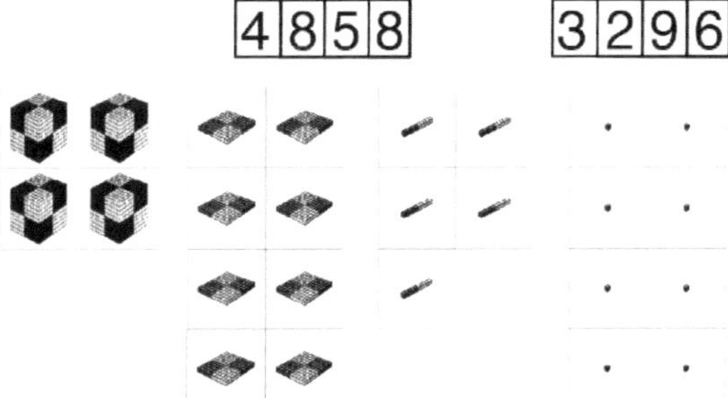

4858 composed with base-10 cards.

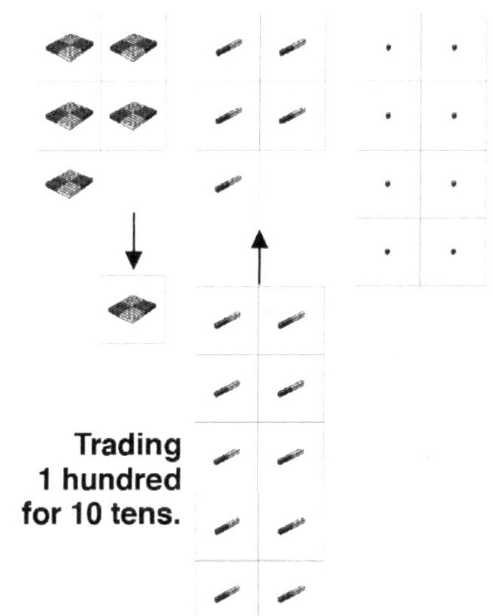

Trading 1 hundred for 10 tens.

Tell him to finish subtracting. The difference is below.

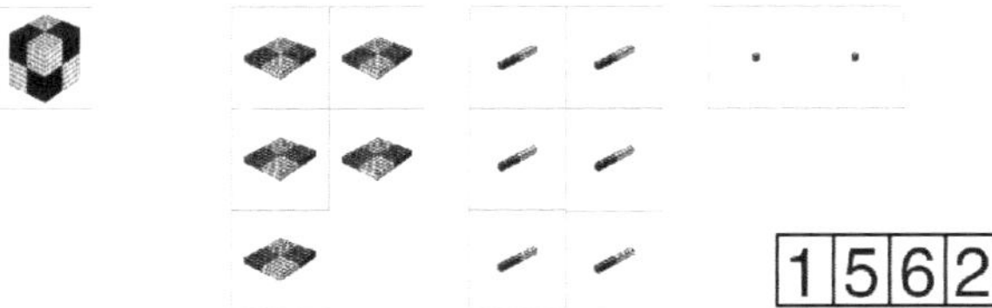

1562

The difference after subtraction.

Tell the child to complete the worksheet. Solutions are shown below.

4.		4	5	3	4	5.		5	0	7	2
	–	2	4	1	8		–	2	5	4	5
		2	**1**	**1**	**6**			**2**	**5**	**2**	**7**
6.		6	4	9	1	7.		7	0	8	0
	–	5	7	8	5		–	3	8	2	9
			7	**0**	**6**			**3**	**2**	**5**	**1**
8.		8	2	1	5	9.		9	2	4	7
	–	5	4	3	7		–	5	6	8	5
		2	**7**	**7**	**8**			**3**	**5**	**6**	**2**

In conclusion. Ask: What do you do when you do not have enough hundreds to subtract? [Trade a thousand for 10 hundreds.]

EXPLANATIONS:

To observe which problem the child is working on, the problem number matches the thousands place of the minuend.

It may not be necessary for the child to do all nine exercises.

LESSON 89: SUBTRACTING ON SIDE 2 OF THE AL ABACUS

OBJECTIVES:

1. To practice trading 4-digit numbers on side 2 of the AL Abacus

MATERIALS:

1. Math journal
2. AL Abacus
3. Worksheet 57, Subtracting on Side 2 of the AL Abacus

ACTIVITIES FOR TEACHING:

Warm-up. Ask: Is there only one way to subtract? [no, there are many]

Ask: How many equations are there for subtracting from 10? [11] How many equations are there for subtracting from 100? [101]

Ask the child to write the answers to the following written problems in his math journal: 85 – 15, [70] 85 – 20, [65] 160 – 15, [145] and 140 – 15. [125]

Ask: How many ones do you need to make 10? [10] How many tens do you need to make 100? [10] How many hundreds do you need to make 1000? [10]

Subtracting on side 2. Tell the child that today he will start with 4995 and then subtract 111, 222, 333, all the way to 999. Tell the child to enter 4995 on side 2 of the abacus as shown below on the left.

EXPLANATIONS:

Lay the abacus flat with side 2 visible to the child.

Write the following in the vertical format:

$$\begin{array}{r} 4995 \\ -\ 111 \\ \hline \end{array}$$

Quantities are entered in the normal order, first thousands. then hundreds, tens, and ones.

Ask: What number do we subtract first? [1 hundred] See the figure below on the right. Continue with 1 ten and 1 one.

This activity focuses on the subtracting process, not on the recording on paper.

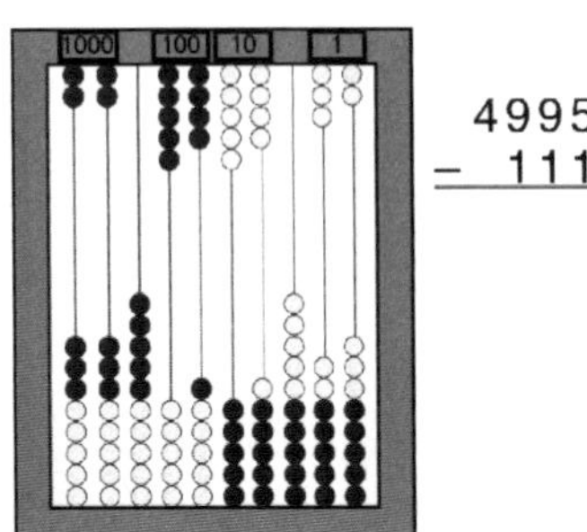

4995 entered.

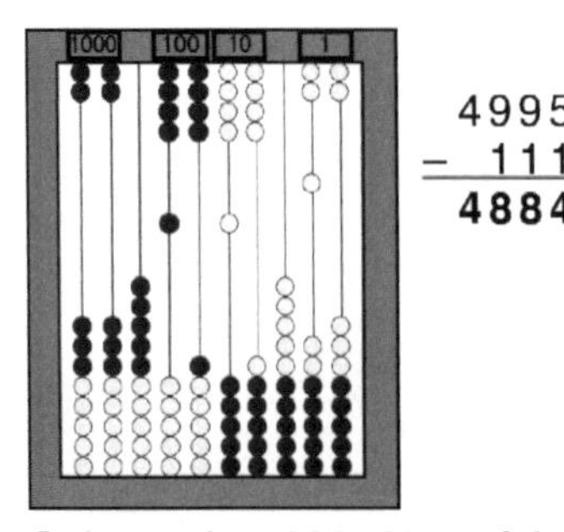

Subtracting 100, 10 and 1.

Then ask him to subtract 222. No trading is necessary. Continue with subtracting 333, where trading is necessary. The trading is shown on the next page.

The child will repeat these subtractions on his worksheet. Answers are at the bottom of the next page.

ACTIVITIES FOR TEACHING:

EXPLANATIONS:

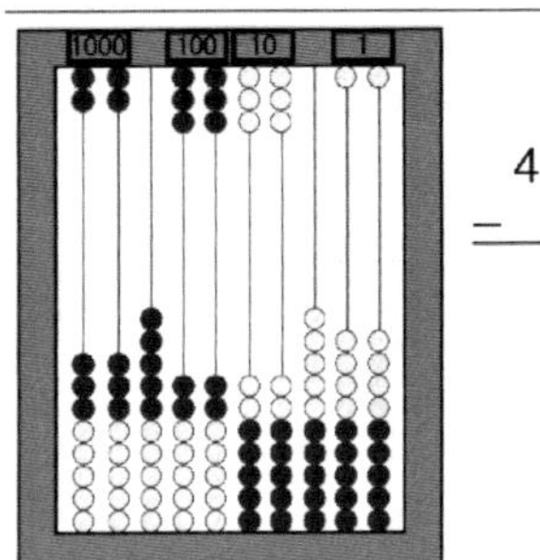

4662
− 333

Subtracting 333.

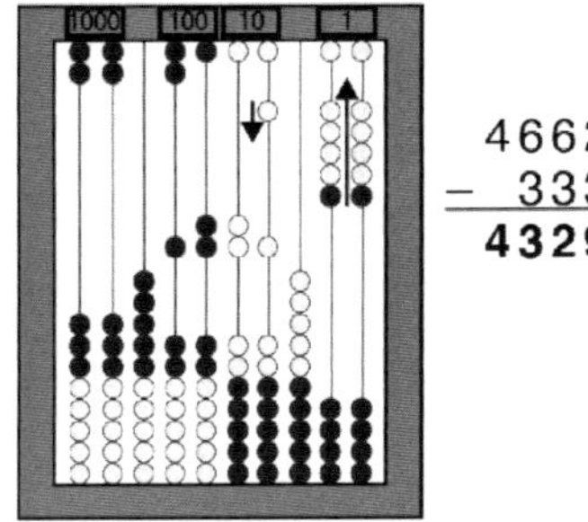

4662
− 333
4329

Trading 1 ten for 10 ones.

Tell the child to subtract 444. See below.

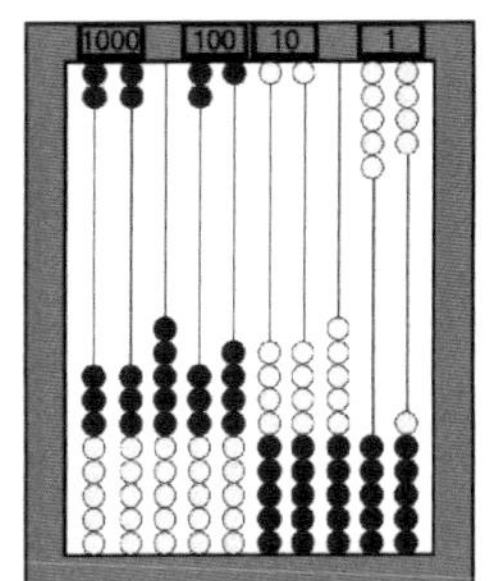

4329
− 444

Subtracting 444.

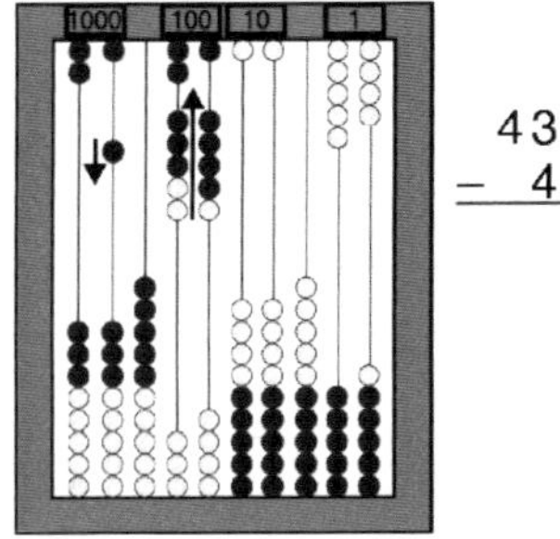

4329
− 444

Trading.

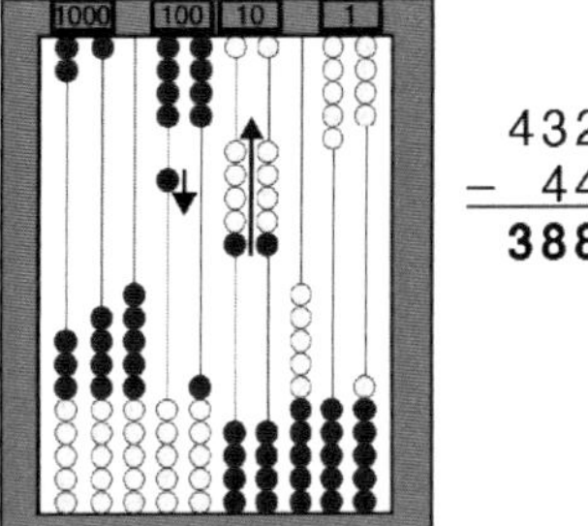

4329
− 444
3885

Another trade.

Tell the child to subtract 555, which requires no trading. Continuing with subtracting 666 and 777, each of which requires three trades. Subtracting 888 requires making a more difficult trade, shown below.

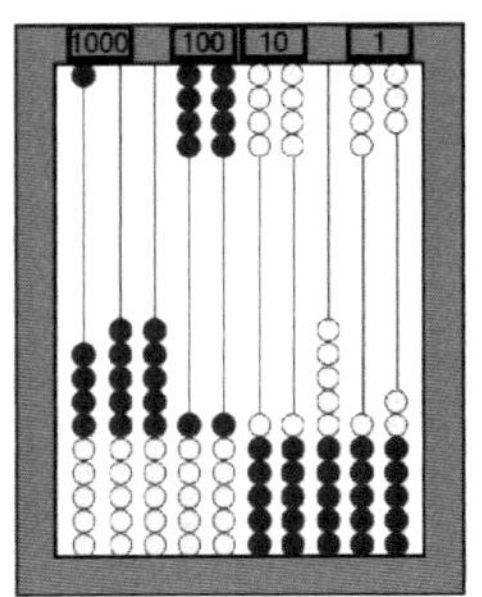

1887
− 888

Subtracting 888.

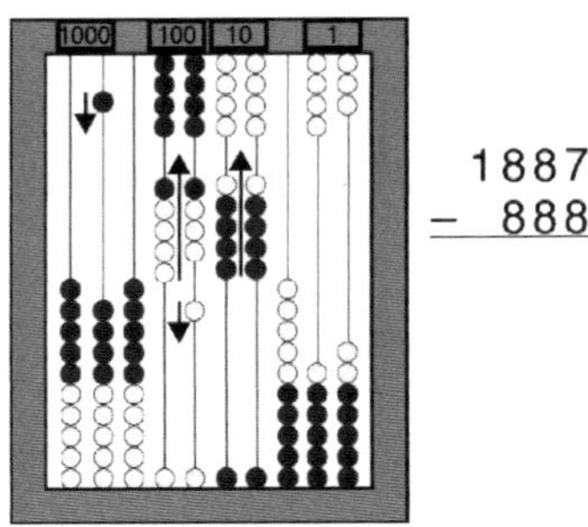

1887
− 888

Trading twice.

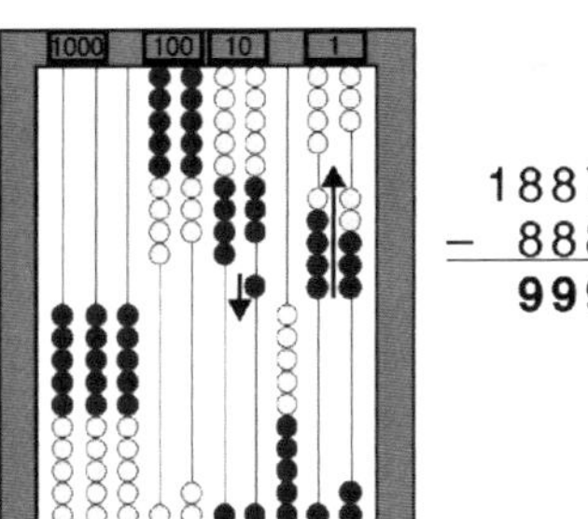

1887
− 888
999

Another trade.

The final subtraction of 999 gives the difference of 0.

Worksheet 57. Give the child the worksheet. See solutions at the right. The first column is the same subtraction done together. The second column is a bit more challenging at the beginning, but ultimately both columns have 12 trades.

In conclusion. Ask: Do you think it makes a difference what order you subtract those numbers? [no]

4 9 9 5	4 9 9 5
− 1 1 1	− 9 9 9
4 8 8 4	**3 9 9 6**
− 2 2 2	− 8 8 8
4 6 6 2	**3 1 0 8**
− 3 3 3	− 7 7 7
4 3 2 9	**2 3 3 1**
− 4 4 4	− 6 6 6
3 8 8 5	**1 6 6 5**
− 5 5 5	− 5 5 5
3 3 3 0	**1 1 1 0**
− 6 6 6	− 4 4 4
2 6 6 4	**6 6 6**
− 7 7 7	− 3 3 3
1 8 8 7	**3 3 3**
− 8 8 8	− 2 2 2
9 9 9	**1 1 1**
− 9 9 9	− 1 1 1
0	**0**

Lesson 90: Recording Subtracting on Paper

OBJECTIVES:

1. To write each subtraction step on paper as it is performed on the AL Abacus in preparation for subtracting without the AL Abacus

MATERIALS:

1. Math journal
2. AL Abacus
3. Worksheet 58, Recording Subtracting on Paper

ACTIVITIES FOR TEACHING:

Warm-up. Ask: How many equations are there for subtracting from 10? [11] How many equations are there for subtracting from 100? [101]

Ask the child to write the answers to the following written problems in his math journal: 95 – 20, [75] 75 – 15, [60] 130 – 15, [115] and 150 – 20. [130]

Ask: How many ones do you need to make 10? [10] How many tens do you need to make 100? [10] How many hundreds do you need to make 1000? [10]

Subtracting on side 2. Tell the child that he will learn to write his differences on paper as he subtracts.

Write the following in the vertical format:

$$\begin{array}{r} 6829 \\ -\ 2637 \\ \hline [4192] \end{array}$$

Tell the child to enter the larger number on the abacus. See the left figure below. Ask: What do we subtract first? [2 thousand] Ask: Before we write 4 thousand, we need to think, should we save a thousand for trading? We do not need to because 829 is more than 637. Then write the 4 thousand as shown in the right figure below.

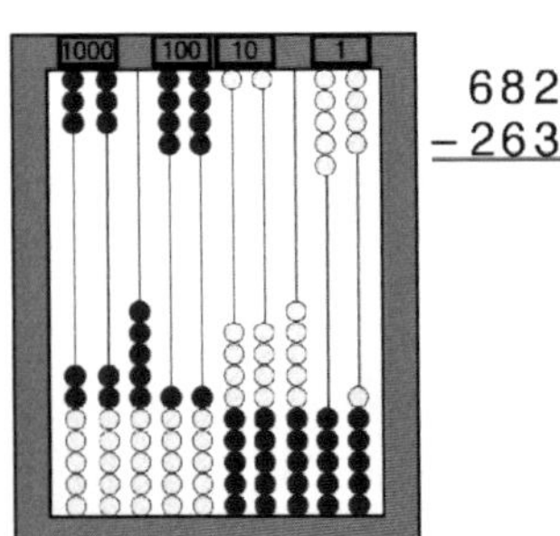

6829 entered.

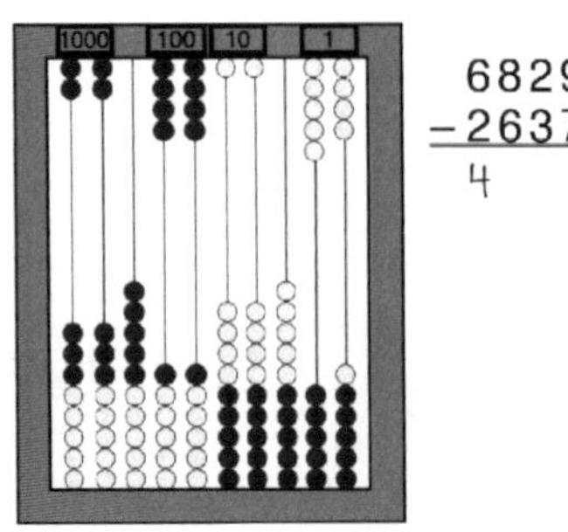

Subtracting 2000.

Ask: What do we subtract next? [6 hundred] Eight hundred minus 6 hundred is what? [2 hundred] Should we save a hundred for trading? [yes] How do we know? [29 is less than 37] Do the trade then ask:

EXPLANATIONS:

Lay the abacus flat with side 2 visible to the child.

Quantities are entered in the normal order, first thousands. then hundreds, tens, and ones.

The subtraction algorithm taught here proceeds from left to right like division. Children naturally prefer to work from left to right.

ACTIVITIES FOR TEACHING:

How many tens do we have now? [12] Show him how to write a little one before the 2 to make it look like 12. Ask: How many hundreds do we have after subtracting 6 and using a hundred to trade? [1 hundred] See the left figure below.

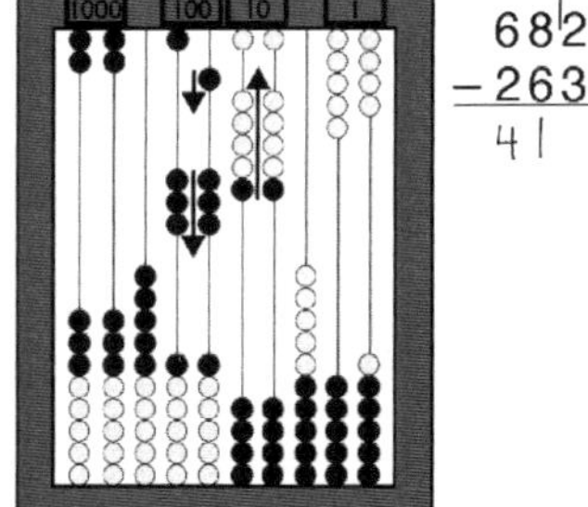

Subtracting hundreds.

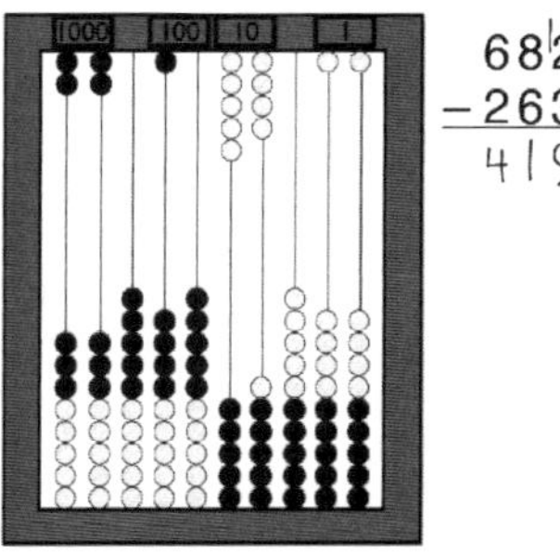

Subtracting tens and ones.

Ask: What do we subtract next? [3-ten] So, 12-ten minus 3-ten is what? [9-ten] Should we save a ten for trading? [no] How do we know? [9 is more than 7] Ask the child to complete the subtraction. See the right figure above.

Second example. Write:

$$\begin{array}{r} 7094 \\ -\ 3528 \\ \hline [3566] \end{array}$$

Tell the child to enter the larger number, left figure below.

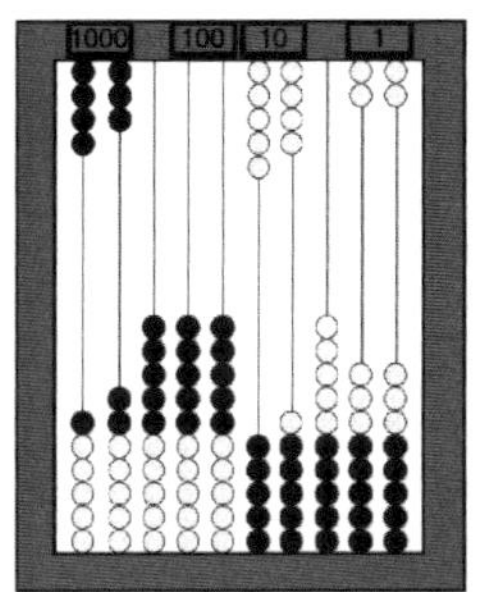

Subtracting hundreds.

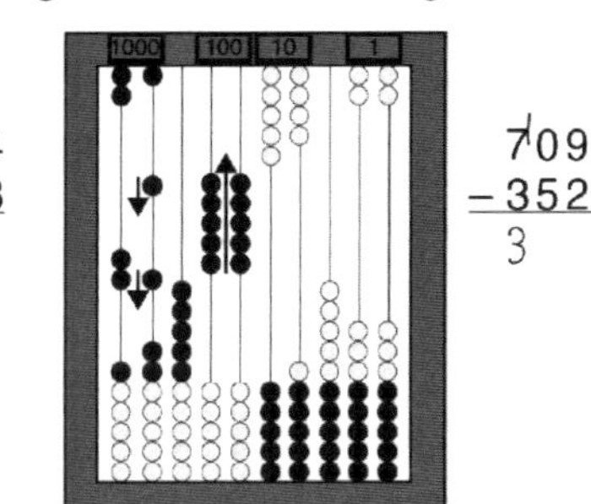

Subtracting tens and ones.

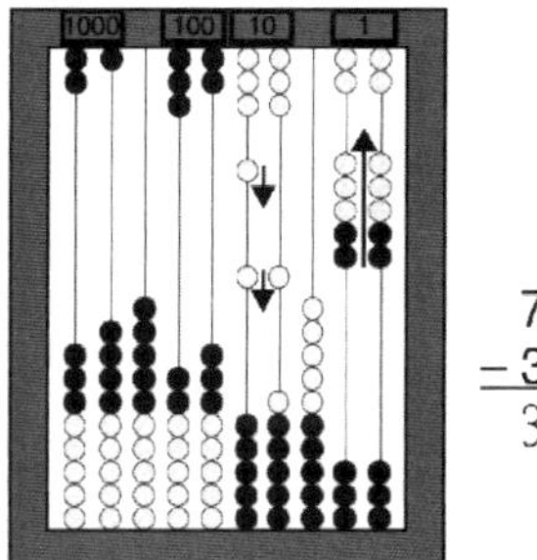

Subtracting tens and ones.

Ask: What is the first subtraction? [7000 – 3000] Should we save a thousand? [yes] What do we write down? [a 1 to show 10 hundred and 3000] See the second figure above.

Ask: What is next? [subtract 5 hundred] Should we save a hundred? [no] Write 5 hundred. Ask: What is next? [subtract 2-ten] Should we save a ten? [yes] See the third figure above. Ask: What do we write down? [a 1 to show 14 ones and 6-ten] What is next? [subtract 8 and write 6]

Worksheet 58. Give the child the worksheet and tell him to complete only the first six subtractions problems. Solutions are at the right.

In conclusion. Ask: Which is easier to use to subtract, base-10 cards or the abacus?

EXPLANATIONS:

In this example, there is no reason to cross out the 8 and write 7 above it. If after subtracting 8 – 6 and before writing the 2, the child discovers 1 hundred is needed for 10 tens, they write 1 less, or 1. The child does not subtract 6 from 7.

Writing the small numbers to indicate trading will also be done for short division.

1.		6	8	^{1}2	9	2.		7	^{1}0	9	^{1}4
	−	2	6	3	7		−	3	5	2	8
		4	**1**	**9**	**2**			**3**	**5**	**6**	**6**
3.		6	8	^{1}3	4	4.		3	^{1}4	5	8
	−	1	5	6	3		−	1	8	2	5
		5	**2**	**7**	**1**			**1**	**6**	**3**	**3**
5.		4	^{1}0	5	^{1}8	6.		9	^{1}2	^{1}4	7
	−	2	7	4	9		−	5	6	6	5
		1	**3**	**0**	**9**			**3**	**5**	**8**	**2**

The remaining portion of this worksheet will be completed in the next few lessons.

Lesson 91: Subtraction Activities

OBJECTIVES:

1. To practice subtraction through playing games
2. To improve precision in subtraction through repeated subtraction

MATERIALS:

1. Worksheet 58, Recording Subtracting on Paper
2. AL Abacus
3. *Math Card Games* book, S9 and S30
4. Math journal
5. Worksheet 59, Subtraction Activities

ACTIVITIES FOR TEACHING:

Warm-up. Ask the child to do problems 7 and 8 on the Worksheet 58, using the abacus.

$$\begin{array}{r} 453{}^{1}4 \\ -2418 \\ \hline \mathbf{2116} \end{array} \qquad \begin{array}{r} 5{}^{1}07{}^{1}2 \\ -2545 \\ \hline \mathbf{2527} \end{array}$$

Ask: Which is more, one hundred or one thousand? [one thousand] Which is more, ten hundreds or one thousand? [same]

Ask: What is the mathematical word for more? [greater] What is the opposite of greater? [less] Tell him to name all numbers greater than five and less than nine. [6, 7, and 8]

Ask: How many ones do you need to make 20? [20] How many tens do you need to make 200? [20] How many hundreds do you need to make 2000? [20]

Zero Corners™ game. Have the child play this variation of the Zero Corners™ game, found in the *Math Card Games* book, S9. Tell him we will use 365, the number of days in a year, as the starting number. If no player reaches zero, the player with the lowest score at the end of the game is the winner.

Scoring is recorded by writing down only the last score in his math journal. Tell the child to subtract any way he likes. See below for a sample scoring for a player.

365
355
340
330
305
295
290
270

EXPLANATIONS:

ACTIVITIES FOR TEACHING:

Worksheet 59. Give the child the worksheet. This worksheet is a variation of the Repeated Subtraction Solitaire game found in the *Math Card Games* book, S30.

Ask: What is special about the first two numbers? See the figure below. [The second number is like the first number without the zero at the end.] How many times do you subtract the second number? [10]

Tell him to only do the first column. Also tell him the last answer will be special. [0] Answers shown below.

$$
\begin{array}{rcccc}
 & 3 & 5 & 7 & 0 \\
- & & 3 & 5 & 7 \\
\hline
 & \mathbf{3} & \mathbf{2} & {}^{1}\mathbf{1} & {}^{1}\mathbf{3} \\
- & & 3 & 5 & 7 \\
\hline
 & \mathbf{2} & \mathbf{8} & {}^{1}\mathbf{5} & {}^{1}\mathbf{6} \\
- & & 3 & 5 & 7 \\
\hline
 & \mathbf{2} & \mathbf{4} & \mathbf{9} & \mathbf{9} \\
- & & 3 & 5 & 7 \\
\hline
 & \mathbf{2} & {}^{1}\mathbf{1} & {}^{1}\mathbf{4} & {}^{1}\mathbf{2} \\
- & & 3 & 5 & 7 \\
\hline
 & \mathbf{1} & \mathbf{7} & \mathbf{8} & {}^{1}\mathbf{5} \\
- & & 3 & 5 & 7 \\
\hline
 & \mathbf{1} & \mathbf{4} & {}^{1}\mathbf{2} & \mathbf{8} \\
- & & 3 & 5 & 7 \\
\hline
 & \mathbf{1} & {}^{1}\mathbf{0} & \mathbf{7} & {}^{1}\mathbf{1} \\
- & & 3 & 5 & 7 \\
\hline
 & & \mathbf{7} & {}^{1}\mathbf{1} & {}^{1}\mathbf{4} \\
- & & 3 & 5 & 7 \\
\hline
 & & \mathbf{3} & \mathbf{5} & \mathbf{7} \\
- & & 3 & 5 & 7 \\
\hline
 & & & & \mathbf{0}
\end{array}
$$

In conclusion. Ask: What is the easiest thing about subtraction? What is the hardest thing about subtraction?

EXPLANATIONS:

The remaining two columns and the problem will be completed in the next lesson.

Lesson 92: More Subtraction Activities

OBJECTIVES:

1. To learn the term *kilometer*
2. To solve a subtraction problem with three parts
3. To improve precision in subtraction through repeated subtraction

MATERIALS:

1. Worksheet 58, Recording Subtracting on Paper
2. AL Abacus
3. Worksheet 59, Subtraction Activities

ACTIVITIES FOR TEACHING:

Warm-up. Ask the child to do problems 9 and 10 on Worksheet 58, using the abacus.

$$\begin{array}{r} 6\,{}^{1}4\,9\,{}^{1}1 \\ -5785 \\ \hline \mathbf{706} \end{array} \qquad \begin{array}{r} 7\,0\,8\,{}^{1}0 \\ -3829 \\ \hline \mathbf{3251} \end{array}$$

Ask: Which is more, two hundred or two thousand? [two thousand] Which is more, ten tens or one hundred? [same]

Ask: How many ones do you need to make 40? [40] How many tens do you need to make 400? [40] How many hundreds do you need to make 400? [4]

Ask: What do you do when you do not have enough hundreds to subtract? [Trade a thousand for 10 hundreds.]

Worksheet 59. Give the child the worksheet and tell him to read the problem on the worksheet.

> The total distance from Windsor, Canada, to Toronto is 370 km. The distance from Windsor to London is 183 km. The distance from London to Hamilton is 119 km. What is the distance from Hamilton to Toronto? [68 km]

Windsor London Hamilton Toronto

Tell him: The abbreviation *km* means *kilometer.* A kilometer is 1000 meters. Suggest he writes the distances that he knows on the figure. Ask him to think about what he knows and what he needs to find. Give him time to think about the problem. See below.

EXPLANATIONS:

ACTIVITIES FOR TEACHING:	EXPLANATIONS:

Ask him to explain his solution. [68] Ask: Why does the part-whole circle set have three parts? [The distance from Windsor to Toronto has three parts.] See below.

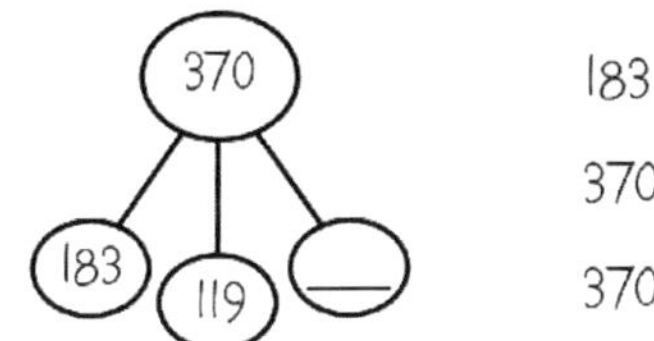

183 + 119 + ___ = 370

370 − 183 − 119 = ___

370 = 183 + 119 + ___

The part-whole circle set and some possible equations.

Ask the child to share the equation he wrote. Ask if it could be written another way. Several options are shown above.

Next ask: How did you the find the distance? One way he may have done it is to add 183 and 119 [302] and go up to 370 to get 68 km. This follows the first equation.

Another way is subtract 370 – 183 [187] and subtract 187 – 119 to get 68 km. This follows the second equation.

Still another way is to add 183 and 119 [302] and then subtract that from 370 to get 68 km. This follows the third equation.

Ask: Does your answer make sense? Is Hamilton 68 km from Toronto? [yes]

Repeated subtraction. For the remaining two repeated subtraction columns on the worksheet, the child can choose his own numbers according to the instructions on the worksheet. If no mistakes have been made, the final differences will be zero.

Some child might want to choose a digit other than zero for the ones place in the top number. They will discover that the final difference will be that digit.

In conclusion. Ask: What is 10 – 1 – 1, [8] 100 – 10 – 10, [80] and 1000 – 10 – 10? [980]

Lesson 93: Review and Games 8

OBJECTIVES:

1. To review recent topics
2. To continue to develope skills through math card games

MATERIALS:

1. Worksheet 60-A or 60-B, Review 8
2. *Math Card Games* book, S9
3. Math journal

ACTIVITIES FOR TEACHING:

EXPLANATIONS:

Worksheet 60-A. Give the child the worksheet. Tell him to listen to the problems and write only the answers on the worksheet. Read each problem twice.

100 – 21   99 – 77   85 + 38

Tell him to complete the worksheet. Solutions are below.

Write only the answers.

79

22

123

Write the answers.

38 + 78 = 116

206 + 49 = 255

306 – 293 = 13

Write the time.

10:43

Draw the hands.

12:20

Subtract.

	4	0	8	5
–	3	8	6	9
		2	1	6

Solve the problem.

The Scenic bus drove 2847 km. The Touring bus drove 529 km farther than the Scenic bus. How far did the Touring bus drive?

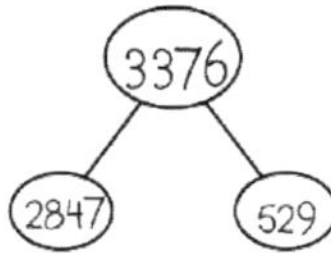

	2	8	4	7	
+		5	2	9	
	3	3	7	6	km

Write >, <, or = on the lines.

2086 < 2806   5371 – 100 = 5271

4253 – 256 < 4253 + 256   399 + 2 > 301

54 – 11 > 54 – 13   6000 – 1 = 5999

Explain what is wrong with this thinking: 64 – 27 = 43.

60 – 20 is 40 and 7 – 4 is 3. So the answer is 40 + 3 = 43.

The ones should be 14 – 7, making the tens to be 30. The answer should be 37.

ACTIVITIES FOR TEACHING:

EXPLANATIONS:

Subtraction Corners™ in the Thousands. Have the child play Subtraction Corners™ in the Thousands, a variation of Zero Corners™, found in the *Math Card Games* book, S9. The players start with a score of 4000. In addition to the points that are the sum, they add 100 points if the colors are green or black and 200 points if the colors are red or blue, then subtract the total from the score.

4000
− 115
3885
− 210
3675
− 215
3460

The subtractions are done in the child's math journal as shown on the right. The winner is the player with the lowest score at the end of game.

Worksheet 60-B. Give the child the worksheet. Tell him to listen to the problems and write only the answers on the worksheet. Read each problem twice.

100 – 32   88 – 66   67 + 43

Tell him to complete the worksheet. Solutions are below.

Write only the answers.

68

22

110

Write the answers.

47 + 86 = 133

307 + 58 = 365

504 – 497 = 7

Write the time.

4:07

Draw the hands.

9:15

Subtract.

	7	8	8	6
–	5	8	6	7
	2	0	1	9

Solve the problem.

The Rail train traveled 1847 km. The Trax train traveled 2073 km. How much farther did the Trax train travel?

2073 → 1847, 226

	2	0	7	3
–	1	8	4	7
		2	2	6 km

Write >, <, or = on the lines.

5901 __>__ 5091

7126 – 1000 __>__ 5126

8146 – 789 __<__ 8146 + 789

499 + 2 __=__ 501

47 – 14 __<__ 47 – 12

7000 – 1 __<__ 7999

Explain what is wrong with this answer 47 – 29 = 22. .

40 – 20 is 20 and 9 – 7 is 2. So the answer is 20 + 2 = 22.

The ones should be 17 – 9 = 8, making the tens to be 10. The answer should be 18.

Lesson 94: Pennies, Nickels, and Dimes

OBJECTIVES:

1. To review the names and value of penny, nickel, and dime
2. To add the value of several coins

MATERIALS:

1. Coins: penny, nickel, dime
2. AL Abacus
3. *Math Card Games* book, M4 or M5
4. Worksheet 61, Pennies, Nickels, and Dimes

ACTIVITIES FOR TEACHING:

Warm-up. Ask the child to count by tens, starting at 75 and ending at 175. [75, 85, 95, . . . , 175]

Ask: What is one half plus one half? [1] What is 11 and one half plus 2 and one half? [14]

Ask: What is 10 – 1 – 1, [8] 100 – 10 – 10, [80] and 1000 – 10 – 10? [980]

Ask: Which is more, five hundred or five thousand? [five thousand] Which is more, ten hundreds or one thousand? [same]

Ask: What is the mathematical word for more? [greater] What is the opposite of greater? [less] Tell him to name all numbers greater than four and less than eight. [5, 6, and 7]

Penny, nickel, and dime. Give the child the penny, nickel, and dime. Lay out the three coins in order of value as shown below. Point to the penny and say: This is a penny, worth 1 cent. Continue with a nickel saying: This is a nickel, worth 5 cents. Point to the dime and say: This is a dime, worth 10 cents.

Penny worth 1¢.

Nickel worth 5¢.

Dime worth 10¢.

Ask him to point to the penny. Continue with the nickel and dime. Ask: How much is the penny worth? [1 cent] Be sure he includes the word *cent.* Repeat for the nickel [5 cents] and dime. [10 cents]

Ask: Do you see any patterns? How is the penny different from the nickel and the dime? [Only the penny is copper-colored and faces right.] Which coin is the thickest? [nickel]

EXPLANATIONS:

Children who are persistent "counters" have a harder time learning the value of coins.

U.S. coins have several obstacles that make learning money difficult for children.

1. The size the dime is smaller than the penny or nickel.
2. The numerical value of the coins is not printed on all the coins.

There is a 25¢ coin, but a $20 bill.

Activities with coins gives children an opportunity to apply their knowledge of tens.

There are four skills to learning money:

3. Learning names and values of the coins
4. Adding the value of several coins
5. Choosing (fewest) coins to make a desired total
6. Starting at a value and choosing the fewest coins to reach a desired total (making change)

ACTIVITIES FOR TEACHING:

EXPLANATIONS:

Say: Except for the dime, the coins get larger in size as they are worth more. The dime is smaller because it used to be made from silver, a very expensive metal.

Entering coin values on the abacus. Ask: What is the name of the coin that is worth 1 cent? [penny] Tell him to enter its value on the abacus. See the left figure below.

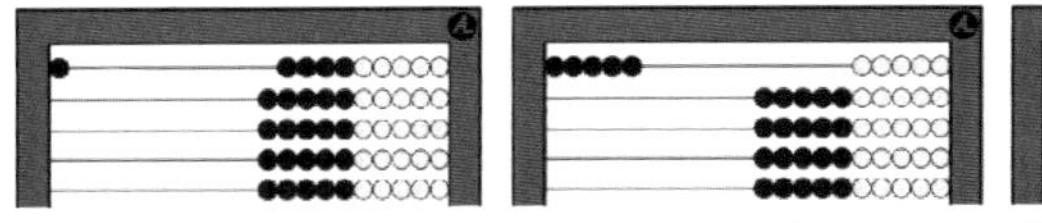

Penny worth 1¢. **Nickel worth 5¢.** **Dime worth 10¢.**

Ask: What is the name of the coin that is worth 5 cents? [nickel] Tell him to enter that amount on the abacus. See the second figure above. Ask: How many pennies does it take to equal 1 nickel? [5]

Ask: What is the name of the coin that is worth 10 cents? [dime] Tell him to enter that value on the abacus. See the third figure above. Ask: How many pennies does it take to equal 1 dime? [10] How many nickels equal 1 dime? [2]

Adding amounts. Tell the child to use his abacus if it helps him to answer the following:

How much is 1 nickel and 2 pennies worth? [7 cents]
How much is 1 nickel and 4 pennies worth? [9 cents]
How much is 6 pennies and 1 nickel worth? [11 cents]
How much is 3 nickels worth? [15 cents]
How much is 4 dimes and 1 penny worth? [41 cents]
How much is 3 dimes and 3 nickels worth? [45 cents]

Money game. From the *Math Card Games* book, play either Money War, M4, or Who Has the Most Money, M5.

Writing the ¢ sign. Show the child how to write 2¢. Explain that the cent sign looks like a "c" with a vertical line through it.

Worksheet 61. Give the child the worksheet and have him complete it. The solutions are below.

7¢	**11¢**	**15¢**
30¢	**22¢**	**15¢**
40¢	**25¢**	**30¢**
16¢	**20¢**	**16¢**

In conclusion. Ask: Of the three coins, penny, nickel, and dime, which coin is smallest in size? [dime] Which coin is worth the least? [penny] Which coin is worth the most? [dime] Which coin is the heaviest? [nickel]

Lesson 95: Adding the Value of Coins

OBJECTIVES:

1. To review or learn the names and value of a *half-dollar* and *quarter*
2. To add the value of several coins

MATERIALS:

1. Worksheet 58, Recording Subtracting on Paper
2. AL Abacus
3. Coins
4. *Math Card Games* book, M5, Variation 1
5. Worksheet 62, Adding the Value of Coins

ACTIVITIES FOR TEACHING:

Warm-up. Ask the child to do problems 11 and 12 on Worksheet 58, using the abacus.

```
  8215      9247
 -5437     -5685
  2778      3562
```

Ask: Of the three coins, penny, nickel, and dime, which coin is smallest in size? [dime] Which coin is worth the least? [penny] Which coin is worth the most? [dime] Which coin is the heaviest? [nickel]

Ask the child to count by fives, starting at 25 and ending at 115. [25, 30, 35, . . . , 115]

Ask the child to count by tens, starting at 45 and ending at 145. [45, 55, 65, . . . , 145]

Half-dollars. Give the child the coins. Ask him to lay a penny, nickel, and dime in a row. Then ask him to add the other two coins as shown below.

1¢

5¢

10¢

25¢

50¢

Coins and their values.

Say: The largest coin is a *half-dollar.* Hardly anyone uses them any more, so they are hard to find. Ask: Since a dollar is worth 100 cents; what is a half-dollar worth? [50 cents] Tell him to show it on his abacus. See the figure below.

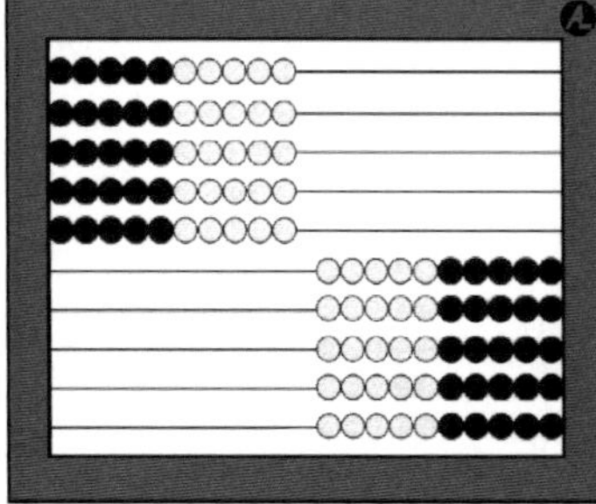

Representing a half-dollar.

EXPLANATIONS:

ACTIVITIES FOR TEACHING:

A quarter of a dollar. Say: The other coin in the row is a *quarter.* Use your abacus to find a quarter of a dollar two different ways. [25¢] See the figures below.

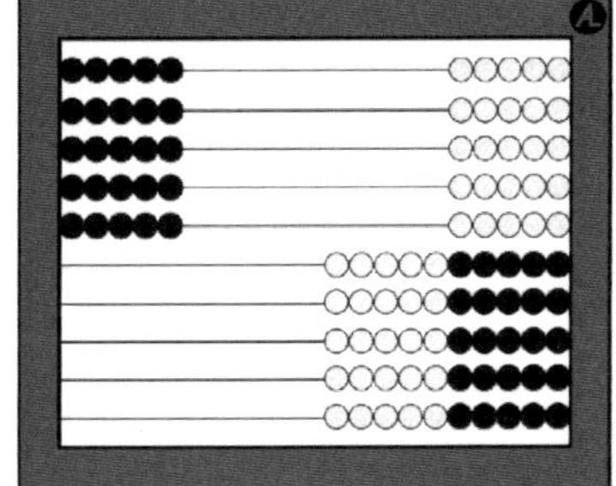

Representing a quarter.

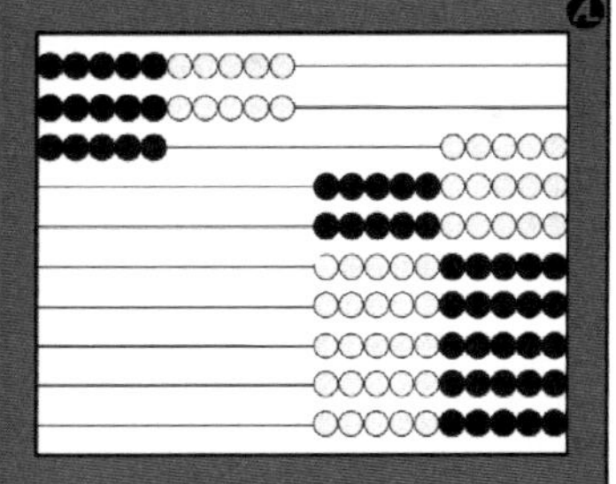

Representing a quarter another way.

Ask: How much are two quarters worth? [50¢] How much are three quarters worth? [75¢] How many quarters are in a dollar? [4] What are two ways to make 50¢? [1 half-dollar or 2 quarters]

Who Has the Most Money game. Play the Who Has the Most Money game, Variation 1, found in the *Math Card Games* book, M5.

Worksheet 62. Give the child the worksheet. Tell him that these problems are puzzles. He can use only three coins to make the amount shown in each row.

Solutions are below.

	Half-dollars	Quarters	Dimes	Nickels	Pennies
7¢				1	2
11¢				2	1
16¢			1	1	1
21¢			2		1
15¢				3	
75¢		3			
76¢	1	1			1
31¢		1		1	1
25¢			2	1	
27¢		1			2
56¢	1			1	1
36¢		1	1		1
61¢	1		1		1
45¢		1	2		

Ask the child to think of other amounts he could make with three coins. [for example, 3¢, 76¢, 36¢, 100¢]

In conclusion. Ask: How much is a dollar? [100 cents] How much is one fourth of a dollar? [25¢] How many fourths are in a dollar? [4] What is another name for one fourth? [quarter] How many quarters equal a dollar? [4]

EXPLANATIONS:

The child may find it easier to think of finding a quarter of a dollar by finding half of a half-dollar.

Lesson 96: Making Change from Fifty Cents

OBJECTIVES:

1. To learn the term *change*
2. To practice making change from 50¢

MATERIALS:

1. Warm-up Practice 1, found after the math journal in the child's worksheet
2. AL Abacus
3. Coins and **Cash box***
4. Dry erase board
5. *Math Card Games* book, M12 or M13

ACTIVITIES FOR TEACHING:

Warm-up. Ask the child to do problems 1 and 2 on Warm-up Practice 1. Use an abacus as needed.

```
 7949      798¹2
-2745     -1929
 5204      6053
```

Ask: How much is a dollar? [100 cents] How much is one fourth of a dollar? [25¢] How many fourths are in a dollar? [4] What is another name for one fourth? [quarter] How many quarters equal a dollar? [4]

Ask: Can you measure more centimeters or more inches on a ruler? [centimeters]

Ask the child to count by fives, starting at 15 and ending at 105. [15, 20, 25, . . . , 105]

Ask the child to count by tens, starting at 75 and ending at 175. [75, 85, 95, . . . , 175]

Ask: What is one half plus one half? [1] What is 16 and one half plus 3 and one half? [20]

Preparation. Place coins in the cash box; quarters in the first box, dimes in the second box, nickels in the third, and pennies in the fourth.

Problem 1. Read the following problem to the child:

> Sam bought a mango for 39¢. Sam gave the clerk two quarters. How much change does Sam receive, or get back?

Explain: *Change* is the amount of money you get back when you pay too much. Draw a part-whole circle set on the dry erase board and ask the child to write the numbers. Ask: What is the whole? [two quarters, or 50 cents] What are the parts? [39 cents and change]

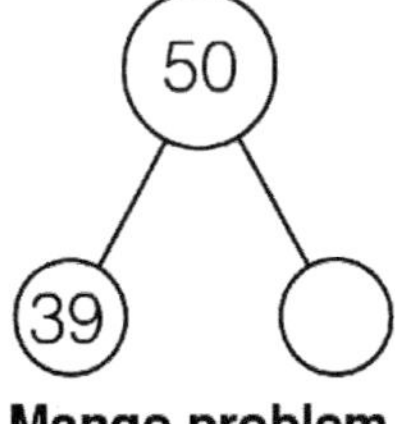

Mango problem.

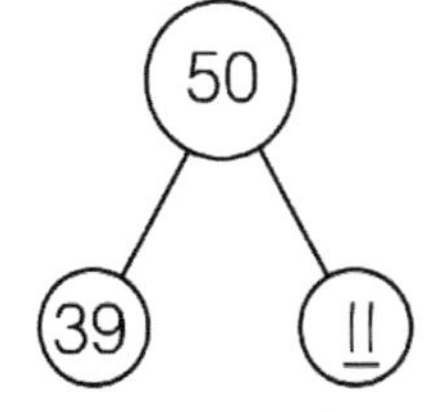

Mango problem solution.

EXPLANATIONS:

*Make a "cash box" by cutting a piece of paper in half the long way and then draw lines dividing it in fourths by estimating. (The paper will not lie flat if it is folded.) This will be used again.

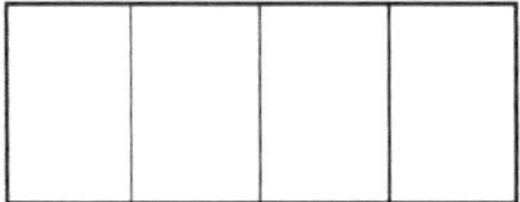

You might want to use the child's name, rather than "Sam."

ACTIVITIES FOR TEACHING:

Ask the child to pretend to buy the mango. Take the 2 quarters and set them nearby, but not inside, the cash box. Then give the child a penny, saying 40, and then a dime, saying 50 cents.

Help the child analyze the transaction by asking: Why did Sam get money back? [Sam gave the clerk too much money.] How much money did Sam receive? [11¢] Why was it 11¢? [39 + 11 = 50] Is this a fair trade? [Yes, the clerk has 50¢ and Sam has the mango worth 39¢ and 11¢.] Is the 11¢ a part or a whole? [part] What is the other part? [39¢] Tell him that the 11¢ is the change.

Show it on the abacus as shown below.

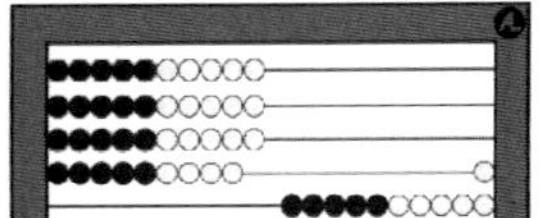

Starting at 39¢.

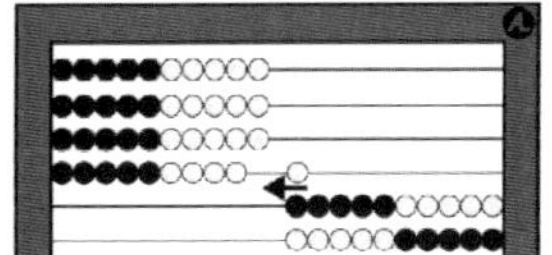

One cent to 40¢.

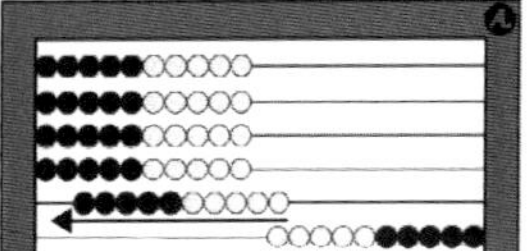

Ten cents to 50¢.

Problem 2. Change the scenario:

> Kelly wanted to buy an eraser that costs 13¢. Kelly did not have any pennies, so Kelly paid for the eraser with a quarter. How much change did the clerk give Kelly? [12¢]

Tell the child to show it on the abacus. See below.

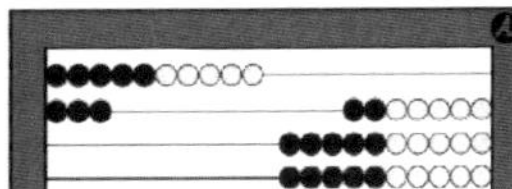

Starting at 13¢.

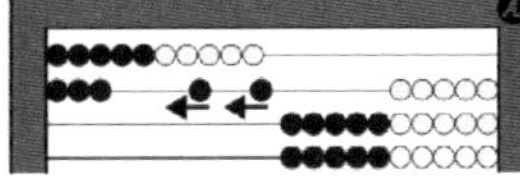

Two cents to 15¢.

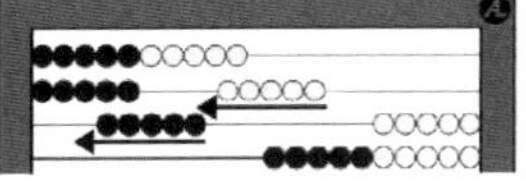

Ten cents to 25¢.

Using coins, count the change to the child: give 2 pennies, saying 14, 15, and giving a dime, saying 25¢.

Change from Fifty Cents game. Have the child play the Change from Fifty Cents game found in the *Math Card Games* book, M12. If desired, play Change from Fifty Cents Solitaire, M13. Several people can play the solitaire together, where they work together trying to beat the cards.

In conclusion. Ask: Why does a person sometimes get change back? [They gave more than the purchase price.] Why doesn't a person always get change back? [They paid the exact amount.]

EXPLANATIONS:

Set the coins near the cashbox, but not inside, so that there is no confusion with the amount given by the purchaser. If any questions arise regarding the original amount, it will be available for reference.

Lesson 97: Ways to Make a Dollar

OBJECTIVES:

1. To practice adding coins up to a dollar
2. To introduce using multiplication to simplify writing equations

MATERIALS:

1. Warm-up Practice 1 and AL Abacus, if needed
2. Coins
3. Dry erase board
4. Worksheet 63, Ways to Make a Dollar

ACTIVITIES FOR TEACHING:

Warm-up. Ask the child to do problems 3 and 4 on Warm-up Practice 1. Use an abacus as needed.

$$\begin{array}{r} 6651 \\ -5928 \\ \hline \mathbf{723} \end{array} \qquad \begin{array}{r} 5057 \\ -3617 \\ \hline \mathbf{1440} \end{array}$$

Read and ask the child to solve the following problem:

Joan bought a banana for 38¢. Joan gave the clerk two quarters. How much change does Joan receive, or get back? [12¢]

Ask: Why does a person sometimes get change back? [They gave more than the purchase price.] Why doesn't a person always get change back? [They paid the exact amount.]

Ask the child to count by fives, starting at 20 and ending at 115. [20, 25, 30, . . . , 115]

Ask the child to count by tens, starting at 65 and ending at 165. [65, 75, 85, . . . , 165]

Ask: What is one half plus one half? [1] What is 10 and one half plus 3 and one half? [14]

Ways to make 30¢. Give the child the coins. Ask: Can you find two coins that total 30¢? [a quarter and a nickel] Tell the child to write the equation on his dry erase board.

30¢ = 25¢ + 5¢

Then ask: Can you make 30¢ using three coins? [3 dimes] Tell the child to write the equation below the first equation.

30¢ = 10¢ + 10¢ + 10¢

Next ask: Can you make 30¢ using four coins? [2 dimes and 2 nickels] Tell the child to write the equation below the last equation.

30¢ = 10¢ + 10¢ + 5¢ + 5¢

Continue with five, six, eight, nine, and ten coins. It is not possible to make 30¢ with seven coins. The equations are on the next page.

EXPLANATIONS:

ACTIVITIES FOR TEACHING:

30¢ = 10¢ + 5¢ + 5¢ + 5¢ + 5¢ (5 coins)

30¢ = 5¢ + 5¢ + 5¢ + 5¢ + 5¢ + 5¢ (6 coins)

30¢ = 10¢ + 10¢ + 5¢ + 1¢ + 1¢ + 1¢ + 1¢ + 1¢ (8 coins)

Tell the child there is another way they could write the last equation, as shown below. Write and read it as: 30 cents equals 10 cents multiplied by 2 plus 5¢ plus 1¢ multiplied by 5.

30¢ = 10¢ × 2 + 5¢ + 1¢ × 5 (8 coins)

The equations for 9 and 10 coins are shown.

30¢ = 10¢ + 5¢ × 3 + 1¢ × 5 (9 coins)

30¢ = 5¢ × 5 + 1¢ × 5 (10 coins)

Ask: What is the greatest number of coins you could use to make 30¢? [30 pennies] What is the fewest? [2, a quarter and a nickel]

Worksheet 63. Give the child the worksheet. Say: The worksheet asks you to find ways to make a dollar using 2 coins all the way to 20 coins. Half-dollars are included, but no pennies. Sometimes there is more than one way to find the coins to equal one dollar. You do not need to write the equations. Some solutions are below.

Number of coins	Half-dollars	Quarters	Dimes	Nickels
2	2			
3	1	2		
4		4		
5	1	1	2	1
6	1		5	
7		2	5	
8		2	4	2
9		1	7	1
10			10	

Number of coins	Half-dollars	Quarters	Dimes	Nickels
11			9	2
12			8	4
13			7	6
14			6	8
15			5	10
16			4	12
17			3	14
18			2	16
19			1	18
20				20

In conclusion. Ask: What is the name of the coin worth one half of a dollar? [half-dollar] What is the name of the coin worth one fourth of a dollar? [quarter] What is the name of the coin worth one tenth a dollar? [dime] What is the name of the coin worth one twentieth of a dollar? [nickel]

EXPLANATIONS:

After writing out the long series of repeated values, the child will appreciate how multiplication simplifies writing equations.

Lesson 98: Making Change from a Dollar

OBJECTIVES:

1. To practice making change from 1 dollar

MATERIALS:

1. Warm-up Practice 1 and AL Abacus, if needed
2. Coins and **Cash box***
3. Dry erase board
4. *Math Card Games* book, M14 or M15
5. Worksheet 64, Making Change from a Dollar

ACTIVITIES FOR TEACHING:

Warm-up. Ask the child to do problems 5 and 6 on Warm-up Practice 1. Use an abacus as needed.

$$\begin{array}{r} 8157 \\ -6561 \\ \hline \mathbf{1596} \end{array} \qquad \begin{array}{r} 9614 \\ -5146 \\ \hline \mathbf{4468} \end{array}$$

Ask: What is the name of the coin worth one half of a dollar? [half-dollar] What is the name of the coin worth one fourth of a dollar? [quarter] What is the name of the coin worth one tenth a dollar? [dime] What is the name of the coin worth one twentieth of a dollar? [nickel]

Ask: Why does a person sometimes get change back? [They gave more than the purchase price.] Why doesn't a person always get change back? [They paid the exact amount.]

Ask the child to count by fives, starting at 10 and ending at 110. [10, 15, 20, . . . , 110]

Ask the child to count by tens, starting at 18 and ending at 98. [18, 28, 38, . . . , 98]

Problem 1. Set up the cash register as in a previous lesson. Read the problem:

> Rosa bought some peanuts for 69¢. She gave the clerk a dollar. How much change does she receive?

Draw a part-whole circle set on the dry erase board and ask the child to write the numbers.

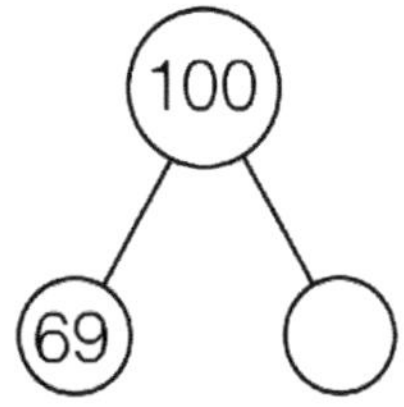

Peanuts problem.

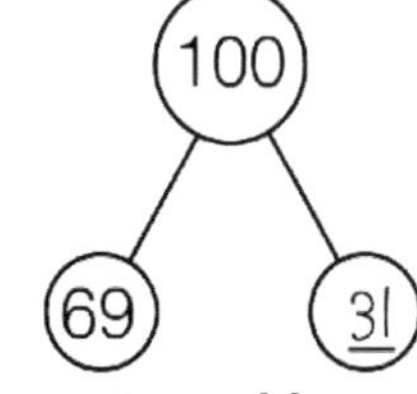

Peanuts problem solution.

Tell the child to show how to make change with the abacus as shown on the next page.

Then ask the child to be the seller. Offer a dollar, which the child places near the cash box. Then he gives a penny, saying 70, and then a nickel, saying 75, and then a quarter, saying 1 dollar.

EXPLANATIONS:

*Use the cash box from a prior lesson.

ACTIVITIES FOR TEACHING: | **EXPLANATIONS:**

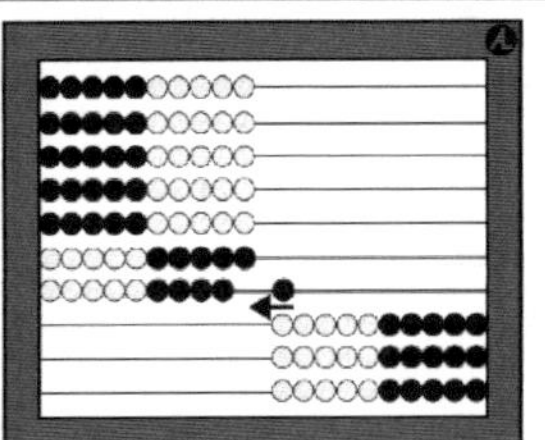

Starting at 69¢: 1 penny, 70¢.

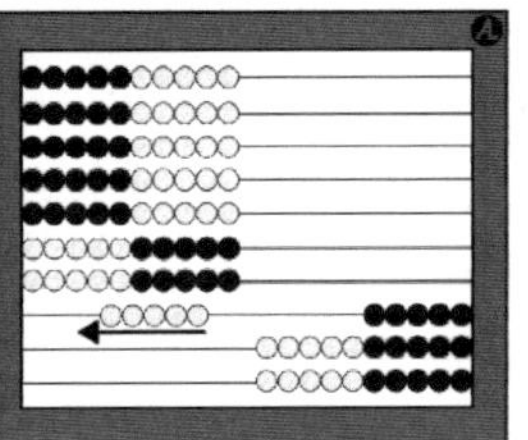

1 nickel: 75¢.

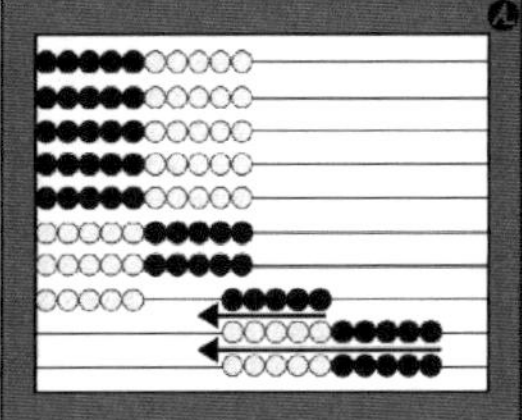

1 quarter: 1 dollar.

Problem 2. Say: This time Miguel buys an orange costing 28¢ with a dollar. Tell the child to enter the quantities on the abacus as the change is being made. See below.

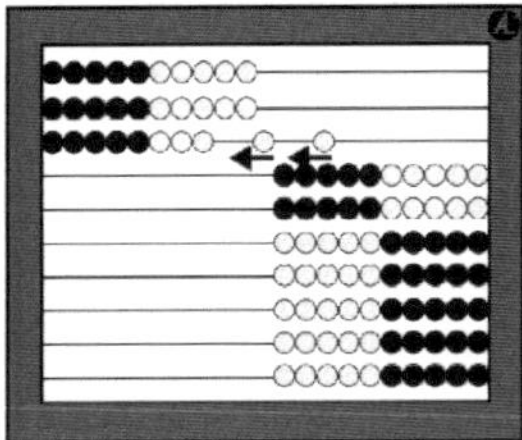

Starting at 28¢: 2 pennies, 29, 30.

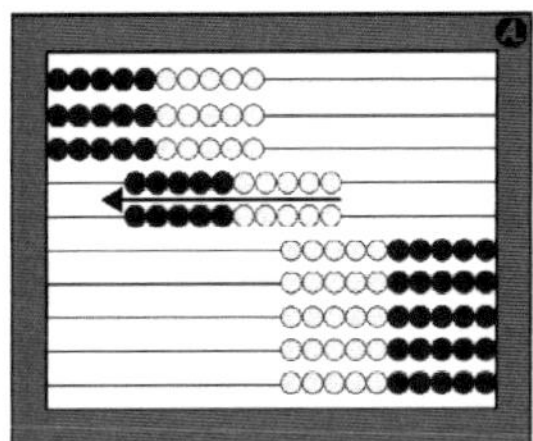

2 dimes: 40, 50.

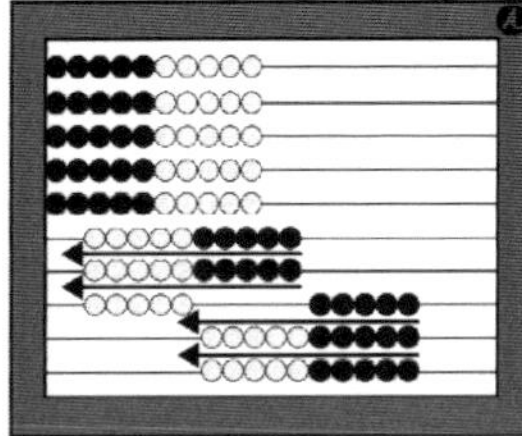

2 quarters: 75, 1 dollar.

The child gives change of 2 pennies [to reach a multiple of 5] saying, 29, 30, then 2 dimes [to reach 50] saying, 40, 50, lastly, gives 2 quarters saying, 75 and 1 dollar.

Change from a Dollar game. Play Change from a Dollar or Change from a Dollar Solitaire found in the *Math Card Games* book, M14 or M15.

Worksheet 64. Give the child the worksheet and have him complete it after reading the instructions. Some solutions are shown below.

A toy costing 38¢: **39, 40, 50¢**
A balloon costing 21¢: **22, 23, 24, 25, 50¢**
A banana costing 15¢: **25, 50¢**
A book costing 29¢: **30, 40, 50¢**
Two apples costing 18¢ each: **37, 38, 39, 40, 50¢**
Three pencils costing 11¢ each: **34, 35, 45, 50¢**

A pen costing 73¢: **74, 75, 1 dollar**
An orange costing 34¢: **35, 40, 50, 75, 1 dollar**
A token costing 85¢: **90, 1 dollar**
A notebook costing 59¢: **60, 70, 75, 1 dollar**
Four apples costing 20¢ each: **90, 1 dollar**
Two toys costing 22¢ each: **45, 50, 75, 1 dollar**

In conclusion. Ask: When you are making change, what coin do you use to get to the next multiple of five? [penny] What coin takes you from 30¢ to 40¢? [dime] What coin takes you from 75¢ to 1 dollar? [quarter]

Lesson 99: Dollars and Cents

OBJECTIVES:

1. To learn the term *decimal point*
2. To write and read money amounts using decimal points
3. To add the value of several coins

MATERIALS:

1. Warm-up Practice 1 and AL Abacus, if needed
2. Geared clock
3. Dry erase board
4. Worksheet 65, Dollars and Cents

ACTIVITIES FOR TEACHING:

Warm-up. Ask the child to do problems 7 and 8 on Warm-up Practice 1. Use an abacus as needed.

3339	6512
−1377	−1113
1962	**5399**

Ask: When you are making change, what coin do you use to get to the next multiple of five? [penny] What coin takes you from 30¢ to 40¢? [dime] What coin takes you from 75¢ to 1 dollar? [quarter]

Put 2:04 on the clock and ask: What time is showing on the clock? [2:04] Put 6:43 on the clock and ask: What time is showing on the clock? [6:43] Repeat for 5:09, 8:23, and 7:55.

Writing whole dollar amounts. Say: Today you will learn how to write dollar amounts. There is a special way to write dollars using a dollar sign. Here is how we write one dollar. Write:

$1

Explain that the dollar sign is written like an S with a vertical line through it. Ask: Where is the dollar sign written, before or after the amount? [before] Where is the cent sign written, before or after the amount? [after]

Tell the child to use the dollar sign to write one dollar on his dry erase board. Ask him to write the following: $46, $106, and $2,380.

Writing dollars and cents. Explain: When we write an amount with both dollars and cents, we use a dot between the dollars and the cents. Write:

$2.35

Say: We read this as two dollars and thirty-five cents. The dot is called a *decimal point*. We say *and* when we come to the decimal point.

Explain: We cannot use both a dollar sign and a cent sign for the same amount.

EXPLANATIONS:

Some countries write the dollar sign *after* rather than before the amount.

ACTIVITIES FOR TEACHING:	EXPLANATIONS:

Ask him to write the cost of a plant that sells for three dollars and 98 cents. [$3.98] Continue with the following: 18 dollars and 64 cents, [$18.64] 13 dollars and 98 cents, [$13.98] and 65 dollars and 50 cents. [$65.50]

Say: Write the time for 2 minutes after 3 o'clock. [3:02] Did you remember to write the zero before the 2?

Write:

$3.02

Say: When we write 3 dollars and 2 cents, we need to write a zero before the 2, like the minutes.

Say: Write the price of a notebook costing 2 dollars and 5 cents. [$2.05]

Ask him to write the following:

31 dollars and 1 cent [$31.01]

15 dollars and 9 cents [$15.09]

17 dollars and 14 cents [$17.14]

Reading dollar amounts. Write:

$24.98

Ask the child to read it. [24 dollars and 98 cents]

Write and ask him to read the following:

$36.51 [36 dollars and 51 cents]

$25.03 [25 dollars and 3 cents]

$301.02 [301 dollars and 2 cents]

$0.40 [40 cents]

Say: If there is no dollar amount, we write a zero before the decimal point.

Worksheet 65. Give the child the worksheet. Explain: You are to find the amounts and write the answer using the dollar sign. Tell the child to add the larger coins first.

The solutions are shown below.

$1.15	**$1.32**	**$2.05**
$0.92	**$1.20**	**$0.66**
$0.82	**$1.06**	**$0.70**

If you are using the Canadian version of the worksheets, the answers are shown below.

$1.15	**$2.32**	**$3.05**
$0.92	**$1.20**	**$0.66**
$0.82	**$1.56**	**$0.70**

In conclusion. Ask: Where do we write the cent symbol, before or after the amount? [after] Where do we write the dollar sign? [before] Which is less, 2¢ or $2? [2¢] Which is more, 100¢ or $1? [same]

Lesson 100: Money Problems

OBJECTIVES:

1. To solve story problems involving money
2. To add four money amounts

MATERIALS:

1. Warm-up Practice 1
2. Worksheet 66, Money Problems

ACTIVITIES FOR TEACHING:

Warm-up. Ask the child to do problems 9 and 10 on Warm-up Practice 1. Use an abacus as needed.

```
  1314       3924
 -1282      -3585
    32        339
```

Ask: Where do we write the cent symbol, before or after the amount? [after] Where do we write the dollar sign? [before] Which is more, 5¢ or $5? [$5] Which is less, 100¢ or $1? [same]

Ask: When you are making change, what coin do you use to get to the next multiple of five? [penny] What coin takes you from 20¢ to 30¢? [dime] What coin takes you from 50¢ to 75¢? [quarter]

Worksheet 66. Give the child the worksheet. Ask him to read the first problem.

> Amy has two quarters, three dimes, and two nickels. How much money does she have? Is it more or less than a dollar?

Say: When a problem has two questions, first answer the first question. Let him work quietly for a few minutes. Draw a part-whole circle set as shown below on the left.

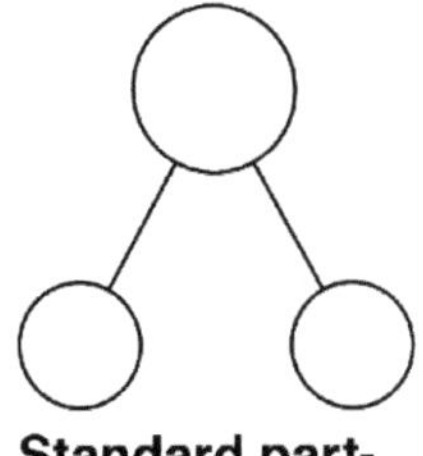
Standard part-whole circle set.

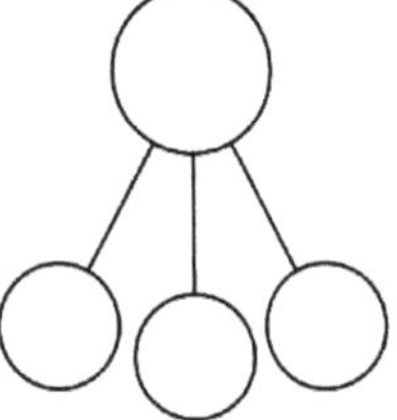
Another part circle added.

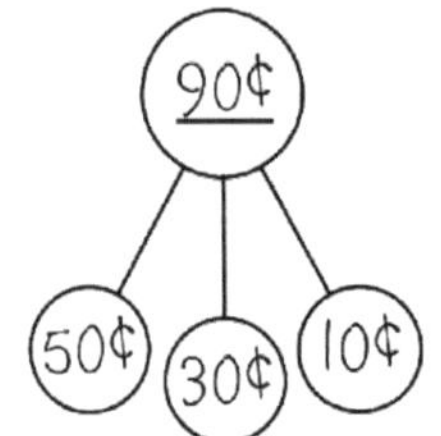

50¢ + 30¢ + 10¢ = 90¢.
Problem 1 solution.

Ask: Will this part-whole circle set work for this problem? [no] Why not? [There are more than two parts.] Tell the child to draw another part. See the second figure above.

EXPLANATIONS:

A mathematical model is a tool, not a rule, for problem solving. Children should feel free to make modifications as needed.

ACTIVITIES FOR TEACHING:

EXPLANATIONS:

Tell the child to solve the problem on his worksheet. Ask him to show the solution. See the third figure on the previous page.

Now tell him to answer the second question in the problem. [No, it is less than a dollar.]

Problem 2. Ask the child to read the second problem.

> Todd wants to buy a gift that costs one dollar. He has 3 quarters and 4 nickels. How much more money does he need? What coins could he use?

Give him a few minutes to think about the problem. When he has solved the first question, ask him to explain his solution. See below.

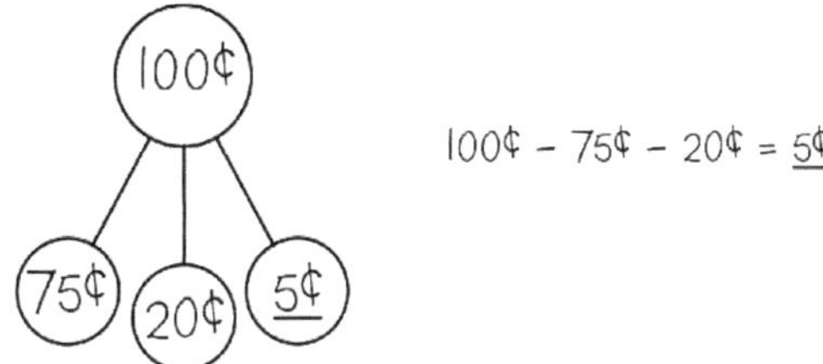

100¢ − 75¢ − 20¢ = <u>5¢</u>

Solution for Problem 2.

Then ask him for his answer to the second question. [a nickel or five pennies]

Problems 3 and 4. Ask the child to read and solve the last two problems.

3. Belle is buying two bananas. Each banana cost 39¢. What is her change from a dollar?

   39¢ + 39¢ + <u>22¢</u> = 100¢

4. Logan has 56¢. He has one quarter, five nickels, and some pennies. How many pennies does he have?

   56¢ = 25¢ + 25¢ + <u>6¢</u>

Problems 5–8. You might remind the child that additions can be done in any order.

The solutions are shown below.

56¢ + 13¢ + 17¢ + 20¢ = **$1.06** $2 + 49¢ + 10¢ + 5¢ = **$2.64**

79¢ + 29¢ + $1.01 + 1¢ = **$2.10** 25¢ + 25¢ + 50¢ + 50¢ = **$1.50**

In conclusion. Ask: Which is more 20 nickels or 10 dimes? [same] Which is less 2 dollars or 6 quarters? [6 quarters] Which is more 2 dollars or 1 dollar and 75 cents? [2 dollars]

Lesson 101: Review and Games 9

OBJECTIVES:

1. To review recent topics
2. To continue to develop skill through playing math card games

MATERIALS:

1. Worksheet 67-A or 67-B, Review 9
2. *Math Card Games* book, M9

ACTIVITIES FOR TEACHING:

EXPLANATIONS:

Worksheet 67-A. Give the child the worksheet. Tell him to listen to the problems and write only the answers on the worksheet. Read each problem twice.

$1 – 42¢ 98¢ – 39¢ $44 + $77

Tell him to complete the worksheet. Solutions are below.

Write only the answers.

58¢

59¢

$121

Write the answers.

3 dimes + 19¢ = 49¢

$3.39 + $0.21 = $3.60

$1.31 – 32¢ = 99¢

Add 284 + 1836.

		2	8	4
+	1	8	3	6
	2	1	2	0

Add.

	4	1	8	5
+	3	8	6	9
	8	0	5	4

Subtract.

	7	7	4	1
–	5	7	6	9
	1	9	7	2

Solve the problem.

Lacey received $1.09 on Wednesday and three quarters and three dimes on Thursday. How much more money did Lacey receive on Wednesday? Write your answer two ways using a ¢ and $ sign.

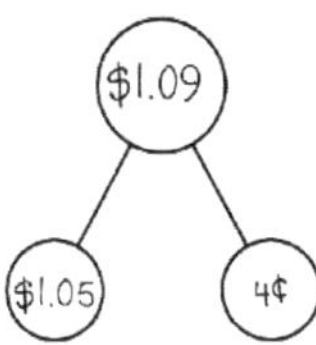

4¢ $0.04

Write >, <, or = on the lines.

1 nickel **<** 1 dime

1 dollar **=** 4 quarters

$0.76 **=** 76¢

6 dimes **>** 11 nickels

3 quarters **<** 8 dimes

Complete the equations.

4 nickels = **2** dimes

75 pennies = 3 quarters

$1.45 = $1 + **45** cents

3 nickels + **1** dimes = 1 quarter

4 dimes + **2** nickels = 2 quarters

ACTIVITIES FOR TEACHING:

EXPLANATIONS:

Make Seventy-Five Cents game. Have the child play the Make Seventy-Five Cents game, found in the *Math Card Games* book, M9.

Worksheet 67-B. Give the child the worksheet. Tell him to listen to the problems and write only the answers on the worksheet. Read each problem twice.

$1 – 57¢   97¢ – 58¢ $66 + $88

Tell him to complete the worksheet. Solutions are below.

Write only the answers.

43¢

39¢

$154

Write the answers.

2 dimes + 39¢ = 59¢

$3.41 + $0.29 = $3.70

$1.26 – 27¢ = 99¢

Add 376 + 4585.

```
    3 7 6
+ 4 5 8 5
  4 9 6 1
```

Add.

```
  6 3 7 4
+ 2 8 1 8
  9 1 9 2
```

Subtract.

```
  5 6 3 7
– 2 6 8 9
  2 9 4 8
```

Solve the problem.

Casey received $1.03 on Monday and three quarters and four nickels on Tuesday. How much less money did Casey receive on Tuesday? Write your answer two ways using a ¢ and $ sign.

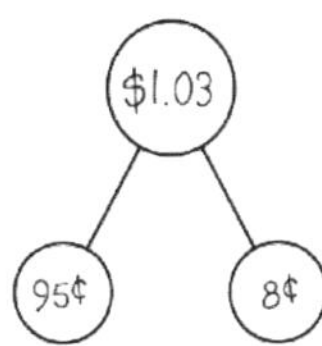

8¢ $0.08

Write >, <, or = on the lines.

1 dime **>** 1 nickel

1 dollar **<** 5 quarters

$0.98 **=** 98¢

42 pennies **<** 9 nickels

3 quarters **>** 7 dimes

Complete the equations.

6 nickels = **3** dimes

15 nickels = 3 quarters

$1.62 = $1 + **62** cents

1 nickel + **2** dimes = 1 quarter

3 dimes + **4** nickels = 2 quarters

Lesson 102: Measuring in Centimeters

OBJECTIVES:

1. To calculate perimeter
2. To write perimeter equations and solutions

MATERIALS:

1. Warm-up Practice 1
2. Worksheet 68, Measuring in Centimeters
3. Centimeter cubes
4. 4-in-1 ruler

ACTIVITIES FOR TEACHING:

Warm-up. Ask the child to do problems 11 and 12 on Warm-up Practice 1. Use an abacus as needed.

$$\begin{array}{r} 8323 \\ -4657 \\ \hline \mathbf{3666} \end{array} \qquad \begin{array}{r} 7050 \\ -2468 \\ \hline \mathbf{4582} \end{array}$$

Ask: Which is more 20 nickels or 10 dimes? [same] Which is less 2 dollars or 7 quarters? [7 quarters] Which is more 2 dollars or 1 dollar and 75 cents? [2 dollars]

Ask: Where do we write the cent symbol, before or after the amount? [after] Where do we write the dollar sign? [before] Which is more, 5¢ or $5? [$5] Which is more, 200¢ or $2? [same]

Ask: Can you measure more centimeters or more inches on your ruler? [centimeters]

Worksheet 68. Give the child the worksheet, centimeter cubes, and 4-in-1 ruler.

Problem 1. Tell the child to find the two lines, one on the left side of the paper and one on the right. Ask: Which one is longer and how much longer? Give the child some quiet time to work. [Line B is $\frac{1}{2}$ cm longer.] Ask him to explain how he did it.

Show the child the centimeter cube and remind him the edge of the cube is 1 cm long. Ask: If you put three cubes together in a row, how long would it be? [3 cm]

Problem 2. Ask him to read the first sentence in problem 2. Say: Think about what perimeter means. Wait a few seconds and then say: Perimeter is the distance around a figure. Write the word and explain that the "peri" part means around similar to periscope. The "meter" part means measure.

(peri)(meter)

"peri" means around
"meter" means measure

EXPLANATIONS:

Giving the definition of perimeter following a short wait time affirms those who know it and helps those still learning it.

Recalling a definition enhances remembering it. However, some child, upon hearing a wrong definition, find it very difficult to unlearn it.

ACTIVITIES FOR TEACHING: | **EXPLANATIONS:**

Ask: What do you need to do first to find the perimeter? [measure the sides] Tell him to measure each side with his ruler and write the measurement near the side as shown below.

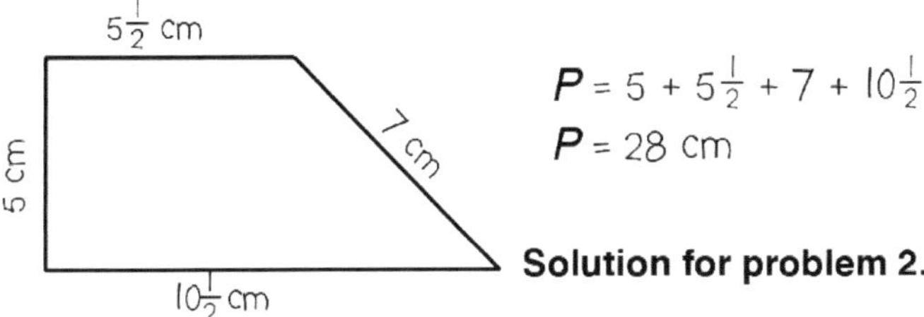

$P = 5 + 5\frac{1}{2} + 7 + 10\frac{1}{2}$
$P = 28$ cm

Solution for problem 2.

Ask: What do you do next for finding the perimeter? [Add the lengths of the sides.] Tell him to write the answers as shown above. Ask: If an ant walked around the trapezoid, how far would it walk? [28 cm]

Problem 3. Tell the child to read problem 3.

> Find the perimeter of the regular pentagon. Write the equations two ways: using addition and using multiplication.

Ask: What is a regular polygon? [a polygon with all sides and angles equal] Tell him to find the perimeter. Then ask the child to explain his answer. The solution is below.

$P = 3\frac{1}{2} + 3\frac{1}{2} + 3\frac{1}{2} + 3\frac{1}{2} + 3\frac{1}{2}$
$P = 3\frac{1}{2} \times 5$
$P = 17\frac{1}{2}$ cm

Problem 4. Ask the child to find the perimeter of the star. Then ask him to explain his answer. The solution is below.

$P = 2 \times 10$
$P = 20$ cm

Ask: Which figure, the pentagon or the star, has the greatest distance around it? [star] Which has the greater perimeter? [star] What would the perimeter of the pentagon be if each side were one half centimeter longer? [20 cm]

In conclusion. Ask: Can you measure how long a pencil is with centimeters? [yes] Can you measure time with centimeters? [no] Can you measure how cold it is outside with centimeters? [no] Can you measure how tall you are with centimeters? [yes]

Lesson 103: Measuring in Centimeters and Inches

OBJECTIVES:

1. To draw rectangles using centimeters and inches
2. To compare perimeters

MATERIALS:

1. Warm-up Practice 2
2. Worksheet 69, Measuring in Centimeters and Inches
3. Drawing board
4. T-square and 30-60 triangle
5. 4-in-1 ruler

ACTIVITIES FOR TEACHING:

EXPLANATIONS:

Warm-up. Ask the child to do problems 1 and 2 on Warm-up Practice 2. Use an abacus as needed.

$$\begin{array}{r} {}^{1}8\,7\,{}^{1}3\,8 \\ +1\,6\,3\,5 \\ \hline \mathbf{10\,373} \end{array} \qquad \begin{array}{r} 6\,8\,6\,{}^{1}1 \\ -2\,8\,3\,9 \\ \hline \mathbf{4\,0\,2\,2} \end{array}$$

Ask: Can you measure how long a piece a paper is with centimeters? [yes] Can you measure time with centimeters? [no] Can you measure how warm it is outside with centimeters? [no] Can you measure how tall your friend is with centimeters? [yes]

Ask the child to count by tens, starting at 65 and ending at 185. [65, 75, 85, . . . , 185]

Worksheet 69. Give the child the drawing board with worksheet attached, T-square, 30-60 triangle, and 4-in-1 ruler. Tell him that today he will draw rectangles using centimeters and inches.

Rectangle 1. Tell the child to read the instructions for the first problem.

> Draw a rectangle that measures $7\frac{1}{2}$ cm by 3 cm. Start at the dot.

Proceed with the child as follows, saying: Starting at the dot, draw a horizontal line. Ask: Do we know how long to draw it? [no] See the left figure below. Next use the centimeter side of the ruler and measure $7\frac{1}{2}$ cm. Use a tick mark to show it. See the right figure below.

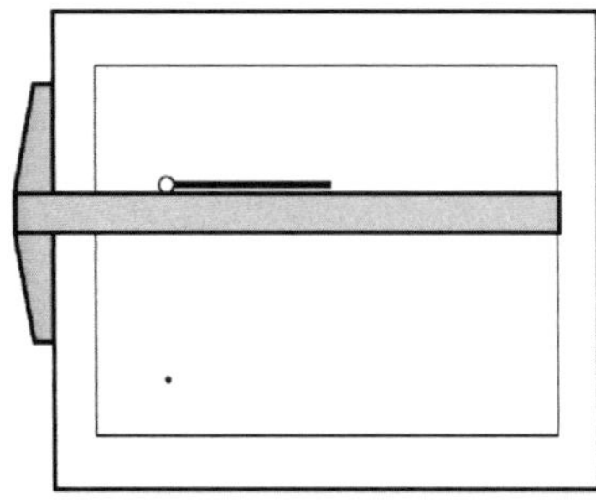

Drawing the horizontal line.

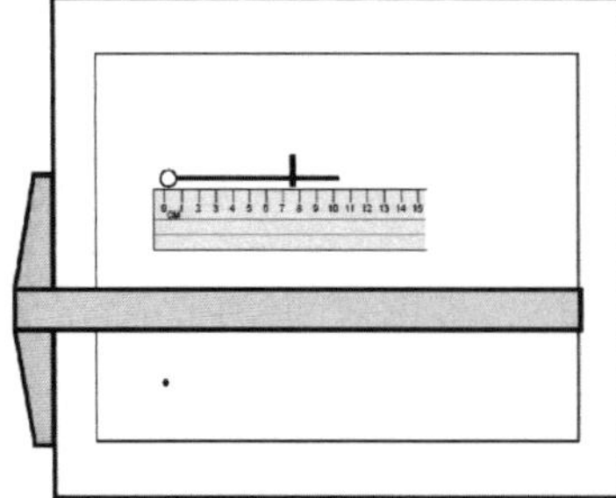

Drawing a tick mark at $7\frac{1}{2}$ cm.

ACTIVITIES FOR TEACHING:

Next draw a side as shown in the left figure below. Measure and mark 3 cm as shown in the right figure.

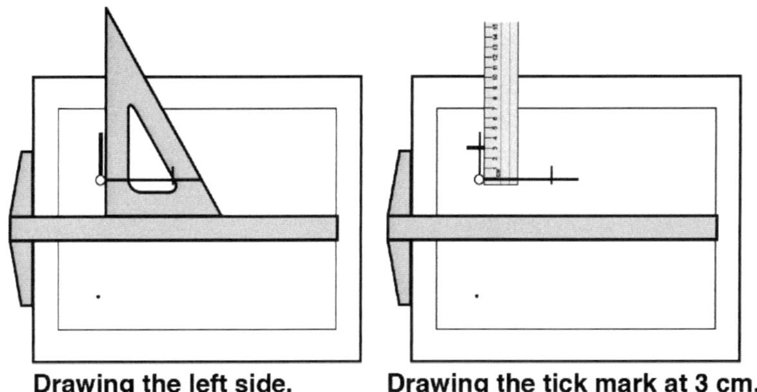

Drawing the left side. **Drawing the tick mark at 3 cm.**

Ask: What should we do next? [Draw the other two sides.] See the figures below.

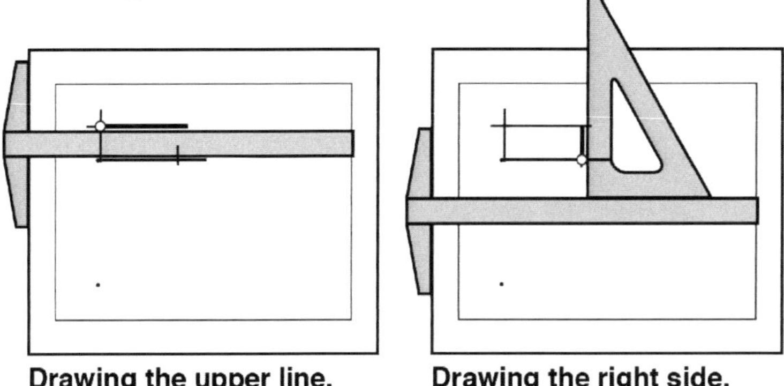

Drawing the upper line. **Drawing the right side.**

Problem 2. Ask the child to draw the next rectangle on his worksheet. Remind him to use inches. The rectangle is shown below on the right.

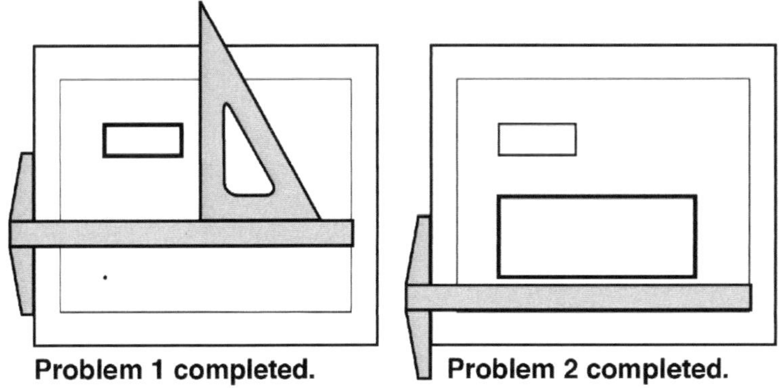

Problem 1 completed. **Problem 2 completed.**

Perimeter. Ask the child to find the perimeters for each rectangle, using centimeters for problem 1 and inches for problem 2. Solutions are shown below.

Problem 1: $P = 7\frac{1}{2} + 3 + 7\frac{1}{2} + 3$ $P = 21$ cm

Problem 2: $P = 7\frac{1}{2} + 3 + 7\frac{1}{2} + 3$ $P = 21$ in

In conclusion. Ask: Are the perimeters the same for the two rectangles? [no] Why not? [The units are different.]

EXPLANATIONS:

Lesson 104: Measuring in Feet

OBJECTIVES:

1. To learn the meaning of a *foot* and *ft*
2. To learn the terms *yard* and *yardstick*
3. To measure in feet

MATERIALS:

1. Warm-up Practice 2
2. Tiles
3. 4-in-1 ruler
4. Folding meter stick
5. **2 pieces of $8\frac{1}{2}$" × 11" paper***
6. Math journal

ACTIVITIES FOR TEACHING:

Warm-up. Ask the child to do problems 3 and 4 on Warm-up Practice 2. Use an abacus as needed.

$$\begin{array}{r} 7\overset{1}{7}4\overset{1}{3} \\ -5817 \\ \hline \mathbf{1926} \end{array} \qquad \begin{array}{r} 60\overset{1}{5}7 \\ +4537 \\ \hline \mathbf{10\,594} \end{array}$$

Ask: Can you measure more centimeters or more inches on your ruler? [centimeters]

Ask the child to count by tens, starting at 55 and ending at 165. [55, 65, 75, . . . , 165]

Ask: What is one half plus one half? [1] What is 11 and one half plus 2 and one half? [14]

One foot. Give the child the tiles and the 4-in-1 ruler. Tell him to lay out 12 tiles in a row. Ask: How long do you think the line is in inches? [12 in.] Tell him to measure it with his ruler. See below.

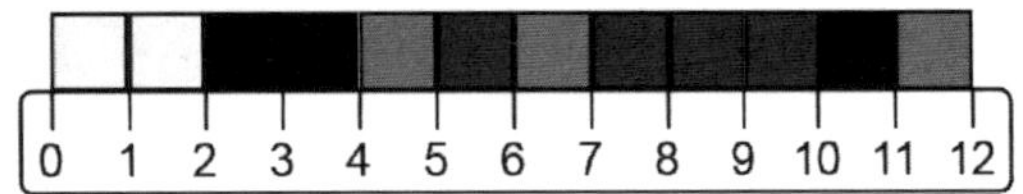

Tiles lined up against the ruler.

Tell him that there is a special name for 12 inches; it is called one *foot*. Hundreds of years ago, 12 inches was the length of a certain person's foot.

Show the length of 1 foot between your hands. Ask: Does your own foot measure more or less than the measuring foot? [less] How long is a foot in inches? [12 in.] Is 13 inches more or less than a foot? [more] Is 9 inches more or less than a foot? [less] How much is half of a foot? [6 in.] How much is a fourth of a foot? [3 in.] How much is a quarter of a foot? [3 in.]

One yard. Give the child the folding meter stick. Tell him to open the meter stick and turn it so the inches are visible. Ask: How many inches do you see? [36] Tell him that thirty-six inches equals 1 *yard*. Ask: How many inches in 1 yard? [36]

EXPLANATIONS:

* Two pieces of paper will be needed again in a few days.

The folding meter stick is somewhat fragile, so remind the child to treat it carefully.

ACTIVITIES FOR TEACHING:

EXPLANATIONS:

Tell him to use his 4-in-1 ruler and find out how many feet are in a yard. [3] See the figures below.

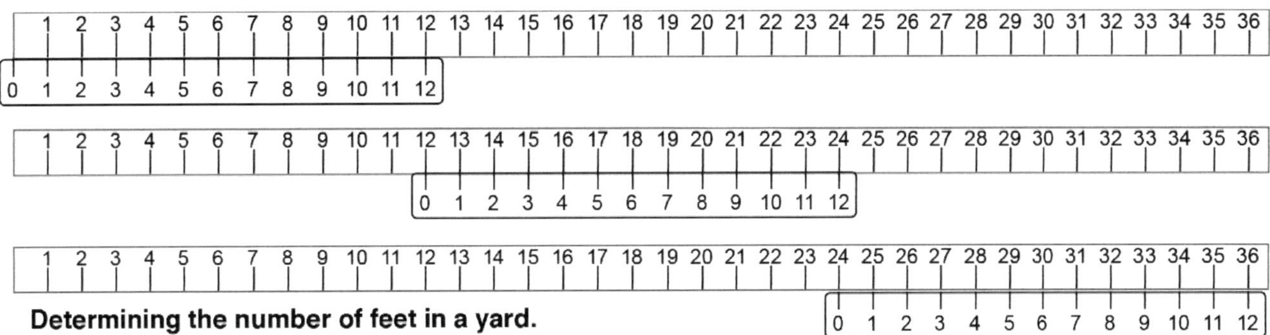

Determining the number of feet in a yard.

Ask: How many feet are in a yard? [3] Tell him that a measuring stick that is 1 yard long is called a *yardstick*. Ask: Where do you start measuring on the yardstick? [the end] Where do you start measuring on the ruler? [the 0]

Problem 1. Give the child two pieces of paper. Tell him to make a rectangle by laying the two pieces of paper side by side, as shown on the right. Tell him to draw a picture of it in his math journal.

1 ft 5 in.

1 ft 8 in.

Two pieces of paper side-by-side.

Tell him to measure the width of the papers in feet and inches. [1 ft 5 in.] Tell him the abbreviation for foot is *ft*; ask him to write the measurements on his drawing. Ask: How wide are the two pieces of paper in inches? [17 in.]

There is no "and" spoken between the word "foot" and the number of inches.

There is no standard for writing abbreviations for the U.S. Customary system, especially whether "ft" should be followed by a period. In this manual, only the abbreviation for "inches" will have a period; this will distinguish it from the word "in".

Next ask him to measure the diagonal of the papers in feet and inches to the closest inch. [1 ft 8 in.] Tell him to write on his drawing. Ask the child to explain how he found the diagonal when the number 20, was missing on the folding meter stick. [1 less than 21 or used the ruler]

Problem 2. Then tell him to place the two sheets of paper end to end as shown on the right. Tell him to draw it in his journal and to find the height and diagonal of the papers in feet and the nearest inch. [1 ft 10 in. and 2 ft]

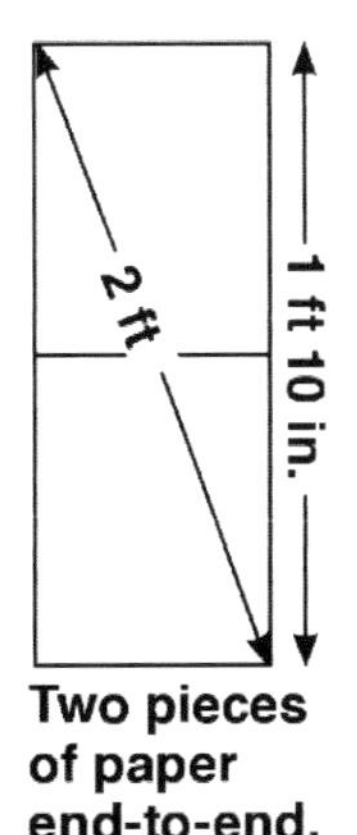

Two pieces of paper end-to-end.

In conclusion. Ask: How many inches are in a foot? [12 in.] How many inches are in a yard? [36 in.] How many feet are in a yard? [3] How many inches are in 2 feet? [24 in.]

Lesson 105: Problems Using Feet

OBJECTIVES:

1. To solve problems involving feet and yards
2. To explore how to use a calculator

MATERIALS:

1. Warm-up Practice 2
2. 4-in-1 ruler
3. Folding meter stick
4. Worksheet 70, Problems Using Feet
5. Casio SL-450S calculator

ACTIVITIES FOR TEACHING:

Warm-up. Ask the child to do problems 5 and 6 on Warm-up Practice 2. Use an abacus as needed.

$$\begin{array}{r} 7{}^{1}2\,5{}^{1}1 \\ -2432 \\ \hline \mathbf{4819} \end{array} \qquad \begin{array}{r} 9623 \\ +4165 \\ \hline \mathbf{13788} \end{array}$$

Ask: How many inches are in a foot? [12 in.] How many inches are in a yard? [36 in.] How many feet are in a yard? [3] How many inches are in 2 feet? [24 in.]

Ask: Can you measure more centimeters or more inches on your ruler? [centimeters]

Ask: Can you measure how long a pencil is with centimeters? [yes] Can you measure time with centimeters? [no] Can you measure how warm it is outside with centimeters? [no] Can you measure how tall your neighbor is with centimeters? [yes]

Ask: What is one half plus 1 and one half? [2] What is 9 and one half plus 7 and one half? [17]

Worksheet 70. Give the child the 4-in-1 ruler, folding meter stick, and worksheet.

Problem 1. Tell the child to read the first problem.

> Measure your height and another person's height in inches. Then change the measurements to feet and inches.

Suggest he measures to the nearest half inch. You might want him to mark the height of each person on the wall and then measure from the floor to the marks.

Problem 2. Have the child read the second problem.

> An amusement park has a ride that only children shorter than 1 yard can ride. Can the following children ride:
>
> Ian, 2 ft 6 in. yes Lily, 3 ft no Jordan, 3 ft 3 in. no

Ask the child to discuss his answers and reasons. Lily cannot ride because she is equal to, but not less than 1 yard tall.

EXPLANATIONS:

ACTIVITIES FOR TEACHING:

EXPLANATIONS:

Problem 3. Tell the child to read the third problem.

A dog is in a backyard that is in the shape of a square. One side of the backyard is 38 feet. How far does the dog walk when it walks around the whole backyard? [152 ft]

Give the child time to work independently on this problem. Then ask him to share how he solved it. Drawing a square might be helpful.

Problem 4. Have the child read the fourth problem.

A basketball player is 6 feet 10 inches tall. How tall is that in inches? Explain how you found the number of inches. [82 in.]

Give the child time to work independently on this problem before explaining his work and solutions. One way to convert the 6 ft. to inches is to recall that 3 ft. is 36 in., so 6 ft. is 72 in. Ten inches added to 72 gives 82 in.

Calculator. Give the child the calculator and challenge him to figure out how to find the answer to the previous problem using the calculator. Ask him to share his procedure. One procedure is to add 6 twelve times and then add 10. Another procedure uses multiplication as follows:

Press 12 (×) 6 (=), (72 will show).

Then press (+) 10 (=), (82 will show).

Ask: Which is method is easier? [using multiplication]

Write:

2 ft 4 in.

Ask the child to use his calculator to change it into inches. [12 × 2 + 4 = 28 in.]

If addition is performed before multiplication, for example, 4 + 2 × 12, a basic calculator will give 72 for the answer. The calculator first added the 4 and 2 to get 6 and then multiplied 6 by 12 to get 72.

Scientific calculators multiply before adding, so the answer would be 28 for either 2 × 12 + 4 or 4 + 2 × 12.

Problems 5–10. Ask him to do the group of exercises. Solutions are shown below.

4 ft 6 in. = **54 in.**	2 ft 8 in. = **32 in.**	5 ft 3 in. = **63 in.**
8 ft 7 in. = **103 in.**	11 ft 9 in. = **141 in.**	10 ft 5 in. = **125 in.**

Problem 11. Ask the child to read problem 11.

In most newer houses, the ceiling is 8 feet above the floor. How far from the ceiling is the basketball player's head in the fourth problem? [1 ft 2 in., or 14 in.]

After he has solved the problem, ask him to explain his solution. The simplest solution is going up. Starting at 6 ft. 10 in. it takes 2 in. to reach 7 feet, then 1 more foot to 8 feet. So the answer is 1 ft 2 in.

In conclusion. Ask: Which is more, 3 ft or 1 yard? [same] How many inches is 1 yard + 1 foot + 1 inch? [49 in.]

Lesson 106: Measuring with the Meter Stick

OBJECTIVES:

1. To learn the term *meter*
2. To learn that 1 meter is 100 centimeters
3. To measure in meters

MATERIALS:

1. Warm-up Practice 2
2. Centimeter cubes and 4-in-1 ruler
3. Folding meter stick
4. **2 pieces of $8\frac{1}{2}$" × 11" paper**
5. Math journal
6. AL Abacus

ACTIVITIES FOR TEACHING:

EXPLANATIONS:

Warm-up. Ask the child to do problems 7 and 8 on Warm-up Practice 2. Use an abacus as needed.

$$\begin{array}{r} 4\overset{1}{4}48 \\ +1366 \\ \hline \mathbf{5814} \end{array} \qquad \begin{array}{r} 46\overset{1}{2}\overset{1}{2} \\ -3365 \\ \hline \mathbf{1257} \end{array}$$

Ask: How many inches are in a foot? [12 in.] How many inches are in a yard? [36 in.] How many feet are in a yard? [3] How many inches are in 2 feet? [24 in.] Which is more, 3 ft or 1 yard? [same] How many inches is 1 yard + 1 foot + 2 inches? [50 in.]

Ask: Can you measure how long a broom is with inches? [yes] Can you measure hours with inches? [no] Can you measure how windy it is with inches? [no] Can you measure how tall your pet is with inches? [yes]

One meter. Give the child the centimeter cubes and the 4-in-1 ruler. Say: Lay out 10 centimeter cubes in a row. Find the centimeter scale on your ruler. Ask: How long do you think the line is in centimeters? [10 cm] Tell him to measure it with his ruler.

Give the child the folding meter stick and two pieces of paper. Tell him to open the meter stick and turn it so the centimeters are visible.

Tell him to measure the line of cubes with the meter stick. [10 cm] Ask: How many centimeters do you see on the whole meter stick? [100] Tell him that one hundred centimeters equals 1 *meter.* Ask: How many centimeters are in 1 meter? [100]

Tell the child to compare both sides of his meter stick. Ask: Which is longer, a meter or a yard? [meter] About how many centimeters does it take to equal a foot? [30 cm] Where do you start measuring on the meter stick? [the end] Where do you start measuring on the ruler? [the 0]

Problem 1. Give the child two pieces of paper. Tell him to make a rectangle by laying the two pieces of paper side by side, as shown on the top of the next page.

ACTIVITIES FOR TEACHING:

EXPLANATIONS:

Tell him to draw a picture of it in his math journal the same size as he did in a prior lesson.

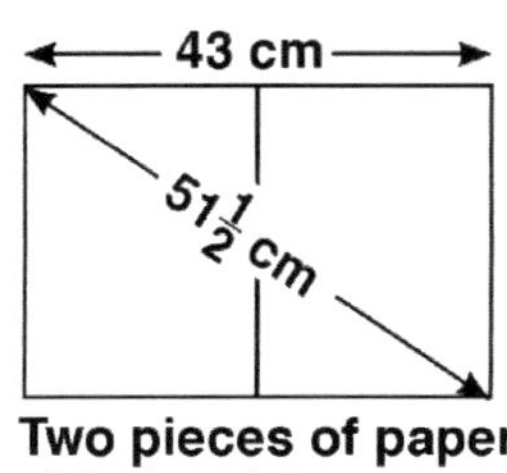

Two pieces of paper side-by-side.

Tell him to measure the width of the papers in centimeters to the nearest half centimeter. [43 cm] Tell him to write the measurement on his drawing.

Tell him to measure the diagonal of the papers in centimeters to the closest half centimeter [$51\frac{1}{2}$ cm] and write it on his drawing. Now measure the other diagonal on the papers and record. [$51\frac{1}{2}$ cm]

Although fractions are not common within the metric system, they are permissible.

Ask: How do your centimeter measurements compare to your feet and inch measurements from the prior day's work? [Centimeter measurements are higher.]

Problem 2. Ask him to place the two sheets of paper end to end as shown on the right. Tell him to draw it in his journal and to find the height and diagonal of the papers in centimeters to the nearest half centimeter and record. [56 cm and 60 cm]

60 cm
56 cm

Two pieces of paper end-to-end.

Ask: Why are the numbers you recorded greater for centimeters? [Centimeters are smaller.]

Problem 3. Give the child the abacus. Tell him to imagine that all the beads on the abacus were entered on one long wire. Ask: What would be the width of all the beads? [100 cm, which is 1 m] Tell him to write how he solved the problem in his math journal. [Each row measures 10 cm, so 10 rows is 100 cm.]

Measuring objects with centimeters. Choose several objects that the child can measure, such as a table, chairs, aquarium, shelves, and so forth. Point these out and explain he is to measure them in centimeters. Then he records the measurements with words and pictures in his math journal.

Measuring in meters. Ask the child to measure the length of a wall or hallway in meters.

In conclusion. Ask: How many centimeters are in a meter? [100] Which is longer, 1 meter or 1 yard? [1 meter] About how long is a foot in centimeters, 3 centimeters or 30 centimeters? [30 cm]

Exact calculations between centimeters and inches is not required; this is to develop perspective and relationships between measurement units.

Lesson 107: Estimating Lengths

OBJECTIVES:

1. To estimate lengths
2. To compare estimates with actual measurements

MATERIALS:

1. Warm-up Practice 2
2. 4-in-1 ruler and Folding meter stick
3. Worksheet 71, Estimating Lengths
4. AL Abacus and Centimeter cubes
5. **A list of objects to be measured***
6. **Measuring tape, optional**

ACTIVITIES FOR TEACHING:

Warm-up. Ask the child to do problems 9 and 10 on Warm-up Practice 2. Use an abacus as needed.

```
  1623      3814
+1453     −3277
  3076        537
```

Ask: How many centimeters are in a meter? [100] Which is longer, 1 meter or 1 yard? [1 meter] About how long is 2 feet in centimeters, 6 centimeters or 60 centimeters? [60 cm]

Ask: How many inches are in a foot? [12 in.] How many inches are in a yard? [36 in.] How many feet are in a yard? [3] Which is more, 3 ft or 3 yards? [3 yards] How many inches is 1 yard + 1 foot? [48 in.]

Worksheet 71. Give the child the worksheet, abacus, centimeter cubes, and the measuring tools. Ask him to show with his hands about how much is 10 cm. Remind him that 10 beads on the abacus measures 10 cm.

Look at the worksheet with the four columns as shown.

Object	Guess	Measured	Difference

Ask the child to guess how wide the abacus is to the closest centimeter. Tell him to write "width ab" and the guess on the worksheet as shown below.

Object	Guess	Measured	Difference
width ab	20 cm		

Tell the child to measure the abacus and record the measurement. [25 cm]

Object	Guess	Measured	Difference
width ab	20 cm	25 cm	

Ask: How close is the guess; what is the difference between the guess and the measurement? [5 cm, for this example]

Object	Guess	Measured	Difference
width ab	20 cm	25 cm	5 cm

EXPLANATIONS:

*These are objects in the room or outdoors that the child can measure in centimeters, meters, inches, feet, and yards, such as chairs, tables, windows, doors, walls, picture frames, shrubs, cars, and so forth.

Remember, exact calculations between centimeters and inches is not required; this is to develop perspective and relationships between measurement units.

ACTIVITIES FOR TEACHING:

EXPLANATIONS:

Tell the child to guess the height of the abacus and write it on his worksheet. Then tell him to measure it and find the difference. See below.

Object	Guess	Measured	Difference
width ab	20 cm	25 cm	5 cm
height ab	22 cm	19 cm	3 cm

Estimating a row of centimeter cubes. Say: Take a large handful of cubes and put them into a long line without counting. Guess how long your line is to the nearest centimeter and write your guess on your worksheet. Then tell him to measure the line and write it down and find the difference.

The child can decide which tool to use to measure. Deciding which tool to use is part of being competent in measuring.

Tell him to take another handful and do the process again.

Estimating the rows in inches. Tell the child to turn his ruler to the side with inches and to see what 10 inches looks like. Say: Now guess how long the rows of cubes are in inches and write that down. Then measure them and find the differences.

Measuring a row of cubes in centimeters and inches could be repeated using different handfuls of cubes.

More estimating. Give the child some suggestions for estimating and measuring other objects. Include lengths long enough to use the folding meter stick. Ask him to write the name of the object or draw a simple picture on his worksheet.

In conclusion. Ask: If your difference column on your worksheet had a zero, what would that mean? [guessed exactly right]

Lesson 108: Reading Rulers

OBJECTIVES:

1. To read a ruler when measurement is not started at zero

MATERIALS:

1. Warm-up Practice 2
2. Worksheet 72, Reading Rulers

ACTIVITIES FOR TEACHING:

EXPLANATIONS:

Warm-up. Ask the child to do problems 11 and 12 on Warm-up Practice 2. Use an abacus as needed.

$$\begin{array}{r} 7214 \\ -3548 \\ \hline \mathbf{3666} \end{array} \qquad \begin{array}{r} 7050 \\ -1376 \\ \hline \mathbf{5674} \end{array}$$

Ask: How many centimeters are in a meter? [100] Which is longer, 1 meter or 1 yard? [1 meter] About how long is a foot in centimeters, 3 centimeters or 30 centimeters? [30 cm]

Ask: How many inches are in a foot? [12 in.] How many inches are in a yard? [36 in.] How many feet are in a yard? [3] How many inches are in 3 feet? [36 in.]

Worksheet 72. Give the child the worksheet.

Problem 1. Tell the child to look carefully at the first figure on the worksheet. See below.

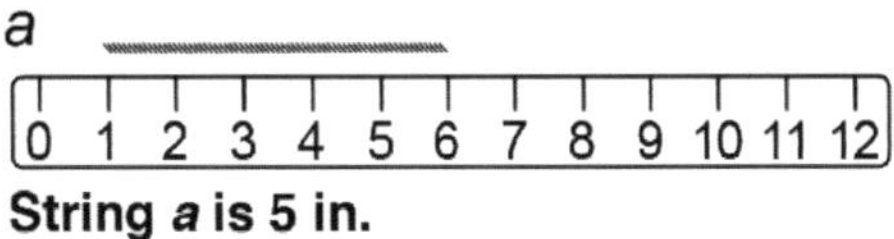

String *a* is 5 in.

Tell him to write down his answer and explain how he got it. [5 in.] He may have said that there are five inches between 1 and 6. Or, since the measuring started at 1, it is 1 in. too long, so the length is 5 in.

Problem 2. Repeat for problem 2. Here the string measures 3 in. See below.

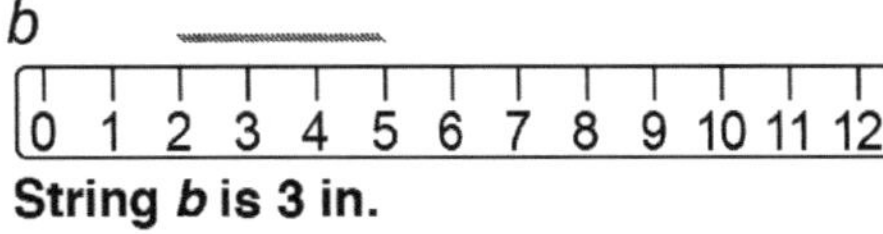

String *b* is 3 in.

ACTIVITIES FOR TEACHING:

Problems 3 and 4. Continue with problems 3 and 4. See below.

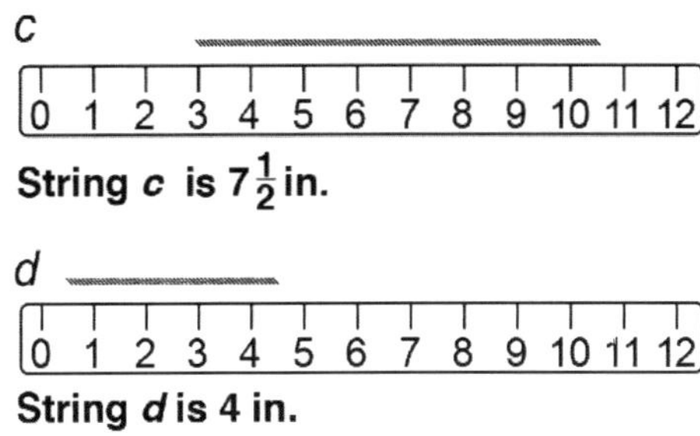

String *c* is $7\frac{1}{2}$ in. long and string *d* is 4 in. long. For string *d*, ask the child to mentally move the ruler so the end of the string lines up with 0. Ask: Now how long is the string? [4 in.]

Problem 5. Tell the child to do the next problem. Then ask him to explain how he solved the problem.

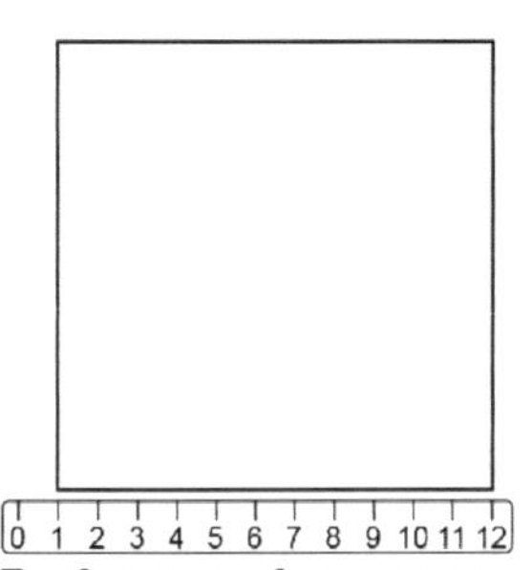

Perimeter of a square.

One way to solve it is to add 11 four times, 44 in., then think that 1 yard is 36 in. So 44 in. is 1 yard 8 in. That makes 3 ft 8 in.

Another way is to think 11 in. is 1 in. less than 1 ft. So the perimeter is 4 ft minus 4 in., which is 3 ft 8 in.

Problems 6. Tell the child to solve the last problem. Then tell him to explain his solution.

The lengths are shown below.

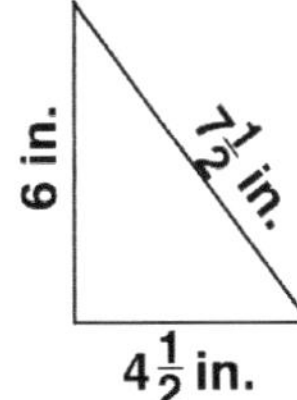

In conclusion. Ask: Where on a ruler is the best place to start measuring? [at the zero] Do you have to start at the zero? [no] When you are finding the perimeter of a square, why do you need to measure only one side of the square? [The sides are all the same.]

EXPLANATIONS:

For child experiencing difficulty, encourage him by asking questions, such as "What is perimeter?" [distance around] or "What is special about the sides of a square?" [all the same]

Lesson 109: Measuring Area

OBJECTIVES:

1. To discuss measurement in general
2. To learn to write square inches as in^2
3. To learn to write square centimeters as cm^2

MATERIALS:

1. Warm-up Practice 3
2. Tiles
3. Math journal
4. Centimeter cubes
5. Worksheet 73, Measuring Area
6. **Colored pencils or crayons, optional**

ACTIVITIES FOR TEACHING:

Warm-up. Ask the child to do section 1 on Warm-up Practice 3. Use an abacus as needed. Answers are 91, 100, 112, and 70.

Ask: Where on a ruler is the best place to start measuring? [at zero] Do you have to start at the zero? [no]

Ask: How many centimeters are in a meter? [100] Which is longer, 1 meter or 1 yard? [1 meter] About how long is 2 feet in centimeters, 6 cm or 60 cm? [60 cm]

Measuring. Discuss measurement in general by asking the child what kinds of things can be measured. Make a list similar to the one below.

Measure	What it tells us
Length	How long
Area	How much flat space
Temperature	How warm or cold
Weight	How heavy
Time	When something happens
Angle	Amount space between two lines with a common point
Price	What something costs

Square inch. Give the child the tiles. Remind him that earlier in the year, he measured area with these tiles. Show a tile and ask: How long is each side of a tile? [1 in.] What shape are they? [square] Remind him that they are called a square inch and they can also be used to measure area.

Square inch problem. Ask the child to use the tiles to make a rectangle that is 3 in. by 4 in. See the figure on the next page.

EXPLANATIONS:

This lesson emphasizes the measurement part of area. Earlier lessons introduced area from the standpoint of arrays and multiplication.

ACTIVITIES FOR TEACHING:

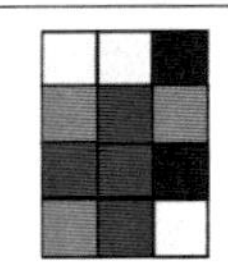
3 by 4 rectangle.

Two rectangles with same areas.

Ask: How many square inches do you need to cover the area? [12] What is the area of the rectangle measured in square inches? [12 square inches]

Write:

$$12 \text{ in}^2$$

Say: We write square inches with a little raised 2 after "in" and do not use a period after the "n". The little 2 means we have inches in two directions.

Equal areas. Ask the child to make another rectangle that has the same area as his first rectangle. See the two possibilities above in the right figures.

Tell him to write the equations to find the area and perimeters of the new rectangles in his math journal. The equations are shown below.

$A = 3 \times 4$	$A = 6 \times 2$	$A = 12 \times 1$
$A = 12 \text{ in}^2$	$A = 12 \text{ in}^2$	$A = 12 \text{ in}^2$
$P = 14$ in.	$P = 16$ in.	$P = 26$ in.

Ask: Are the areas equal? [yes] Are the perimeters equal? [no]

Square centimeter. Give the child the centimeter cubes. Show an edge of the cube and ask: How long is each edge of this cube? [1 cm] Point out the square and ask: What shape is this? [square] Say: It is a square centimeter. It can be used to measure area in square centimeters.

Write:

$$1 \text{ cm}^2$$

Say: This is how we write 1 square centimeter.

Worksheet 73. Give the child the worksheet. The first problem on the worksheet is similar to the above problem, but in centimeters. The solutions are shown at the right.

In conclusion. Ask: If the areas of two rectangles are the same, does that mean their perimeters will be the same? [no] Which is larger, 1 inch or 1 centimeter? [1 inch] Which is larger, 1 in^2 or 1 cm^2? [1 in^2]

EXPLANATIONS:

There are over a dozen ways of abbreviating *square inches.* The form used here, "in^2", corresponds to the standard for the metric system, cm^2.

Be sure to read *12 in^2* as "twelve square inches." Avoid saying "twelve inches squared," which has an entirely different meaning.

12 square inches could be an area 4 in. by 3 in. It is a measurement of area written as "12 in^2."

12 squared is 144. Extending that, *12 inches squared,* is 144 inches, which is incorrect.

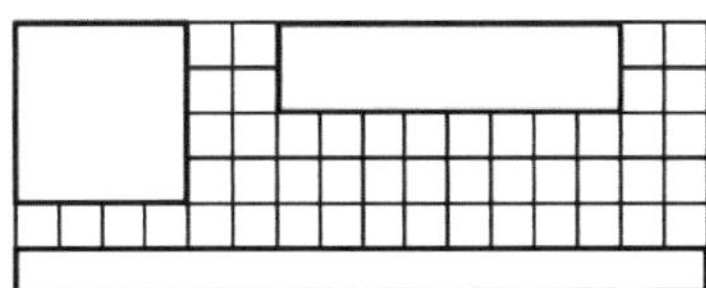

$A = 4 \times 4 = 16$ cm^2, $P = 16$ cm

$A = 8 \times 2 = 16$ cm^2, $P = 20$ cm

$A = 16 \times 1 = 16$ cm^2, $P = 34$ cm

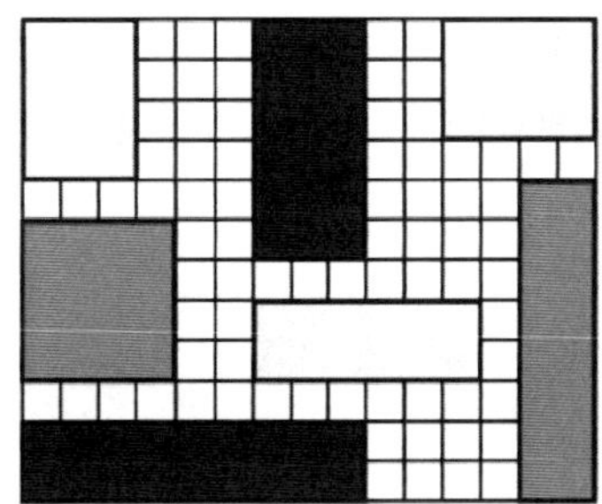

Lesson 110: Area on Geoboards

OBJECTIVES:

1. To find areas on the geoboard
2. To work with square units
3. To work with halves of square units

MATERIALS:

1. Warm-up Practice 3
2. Geoboard
3. Worksheet 74, Area on Geoboards

ACTIVITIES FOR TEACHING:

Warm-up. Ask the child to do section 2 on Warm-up Practice 3. Use an abacus as needed. Solutions are 1 and 1.

Ask: If the areas of two rectangles are the same, does that mean their perimeters will be the same? [no] Which is smaller, 1 inch or 1 centimeter? [1 centimeter] Which is smaller, 1 in^2 or 1 cm^2? [1 cm^2]

Ask: How many centimeters are in a meter? [100] Which is longer, 1 meter or 1 yard? [1 meter] About how long is 3 feet in centimeters, 10 centimeters or 100 centimeters? [100 cm]

Ask: Where on a ruler is the best place to start measuring? [at the zero] Do you have to start at the zero? [no] When you are finding the perimeter of a square, why do you need to measure only one side of the square? [The sides are all the same.]

Square units. Give the child a geoboard. Ask him to make the smallest possible square on the geoboard. See the left figure below. Ask: Is your square a square centimeter? [no] Tell him it is also too large to be a square inch, so we will call it a square unit. Ask: What is the area of your square? [1 square unit] Demonstrate how to write it.

1 unit^2

Rectangles. Tell the child to make a rectangle with 2 unit^2. See the second figure below. Next ask him to make two rectangles on his geoboard each having four square units. See the right figure below.

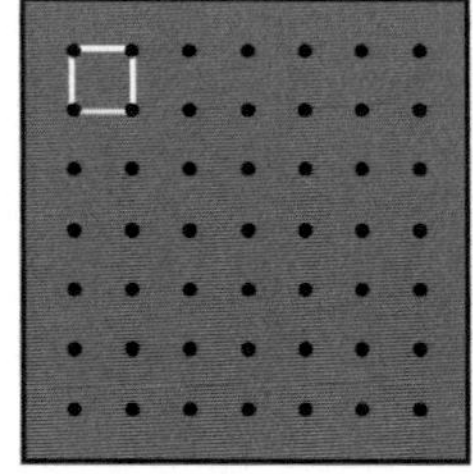

A 1 unit^2.

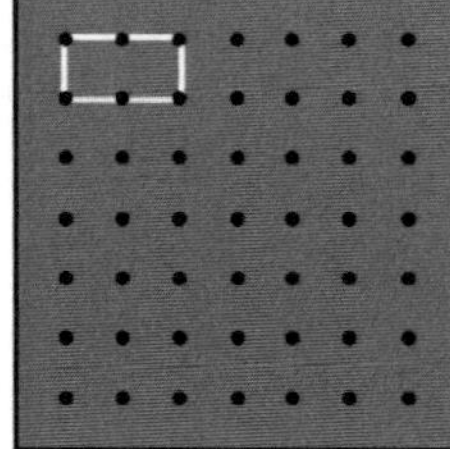

A rectangle having 2 unit^2.

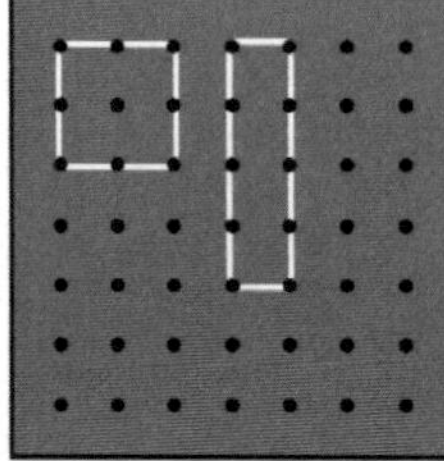

Two rectangles having 4 unit^2.

EXPLANATIONS:

ACTIVITIES FOR TEACHING:

EXPLANATIONS:

One half of a square unit. Tell the child: Make a rectangle having one square unit. See the first figure on the right. Say: Now make a triangle with half the area. See the first triangle in the figure at the right. Say: The area of the triangle is one half square unit.

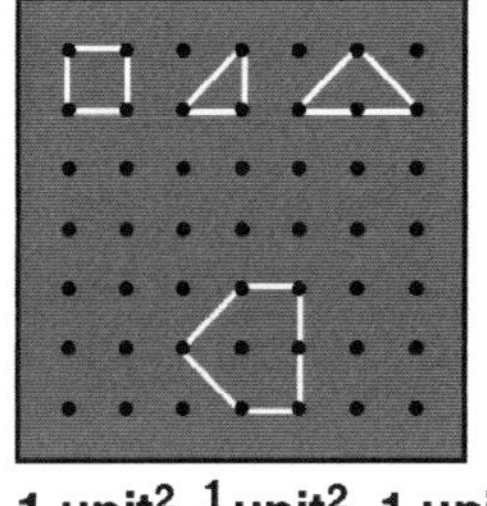

1 unit^2, $\frac{1}{2}$unit^2, 1 unit^2
3 unit^2

Tell the child to make a triangle that is twice as large as the first triangle. See the second triangle in the figure above as one possible example. Ask: What is the area of your new triangle? [1 unit^2] How do you know? [two halves makes a whole] Does it look like it has the same area as the square? [yes]

Make the last shape in the figure above and ask: What is the area of this shape? [3 unit^2] How do you know? [Two square units and two halves makes 3 unit^2.]

Worksheet 74. Give the child the worksheet. Point out that the dotted squares on the worksheet are square centimeters. Tell him to only complete problem 1; the solution is below.

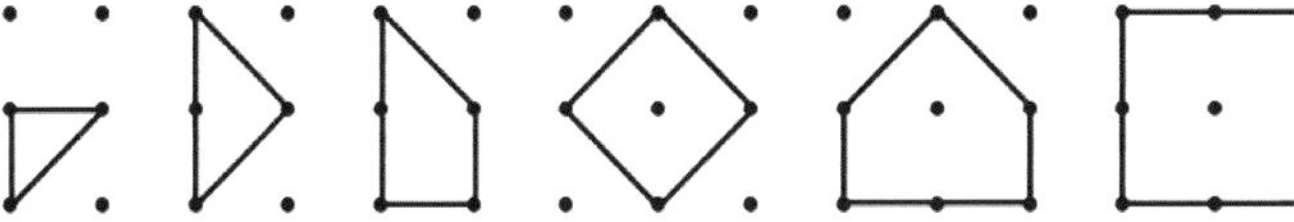

Another half of a square unit. Tell the child to make a 2 by 1 rectangle. See the first shape in the figure. Then tell him to make a triangle by dividing the rectangle in half with a diagonal. See the next figure on the right. Ask: What is the area of the triangle? [one square unit] How do you know? [The rectangle is 2 square units and the triangle is half of the rectangle, so it must be 1 square unit.]

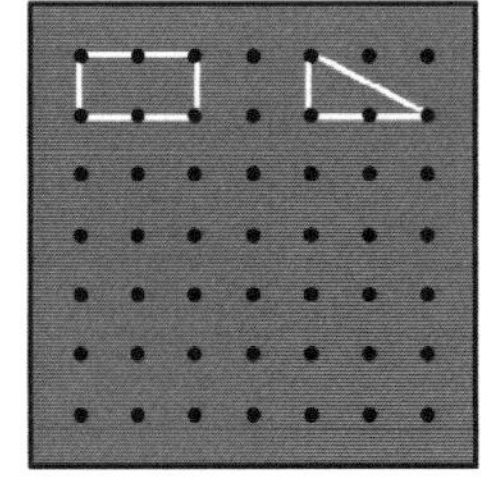

Rectangle: 2 unit^2.
Triangle: 1 unit^2.

Problem 2. Ask the child to finish the worksheet. Ask him to discuss his solutions. The solutions are below.

A. **2 cm^2**	*B.* **2 cm^2**	*C.* **2 cm^2**
D. **3 cm^2**	*E.* **1 cm^2**	*F.* **$1\frac{1}{2}$ cm^2**
G. **$1\frac{1}{2}$ cm^2**	*H.* **3 cm^2**	*I.* **2 cm^2**

To find these areas, many children will find it helpful to mentally move parts of the shape to a more advantageous location.

This worksheet will be used in a future lesson.

In conclusion. Ask: What is 2 square centimeters plus 4 square centimeters? [6 cm^2] What is $2\frac{1}{2}$ square centimeters plus $2\frac{1}{2}$ square centimeters? [5 cm^2] What is 3 square centimeters minus $1\frac{1}{2}$ square centimeters? [$1\frac{1}{2}$cm^2]

Lesson 111: Review and Games 10

OBJECTIVES:

1. To review recent topics
2. To continue to develop skill through playing math card games

MATERIALS:

1. Worksheet 75-A or 75-B, Review 10
2. 4-in-1 ruler
3. *Math Card Games* book, A9 or S9
4. Math journal for scoring

ACTIVITIES FOR TEACHING:

Worksheet 75-A. Give the child the worksheet and 4-in-1 ruler. Tell him to listen to the problems and write only the answers on the worksheet. Read each problem twice.

1 m – 57 cm   37¢ – 18¢ $15 + 89¢

Tell him to complete the worksheet. Solutions are below.

Write only the answers.

43 cm

19¢

$15.89

Write the answers.

4 dimes + 17¢ = 57¢

86 + 17 = 103

5 × 5 = 25

Solve the problem.

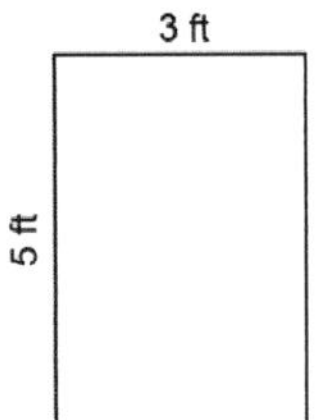

Alex and friends want to make a fence for a pet. They have 4 yards of fencing material. Is it enough to make the pen shown? Explain.

P = 5 + 3 + 5 + 3 = 16 ft
Each yard is 3 ft, so they have 12 ft. It is not enough.

Measuring problem.

Use your centimeter ruler and find the perimeter and area of the rectangle below.

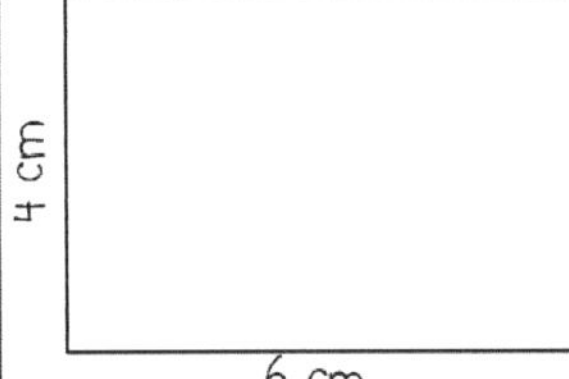

P = 6 + 4 + 6 + 4 = 20 cm

A = 6 × 4 = 24 cm^2

Write >, <, or = on the lines.

3 ft = 1 yard

4 cm < 4 in.

24 in. > 1 ft 10 in.

1 meter > 1 yard

4 in. = 10 cm

Complete the equations.

3 ft = 36 in.

12 in. = 1 ft

1 meter = 100 cm

2 ft + 6 in. = 30 in.

4 ft – 12 in. = 1 yard

EXPLANATIONS:

ACTIVITIES FOR TEACHING:

EXPLANATIONS:

Corners™ game. Have the child play a Corners™ game found in the *Math Card Games* book, A9 or S9.

Subtraction Corners™ in the Thousands. Have the child play Subtraction Corners™ in the Thousands, a variation of Zero Corners™, found in the *Math Card Games* book, S9. The players start with a score of 4000. In addition to the points that are the sum, they add 100 points if the colors are green or black and 200 points if the colors are red or blue, then subtract the total from the score.

```
 4000
- 115
 3885
- 210
 3675
- 215
 3460
```

The child's subtractions are done in his math journal as shown on the right. The winner is the player with the lowest score at the end of game.

Worksheet 75-B. Give the child the worksheet and 4-in-1 ruler. Tell him to listen to the problems and write only the answers on the worksheet. Read each problem twice.

1 m – 38 cm   62¢ – 27¢ $19 + 67¢

Tell him to complete the worksheet. Solutions are below.

Write only the answers.

62 cm

35¢

$19.67

Write the answers.

5 dimes + 21¢ = 71¢

74 + 49 = 123

5 × 4 = 20

Solve the problem.

Robin and Morgan made a sandbox for their sister. It has four sides each 1 meter long. What is the distance around the sandbox in centimeters?

P = 1 + 1 + 1 + 1 = 4 m
Each meter is 100 cm, so
distance is 400 cm.

Measuring problem.

Use inches on your ruler and find the perimeter and area of the rectangle below.

1 in.

3 in.

P = 3 + 1 + 3 + 1 = 8 in.

$A = 3 \times 1 = 3\ in^2$

Write >, <, or = on the lines.

1 yard < 1 meter

3 in. > 3 cm

21 in. = 1 ft 9 in.

36 in. = 1 yard

2 in. = 5 cm

Complete the equations.

3 ft = 36 in.

12 in. = 1 ft

2 meter = 200 cm

10 in. + 1 ft = 22 in.

1 yard – 1 ft = 24 in.

Lesson 112: Introducing Line Plots

OBJECTIVES:

1. To learn the term *line plots*
2. To construct a line plot with data
3. To gather data

MATERIALS:

1. Warm-up Practice 3
2. Tiles
3. Worksheet 76, Introducing Line Plots

ACTIVITIES FOR TEACHING:

Warm-up. Ask the child to do section 3 on Warm-up Practice 3. Use an abacus if needed. Problems and solutions are shown below.

399 + 19 = **418**	372 + 108 = **480**
543 + 21 = **564**	293 + 40 = **333**
146 + 18 = **164**	731 + 60 = **791**

Ask: Can you measure more centimeters or more inches on your ruler? [centimeters]

Ask the child to count by tens, starting at 75 and ending at 175. [75, 85, 95, . . . , 175]

Ask: What is one half plus one half? [1] What is 19 and one half plus 2 and one half? [22]

Ask: What is 2 square centimeters plus 4 square centimeters? [6 cm^2] What is 2 square centimeters plus 2 square centimeters? [4 cm^2] What is 3 square centimeters minus 1 and a half square centimeters? [$1\frac{1}{2}$ cm^2]

Tabulating tiles by color. Take a large handful of tiles. Tell the child that we are going to make a line plot to show how many of each color we have. Make a chart as shown below:

Blue	
Red	
Green	
Yellow	

Pick up one tile at a time and tell the child to make a tally mark after that color on the chart. Continue with the remaining tiles. See below.

Blue	II
Red	𝍸 II
Green	𝍸 I
Yellow	𝍸 I

EXPLANATIONS:

ACTIVITIES FOR TEACHING:

EXPLANATIONS:

Making a line plot. Say: We will now put this data on a line plot. A *line plot* is a type of chart that shows a picture of data.

Say: First you draw a line. Then you draw little marks for the number of categories; colors, in this case. Ask: How many colors do we have? [4] Say: So we need four marks. Below the marks, write the name of the colors. See below.

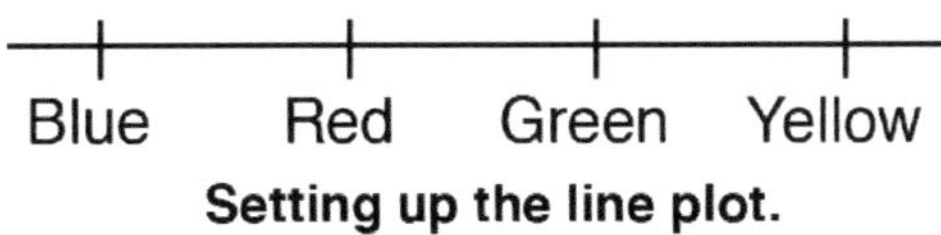

Setting up the line plot.

Ask: How many blue tiles are there? [in our example, 2] Draw two x's in the blue column. See below. Ask the child to complete the other columns. Remind him that the x's must be the same size, the same distance apart, and in straight lines.

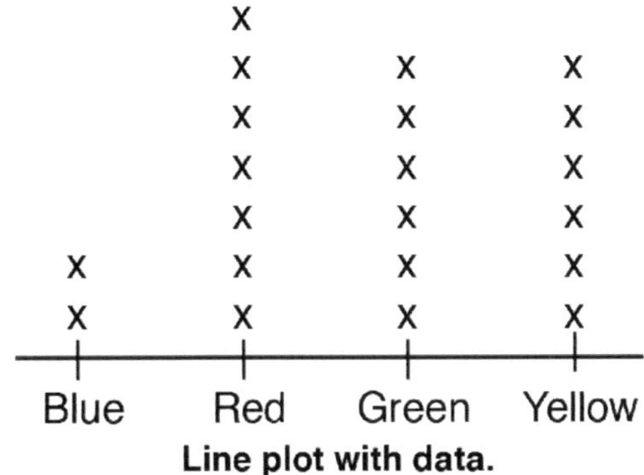

Line plot with data.

Worksheet 76. Give the child the worksheet. Tell the child to take his own handful of tiles and make his own line plot.

Birthday data. Tell the child to read the instructions for the second line plot. Let him decide how to gather the data he needs; that is, how to determine in which month his family and friends have their birthdays. Try to gather about 15 to 20 dates.

After he draws his line plot, discuss the questions:

What month has the fewest birthdays?

How many birthdays are in June, July, and August?

In what month is your birthday?

How many birthdays are in the month of your birthday?

In conclusion. Ask: What does a line plot show you? [a picture of data that shows how many things are in a group]

Lesson 113: Addition Sums Line Plot

OBJECTIVES:

1. To determine the number of facts for sums from 2–18
2. To construct a line plot with these numbers
3. To review addition facts

MATERIALS:

1. Warm-up Practice 3
2. Worksheet 77, Addition Sums Line Plot
3. *Math Card Games* book, A44*

ACTIVITIES FOR TEACHING:

Warm-up. Ask the child to do section 4 on Warm-up Practice 3. Problems and solutions are shown below.

87 + **13** = 100	437 + **21** = 458
243 + **10** = 253	372 + **28** = 400
689 + **110** = 799	731 + **99** = 830

Ask: What can a line plot show you? [a picture of data that shows how many things are in a group]

Ask: What is 46 square centimeters plus 34 square centimeters? [80 cm^2] What is 77 square centimeters plus 66 square centimeters? [143 cm^2] What is 10 cm^2 minus 1 and a half cm^2? [8 and a half cm^2]

Addition facts. Write:

11 =

Say: Name all the facts that have 11 as a sum. These facts cannot have any addends greater than 9, any duplicates, nor any facts with a zero. Write his responses as shown below:

11 = 9 + 2
11 = 8 + 3
11 = 7 + 4
11 = 6 + 5

Ask: Is 11 = 5 + 6 another fact? [no, it is a duplicate] Is 11 = 10 + 1 another fact? [no, 10 cannot be an addend] Is 11 = 6 + 6 another fact? [no, 11 does not equal 6 + 6] How many facts does 11 have? [4]

Worksheet 77. Give the child the worksheet and tell him that he will make a line plot showing how many addition facts there are for each sum from 2 to 18.

Tell him to complete both tables. Remember that facts cannot have any addends greater than 9, any duplicates, nor any facts with a zero. The completed tables are shown on the next page.

EXPLANATIONS:

*Use a deck with ten cards of each number from 1–9 for the Addition War game. This will provide the players with the 45 facts that are needed for their line plots.

Sometimes the term *combinations* is used in place of *facts*.

ACTIVITIES FOR TEACHING:

EXPLANATIONS:

Sum	Facts
2	1
3	**1**
4	**2**
5	**2**
6	**3**
7	**3**
8	**4**
9	**4**
10	**5**

Sum	Facts
11	4
12	**4**
13	**3**
14	**3**
15	**2**
16	**2**
17	**1**
18	**1**

Line plot. Tell the child to use his data and make a line plot. See below.

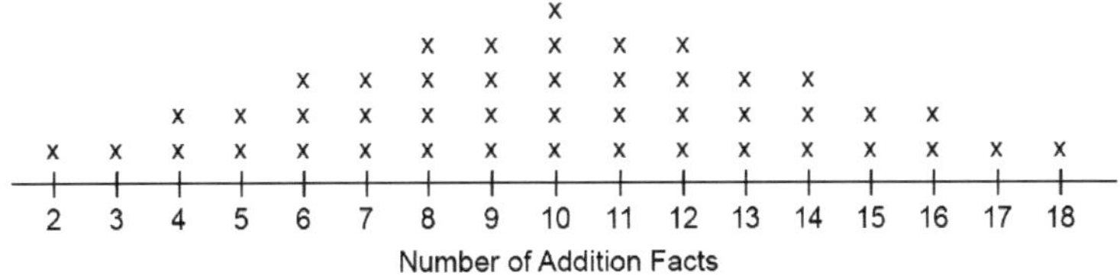

Ask: Are you surprised at how your line plot looks? Is the design symmetrical? [yes] Where is the line of symmetry? [at 10]

Tell him to answer the next five worksheet questions.

3. Which sum has the greatest number of facts? **10**
4. Which sums have four facts? **8, 9, 11, 12**
5. How many facts are on your line plot? **45**
6. How many facts have sums greater than ten? **20**
7. Are there more facts less than ten or more facts greater than ten? **same**

Addition War game. Have the child play the Addition War game found in the *Math Card Games* book, A44, using ten cards of each number from 1–9. The game is over when all the cards are played.

Say: For every turn, after you find the sums, write an "x" in the correct place on the second line plot on your worksheet, unless it is already marked. Write an "x" for the sum of your cards and write an "x" for the sum of the other player's cards. When you have a war, take a peek at the cards that are placed face down, find those sums and enter them on the line plot also.

Questions 8–9. Discuss the last two questions.

9. How many facts are there on your line plot? **45**
10. How is this line plot different from the one above?

These line plots will be slightly different from the first line plot.

In conclusion. Ask: Are you surprised at how few addition facts there are?

Lesson 114: Area Line Plots

OBJECTIVES:

1. To read and follow written instructions
2. To learn the term *include*
3. To make a line plot from areas of shapes

MATERIALS:

1. Warm-up Practice 3
2. Worksheet 78, Area Line Plots
3. Worksheet 74, Area on Geoboards
4. Geoboards, optional

ACTIVITIES FOR TEACHING:

Warm-up. Ask the child to do section 5 on Warm-up Practice 3. Answers are shown below.

7, 12, 24, 60, 30, 15

Ask: Can you measure more centimeters or more inches on a ruler? [centimeters]

Ask: What does a line plot show you? [a picture of data that shows how many things are in a group]

Ask: What is 3 square centimeters plus 6 square centimeters? [9 cm^2] What is 4 square centimeters plus 4 square centimeters? [8 cm^2] What is 4 and one half square centimeters minus 2 and a half square centimeters? [2 cm^2]

Worksheet 78. Give the child the worksheet and ask him to take out Worksheet 74 that was completed in a prior lesson.

Tell him to read the first two instructions on Worksheet 78. Ask: What does it tell you to do? [Fill in the tables with data from Worksheet 74, then make a line plot.]

The tables are shown below and the line plot on the next page.

Shape	Area in cm^2
I	2
II	4
III	3
IV	$1\frac{1}{2}$
V	1
VI	$\frac{1}{2}$

Shape	Area in cm^2
A	2
B	2
C	2
D	3
E	1
F	$1\frac{1}{2}$
G	$1\frac{1}{2}$
H	3
I	2

EXPLANATIONS:

Learning to read and understand written instructions is a necessary skill for children to master.

ACTIVITIES FOR TEACHING:

EXPLANATIONS:

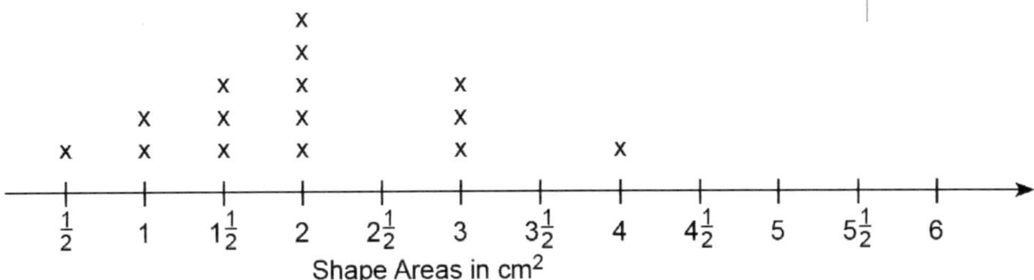

Question 3. Tell the child to read question 3.

> Sketch at least four shapes on the grid. Include a rectangle, a pentagon, and a hexagon. Fill in the table below.

Ask: What does *include* mean? [it is part of the whole] Do you need to make a triangle? [no] Do you have to make six shapes? [no, the directions say at least four] Can you make five shapes? [yes] How many sides does a pentagon have? [5] How many sides does a hexagon have? [6]

Some children may benefit from making their shapes on the geoboard before drawing them on the grid.

Question 4. Tell him to read question 4.

> Add the areas of these shapes to the line plot above. Underline the x's of your new areas.

Questions 5–8. Tell him to complete the worksheet Discuss the remaining questions. Answers will vary.

> 5. Which shape has the least area?
> 6. Which shape has the greatest area?
> 7. What area is the most common?
> 8. How many different areas are on your line plot?

In conclusion. Ask: Are squares parallelograms? [yes] Are triangles included parallelograms? [no] Are rectangles included parallelograms? [yes]

Lesson 115: Making Squares with Tangrams

OBJECTIVES:

1. To compare areas of the tangram pieces
2. To draw shapes using the 45 triangle

MATERIALS:

1. Warm-up Practice 4
2. Tangrams
3. Drawing board
4. Worksheet 79, Making Squares with Tangrams
5. T-square and 45 triangle*

ACTIVITIES FOR TEACHING:

Warm-up. Ask the child to do section 1 on Warm-up Practice 4. The problems and hundred chart are below.

7 + 5 = **12**	9 tens and 3 ones = **93**
40 − 19 = **21**	39 + 41 = **80**
10 × 8 + 2 = **82**	100 − 92 = **8**
35 − 16 = **19**	2 less than 100 = **98**
6 × 5 = **30**	Number of quarters in 75¢ = **3**
96 − 7 = **89**	Odd number before 72 is **71**

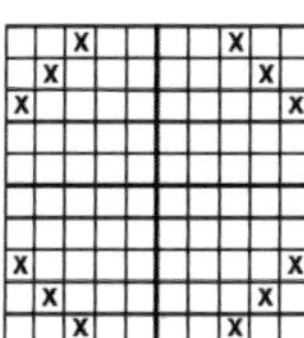

The tangram pieces. Give the child a set of tangrams. Ask: How many pieces are there? [7] How many different shapes? [3] What are they? [right triangle, square, and parallelogram] How many right triangles altogether do the pieces have? [5] Are any triangles congruent? [two smallest and two largest] Tell him that when we talk about the triangles, we will name the triangles: small, medium, and large.

Constructing shapes with small triangles. Ask the child to use the small tangram triangles to construct the square, the parallelogram, and the medium triangle. See the figures below.

Square

Parallelogram

Medium triangle

Ask: Compared to the small triangle, how much area does the medium triangle have? [twice as much] Compared to the small triangle, how much area does the square have? [twice as much] Compared to the small triangle, how much area does the parallelogram have? [twice as much] Ask: What does this tell you about the areas of the square, parallelogram, and medium triangle? [They are equal.]

EXPLANATIONS:

*This 45 triangle is not the same triangle that was used in earlier lessons. That was the 30-60 triangle.

Even though the square is also a parallelogram, the term *parallelogram* will refer to the non-square parallelogram.

Comparing areas in different configurations is a prerequisite for understanding fractions. Fractions are traditionally taught using an area model.

ACTIVITIES FOR TEACHING:

Constructing squares. Ask the child to make squares with his tangram pieces. The following squares can be made:

Using the two small triangles,
Using the three smaller triangles,
Using the two large triangles,
Using the three smaller triangles, the square, and the parallelogram.

See the figures below.

Squares of three different sizes.

Worksheet 79. Give the child the drawing board with the worksheet attached, T-square, and 45 triangle.

Refer to the first figure below while demonstrating how to draw the square. Start with a horizontal line. The sides can be drawn first, but the diagonal must be drawn before the top line can be drawn. See figure below on the right.

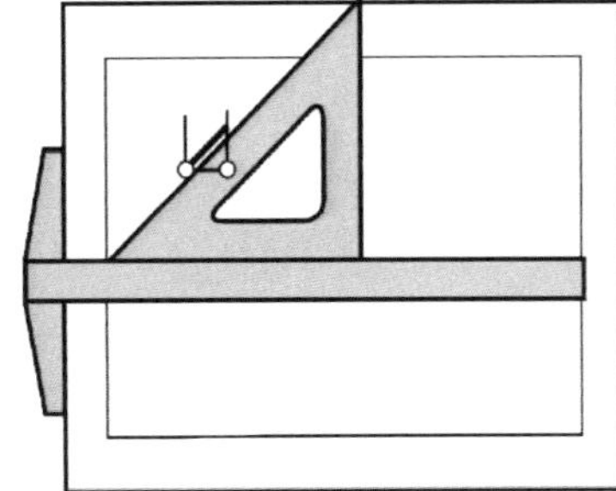

Drawing sides and diagonal.

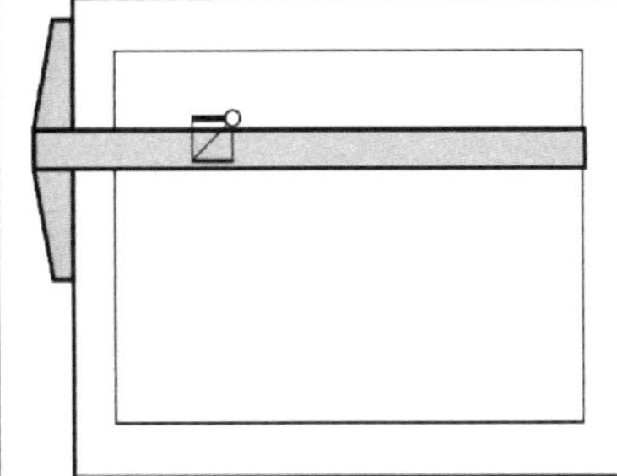

Drawing the top line.

Tell the child to complete the worksheet. Remind him to first make the figure with his tangrams. The solutions are below. There are additional solutions that are mirror images.

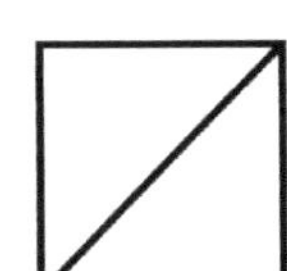
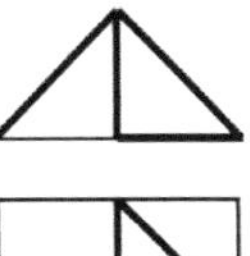

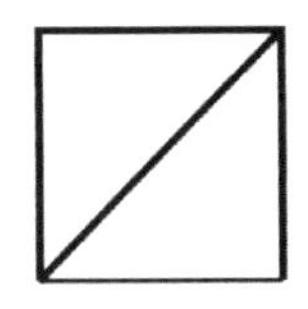
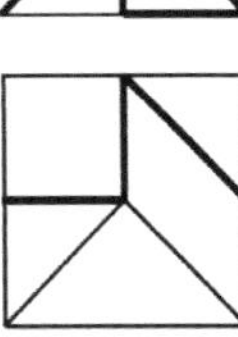

In conclusion. Ask: What do you need before you can draw a line with your drawing tools? [a starting point]

EXPLANATIONS:

Some children might need this hint for the fourth square: The largest side of the medium triangle forms a side of the square.

Another square can be made, which uses all seven pieces, but is more challenging.

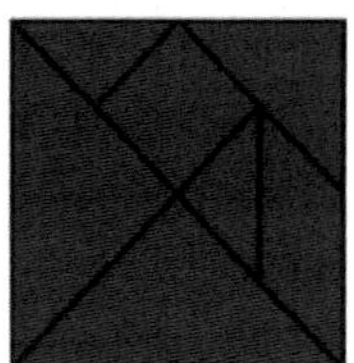

A common error is to guess where the top line of the square should be rather than do the necessary constructions to find the starting point.

Help the child realize the quality of his work results from his attention to precision.

LESSON 116: MAKING RECTANGLES WITH TANGRAMS

OBJECTIVES:

1. To make rectangles of different sizes
2. To draw rectangles by adding other shapes

MATERIALS:

1. Warm-up Practice 4
2. Tangrams
3. Drawing board
4. Worksheet 80, Making Rectangles with Tangrams
5. T-square and 45 triangle

ACTIVITIES FOR TEACHING:

Warm-up. Ask the child to do section 2 on Warm-up Practice 4. The problems and hundred chart are shown below.

13 + 10 = **23**	15 + 10 = **25**
53 + 10 = **63**	65 + 2 = **67**
29 + 20 = **49**	39 + 30 = **69**
30 − 1 = **29**	23 + 18 = **41**
25 + 2 = **27**	45 + 20 = **65**
100 − 79 = **21**	87 − 26 = **61**

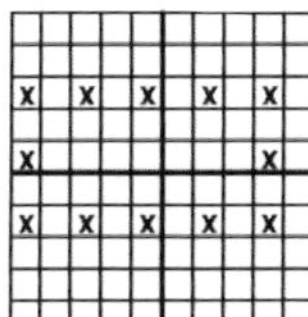

Constructing rectangles. Give the child a set of tangrams. Tell him to make a rectangle that is not a square using three tangram pieces. See the figures below. Ask him if he can find another solution.

Rectangles made with three tangram pieces.

Remind him that solving these problems are like doing a jigsaw puzzle. Sometimes he will need to try many different pieces before he finds one that works.

Next tell him to make rectangles that are not squares using four tangram pieces. Ask him if he can find more than one solution. See the figures below.

Rectangles using four tangram pieces.

EXPLANATIONS:

This type of geometry work encourages a child to persevere.

There are other solutions if two sets of tangrams are used.

ACTIVITIES FOR TEACHING:

EXPLANATIONS:

Tell him to make rectangles using five pieces. See the figures below.

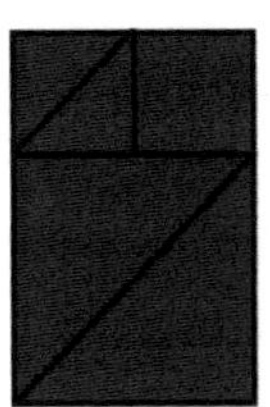
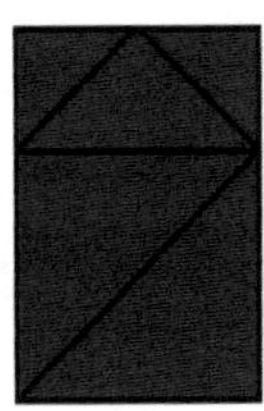
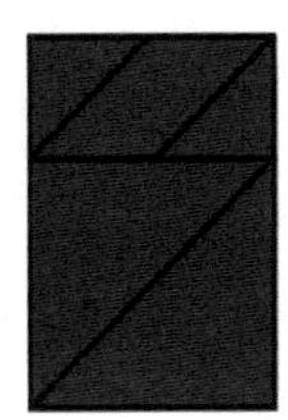

Rectangles using five tangram pieces.

Worksheet 80. Give the child the drawing board with the worksheet attached, T-square, and 45 triangle.

Say: The worksheet has part of the rectangle drawn. The first thing to do is make the rectangle with your tangrams. Then you complete the rectangles on the worksheet using your drawing tools.

The solutions are shown below.

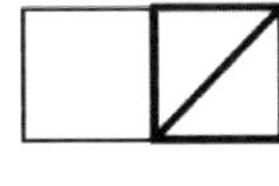
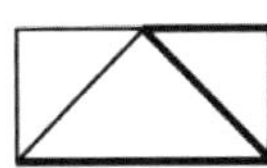

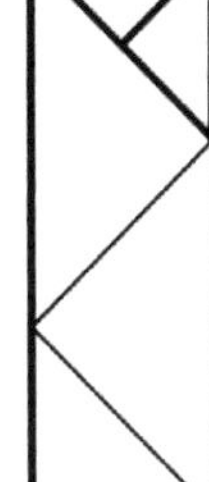
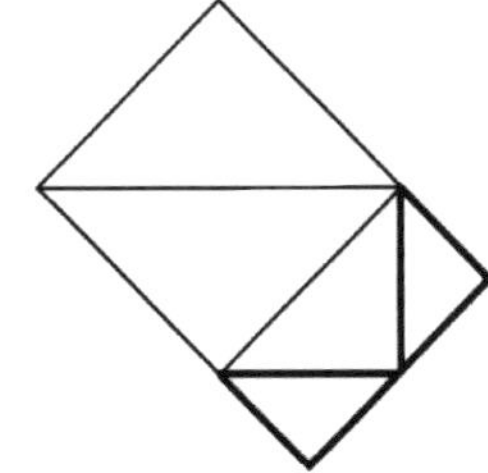

In conclusion. Ask: How many pairs of parallel sides does a rectangle have? [two] How many angles does a rectangle have? [four] What are two names for the angles in a rectangle? [right angle and 90°] What is the name of a special rectangle with all four sides congruent? [square]

Lesson 117: Making Trapezoids with Tangrams

OBJECTIVES:

1. To review trapezoids
2. To find several solutions to make a trapezoid with tangram pieces

MATERIALS:

1. Warm-up Practice 4
2. Tangrams
3. Drawing board
4. Worksheet 81, Making Trapezoids with Tangrams
5. T-square and 45 triangle

ACTIVITIES FOR TEACHING:

Warm-up. Ask the child to do section 3 on Warm-up Practice 4. The problems and hundred chart are shown below.

18 + 17 = **35**	92 – 37 = **55**
5 × 3 = **15**	2 × **5** = 10
29 + 36 = **65**	Third multiple of 2 is **6**
52 – 48 = **4**	60 – 15 = **45**
51 – 44 = **7**	3 quarters is **75¢**
5 × 5 = **25**	Sides in a triangle is **3**

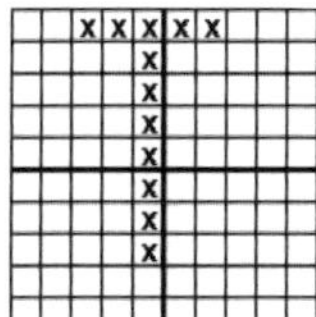

Constructing trapezoids. Give the child the tangrams. Ask: A rectangle has how many pairs of parallel lines? [two] But a trapezoid can only have how many pairs of parallel lines? [one] Emphasize: A trapezoid has four sides with one and only one of the sides parallel.

Tell the child to make five different trapezoids using two tangram pieces. See the figures below.

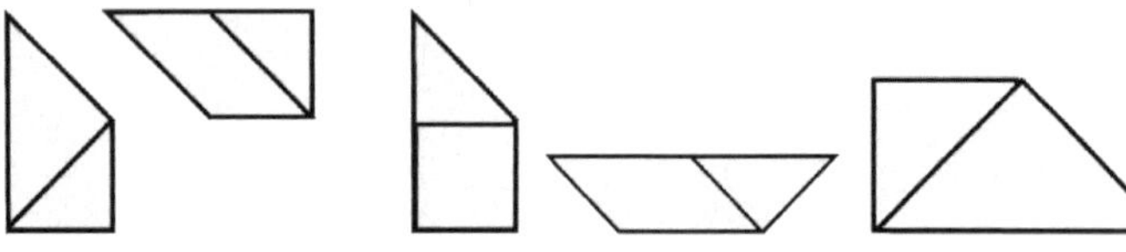

Trapezoids made with two tangram pieces.

Large trapezoids. Challenge the child to make as large a trapezoid as he can. Two possibilities are shown are the next page.

EXPLANATIONS:

In British English, this figure is often called a *trapezium*.

ACTIVITIES FOR TEACHING:

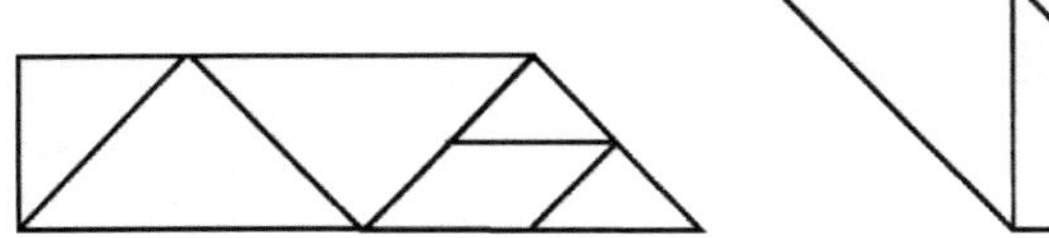

Two large trapezoids.

After the child has made the above two trapezoids, ask: Which trapezoid is larger? [the trapezoid on the right] How do you know? [It uses all 7 pieces; the left one does not use the square.]

Worksheet 81. Give the child the drawing board with the worksheet attached, T-square, and 45 triangle.

Say: The worksheet has a large shaded trapezoid near the top of the page. Use your tangrams to make a trapezoid that fits the shaded area. Then draw that trapezoid with your drawing tools. Do this for six different trapezoids.

Possible solutions are shown below.

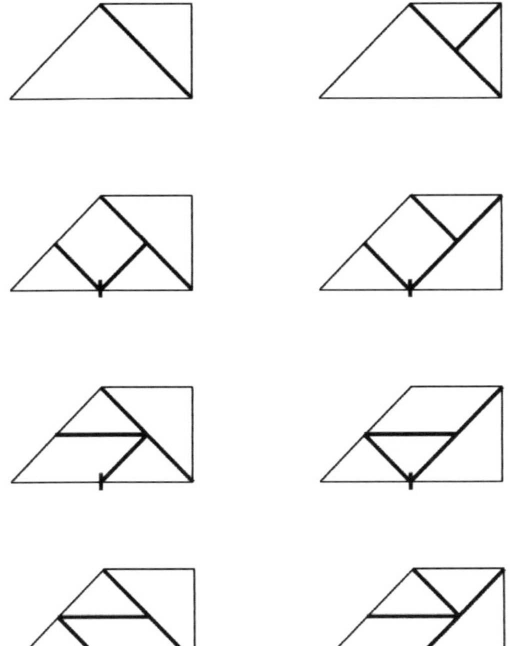

In conclusion. Ask: How many pairs of parallel sides does a trapezoid have? [one] How many angles does a trapezoid have? [four] Can a trapezoid have a right angle? [yes] Does a trapezoid always have a right angle? [no]

EXPLANATIONS:

Finding the tick mark (Lesson 66) is shown below.

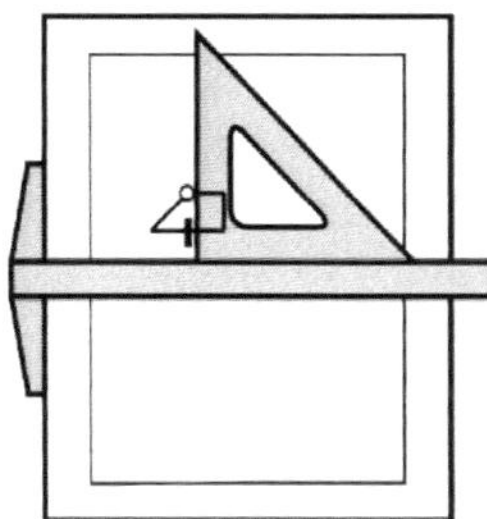

The starting point can also be found without a tick mark by drawing from the upper right corner as shown in the figure below.

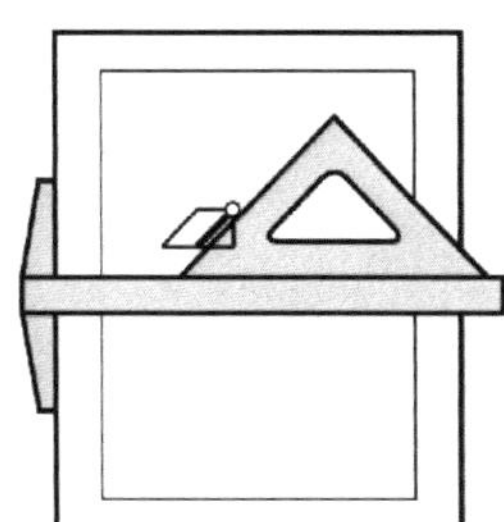

Lesson 118: Making Reflections with Tangrams

OBJECTIVES:

1. To understand what a reflection is
2. To review line of symmetry
3. To visualize a reflection
4. To draw reflections of shapes made with tangrams

MATERIALS:

1. Warm-up Practice 5
2. Tangrams
3. Geometry reflector
4. Worksheet 82, Making Reflections with Tangrams
5. Drawing board, T-square, and 45 triangle

ACTIVITIES FOR TEACHING:

Warm-up. Ask the child to do section 1 on Warm-up Practice 5. The problems and hundred chart are shown below.

19 + 32 = **51**	10 × 3 + 3 = **33**
80 – 38 = **42**	3 quarters = **75¢**
80 – 7 = **73**	56 less than 100 = **44**
7 tens and 2 ones **72**	First odd number after 60 is **61**
100 – 45 = **55**	5 tens and 21 ones = **71**
37 + 37 = **74**	2 quarters & 3 nickels = **65**

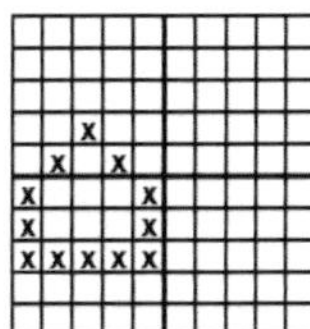

Making reflections with the reflector. Give the child the tangrams.

Set a geometry reflector between you and the child. Then place a large tangram triangle next to the reflector as shown below in the left figure.

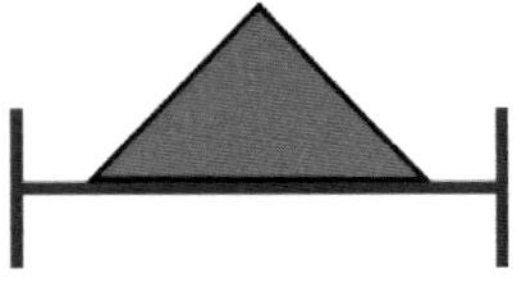

A triangle on one side of the reflector.

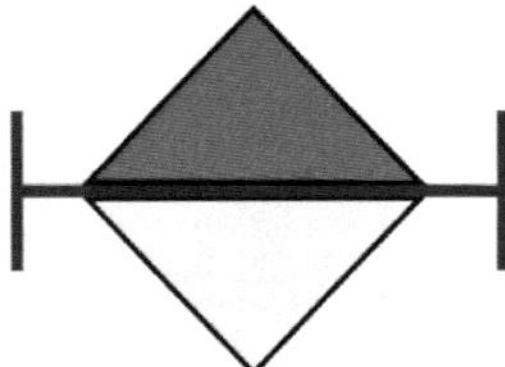

A second triangle on the other side.

Ask: What do you see in the reflector? [the triangle] Ask the child to place the other large triangle exactly on top of the reflection. See the right figure above.

Next add another tangram piece. A parallelogram is added in the left figure shown on the next page.

EXPLANATIONS:

Be sure the child is seated in front of you for this lesson until he does the worksheet.

Reflections are easier to see if the background surface is light-colored, especially when red tangram pieces are used.

ACTIVITIES FOR TEACHING:

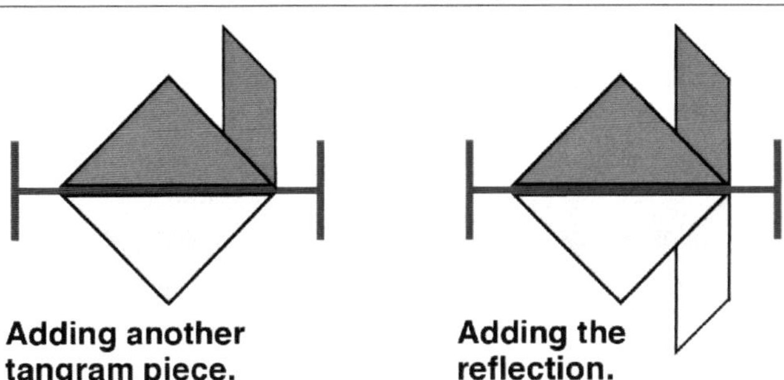

Adding another tangram piece.

Adding the reflection.

Ask the child to look at the reflection, find the new addition, and place the corresponding tangram piece on top of the reflection. See the right figure above.

Now remove the reflector. See the figure on the right.

line of symmetry

Ask: What do you see?
[One figure is the reflection of the other figure.] Say: The imaginary line where the reflector was is the line of symmetry.

Making reflections. Have the child make a shape on one side of the reflector with 2 to 3 tangram pieces. You make the reflection. Then remove the reflector. Exchange roles and do it again.

Worksheet 82. Give the child the drawing board with attached worksheet, T-square, and 45 triangle. Tell him to read the instructions. Ask him to imagine what a reflection looks like before drawing it. Remind him every line needs to start at a vertex. Encourage him to check his work with a reflector. Solutions are below.

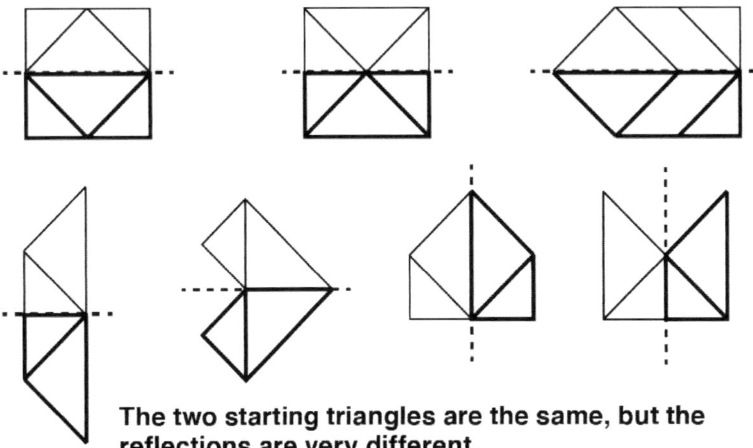

The two starting triangles are the same, but the reflections are very different.

In conclusion. Ask: When you look yourself in the mirror, is your reflection the way you actually look? [no] Where is your right hand in the mirror? [on the left]

EXPLANATIONS:

LESSON 119: MISSING FACTORS

OBJECTIVES:

1. To learn the term *factor*
2. To find the missing factor that tells how many groups
3. To use Take and Give Strategy to find missing factors

MATERIALS:

1. Warm-up Practice 5
2. AL Abacus
3. Worksheet 83, Missing Factors

ACTIVITIES FOR TEACHING:

Warm-up. Ask the child to do section 2 on Warm-up Practice 5. The questions and hundred chart are shown below.

100 – 45 = **55**	19 + 26 = **45**
29 + 8 = **37**	4 × 5 + 3 = **23**
116 – 60 = **56**	50 + 17 = **67**
14 + 20 = **34**	58 + 15 = **73**
95 – 17 = **78**	7 + 9 + 8 + 4 = **28**
32 + 14 = **46**	Even number after 62 is **64**

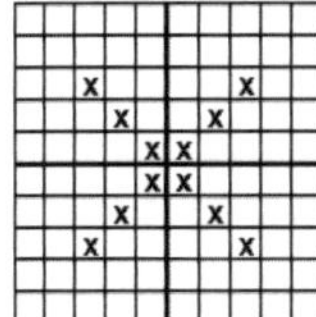

Introducing factors. Write:

5 × 4 = 20

Ask the child to read it. [5 multiplied by 4 equals 20] Ask: Which number is the product? [20] Tell him the other numbers in the equation, the 5 and the 4, are called *factors.*

Ask the child to enter the equation on his abacus as shown on the figure at the right. Ask: Where on the abacus do you see the first factor? [the number of beads in a row] Where on the abacus do you see the second factor? [the number of rows] Where on the abacus is the product? [all the beads]

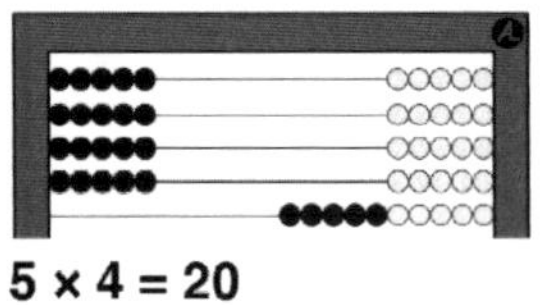

5 × 4 = 20

Finding the missing factor. Write the following:

6 × ___ = 24

Explain that he will be using his abacus to find the missing factor. Ask: Which factor is missing, the number in a row or the number of rows? [number of rows]

Demonstrate the procedure shown on the next page.

EXPLANATIONS:

Sometimes 8 × 4 is thought of as "8 groups of 4." However, consistency with the other arithmetic operations requires a closer look. To add 8 + 4, we start with 8 and transform it by adding 4. To subtract 8 – 4, we start with 8 and transform it by removing 4. To divide 8 ÷ 4, we start with 8 and transform it by dividing it into 4 groups or into groups of 4s. Therefore, to multiply 8 × 4, we start with 8 and transform it by duplicating it a total of 4 times.

The division problem of finding how many groups is often referred to as *measurement, quotative,* or *repeated subtraction* division.

ACTIVITIES FOR TEACHING:	EXPLANATIONS:

Ask: How many beads do we start with? [24] See the left figure below. Ask: How many beads do we want on each row? [6] What do we need to do? [Move the extra beads to other rows.] See the right two figures below.

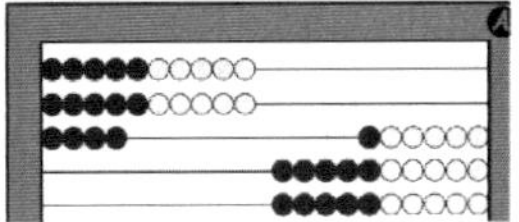
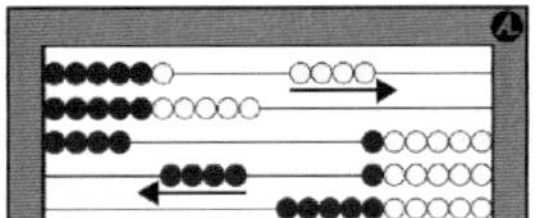
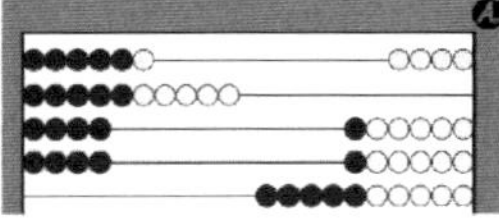

24 entered. **Taking 4 from row 1 and Giving 4 to row 4.**

Using the Take and Give Strategy, remind him to use his right hand to take the beads and his left hand to give the same number of beads to another row.

Many children really enjoy performing this procedure.

Continue by taking two beads from the second row and giving them to the third row. See the figures below.

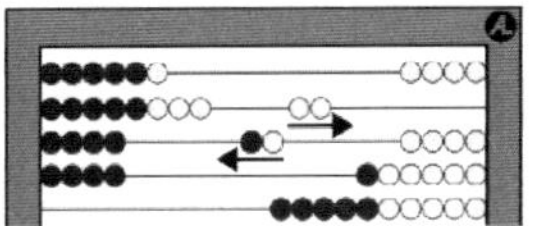
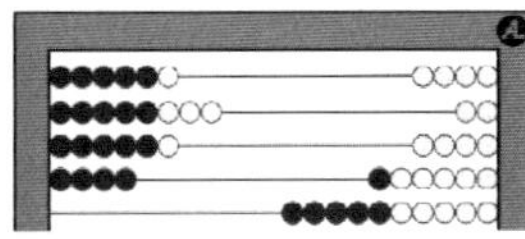

Taking 2 from row 2 and Giving 2 to row 4.

There are many different ways 24 could have been transformed into the 6 × 4 array.

Ask: What else do we need to do? [Move two beads from the second row to the fourth row.] See the figures below.

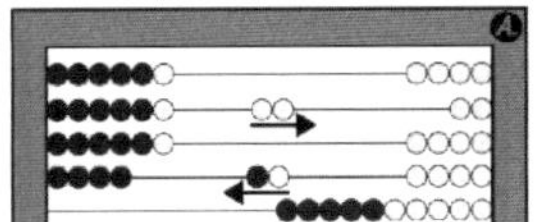

Take and Give the last 2.

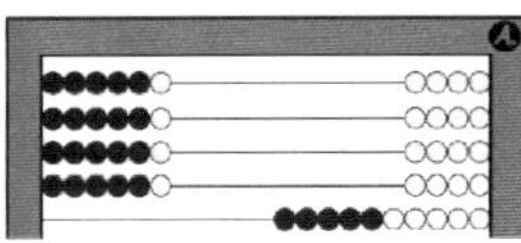

6 × <u>4</u> = 24

Ask: What does the array show? [6 × 4] Does it have the same number of beads that we had at the beginning? [yes]

Another example. Give the child 7 × ___ = 35 to do independently. [5] Ask him to explain his procedure.

Worksheet 83. Give the child the worksheet. Tell him to find the missing factors in only the top section, down to the dotted line.

The child will do only part of this worksheet for this lesson; the remainder will be completed in the following lesson.

The equations and solutions are below.

6 × **3** = 18	7 × **4** = 28	12 = 6 × **2**
5 × **6** = 30	5 × **3** = 15	20 = 4 × **5**
8 × **7** = 56	5 × **10** = 50	72 = 9 × **8**
9 × **5** = 45	8 × **6** = 48	72 = 8 × **9**
5 × **9** = 45	6 × **8** = 48	32 = 8 × **4**
6 × **9** = 54	8 × **8** = 64	25 = 5 × **5**

In conclusion. Ask: What do you call the answer when you multiply? [product] What do you call the two numbers you need to multiply? [factors] When you use Take and Give, how many numbers can you move at a time? [as many as you want]

Lesson 120: More Missing Factors

OBJECTIVES:

1. To find the missing factor that tells how many in a group

MATERIALS:

1. Warm-up Practice 5
2. AL Abacus
3. Worksheet 83, Missing Factors

ACTIVITIES FOR TEACHING:

Warm-up. Ask the child to do section 3 on Warm-up Practice 5. The questions and hundred chart are shown below.

24 + 24 = **48**
83 – 49 = **34**
60 – 13 = **47**
13 doubled = **26**
18 + 19 = **37**
22 × 2 = **44**

62 – 58 = **4**
Days in 2 weeks = **14**
5 × 3 = **15**
One half of 90° = **45°**
12 + 12 = **24**
First multiple of 2 after 45 is **46**

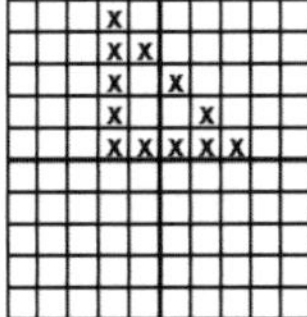

Finding the missing factor. Write the following equation:

$$\_\_\_ \times 4 = 12$$

Ask: Which factor is missing, the number in a row or the number of rows? [number in a row] Demonstrate the procedure as shown below using the Take and Give.

Ask: How many beads do we start with? [12] See the left figure below.

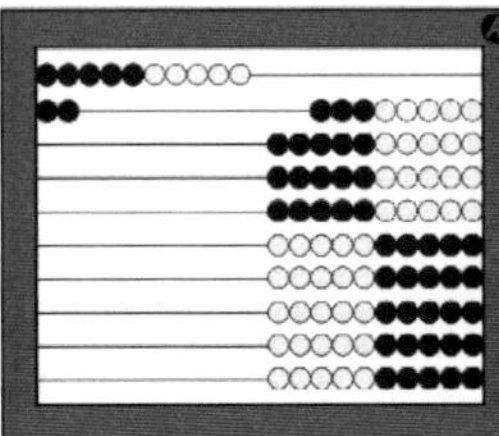

12 entered.

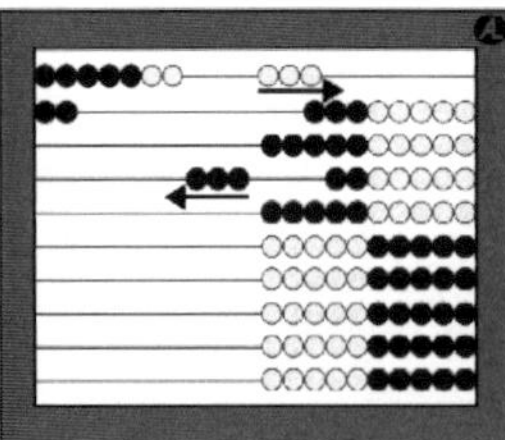

Taking 3 from row 1 and Giving 3 to row 4.

Ask: How many rows do we need? [4] What do we need to do? [Move the extra beads to other rows.] Take three beads and give them to the fourth row. See the right figure above.

EXPLANATIONS:

The number of beads moved at a time is arbitrary.

ACTIVITIES FOR TEACHING:	EXPLANATIONS:

Continue by taking three more beads from the first row and giving them to the third row. See the figures below.

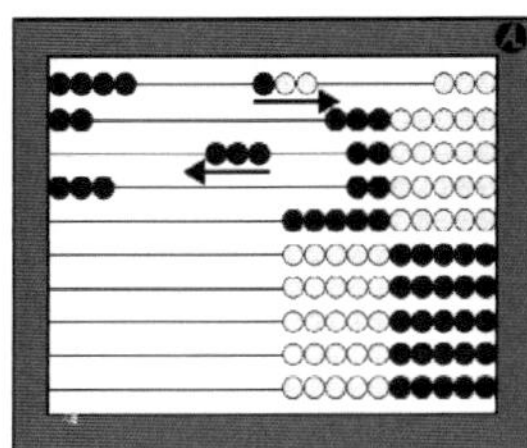
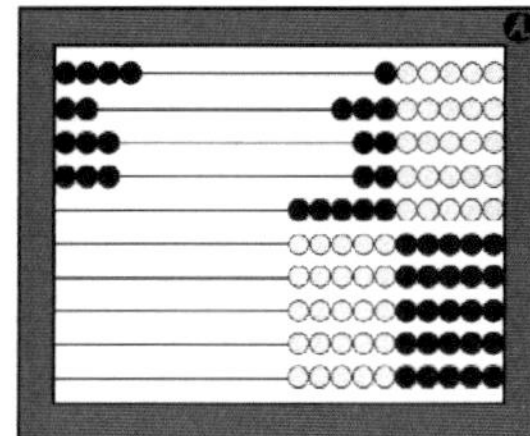

Taking 3 from row 1 and Giving 3 to row 3.

Ask: What do we need to do next? [Move one bead from the first row to the second row.] See the figures below.

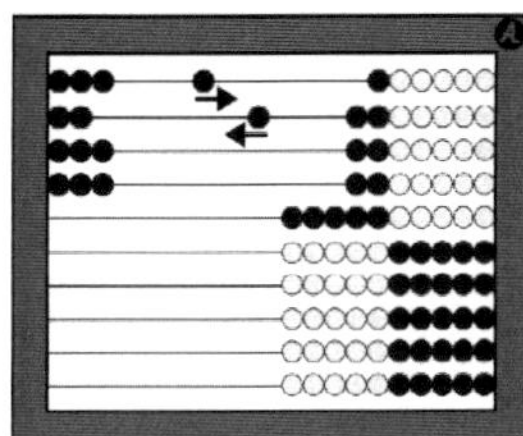
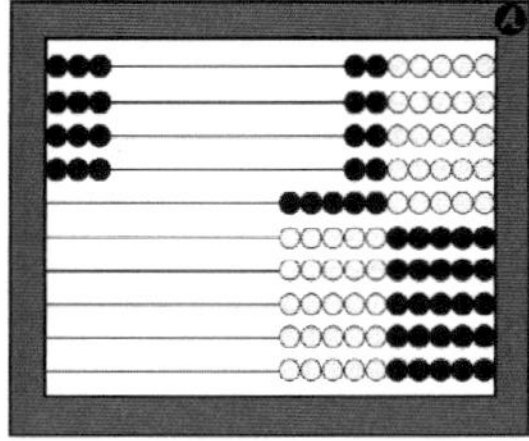

Take and Give the last bead. **$\underline{3}\times 4 = 12$**

Ask: What does the array show? [$3 \times 4 = 12$] Is that the same number of beads that we had at the beginning? [yes]

Another example. Write:

$$\_\_\_\times 3 = 15\ [5]$$

Tell him to do the equation independently. Ask him to explain his procedure.

Worksheet 83. Give the child the worksheet from the previous lesson. Tell him to complete the worksheet.

The equations and solutions are shown below.

8 × 4 = 32	**7** × 5 = 35	32 = **4** × 8
6 × 3 = 18	**7** × 6 = 42	12 = **6** × 2
4 × 10 = 40	**6** × 7 = 42	36 = **6** × 6
5 × 7 = 35	**5** × 4 = 20	72 = **9** × 8
9 × 9 = 81	**3** × 6 = 18	72 = **8** × 9

In conclusion. Ask: In multiplication, what do you call the size of the group? [factor] What do you call how many groups? [factor] What do you call the answer? [product]

Lesson 121: Introducing Division

OBJECTIVES:

1. To introduce division problems
2. To introduce writing division expressions

MATERIALS:

1. Warm-up Practice 6
2. Worksheet 84, Introducing Division
3. AL Abacus
4. Dry erase board

ACTIVITIES FOR TEACHING:

Warm-up. Ask the child to do section 1 on Warm-up Practice 6. The problems and hundred chart are shown below.

3 × 3 = **9**

102 – 10 = **92**

4 × 5 = **20**

Zero plus one is **1**

100 – 89 = **11**

200 – 109 = **91**

10 × 9 – 9 = **81**

Diagonals in a square is **2**

Tens in 100 is **10**

Odd number before 100 is **99**

Centimeters in a meter is **100**

45 × 2 = **90**

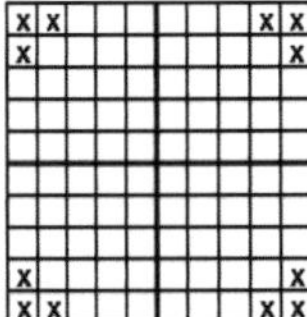

Worksheet 84. Give the child the worksheet and abacus and tell him to read the first problem.

> Mickey has 24 ounces of lemonade and is pouring 6 ounces into each glass. How many glasses of lemonade can Mickey fill?

Ask the child to write the missing factor equation on his worksheet. Use Take and Give on his abacus to solve the problem. Then have him complete the equation. See below.

$$6 \times \_\_ = 24$$

$$6 \times \underline{4} = 24$$

Say: Your worksheet has a whole-circle. How many parts do you need? [4] Tell the child to draw the parts and write the numbers on his worksheet. See below. Ask: Does Mickey have enough lemonade for four glasses? [yes]

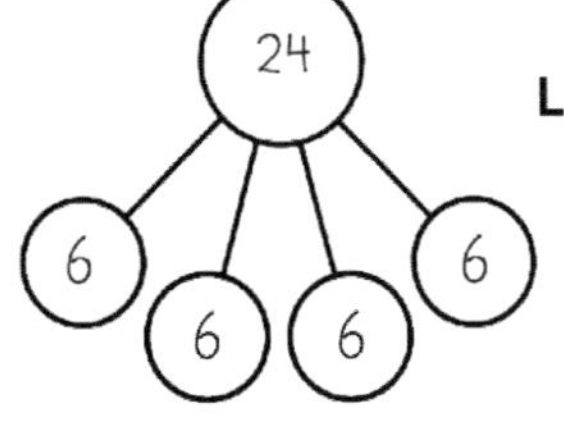

Lemonade fits in 4 glasses.

EXPLANATIONS:

The division problem of finding the how many in a group is often referred to as *partitive* or *sharing* division.

ACTIVITIES FOR TEACHING:

Dividing. Explain: There is another way to write the equation for this problem. Mickey is *dividing* the lemonade by pouring 6 ounces at a time into four glasses. As you write the following, say: 24 divided by 6 equals 4.

$$\frac{24}{6} = 4$$

Problem 2. Have the child read the second problem.

> Dana has 24 ounces of chocolate milk and is pouring the same amount into 3 glasses. How much can Dana pour into each glass? [8 ounces]

Ask the child to write the missing factor equation.

$$\underline{8} \times 3 = 24$$

Ask: How many parts does your part-whole circle set need this time? [3] Tell him to draw the parts and write the numbers. See below.

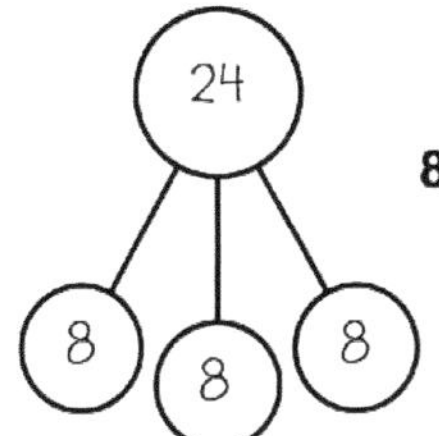

8 ounces of milk in each glass.

Tell the child to write as you say the following: 24 divided by 3 equals 8.

$$\frac{24}{3} = 8$$

Division practice. Write the following division problems on the dry erase board for the child to solve:

$\frac{10}{2}$ = [5] $\frac{16}{4}$ = [4] $\frac{20}{2}$ = [10]

Tell him to solve the problems any way he likes. Ask him to explain his solutions.

Worksheet 84. Tell the child to complete the worksheet. The equations and solutions are below.

$\frac{8}{4} = 2$	$\frac{12}{4} = 3$	$\frac{28}{4} = 7$
$\frac{10}{2} = 5$	$\frac{15}{5} = 3$	$\frac{25}{5} = 5$
$\frac{20}{5} = 4$	$\frac{40}{8} = 5$	$\frac{30}{5} = 6$
$\frac{16}{4} = 4$	$\frac{20}{4} = 5$	$\frac{48}{8} = 6$

In conclusion. Ask: What is 2 multiplied by 2? [4] What is 4 divided by 2? [2] What is 5 multiplied by 3? [15] What is 15 divided by 5? [3] What is 15 divided by 3? [5]

EXPLANATIONS:

This form of writing division is introduced here because it correlates to fractions, which will be addressed next.

Lesson 122: Unit Fractions

OBJECTIVES:

1. To review unit fractions

MATERIALS:

1. Warm-up Practice 6
2. Fraction pieces
3. Worksheet 85, Unit Fractions

ACTIVITIES FOR TEACHING:

EXPLANATIONS:

Warm-up. Ask the child to do section 2 on Warm-up Practice 6. The problems and hundred chart are shown below.

28 + 19 = **47**	8 tens and 17 ones is **97**
70 − 32 = **38**	1 quarter + 12¢ = **37¢**
90 − 21 = **69**	61 less than 100 = **39**
10 × 9 − 3 = **87**	First odd number after 56 is **57**
10 × 4 = **40**	Twice 34 = **68**
42 + 15 + 20 = **77**	6 dimes & 7 pennies = **67**

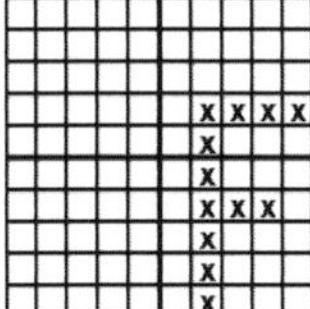

Dividing one into parts. Remind the child that in the previous lesson he divided more than one into equal groups. Say: Now we will divide one into parts. Read the following problem:

> Lu and Joe are dividing a granola bar between them. How much does each person get? [1/2]

Draw a part-whole circle set. Ask: How many parts do we need? [2] What do we write in the part-circles? [1/2] See the left figure below.

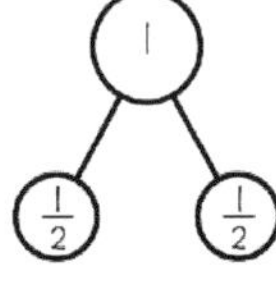

1 divided by 2.

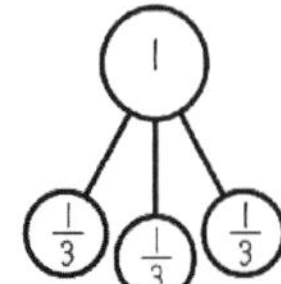

1 divided by 3.

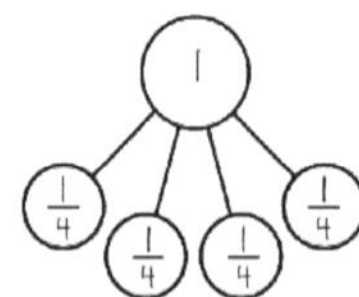

1 divided by 4.

Tell the child that the problem is changed and say:

> Before Lu and Joe get to break their bar, Will joins them. Now how much would each one get? [1/3]

Again draw the part-circles. Ask: How many part-circles do we need? [3] What do we write in them? [1/3] See the center figure above.

ACTIVITIES FOR TEACHING:

Change the problem again and say:

> Oh look, Sofie just arrived. Now how much would each person get? [1/4]

Again draw the part-circles. Ask: How many part-circles do we need? [4] What do we write in them? [1/4] See the third figure on the previous page.

Fraction stairs. Give the child the fractions pieces. Ask: Are any pieces the same? [yes] Tell him to take one fraction strip of each size. Ask: How many different size strips are there? [10] Then ask him to build the fraction stairs with the longest strip on the bottom. See the figure at the right.

When the stairs are completed, ask: How do the fraction stairs differ from the abacus stairs? Could you walk up the fractions stairs? [No, the steps get smaller near the top.]

Fraction names. Have the child say the ordinal numbers from 1–12. [first, second, third, . . . , twelfth] Say: Except for one half, the names of unit fractions are the same as the ordinal numbers. Tell him to read the names of the fractions, starting with 1. [one half, one third, one fourth, . . . , one tenth]

The fraction chart. Have the child assemble the fraction chart with the 1 at the top.

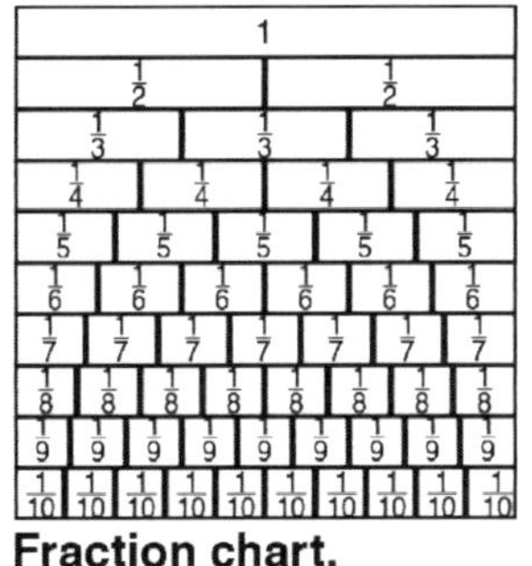

Fraction chart.

Ask: Which row shows dividing the granola bar into two pieces? [the second row, with halves] Which row shows dividing the granola bar into three pieces? [the third row, with thirds] Which row show dividing the granola bar into four pieces? [the fourth row, with fourths]

Worksheet 85. Give the child the worksheet and have him complete it. Solutions are shown below and on the right.

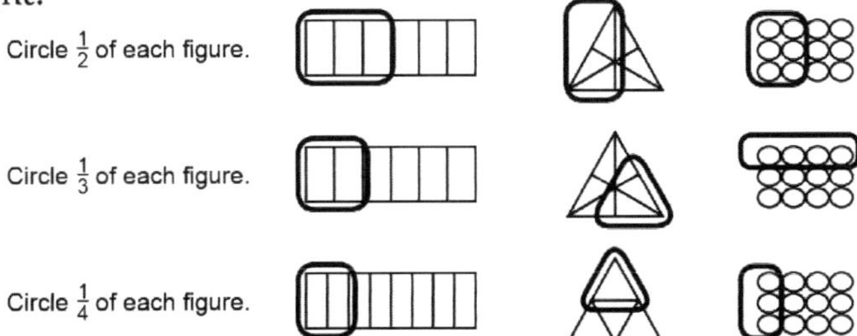

In conclusion. Ask: What do we call 1 divided by 2? [one half] What do we call 1 divided by 4? [one fourth] What do we call 1 divided by 12? [one twelfth]

EXPLANATIONS:

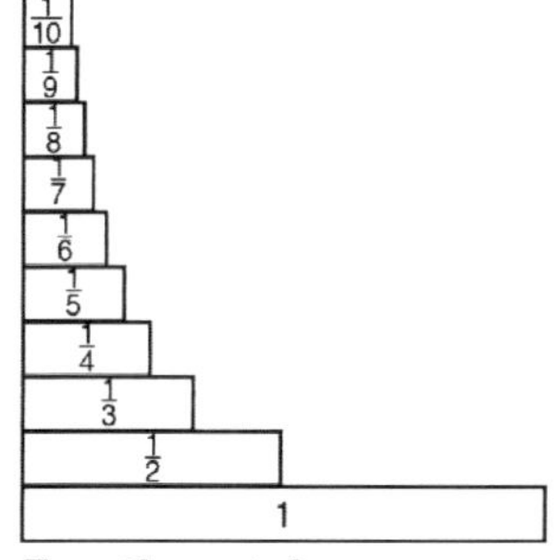

Fraction stairs.

$\frac{1}{2}$ $\frac{1}{3}$ $\frac{1}{4}$ $\frac{1}{5}$ $\frac{1}{6}$ $\frac{1}{7}$ $\frac{1}{8}$ $\frac{1}{9}$ $\frac{1}{10}$

Enrichment Lesson 123: Fraction Chart Project

OBJECTIVES:

1. To build a large paper fraction chart

MATERIALS:

1. Fraction pieces
2. Warm-up Practice 6
3. **Wide paper, ideally 36" by 36" long (1 m × 1 m)***
4. 4-in-1 ruler
5. **Scissors and marker**

ACTIVITIES FOR TEACHING:

Warm-up. Ask the child to assemble the fraction chart. Then tell him to do section 3 on Warm-up Practice 6. The problems and solutions are shown below.

3 thirds + 3 = **4**	8 fourths is **2**
81 – 36 = **45**	2 quarters + 17¢ = **67¢**
402 – 390 = **12**	2 tens + 2 halves = **21**
3 fourths + 1 fourth = **1**	Even number before 36 is **34**
30 tenths = **3**	Twice 15 + twice one half = **31**
42 – 15 – 4 = **23**	10 halves + 6 = **11**
109 + 20 – 73 = **56**	

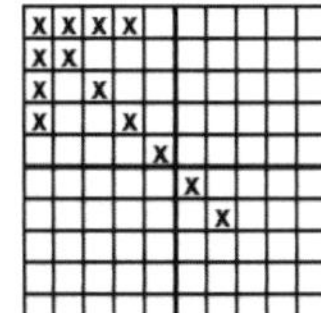

The fraction project. Explain to the child that today he will make a large fraction chart for the wall. Show him the large piece of paper folded into 10 strips. Say: First you will cut the strips apart. Next you will cut the strips into the different fractions and write the fraction on the pieces. Then we will attach it to the wall.

Cutting the strips. Give the child the scissors and have him cut the strips apart.

Making the one. The 1-piece needs only *1* written in the middle. Tell the child to write a large 1.

Making the halves, fourths, and eighths. Tell the child to fold a strip in half to make the two halves and then cut it apart. Label each piece with the correct fraction.

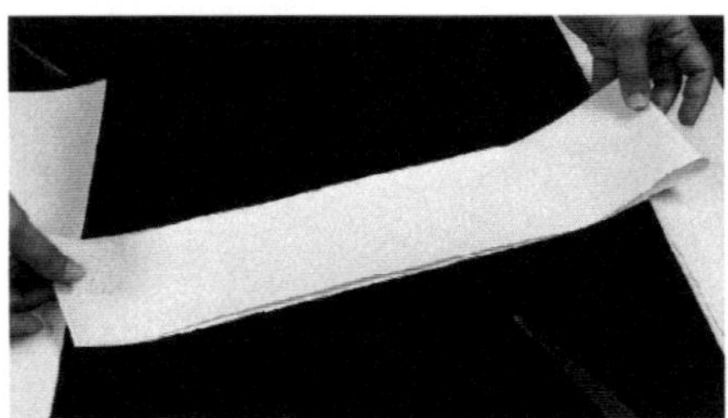

Folding a strip in half.

Folding into fourths.

EXPLANATIONS:

*Prepare the paper as follows: Along the bottom of the paper, measure and mark 3.6" (one tenth of the width of 36" paper) on both edges and in the middle. Then use accordion folding to mark the 10 strips. See the figures below.

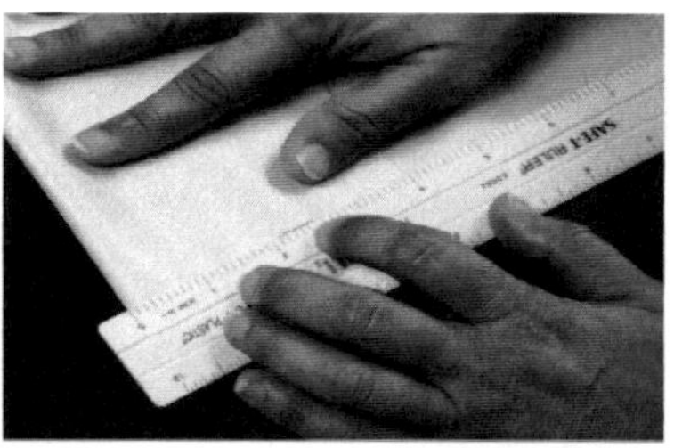

Only use one color of marker so the child does not associate a color with a particular fraction.

ACTIVITIES FOR TEACHING:

To make the fourths, fold another strip in half twice. Cut the fourths apart. See the figures on the previous page. Remind the child to write the correct fraction on each piece.

Likewise, making eighths requires folding a strip in half three times.

Making the thirds, sixths, and ninths. Ask the child to fold a strip into thirds as shown below.

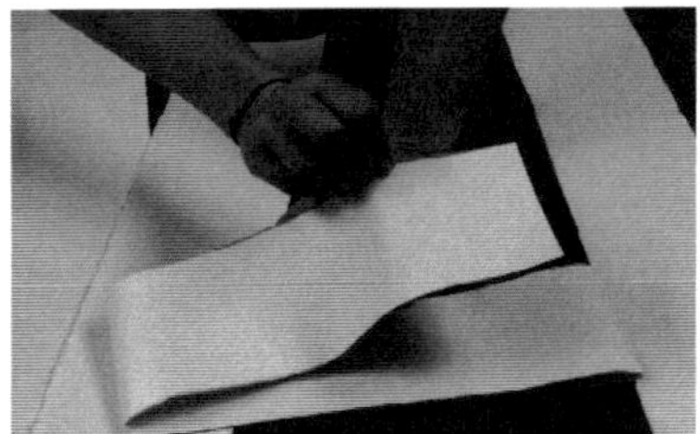

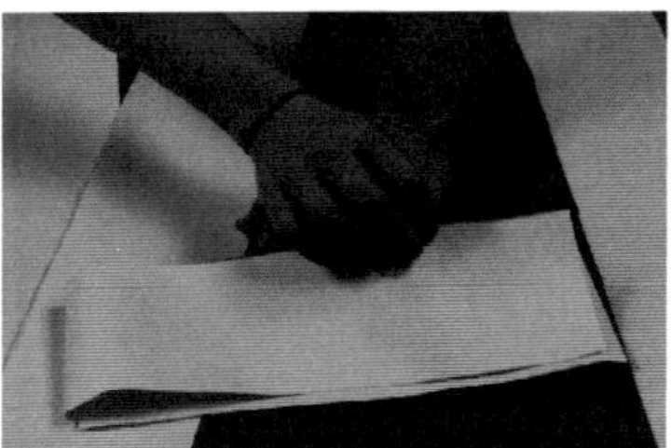

Folding a strip into thirds.

To make the sixths, fold another strip into thirds and divide each piece in half. To make the ninths, fold a third strip into thirds and divide each piece in thirds.

Making the fifths and tenths. For the fifths, mark the first fold one fifth from a side; for 36" wide paper, one fifth is 7.2". Then ask the child to use accordion folding to make the other four fifths.

To make the tenths, divide another strip into fifths and divide each piece in half.

Making the sevenths. For the sevenths, mark the first fold one seventh from a side. For 36" wide paper, one seventh is 5.1". Then ask the child to use accordion folding to make the other six sevenths.

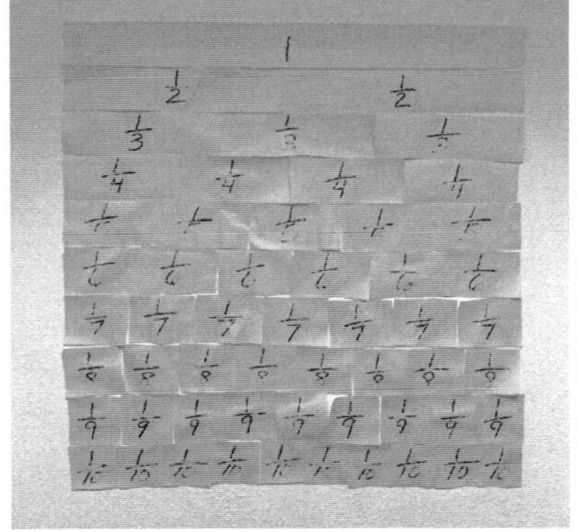

Completed fraction chart.

Attaching to the wall. Attach the fraction pieces to the wall. An example is shown.

In conclusion.
Ask: Which fraction pieces were the easiest to make? [probably halves, fourths, and eighths] How many of each fraction did you need? [2 halves, 3 thirds, 4 fourths, and so forth]

EXPLANATIONS:

Lesson 124: Non-Unit Fractions

OBJECTIVES:

1. To introduce non-unit fractions
2. To learn non-unit fractions

MATERIALS:

1. Warm-up Practice 7
2. Fraction pieces
3. Worksheet 86, Non-Unit Fractions

ACTIVITIES FOR TEACHING:

Warm-up. Ask the child to do section 1 on Warm-up Practice 7. The problems and hundred chart are shown below.

110 – 68 = **42**
6 dimes + 15¢ = **75¢**
27 less than 100 = **73**
2 × 2 = **4**
10 × 4 + 6 = **46**
185 – 122 = **63**
17 + 18 + 8 = **43**
40 + 60 – 15 = **85**

$\frac{1}{2}$ of 28 = **14**
1 quarter + 20¢ = **45¢**
1 hour and 5 minutes = **65**
Eighteen plus six is **24**
Twenty-two doubled is **44**
Eight tens minus six = **74**

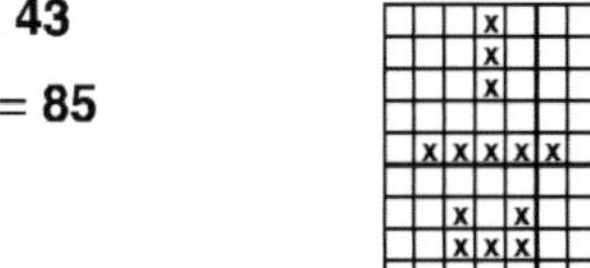

Can You Find game, Version 1. Give the child the fraction pieces. Tell him to assemble the chart. Tell him he will play the Can You Find game with the fraction pieces. Say: Can you find and set aside the following fraction pieces:

3 fourths	4 sevenths	3 tenths
5 eighths	3 ninths	2 tenths
2 ninths	2 fifths	1 third

Tell him we will continue the game in a few minutes.

Reading non-unit fractions. Write the fraction:

$$\frac{2}{3}$$

Say: This is the way we write two thirds. Write the following fractions and tell the child to pick up the corresponding fraction pieces:

$\frac{2}{3}$ $\frac{3}{5}$ $\frac{4}{6}$ $\frac{3}{8}$ $\frac{1}{7}$ $\frac{2}{2}$

$\frac{1}{4}$ $\frac{2}{6}$ $\frac{2}{7}$ $\frac{4}{9}$ $\frac{3}{10}$ $\frac{2}{10}$

EXPLANATIONS:

A unit fraction has 1 as the numerator; a non-unit fraction does not. There is little reason for the students to learn this distinction.

There is no hurry to introduce the terms, *numerator* and *denominator*. Either the word or the concept should be familiar to the student before attaching the two. Here the concept is still being developed and the terms are unknown.

ACTIVITIES FOR TEACHING:	EXPLANATIONS:

At the end of the game the only remaining fraction piece will be the 1.

Can You Find game, Version 2. Tell the child that he will play the game again, but this time the fraction pieces will be scattered. Use the same list of fractions from the first game.

This version is harder because the players need to keep the size of the fraction pieces in mind in order to quickly find them, rather than look at the rows.

Worksheet 86. Give the child the worksheet and ask him to do only the top part of the worksheet. The solutions are below.

The child will do only the top part of this worksheet for this lesson; the remainder will be completed in a following lesson.

	1
$\frac{2}{2}$	$\frac{1}{2}$ $\frac{1}{2}$
$\frac{2}{3}$	$\frac{1}{3}$ $\frac{1}{3}$ $\frac{1}{3}$
$\frac{3}{4}$	$\frac{1}{4}$ $\frac{1}{4}$ $\frac{1}{4}$ $\frac{1}{4}$
$\frac{1}{5}$	$\frac{1}{5}$ $\frac{1}{5}$ $\frac{1}{5}$ $\frac{1}{5}$ $\frac{1}{5}$
$\frac{3}{6}$	$\frac{1}{6}$ $\frac{1}{6}$ $\frac{1}{6}$ $\frac{1}{6}$ $\frac{1}{6}$ $\frac{1}{6}$
$\frac{5}{7}$	$\frac{1}{7}$ $\frac{1}{7}$ $\frac{1}{7}$ $\frac{1}{7}$ $\frac{1}{7}$ $\frac{1}{7}$ $\frac{1}{7}$
$\frac{2}{8}$	$\frac{1}{8}$ $\frac{1}{8}$ $\frac{1}{8}$ $\frac{1}{8}$ $\frac{1}{8}$ $\frac{1}{8}$ $\frac{1}{8}$ $\frac{1}{8}$
$\frac{4}{9}$	$\frac{1}{9}$ $\frac{1}{9}$ $\frac{1}{9}$ $\frac{1}{9}$ $\frac{1}{9}$ $\frac{1}{9}$ $\frac{1}{9}$ $\frac{1}{9}$ $\frac{1}{9}$
$\frac{3}{10}$	$\frac{1}{10}$ $\frac{1}{10}$ $\frac{1}{10}$ $\frac{1}{10}$ $\frac{1}{10}$ $\frac{1}{10}$ $\frac{1}{10}$ $\frac{1}{10}$ $\frac{1}{10}$ $\frac{1}{10}$

In conclusion. Ask: What do we call 3 one fourths? [three fourths] Which is more, one fourth or one third? [one third] Which is more, two fourths or two thirds? [two thirds] Which is more, three fourths or three thirds? [three thirds]

Lesson 125: Solving Fractional Problems

OBJECTIVES:

1. To solve fractional problems, like three divided by four

MATERIALS:

1. Warm-up Practice 7
2. Fraction chart
3. Worksheet 87, Solving Fractional Problems
4. **Scissors and tape**

ACTIVITIES FOR TEACHING:

Warm-up. Tell the child to do section 2 on Warm-up Practice 7. The problems and hundred chart are shown below.

682 – 652 = **30**	$\frac{1}{2}$ of 48 = **24**
Inches in a yard is **36**	Dollar – sixty cents = **40¢**
Quarter – two cents = **23¢**	Five fives plus one = **26**
110 – 71 = **39**	20 – 1 + 14 = **33**
10 × 5 – 23 = **27**	3 ft + 1 in. = **37 in**.
33 + two halves = **34**	102 – 73 = **29**

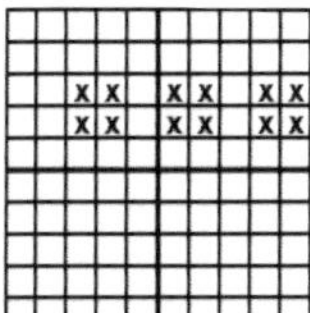

Worksheet 87. Give the child the fraction chart, worksheet, scissors, and tape.

Problem 1. Tell the child to read the first problem.

> There are 3 granola bars to be split equally among 4 friends. How many fourths does each friend get? [three]

Say: The three rectangles on the worksheet are the same size as the 1-piece on the fraction chart. Cut them out to represent the granola bars. Tape them together, then fold them into fourths. Cut them into fourths on the fold lines.

When the child has solved the problem, ask him to explain the solution.

To find the fraction, compare it to the fourths of the fraction chart. See figures below.

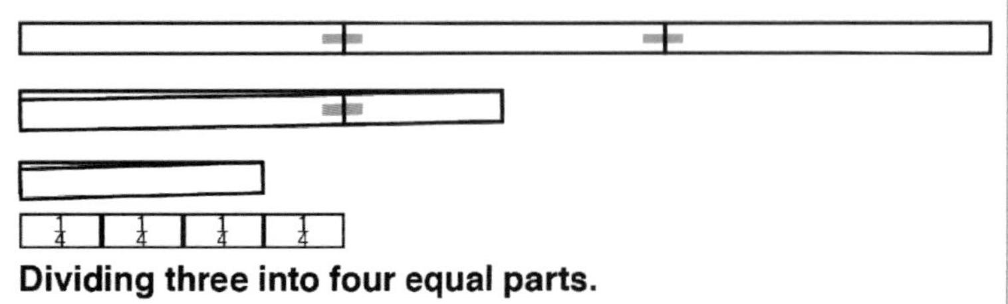

Dividing three into four equal parts.

EXPLANATIONS:

This lesson emphasizes the mathematical meaning of fractions; that is, *a* divided by *b*, where *b* is not zero.

ACTIVITIES FOR TEACHING:

It may be helpful to align the four equal parts to see the three 1s. See below.

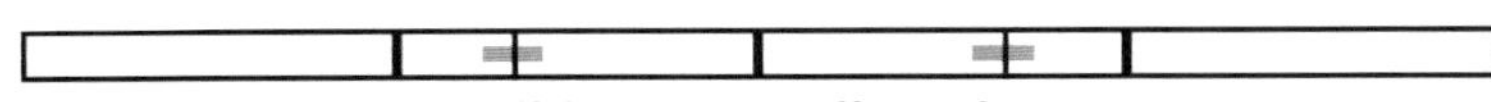

Four equal parts visible once realigned.

A second solution is to fold and cut each strip into fourths and dole out the pieces equally to the four friends, with each friend receiving an amount equal to three fourths. See below.

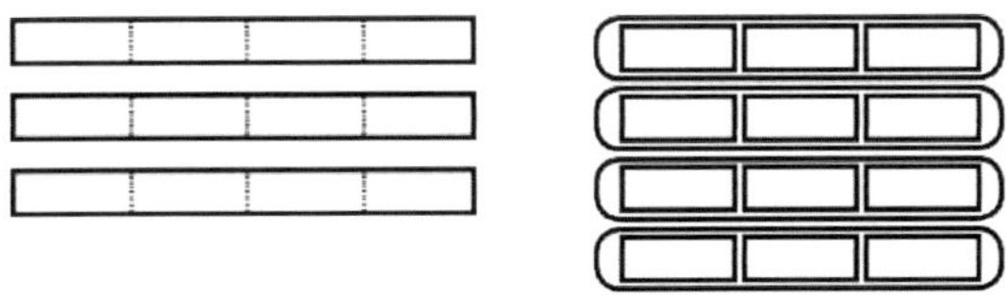

Dividing the fourths among the four friends.

3 divided by 8. Expand the problem. Say: Each friend has a brother or sister, so the 3 granola bars must be divided by twice as many people. Ask: Now how much does each one get? [three eighths] Encourage the child to explain it, using the pieces as necessary.

Ask: Does each person receive more or less than before? [less, half as much]

2 divided by 4. Write:

$$\frac{2}{4}$$

Ask: If 2 bars are divided among 4 children, how much will each one get? [one half] Why don't they get two fourths? [same thing] Tell him to compare 2 one fourth strips with a one half strip.

Problem 2. Ask the child to solve the second problem on his worksheet. One solution is shown below.

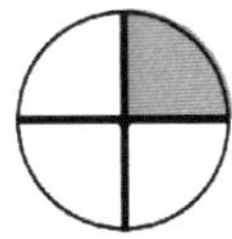 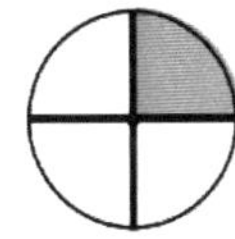 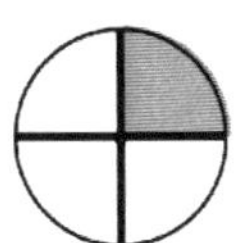

Three friends get the white area in each pizza, while the fourth friend gets the shaded areas.

In conclusion. Ask: Is three fourths the same as 3 one fourths? [yes] Is three fourths the same as three divided by four? [yes]

EXPLANATIONS:

LESSON 126: TWO FRACTIONS EQUALING ONE

OBJECTIVES:

1. To find pairs of fractions equaling one

MATERIALS:

1. Warm-up Practice 7
2. Fraction pieces
3. Fraction cards*
4. *Math Card Games* book, F3
5. Worksheet 86, Non-Unit Fractions

ACTIVITIES FOR TEACHING:

Warm-up. Ask the child to do section 3 on Warm-up Practice 7. The questions and hundred chart are shown below.

102 – 14 = **88**	$\frac{1}{2}$ of 18 = **9**
$1.00 – 41¢ = **59¢**	8 dimes + 2 nickels = **90¢**
31 less than 50 = **19**	Half hour – 1 minute = **29**
Eighty-two – three = **79**	Nine plus nine is **18**
10 × 5 + 19 = **69**	150 – 100 – 1 = **49**
40 – 2 halves = **39**	Ten tens minus eleven = **89**

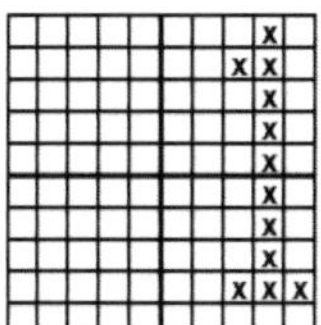

Fractions equaling 1. Give the child the fraction pieces and ask him to assemble the chart. When the fraction chart is complete, ask: How many thirds are needed to equal one? [three] If you have two thirds, how much more do you need to equal one? [one third]

Next ask him to separate the one and to lay the fraction pieces for three fifths under the one. Ask: How many more fifths are needed to make one? [two fifths] See the figure below.

1				
$\frac{1}{5}$	$\frac{1}{5}$	$\frac{1}{5}$	$\frac{1}{5}$	$\frac{1}{5}$

Three fifths and two fifths make one.

Repeat for other fractions, such as one sixth, [five sixths] seven tenths, [three tenths] and one half. [one half]

Write:

$$\frac{3}{8}$$

Ask what is needed to make one. [five eighths] Repeat for one tenth [nine tenths] and two thirds. [one third]

EXPLANATIONS:

*Remove the percentage cards before giving them to the child.

To focus the students' attention on fractions, not arithmetic, avoid teaching the algorithm that the sum of the two numerators equals the denominator.

ACTIVITIES FOR TEACHING:	EXPLANATIONS:

Finding pairs to equal one. Give the child the fraction cards. Tell him to spread his cards out face up. Next he is to pick up a card and find the match so the two cards equals one. Tell him to find ten different pairs.

By finding these matches, the child is sorting the cards they will need to play the Concentrating on One game.

Concentrating on One game. Have the child play the Concentrating on One game, found in the *Math Card Games* book, F3, with the pairs of cards that he found.

If the child has duplicate pairs, he can still play the game, although it may take a bit longer.

Worksheet 86. Give the child the worksheet from a prior lesson and tell him to complete it. The solutions are shown below.

The pairs on the worksheet are fractions not found on the cards, which have only simplified fractions.

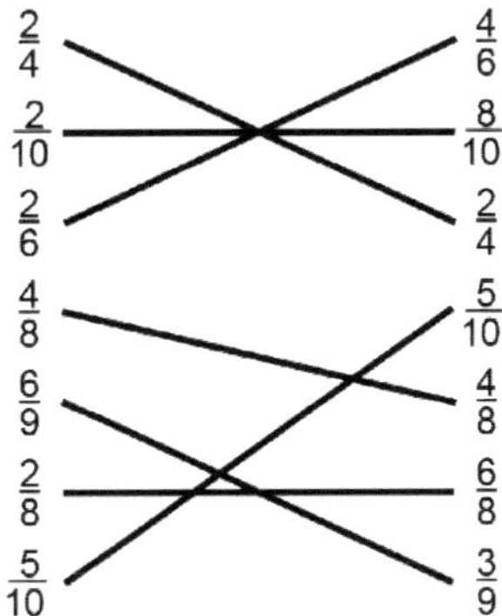

In conclusion. Ask: Why does it take 10 tenths to make 1, but only 3 thirds to make 1? [tenths are smaller] How many twelfths do you need to make a whole? [twelve]

Lesson 127: One Made with Halves, Fourths, & Eighths

OBJECTIVES:

1. To learn the term *expression*
2. To use the partial fraction chart to find equivalent fractions
3. To find fraction expressions that equal one

MATERIALS:

1. Warm-up Practice 8
2. Fraction pieces
3. Math journal

ACTIVITIES FOR TEACHING:

Warm-up. Ask the child to do section 1 on Warm-up Practice 8. The problems and hundred chart are shown below.

5 × 5 = **25**

\$1.00 – 59¢ = **41¢**

750 – 708 = **42**

ninety – forty-six = **44**

8 – 2 + 16 – 1 = **21**

512 – 489 = **23**

1 hour + 1 minute = **61**

28 – 4 halves = **26**

3 ones + 4 tens = **43**

$\frac{1}{2}$ of 8 + 20 = **24**

9 dimes – 9 cents = **81¢**

2 feet + 4 inches = **28**

fifteen plus seven is **22**

38 from one hundred = **62**

sixty minus thirty-three = **27**

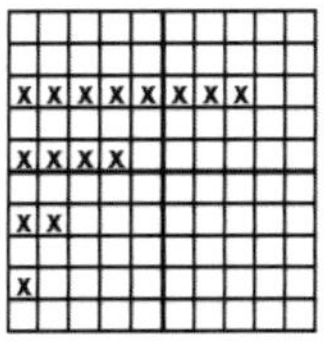

x	x	x	x	x	x	x	x		
x	x	x	x						
x	x								
x									

Partial fraction chart. Give the child the fraction pieces and ask him to construct the fraction chart, using only the 1, halves, fourths, and eighths. See below.

<table>
<tr><td colspan="8">1</td></tr>
<tr><td colspan="4">$\frac{1}{2}$</td><td colspan="4">$\frac{1}{2}$</td></tr>
<tr><td colspan="2">$\frac{1}{4}$</td><td colspan="2">$\frac{1}{4}$</td><td colspan="2">$\frac{1}{4}$</td><td colspan="2">$\frac{1}{4}$</td></tr>
<tr><td>$\frac{1}{8}$</td><td>$\frac{1}{8}$</td><td>$\frac{1}{8}$</td><td>$\frac{1}{8}$</td><td>$\frac{1}{8}$</td><td>$\frac{1}{8}$</td><td>$\frac{1}{8}$</td><td>$\frac{1}{8}$</td></tr>
</table>

Fraction chart with 1, halves, fourths, and eighths.

Mathematical expression. Write:

$$\frac{1}{2} + \frac{1}{4} + \frac{1}{4}$$

Ask: Is this an equation? [no] Why not? [It has no equal sign.] Say: A group of numbers and mathematical symbols without an equal sign is called an *expression.*

Ask: What does this expression equal? [1] Write a 1 before the expression as shown below.

$$1 = \frac{1}{2} + \frac{1}{4} + \frac{1}{4}$$

EXPLANATIONS:

ACTIVITIES FOR TEACHING:

Unit fractions equaling one. Ask: Can you think of another expression that uses only the fractions one half, one fourth, and one eighth to equal one? Tell him to write as many of these equations as he can in his math journal. There are nine different equations. Solutions are below.

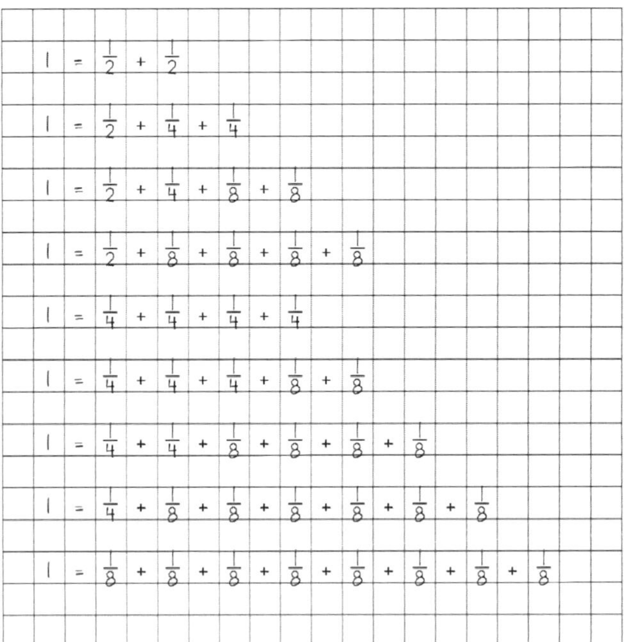

Unit fractions equaling 1.

Two fractions equaling one. Write:

$$1 = \frac{2}{8} + \_\_\_$$

Say: Look at your fraction pieces and decide what you need to solve the equation. [six eighths]

$$1 = \frac{2}{8} + \frac{6}{8}$$

Say: Using only halves, fourths, and eighths, write equations in your math journal that equal one, but use only two fractions. There are 12 possibilities.

Solutions are shown at the right.

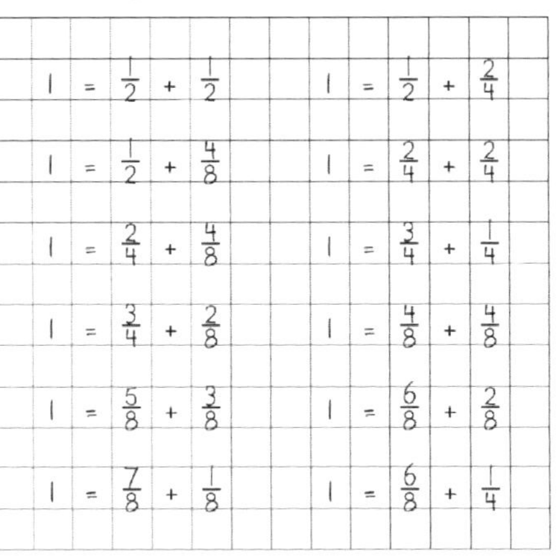

Two fractions equaling 1.

In conclusion. Ask: How much is two halves? [1] How much is eight eighths? [1] How much is six sixths? [1] How much is twelve twelfths? [1]

EXPLANATIONS:

If necessary, remind the child to look at his partial fraction chart to get ideas.

Lesson 128: Fractions Games

OBJECTIVES:

1. To combine fractions to total one
2. To compare fractions with ones, halves, fourths, and eighths

MATERIALS:

1. Warm-up Practice 8
2. Fraction pieces
3. *Math Card Games* book, F6 and F7

ACTIVITIES FOR TEACHING:

Warm-up. Ask the child to do section 2 on Warm-up Practice 8. The questions and hundred chart are shown below.

$5 \times 3 + 2 =$ **17**

a quarter + 8¢ = **33¢**

$350 - 336 =$ **14**

$750 - 712 =$ **38**

$8 + 3 + 5 =$ **16**

$4 \times 5 =$ **20**

$3 \times 2 + 7 =$ **13**

$13 + 35 - 8 - 8 =$ **32**

$\frac{1}{4}$ of 44 = **11**

$1.39 – $1.00 = **39¢**

inches in a foot = **12**

nine doubled is **18**

seventy-two – fifty-three = **19**

quarter of an hour = **15**

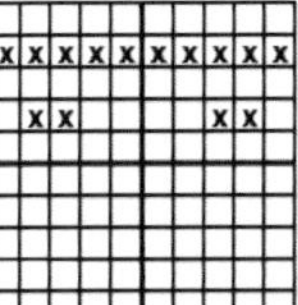

Fraction chart. Give the child the fraction pieces and ask him to assemble the fraction chart as shown below.

1

$\frac{1}{2}$ $\frac{1}{2}$

$\frac{1}{3}$ $\frac{1}{3}$ $\frac{1}{3}$

$\frac{1}{4}$ $\frac{1}{4}$ $\frac{1}{4}$ $\frac{1}{4}$

$\frac{1}{5}$ $\frac{1}{5}$ $\frac{1}{5}$ $\frac{1}{5}$ $\frac{1}{5}$

$\frac{1}{6}$ $\frac{1}{6}$ $\frac{1}{6}$ $\frac{1}{6}$ $\frac{1}{6}$ $\frac{1}{6}$

$\frac{1}{7}$ $\frac{1}{7}$ $\frac{1}{7}$ $\frac{1}{7}$ $\frac{1}{7}$ $\frac{1}{7}$ $\frac{1}{7}$

$\frac{1}{8}$ $\frac{1}{8}$ $\frac{1}{8}$ $\frac{1}{8}$ $\frac{1}{8}$ $\frac{1}{8}$ $\frac{1}{8}$ $\frac{1}{8}$

$\frac{1}{9}$ $\frac{1}{9}$ $\frac{1}{9}$ $\frac{1}{9}$ $\frac{1}{9}$ $\frac{1}{9}$ $\frac{1}{9}$ $\frac{1}{9}$ $\frac{1}{9}$

$\frac{1}{10}$ $\frac{1}{10}$ $\frac{1}{10}$ $\frac{1}{10}$ $\frac{1}{10}$ $\frac{1}{10}$ $\frac{1}{10}$ $\frac{1}{10}$ $\frac{1}{10}$ $\frac{1}{10}$

Fraction chart.

The game of One. Have the child play One, found in the *Math Card Games* book, F6. Tell him that he will be making one in other ways. Besides the fractions from the last lesson, he will also use the thirds, fifths, sixths, and tenths.

EXPLANATIONS:

There are no fraction cards with sevenths or ninths.

ACTIVITIES FOR TEACHING:

Preparation for Fraction War game. Ask the child to change the fraction chart to have only the one, halves, fourths, and eighths as shown below.

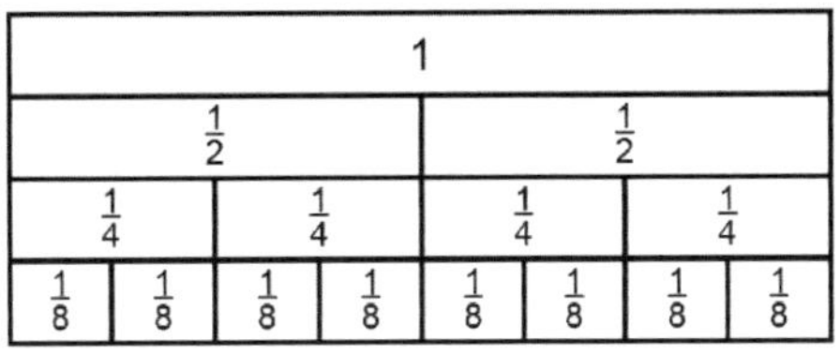

1							
$\frac{1}{2}$				$\frac{1}{2}$			
$\frac{1}{4}$		$\frac{1}{4}$		$\frac{1}{4}$		$\frac{1}{4}$	
$\frac{1}{8}$	$\frac{1}{8}$	$\frac{1}{8}$	$\frac{1}{8}$	$\frac{1}{8}$	$\frac{1}{8}$	$\frac{1}{8}$	$\frac{1}{8}$

Partial fraction chart.

Tell him to collect the ones from the fraction cards, which were set aside from the One game, the halves, fourths, and eighths.

Fraction War game. Have the child play Fraction War, found in the *Math Card Games* book, F7, with the sorted cards.

In conclusion. Ask: Which is greater, seven eighths or one half? [seven eighths] Which is greater, three fourths or one half? [three fourths] Which is less, one half or one sixth? [one sixth] Which is greater, three fourths or five eighths? [three fourths]

EXPLANATIONS:

Lesson 129: Introducing Negative Numbers

OBJECTIVES:

1. To introduce numbers less than one
2. To play Corners™ games involving negative numbers

MATERIALS:

1. Warm-up Practice 8
2. Casio SL-450S calculator
3. *Math Card Games* book, A9 and S10
4. Math journal

ACTIVITIES FOR TEACHING:

Warm-up. Ask the child to do section 3 on Warm-up Practice 8. The problems and hundred chart are shown below.

100 – 48 + 3 = **55**	59 + 32 = **91**
9 dimes – 9¢ = **81¢**	$2.00 – $1.15 = **85¢**
810 – 737 = **73**	1 hour + 1 minute is **61**
eleven + eighty-four = **95**	odd number after 74 is **75**
7 × 10 – 5 = **65**	seventy + twelve + two = **84**
39 + 32 = **71**	half of one hundred + 1 = **51**
23 + 16 + 8 + 15 = **62**	

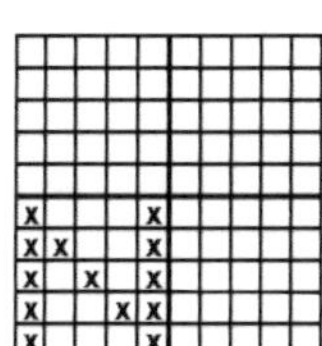

Temperatures below zero. Ask: If it is winter in a cold place and the temperature outside is 10 degrees and it gets 1 degree colder, what would the temperature be? [9 degrees] It's getting colder and the temperature drops 3 more degrees; now what is the temperature? [6 degrees]

Continue by saying: An hour later, the wind comes up and the temperature goes down 6 more degrees. Ask: Now what is the temperature? [0 degrees] Can it get colder? [yes] What is the temperature when it gets 2 degrees colder? [2 below or 2 below 0]

Draw a thermometer as shown on the right:

Say: People usually place a little minus sign before numbers below zero. Then they sometimes say the temperature is minus 4 or minus 10.

Ask the child to find the following on the thermometer:

Where is 3 degrees above zero?
Where is 3 degrees below zero?
Start at 2 degrees and go down 3 degrees.
Start at minus 3 degrees and warm up 4 degrees.

5
4
3
2
1
0
-1
-2
-3
-4
-5

EXPLANATIONS:

Recent research by Bofferding (2014) shows that young child benefit by expanding their understanding of numbers to include negative numbers. Early introduction prevents them from developing incorrect concepts that are hard to correct later.

This scenario works for either Celsius or Fahrenheit scales.

Interestingly, not all thermometers have a minus sign before the negative temperatures.

There is a subtle difference in print between the minus sign indicating subtraction and the minus sign designating a negative number. The subtraction sign is longer (–) followed by a space before the next number. The negative number sign is shorter (-) without a space before the number.

ACTIVITIES FOR TEACHING:

Calculators. Give the child the calculator. Ask him to do the following:

Enter 2 and subtract 1. What did you get? [1]

Subtract 1 again. What did you get? [0]

Do it again. What did you get? [minus 1 or 1 below 0]

Do it again. What did you get? [minus 2 or 2 below 0]

What do you think you would get if you did again? Try it. [minus 3]

What do you think you will get if you add 4? Try it. [1]

Below Zero Corners™ game. With the exception of starting scores, this is the same Corners™ game that is found in the *Math Card Games* book, A9. The players start with a score of minus 100. The winner is the player with the highest score at the end of the game.

Tell him to write his score in his math journal. A sample is shown below.

-50
-35
-30
-10
0
15
25

Negative Corners™ game. In contrast to Below Zero Corners™, which is an addition game, Negative Corners™ is a subtraction game. Have the child play this game, found in the *Math Card Games* book, S10.

50
40
35
20
5
-5
-15

In conclusion. Ask: Which is colder, 5 above or 9 below? [9 below] Which is warmer, zero or 3 below? [zero] Which is colder, 2 above or minus 3? [minus 3]

EXPLANATIONS:

While the term *negative 1* is commonly used in mathematics classes, *minus 1* is usually used in discussing the weather.

Lesson 130: More Negative Numbers

OBJECTIVES:

1. To continue to work with negative numbers

MATERIALS:

1. Warm-up Practice 9
2. Dry erase board
3. *Math Card Games* book, S28 and S11
4. Math journal

ACTIVITIES FOR TEACHING:

Warm-up. Ask the child to do section 1 on Warm-up Practice 9. The problems and hundred chart are shown below.

8 ones and 4 tens = **48**

3 dimes – 12¢ = **18¢**

690 – 612 = **78**

days in 4 weeks = **28**

4 × 10 + 4 = **44**

39 + 29 = **68**

50 – 13 – 10 = **27**

$0.88 – 0 = **88¢**

16 + 20 + 3 + 7 = **46**

nineteen doubled is **38**

seventy – twelve = **58**

three quarters of an hour is **45**

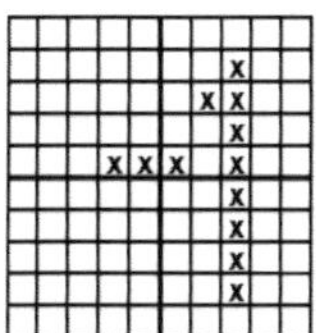

Sums less than zero. Draw the thermometer model from the previous lesson as shown on right. Then write on the dry erase board:

5 – 5 = ___ [0]

Ask the child for the answer. Repeat for:

3 – 5 = ___ [-2]

Tell him to think of the thermometer. Ask how he found the answer.

Continue with:

3 – ___ = -2 [5]

and

2 – 1 – ___ = -3 [4]

5
4
3
2
1
0
-1
-2
-3
-4
-5

On the Number Negative Five game. Have the child play the On the Number Negative Five game, found in the *Math Card Games* book, S28. Rather than the goal of minus 5, use minus 3.

If necessary, explain that a card turned sideways means that number is to be subtracted.

EXPLANATIONS:

Avoid giving the child specific methods for solving these equations. It is much more important for him to think about what it means, rather than trying to apply some rule.

Note that only one row exists at a time. This contrasts to the On the Number game, A55, played earlier in the year.

ACTIVITIES FOR TEACHING:

Top and Bottom Corners™ game. Have the child play Top and Bottom Corners™, found in the *Math Card Games* book, S11, with the following variation: Use four cards and include scoreless matching. Also start with a score of -50.

Tell the child to write his scoring in his math journal.

In conclusion. Ask: What kind of number is between zero and one? [fraction] What number is at the beginning of a ruler or meter stick? [zero] What kind of number is less than zero? [negative number] How many numbers are there? [answers will vary]

EXPLANATIONS:

The name, *Top and Bottom Corners™*, refers to adding the sums of cards played to the top and bottom (green and black), while subtracting sums played to the left and right (red and blue).

When playing the Corners™ game, a player may match colors and numbers, however no points will be earned because the sum is not a multiple of 5. For example, 9 and 9, is a valid play but would result in a score of zero, which is a scoreless match.

Lesson 131: Building Prisms and Pyramids

OBJECTIVES:

1. To review prisms and pyramids
2. To construct four prisms and three pyramids with Geometry panels

MATERIALS:

1. Warm-up Practice 9
2. Geometry panels*
3. Worksheet 88, Building Prisms and Pyramids
4. Geometry solids

ACTIVITIES FOR TEACHING:

Warm-up. Ask the child to do section 2 on Warm-up Practice 9. The problems and hundred chart are shown below:

3 quarters = **75¢**

four + 77 = **81¢**

408 – 314 = **94**

2 quarters + $0.03 = **53¢**

9 × 10 + 2 halves = **91**

29 + 26 = **55**

twelve + forty-nine = **61**

397 – 302 = **95**

18 – 20 + 12 + 41 = **51**

200 – 108 = **92**

80 – 20 plus eleven = **71**

$0.82 – 3 dimes = **52¢**

15 + 50 + 3 + 7 + 10 = **85**

6 tens plus 5 is **65**

59 + 34 = **93**

6 minutes less than 1 hour is **54**

Building a cube. Demonstrate how to make a cube. Take two square panels and align two edges with the white sides together. Hold them together and ask the child to place a rubber band around the edges. Explain that the notches at the vertices keeps the rubber bands in place. Repeat for the remaining edges. See the figure below.

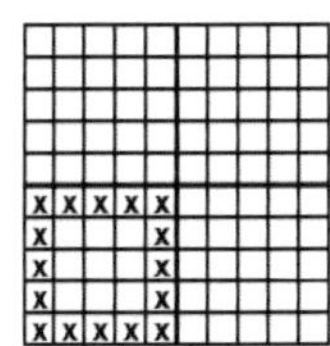

Cube made with geometry panels.

Worksheet 88. Give the child the worksheet. Also give him the geometry panels. Tell him to build the seven shapes pictured on the worksheet.

Prisms. After the shapes are made say: Prisms have two parallel congruent polygons, called bases. Have the child find the prism with congruent triangles at each end. See first figure on the next page. Then have him find the prism with rectangles at each end. See second figure. Say: This solid is also called a cube because all the rectangles are squares.

EXPLANATIONS:

*If the panels have not been used, the edges will need to be creased. Bend the perforated lines near each edge of the panels toward the colored side. Place the edge on a hard surface and bend gently. Bending two at a time works well.

Having the child place the rubber band is modeling how two people can work together.

All seven solids can be made from the set of geometry panels.

ACTIVITIES FOR TEACHING:

Ask him to find the pentagonal prism. See third figure below. Then find the hexagonal prism. See fourth figure.

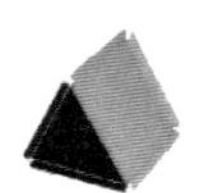
triangular prism

rectangular prism

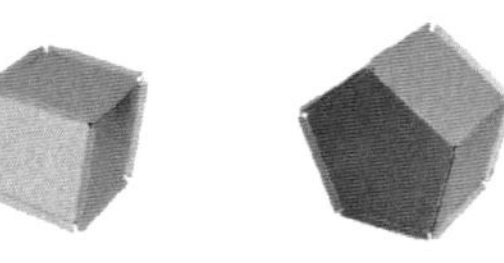
pentagonal prism

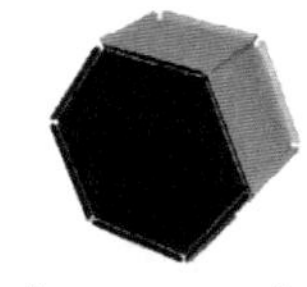
hexagonal prism

Pyramids. Ask: What is special about the other solids? [they have triangles to make a point] Remind the child they are pyramids. Ask: How many pyramids did you make? [3] Pick up each pyramid in turn and ask him to name the polygon base of the solid. [triangle, rectangle, pentagon] See the figures below.

triangular pyramid
rectangular pyramid
pentagonal pyramid

Faces, edges, and vertices. Ask: How many faces, or surfaces, does the triangular pyramid have? [4] How many edges? [6] How many vertices? [4] Repeat the questions for the rectangular prism. [6, 12, 8]

Geometry solids. Show the following geometric solids and ask the child for the names:

rectangular prism

triangular prism

hexagonal prism

rectangular prism

rectangular pyramid

rectangular prism

octagonal prism

Worksheet table. Have the child complete the worksheet. The solutions are shown below.

Shape	Faces	Edges	Vertices
Triangular prism	5	9	6
Rectangular prism	6	12	8
Pentagonal prism	7	15	10
Hexagonal prism	8	18	12
Triangular pyramid	4	6	4
Rectangular pyramid	5	8	5
Pentagonal pyramid	6	10	6

rectangular prism
triangular prism
rectangular prism
hexagonal prism
rectangular prism
rectangular pyramid
octagonal prism

In conclusion. Ask: What group of figures has triangles to make a point? [pyramids] What group of figures have parallel bases? [prisms] In a prism, what polygons are between the bases? [rectangles] In a pyramid, what polygons are between the base and the point? [triangles]

EXPLANATIONS:

The cube will be needed in the next lesson.

Lesson 132: Comparing Cubes

OBJECTIVES:

1. To compare three different sized cubes
2. To introduce the term *volume*

MATERIALS:

1. Warm-up Practice 9
2. Worksheet 89, Comparing Cubes
3. Centimeter cubes
4. Geometry solids, only cube is needed
5. Geometry panels, squares made into a cube
6. 4-in-1 ruler

ACTIVITIES FOR TEACHING:

Warm-up. Ask the child to do section 3 on Warm-up Practice 9. The problems and hundred chart are shown below:

5 × 5 + 1 = **26**
512 – 435 = **77**
9 + 29 = **38**
thirty minus seven = **23**
3 × 10 + 2 = **32**
5 × 5 = **25**
2 quarters – 2¢ = **48¢**
10 × 10 – 59 = **41**
49 + 19 = **68**
37 + 9 = **46**

50 – 13 – 10 = **27**
$0.88 – 6 dimes = **28¢**
-1 + 25 = **24**
forty-three doubled is **86**
seventy – twelve = **58**
1000 – 963 = **37**

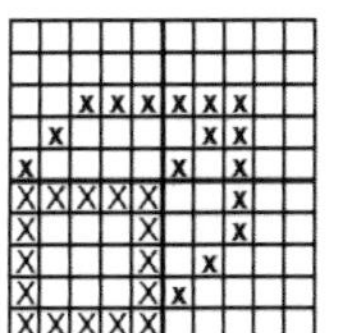

Worksheet 89. Give the child the worksheet, the centimeter cubes, the cube from the geometric solids, and the geometry panel cube made in the previous lesson as shown below.

Centimeter cube

Wooden cube

Yellow geometry panel cube

Comparing cubes. Tell the child to read the three questions on the worksheet and write down his estimates.

1. Compared to the centimeter cube, how many times larger do you think the wooden cube is?
2. Compared to the wooden cube, how many times larger do you think the yellow cube is?
3. Compared to the centimeter cube, how many times larger do you think the yellow cube is?

EXPLANATIONS:

ACTIVITIES FOR TEACHING:

Ask: How can you measure the lengths of the cubes? [4-in-1 ruler or a row of centimeter cubes] Tell the child to measure the length of the three cubes in centimeters and write it in the table on the worksheet. [1 cm, 5 cm, 10 cm] See the table below.

Cube	Edge Length	Face Area	Cube Volume
centimeter cube	**1 cm**	**1 cm^2**	**1 cm^3**
wooden cube	**5 cm**	**25 cm^2**	**125 cm^3**
yellow cube	**10 cm**	**100 cm^2**	**1000 cm^3**

Ask: What is the area of a face of the centimeter cube? [1 cm^2] Tell him to find the area of the faces of the three cubes in square centimeters and write it in the table as shown above. [1 cm^2, 25 cm^2, 100 cm^2] If necessary, remind him that area means how many square centimeters will cover the face.

Introducing volume. Hold up a centimeter cube and say: The amount of space inside a 3D shape is called *volume*. One unit of measurement is this centimeter cube. This is how it is written:

$$1 \text{ cm}^3$$

Explain that the little *3* means it is 1 centimeter in three directions. It is usually read as cubic centimeter.

Tell him to find the volume of the wooden cube and then discuss his solution. [125 cm^3] Mentally stacking five arrays of 5 × 5 gives the volume. To find the total, 25 × 4 = 100, 100 and 25 more is 125 cm^3.

Tell him to find the volume of the yellow cube [1000 cm^3] and discuss his solution. Have him complete the last column of the table. [1 cm^3, 125 cm^3, 1000 cm^3]

Comparison questions. Ask the child to answer the last five questions.

5. **125** 6. **1000** 7. **8** 8. **8** 9. $\mathbf{\frac{1}{8}}$

In conclusion. Ask: Are you surprised how many centimeter cubes fit in the yellow cube? What is the length of the centimeter cube? [1 cm] What is the area of the centimeter cube? [1 cm^2] What is the volume of the centimeter cube? [1 cm^3]

EXPLANATIONS:

With Montessori materials, the smallest cube of the pink tower is 1 cm^3; the largest cube is 1000 cm^3.

Lesson 133: Geometry Review

OBJECTIVES:

1. To review the geometry topics

MATERIALS:

1. Geometry solids
2. Worksheet 90, Geometry Review
3. Fraction pieces

ACTIVITIES FOR TEACHING:

Polygon review. Using the chart below, discuss the characteristics of various polygons. The chart will be completed in the upcoming assessment.

Polygon	Letter	= sides	= angles	Regular	Symmetry	ll lines
Rectangle	G	no	yes	no	yes	2
Rhombus	F	yes	no	no	yes	2
Regular hexagon	D	yes	yes	yes	yes	3
Pentagon	A	no	no	no	yes	0
Right triangle	H	no	no	no	no	0
Equilateral triangle	C	yes	yes	yes	yes	0
Parallelogram	I	no	no	no	no	2
Square	B	yes	yes	yes	yes	2
Trapezoid	E	no	no	no	no	1

Have the child show parallel lines with his arms. Then ask him to answer the following questions.

What makes a polygon regular? [all the sides and angles are equal]

What is a quadrilateral? [a polygon with four sides]

Is a square a rectangle? [yes]

Geometry review. Show the child the cube and square pyramid from the geometry solids. See below.

Cube.

Square pyramid.

Hold up the cube and ask: What shape is this? [cube] How many equal faces does it have? [6]

Then hold up the square pyramid and ask: What shape is this? [square pyramid] How many equal faces does it have? [4]

EXPLANATIONS:

Lessons 133, 135, 137, and 139 are review lessons for the end of year assessments. If preferred, these four reviews may be taught sequentially, then the four assessments may be presented as a single final test.

ACTIVITIES FOR TEACHING:

EXPLANATIONS:

Worksheet 90. Give the child the worksheet. Tell him to complete the first problem. See answers below. Ask him to discuss his solutions.

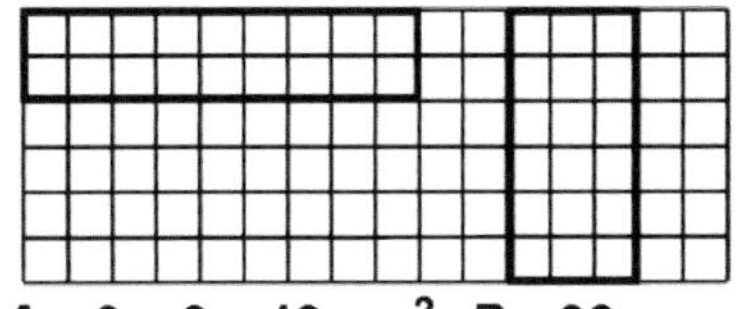

$A = 9 \times 2 = 18$ cm^2, $P = 22$ cm

$A = 3 \times 6 = 18$ cm^2, $P = 18$ cm

Fraction chart. Give the child the fraction pieces and have him assemble the chart. See below.

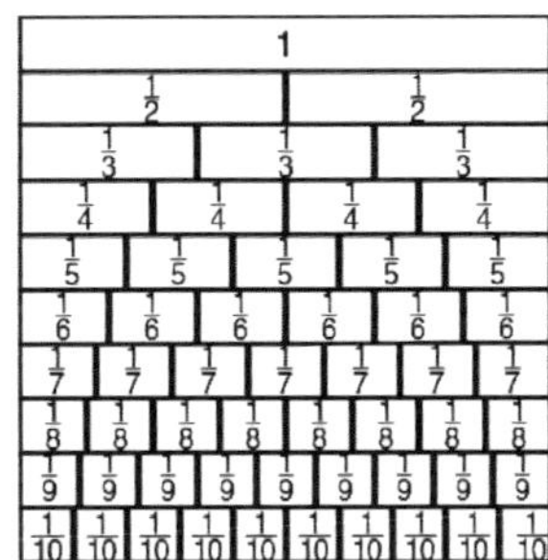

Fraction chart.

Ask the child various questions such as:

How many thirds are in a whole? [3]

If you have one half what do you need to make 1? [one half, 2 fourths, 3 sixths, 4 eighths, or 5 tenths]

If you have three quarters how much more do you need to make 1? [one quarter or one fourth]

How many fourths are in one half? [2 fourths]

Problem 2. Have the child complete the second problem. Some possible answers are shown below. Have him discuss his solutions.

Circle $\frac{1}{2}$ of each figure.

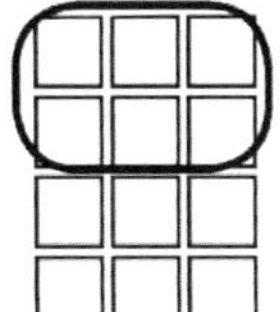

Circle $\frac{1}{3}$ of each figure.

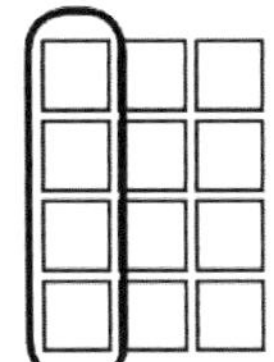

Circle $\frac{1}{4}$ of each figure.

LESSON 134: GEOMETRY ASSESSMENT

OBJECTIVES:

1. To assess the geometry topics

MATERIALS:

1. End of Year Assessment 1 (found in the back of the child's worksheet)

ACTIVITIES FOR TEACHING:

Assessment 1. Give the child the End of Year Assessment 1.

Problems 1–9. Have the child complete the chart.

Polygon	Letter	= sides	= angles	Regular	Symmetry	ll lines
Rectangle	G	no	yes	no	yes	2
Rhombus	F	yes	no	no	yes	2
Regular hexagon	D	yes	yes	yes	yes	3
Pentagon	A	no	no	no	yes	0
Right triangle	H	no	no	no	no	0
Equilateral triangle	C	yes	yes	yes	yes	0
Parallelogram	I	no	no	no	no	2
Square	B	yes	yes	yes	yes	2
Trapezoid	E	no	no	no	no	1

Problems 10–16. Have the child answers the following questions on the assessment.

How many of the polygons have all sides equal? [4]

How many of the polygons have all angles equal? [4]

How many of the polygons are regular? [3]

Which polygon has the most sets of parallel lines? [regular hexagon]

How many of the polygons are quadrilaterals? [5]

How many of the polygons are not quadrilaterals? [4]

What is the name of a special rectangle with all four sides congruent? [square]

Problems 17–20. Tell the child to answer the following questions on the assessment.

What is the first shape? [cube]

How many equal faces does it have? [6]

What is the second shape? [square pyramid]

How many equal faces does it have? [4]

EXPLANATIONS:

ACTIVITIES FOR TEACHING:

Problems 21–23. Tell the child to draw a 4 by 4 rectangle on the centimeter grid. Then have him draw two more rectangles with the same area and write the areas and perimeters of all three rectangles, remembering to label the units.

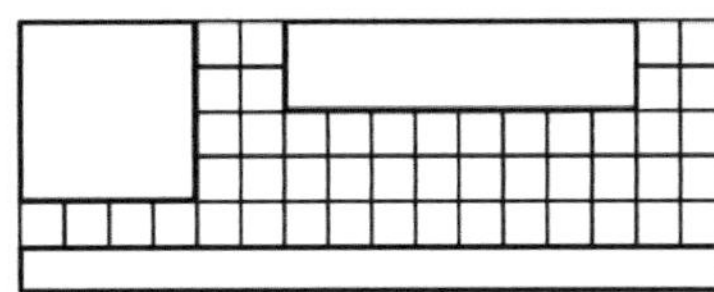

$A = 4 \times 4 = 16\ cm^2$, $P = 16$ cm

$A = 8 \times 2 = 16\ cm^2$, $P = 20$ cm

$A = 16 \times 1 = 16\ cm^2$, $P = 34$ cm

Problems 24. Have the child complete the fraction chart. Answers are shown below.

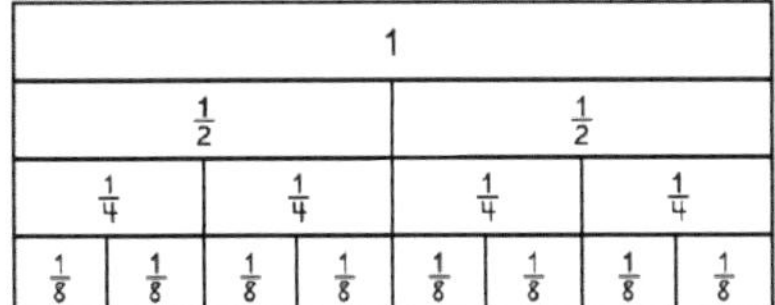

Problems 25-27. Tell the child to divide the rectangle into equal fourths three different ways. See below for possible answers.

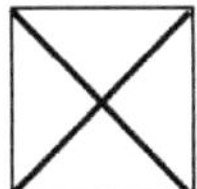 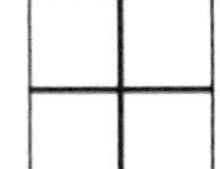 

Problems 28–30. Have the child circle half of each figure on the first line, a third of each figure on the second line, and a fourth of each on the last line. Some possible answers are shown below.

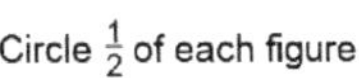

  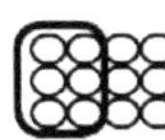

Circle $\frac{1}{3}$ of each figure. 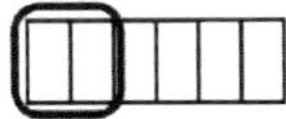  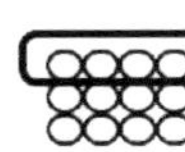

Circle $\frac{1}{4}$ of each figure.  

EXPLANATIONS:

Lesson 135: Measurement and Data Review and Games

OBJECTIVES:

1. To review the measurement and data topics

MATERIALS:

1. Worksheet 91, Measurement and Data Review
2. 4-in-1 ruler
3. *Math Card Games* book, M5

ACTIVITIES FOR TEACHING:

Worksheet 91. Give the child the worksheet and the 4-in-1 ruler. Tell him to estimate the length of line A and line B on his worksheet in centimeters and inches. Have him record his answers in the chart.

	Your Guess	Measured	Difference
Line A in centimeters		9 cm	
Line A in inches		$3\frac{1}{2}$ in.	
Line B in centimeters		14 cm	
Line B in inches		$5\frac{1}{2}$ in.	

After the child has completed his guesses, have him use the 4-in-1 ruler to measure the lines and write the measurements in the chart. Then have him calculate the difference. See completed chart above.

Ask and discuss the following questions:

Which measurement gives you the larger number, centimeters or inches? [cm]

Do you have to start at zero when reading a ruler? [no]

How many inches in a foot? [12]

How many feet are in a yard? [3]

How many inches are in a yard? [36]

How many centimeters are in a meter? [100]

EXPLANATIONS:

ACTIVITIES FOR TEACHING:

Clocks. Tell the child to match the digital clocks in the center to the analog clocks on the sides. Answers shown below.

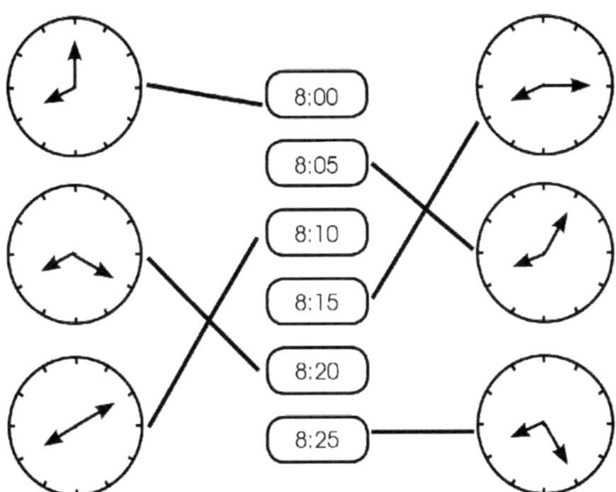

Line plot. Tell the child to read the following problem on his worksheet, then fill in the line plot with the data.

Kat has 3 radishes, 3 potatoes, 2 carrots, and 1 squash for sale. Kim has 1 potato, 2 carrots, 2 radishes and 5 squash for sale. What is the total amount of produce that is for sale? [19 items]

Line plot showing number of pieces of produce for sale.

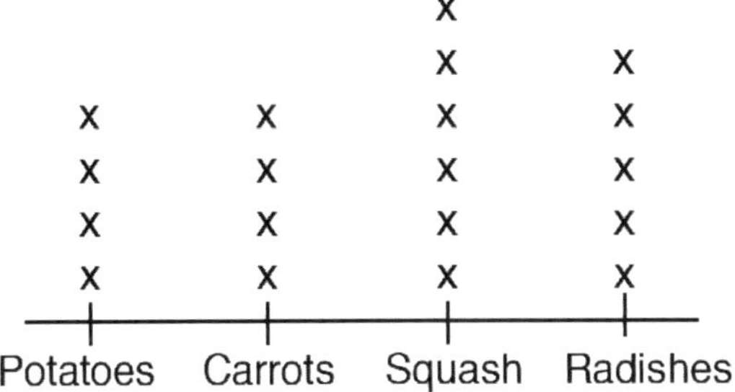

Are there more potatoes or squash for sale? [squash]

How many more squash than potatoes are there? [2]

How many carrots are for sale? [4]

How many more radishes than carrots are there? [1]

Who Has the Most Money game. Play the Who Has the Most Money game, Variation 1, found in the *Math Card Games* book, M5.

EXPLANATIONS:

LESSON 136: MEASUREMENT AND DATA ASSESSMENT

OBJECTIVES:

1. To assess the measurement and data topics

MATERIALS:

1. End of Year Assessment 2
2. 4-in1-ruler

ACTIVITIES FOR TEACHING:

EXPLANATIONS:

Assessment 2. Give the child the End of Year Assessment 2 and the 4-in-1 ruler.

Problems 1–8. Tell the child to estimate the length of both line A and line B in centimeters and inches. Have him record his answers in the chart on the assessment.

	Your Guess	Measured	Difference
Line A in centimeters		5 cm	
Line A in inches		2 in.	
Line B in centimeters		$17\frac{1}{2}$ cm	
Line B in inches		7 in.	

After the child has completed his guesses, have him use the 4-in-1 ruler to measure the lines and write the measurements in the chart. Then have the child calculate the difference. See completed chart above.

Problems 9–13. Have the child answer the following questions on the assessment.

Which measurement gives you the larger number? [cm]

How many inches in a foot? [12]

How many feet are in a yard? [3]

How many inches are in a yard? [36]

How many centimeters are in a meter? [100]

Problems 14–15. Tell the child to complete the next two question on the assessment.

A basketball player is 6 feet 10 inches tall. How tall is that in inches? [82 inches]

In most newer houses the ceiling is 8 feet above the floor. How far from the ceiling is the basketball player's head? [1 ft 2 inches or 14 inches]

Problems 16–17. Ask the child to answer the string problems on the assessment. Answers shown at the top of the next page.

ACTIVITIES FOR TEACHING: | **EXPLANATIONS:**

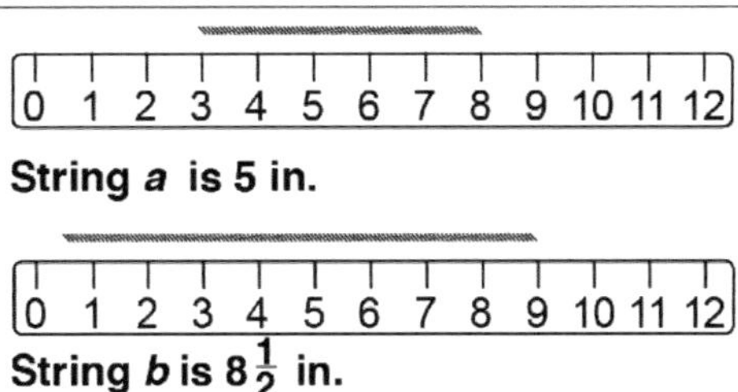

Problems 18–21. Tell the child to write the time and draw the hands on the clocks. Answers shown below.

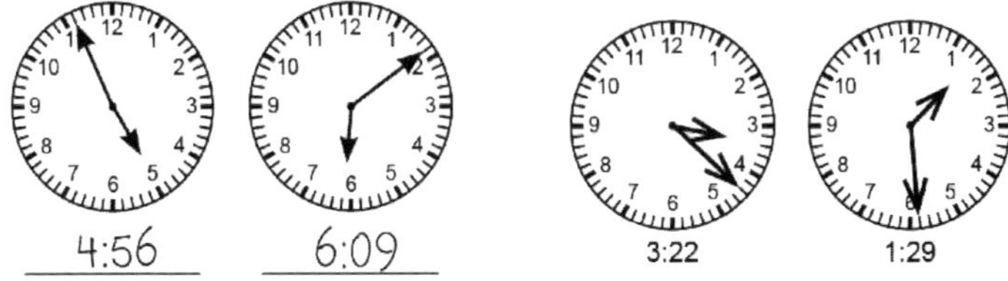

Problems 22–23. Have the child read and solve the problems.

Carrie is buying four pears. Each pear cost 21¢. What is her change from a dollar? [16¢; 21 + 21 + 21 + 21 + 16 = 100¢]

Tyler has 76¢. He has two quarters, four nickels, and some pennies. How many pennies does he have? [6 pennies; 25 + 25 + 5 + 5 + 5 + 5 + 6 = 76¢]

Problems 24–28. Tell the child to read the following problem and then fill in the line plot with the data.

Rita has 2 melons, 3 apples, 2 peaches and 1 pear in her garden basket. Ryan has 1 melon, 2 apples, 2 peaches and 5 pears in his basket.

Line plot showing number of pieces of fruit in both baskets.

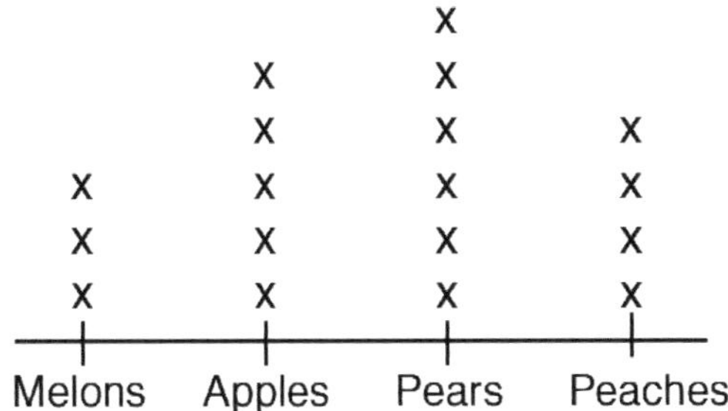

What is the total amount of produce in both baskets? [18 pieces]

Are there more apples or pears in the baskets? [pears]

How many more pears than apples are there? [1]

How many melons are in the baskets? [3]

How many more peaches than melons are there? [1]

LESSON 137: NUMBER & OPERATION IN BASE TEN REVIEW

OBJECTIVES:

1. To review the number and operations in base ten topics

MATERIALS:

1. Worksheet 92, Number & Operation in Base Ten Review
2. *Math Card Games* book, A9 or S9

ACTIVITIES FOR TEACHING:

Addition. Tell the child to listen to the problems and say the answers aloud. Read each problem twice.

543 + 10 = [553] 838 + 100 = [938]

543 – 10 = [533] 838 – 100 = [738]

Place-value. Ask: How many digits are needed after the 1 to write 100? [2] How many digits are needed after the 1 to write 10? [1] How many digits are needed after the 1 to write 1? [0]

Number sequence. Tell the child to count by 2s to 10. [2, 4, 6, . . . , 10] Then have him count by 5s to 120, [5, 10, 15, . . . , 120] by 10s to 300, [10, 20, 30, . . . , 300] and by 100s to 1000. [100, 200, 300, . . . , 1000]

Worksheet 92. Give the child the worksheet and have him fill in the missing numbers on the place-value cards and then write them in standard form. Answers shown below.

6000 + 300 + 50 + 4 6354

1000 + 000 + 30 + 1 1031

3000 + 200 + 00 + 4 3204

EXPLANATIONS:

ACTIVITIES FOR TEACHING:	EXPLANATIONS:

Practice. Tell the child to complete the worksheet. Answers shown below.

321 + 100 **=** 411 + 10

98 + 63 **<** 100 + 85

485 + 10 + 1 **>** 100 + 336

460 + 10 **=** 9 + 461

4356	9565	5876	7265
+ 2345	+ 1245	– 3967	– 3689
6701	**10810**	**1909**	**3576**

15 + 12 + 45 + 18 = **90**

64 + 34 + 16 + 35 = **149**

41 + 56 + 80 + 23 = **200**

32 + 50 + 64 + 36 = **182**

Corners™ games. Have the child play a Corners™ game found in the *Math Card Games* book, A9 or S9.

Lesson 138: Number & Operation in Base Ten Assessment

OBJECTIVES:

1. To review the number and operations in base ten topics

MATERIALS:

1. End of Year Assessment 3

ACTIVITIES FOR TEACHING:

Assessment 3. Give the child the End of Year Assessment 3.

Problems 1–4. Tell him to listen to the problems and write only the answers. Say each problem twice.

483 + 10 = [493]   748 + 100 = [848]

483 – 10 = [473]   748 – 100 = [648]

Problems 5–7. Have the child answer the next three questions on the assessment.

How many digits are needed after the 6 to write 600? [2]

How many digits are needed after the 6 to write 60? [1]

How many digits are needed after the 6 to write 6? [0]

Problems 8–11. Tell the child to write sequential numbers.

Count by 5s starting at 5. [5, 10, 15, . . . , 50]

Count by 5s starting at 85. [85, 90, 95, . . . , 130]

Count by 10s starting at 280. [280, 290. 300, . . . , 370]

Count by 100s starting at 100. [100, 200, 300, . . . , 1000]

Problems 12–13. Have the child fill in the missing numbers on the place-value cards and then write them in standard form. Answers shown below.

2 0 0 0 + **3** 0 0 + **4** 0 + **2**   **2 3 4 2**

1 0 0 0 + **0 0 0** + **3** 0 + **4**   **1 0 3 4**

EXPLANATIONS:

ACTIVITIES FOR TEACHING:

Problem 14–17. Tell the child to solve the following problem using the <, >, or = signs.

611 + 100 **>** 611 + 10 89 + 63 **<** 100 + 73
455 + 10 + 1 **>** 100 + 365 250 + 10 **=** 9 + 251

Problems 18–21. Have the child solve.

2964	9778	6829	7094
+ 5342	+ 1318	– 2637	– 3528
8306	**11096**	**4192**	**3566**

Problem 22–25. Tell the child to solve the following problems.

13 + 11 + 37 + 15 = **76** 54 + 37 + 18 + 25 = **134**
71 + 52 + 70 + 32 = **225** 23 + 70 + 53 + 26 = **172**

Problems 26–27. Tell the child to read the problems, fill in the part-whole circle sets, and write the equation.

Kyle's hamster weighs 80 grams. Stephen's hamster weighs 6 grams less than Kyle's hamster. How much does Stephen's hamster weigh? [80 – 6 = 74 grams]

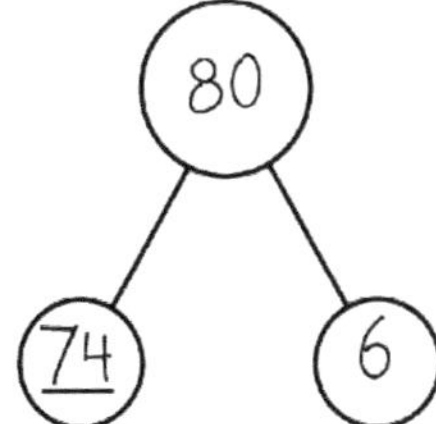

The Heidrich family traveled 18 miles to a wedding. The Haak family traveled 27 miles. How many miles less did the Heidrich family travel? [27 – 18 = 9 miles]

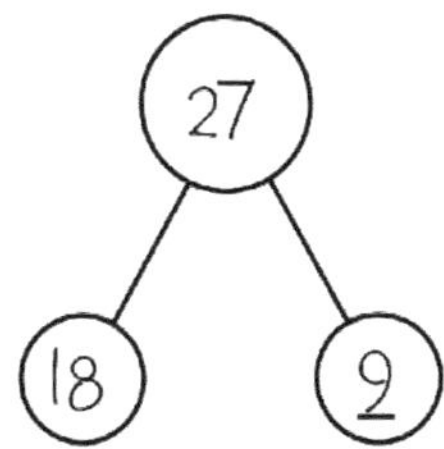

EXPLANATIONS:

Lesson 139: Operation & Algebraic Thinking Review

OBJECTIVES:

1. To review the operation and algebraic thinking topics

MATERIALS:

1. Tiles
2. Dry erase board
3. *Math Card Games* book, P3
4. Math journal

ACTIVITIES FOR TEACHING:

Reviewing even or odd. Give the child 10 to 15 tiles each in two different colors. Tell him to arrange his tiles so someone could tell if they were even or odd without counting. Ask: Do you have an even or odd amount? How do you know?

Adding two even numbers. Now ask the child to make two even numbers, each less than 10. Then ask him to add his two numbers together. See the figure below. Ask: Is your sum even or odd? [even] Ask him to explain why. [All the groups of two tiles stay together.]

Even + even = even.

Adding two odd numbers. Ask the child to make two odd numbers, each less than 10. Again ask him to add his tiles together. See the figure below. Ask: Is your sum even or odd? [even] Ask him to explain why. [The extra ones formed a pair.]

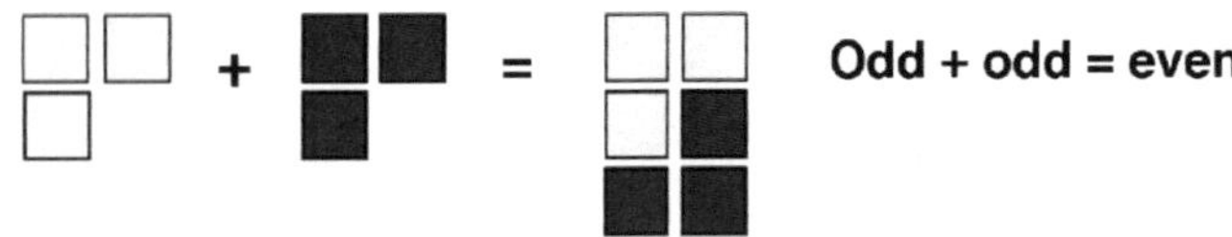

Adding an even and an odd number. Ask: What happens if we add an even number and an odd number? Then tell him to try it. See the figure below. Ask: What happens when you combined them? [odd] Ask him to explain. [The extra 1 from the odd number could not find a partner.]

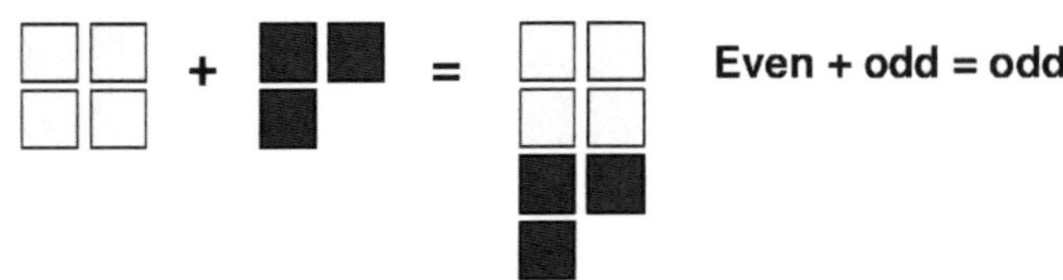

EXPLANATIONS:

ACTIVITIES FOR TEACHING:

Array. Using the tiles, have the child make a 3 by 3 array. See below.

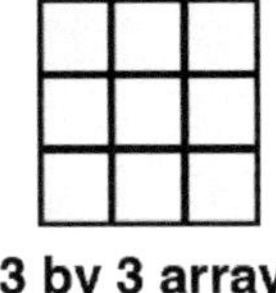

3 by 3 array.

Ask: How many tiles are in your array? [9] Have him write the equation for the array on his dry erase board.

$$3 + 3 + 3 = 9$$

Then have the child make a 2 by 4 array. See below.

2 by 4 array.

Ask: How many tiles are in this array? [8] Have the child write the two equations for the array.

$$2 + 2 + 2 + 2 = 8$$

$$4 + 4 = 8$$

Ask: Which array uses more tiles? [3 by 3] Which array takes more space? [3 by 3] How do you know? [The 3 by 3 needs 9 tiles, and the 4 by 2 needs 8 tiles.]

Sum Rummy game. Tell the child to play the Sum Rummy game, found in the *Math Card Games* book, P3. He may use adding equations or multiplication equations. Tell the child to record his score in his math journal.

EXPLANATIONS:

Lesson 140: Operation & Algebraic Thinking Assessment

OBJECTIVES:

1. To assess the operation and algebraic thinking topics

MATERIALS:

1. End of Year Assessment 4

ACTIVITIES FOR TEACHING:

Assessment 4. Give the child the End of Year Assessment 4.

Problems 1–10. Have the child solve.

7 + 3 = [10]	5 – 4 = [1]
4 + 3 = [7]	3 + 3 = [6]
9 – 6 = [3]	1 + 4 = [5]
8 + 2 = [10]	2 – 1 = [1]
6 – 1 = [5]	9 – 2 = [7]

Problems 11–12. Tell him to read and solve the next two problems on his assessment.

Jack wants to buy a gift that costs one dollar. Jack already has 85¢. How much more money does he need? [15¢]

Some children were lined up. Fourteen more children join the line. Now there are 21 children. How many children were in line at the start? [7]

Problems 13–19. Ask the child to circle the even and underline the odd quantities. Then have him answer the following questions.

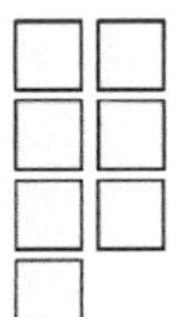
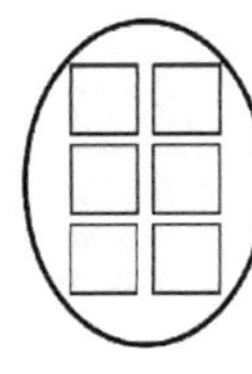
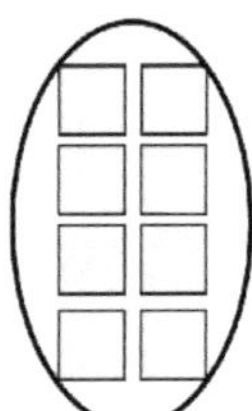
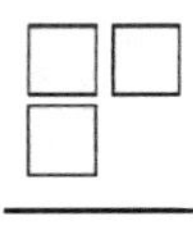

What is even + even = ______ [even]
What is odd + odd = ______ [even]
What is even + odd = ______ [odd]

EXPLANATIONS:

ACTIVITIES FOR TEACHING: | **EXPLANATIONS:**

Problems 20–27. Write the array name and write one of the equations for the following problems. Answers shown below.

5 by 2 **5 + 5 = 10 or 2 + 2 + 2 + 2 + 2 = 10**

3 by 4 **4 + 4 + 4 = 12 or 3 + 3 + 3 + 3 = 12**

5 by 5 **5 + 5 + 5 + 5 + 5 = 25**

4 by 2 **4 + 4 = 8 or 2 + 2 + 2 + 2 = 8**

Problems 28–30. Tell the child to answer the following questions on his assessment.

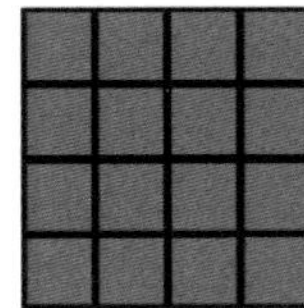

4 by 4 array

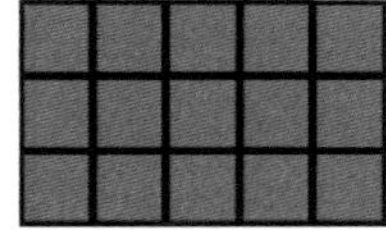

5 by 3 array

Which array is larger? [4 by 4]

Which array takes up more space? [4 by 4]

How do you know? [The 4 by 4 needs 16 squares, but the 5 by 3 needs 15 squares.]

Congratulations!

Your child has completed RightStart™ Mathematics Level C and is now ready for Level D Second Edition.

Certificates of completion are in the back of the child's worksheets.

To move on to RightStart™ Mathematics Level D Second Edition, all you need is the Level D Book Bundle. This can be purchased at RightStartMath.com or by calling 888-272-3291.

APPENDIX

Yellow is the Sun

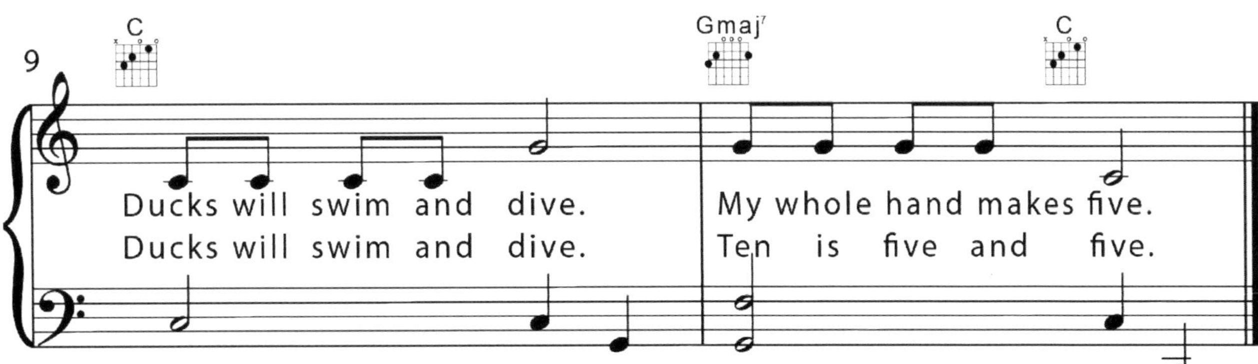

Lyrics by Joan A. Cotter

Composed by Rosine Hermodson-Olsen
Arranged by Barbara Ask

Thirty Days has September

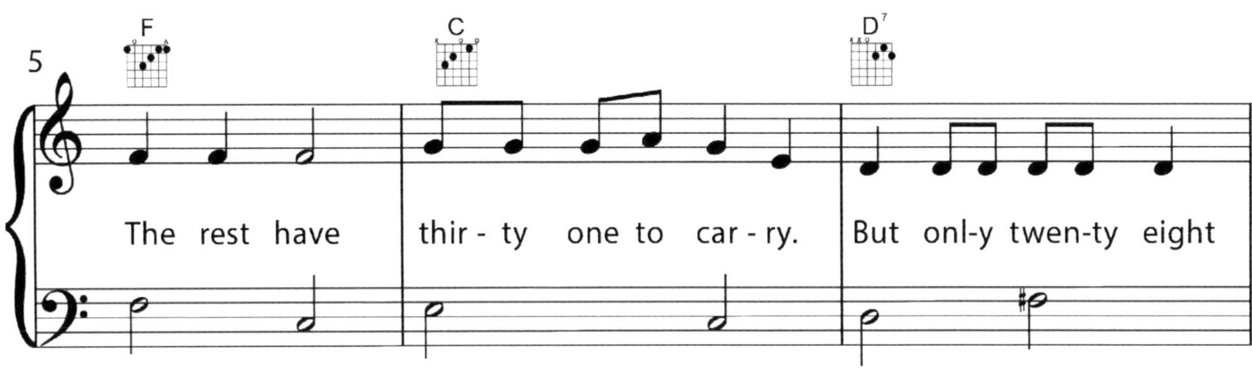

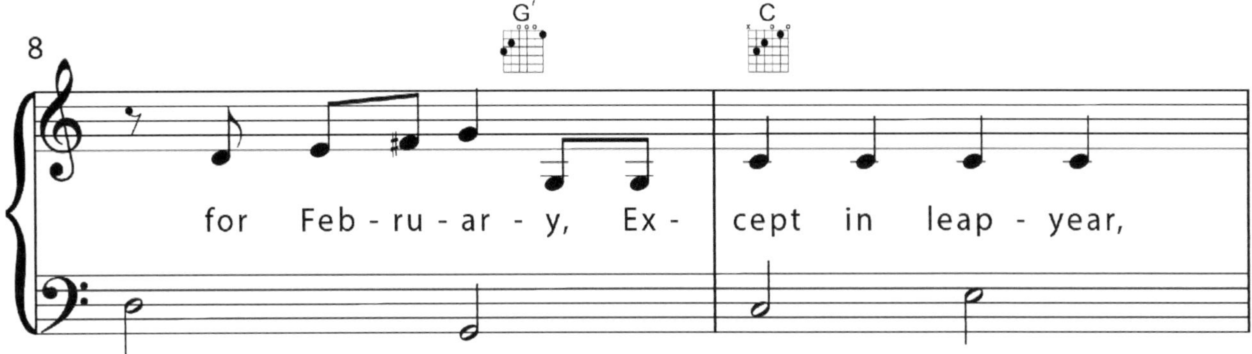

Lyrics by Joan A. Cotter

Composed by Rosine Hermodson-Olsen
Arranged by Barbara Ask

30-60 Triangles

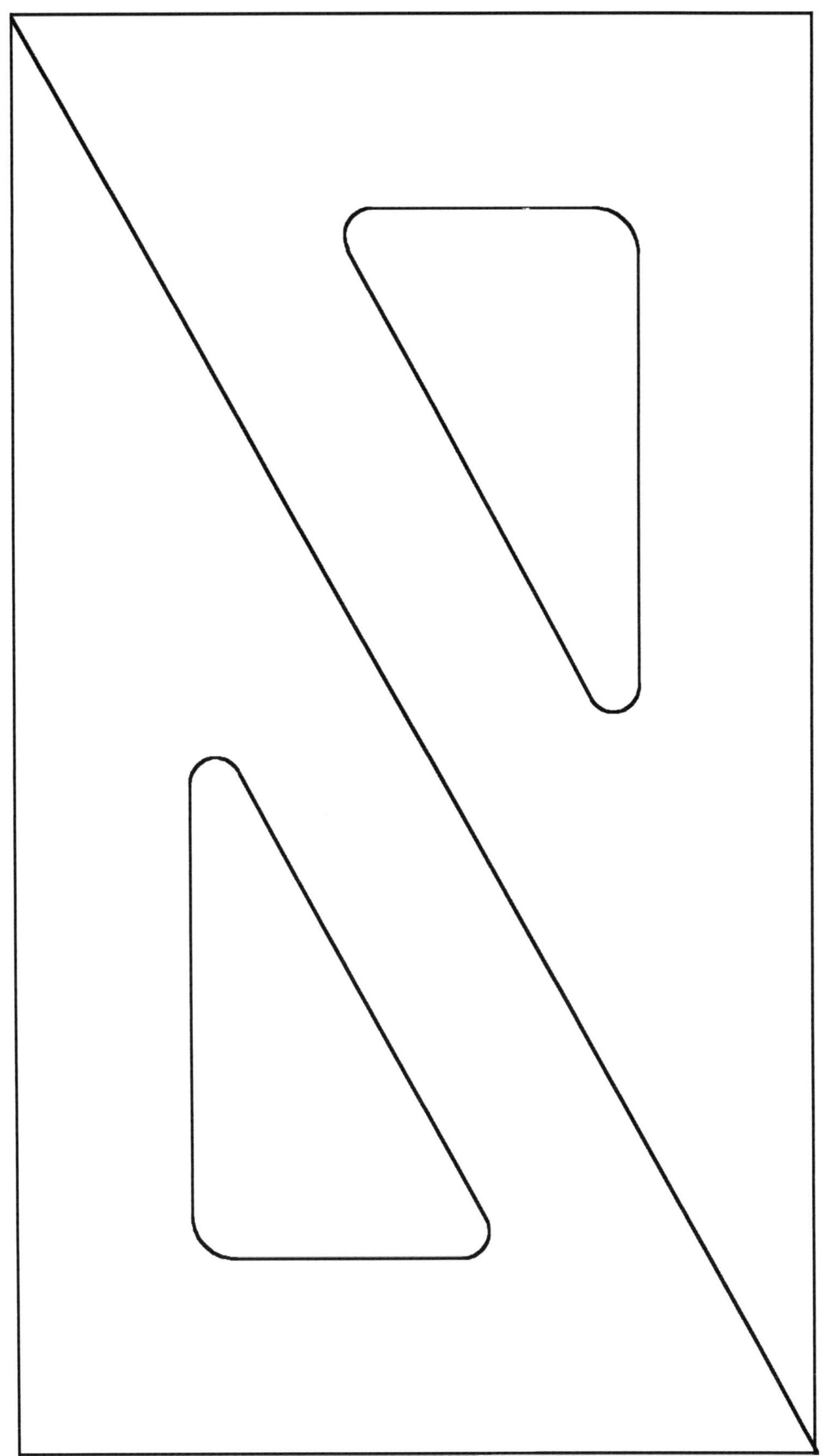